Deepening Integration in the Pacific Economies

NEW HORIZONS IN INTERNATIONAL BUSINESS

General Editor: Peter J. Buckley
Centre for International Business,
University of Leeds (CIBUL), UK

This series is aimed at the frontiers of international business research. The study of international business is important not least because it gives researchers the opportunity to innovate in theory, technique, empirical investigation and interpretation. The area is fruitful for interdisciplinary and comparative research. This series is established as a central forum for the presentation of new ideas in international business.

Titles in the series include:

Japanese Multinationals in the Global Economy
Paul W. Beamish, Andrew Delios and Donald J. Lecraw

Direct Investment in Economies in Transition
Klaus Meyer

Taiwanese Firms in Southeast Asia
Networking Across Borders
Edited by Tain-Jy Chen

Global Competitive Strategies in the New World Economy
Multilateralism, Regionalization and the Transnational Firm
Edited by Hafiz Mirza

Foreign Direct Investment and Corporate Networking
A Framework for Spatial Analysis of Investment Conditions
Robert L.A. Morsink

Structural Change and Cooperation in the Global Economy
Edited by Gavin Boyd and John H. Dunning

Managing the Multinationals
An International Study of Control Mechanisms
Anne-Wil Käthe Harzing

The Origins of the International Competitiveness of Firms
The Impact of Location and Ownership in the Professional Service Industries
Lilach Nachum

Deepening Integration in the Pacific Economies
Corporate Alliances, Contestable Markets and Free Trade
Edited by Alan M. Rugman and Gavin Boyd

The Global Integration of Europe and East Asia
Studies of International Trade and Investment
Edited by Sang-Gon Lee and Pierre-Bruno Ruffini

Foreign Direct Investment and Economic Growth in China
Edited by Yanrui Wu

Multinationals, Technology and National Competitiveness
Marina Papanastassiou and Robert Pearce

Deepening Integration in the Pacific Economies

Corporate Alliances, Contestable Markets and Free Trade

Edited by
Alan M. Rugman

Thames Water Fellow of Strategic Management, University of Oxford, UK

Gavin Boyd

Honorary Professor, Political Science Department, Rutgers University, Newark, USA and Research Associate, Centre for International Business Studies, University of Montreal, Canada

NEW HORIZONS IN INTERNATIONAL BUSINESS

Edward Elgar
Cheltenham, UK • Northampton, MA, USA

Published by
Edward Elgar Publishing Limited
Glensanda House
Montpellier Parade
Cheltenham
Glos GL50 1UA
UK

Edward Elgar Publishing, Inc.
6 Market Street
Northampton
Massachusetts 01060
USA

A catalogue record for this book
is available from the British Library

Library of Congress Cataloguing in Publication Data
Deepening integration in the Pacific economies: corporate alliances, contestable markets, and free trade / edited by Alan M. Rugman, Gavin Boyd.
  —(New horizons in international business series)
  Includes bibliographical references (p.).
  1. Pacific Area—Economic integration. 2. Pacific Area—Foreign economic relations. I. Rugman, Alan M. II. Boyd, Gavin.
  III. Series: New horizons in international business.
  HC681.D43 1999
  337.1'9—dc21   98–31696
                                                                          CIP

ISBN 1 85898 671 0

Printed and bound in Great Britain by Creative print and Design, Wales

Contents

List of figures   vi
List of tables   vii
Notes on contributors   viii
Preface   ix

1 Pacific integration and globalization   1
   Gavin Boyd
2 East Asian crises and regional economic integration   19
   Brian K. MacLean, Paul Bowles and Osvaldo Croci
3 Pacific economic integration and the 'flying geese' paradigm 55
   Terutomo Ozawa
4 Pacific market integration: firms and governments   92
   Terry Ursacki and Ilan Vertinsky
5 Multinational enterprises in APEC   124
   Alan M. Rugman and Cecilia Brain
6 Corporate–government relations in the Pacific   149
   Gavin Boyd
7 Corporate interaction, direct investment and regional
   cooperation in industrializing Asia   193
   Michael G. Plummer
8 Bank loan capitalism and financial crises: Japanese and
   Korean experiences   214
   Terutomo Ozawa
9 Pacific collective management   249
   Gavin Boyd

Index   289

List of figures

3.1 Changes in industrial structures of Asia Pacific countries
and areas, 1982–92   57
3.2 Ratio of machinery and light industry products to total
exports from countries and areas in East Asia   59
3.3 Riding on an S-shaped growth curve   60
3.4 Sequence of postwar structural upgrading under the aegis
of the *Pax Americana*   64
3.5 Trends in Japan's foreign direct investment in East Asia   68
3.6 Japan's trade balance in technology with other major
countries   70
7.1 Costs and benefits of a protective environment to foreign
firms   198
7.2 Costs of protection under alternative input–output coefficient
assumptions   199
8.1 Japan's bank-loan capitalism during the high-growth period
of heavy and chemical industrialization, 1950–74   223
8.2 Korea's financial crisis   242

List of tables

3.1 Recent patterns of inward FDI into and exports from
the NIEs 73
3.2 Recent patterns of inward FDI into and exports from
ASEAN-4 78
3.3 Recent patterns of inward FDI into and exports from China 80
5.1 Multinational enterprises in APEC countries, 1996 126
5.2 The 20 largest APEC MNEs, 1996 127
5.3 The 20 largest US MNEs, 1996 128
5.4 The 20 largest Japanese MNEs, 1996 129
5.5 The 13 largest South Korean MNEs, 1996 129
5.6 MNEs from other APEC economies, 1996 130
7.1 Direct investment in China 204
7.2 Determinants of Korean DFI 208
8.1 Korea's economic indicators 239

Contributors

Paul Bowles is Professor of Economics at the University of Northern British Columbia.

Gavin Boyd is Honorary Professor, Political Science Department, Rutgers University, Newark, New Jersey, and Research Associate, Centre for International Business Studies, Ecole des Hautes Etudes Commerciales, University of Montreal.

Cecilia Brain is a Research Assistant in the Joseph L. Rotman Centre for Management, University of Toronto.

Osvaldo Croci is Chair of the Political Science Department, Laurentian University, Sudbury, Ontario, Canada.

Brian K. MacLean is Associate Professor of Economics, Laurentian University, Sudbury, Ontario, Canada.

Terutomo Ozawa is Professor of Economics at Colorado State University, Fort Collins, Colorado, USA.

Michael G. Plummer is Professor of Economics at Brandeis University, Waltham, Massachusetts, USA.

Alan M. Rugman is Thomas Water Fellow of Strategic Management at Templeton College, University of Oxford, UK.

Terry Ursacki is Professor in the Faculty of Management, University of Calgary, Alberta, USA.

Ilan Vertinsky is Director of International Business Studies in the Faculty of Commerce and Business Administration, University of British Columbia, Vancouver, Canada.

Preface

This book has been planned as a survey of the transnational production and trade linkages between market-economy East Asian and North American states in the Asia Pacific Economic Cooperation (APEC) forum. The linkages are replacing shallow integration (through mostly arm's-length commerce) with deepening integration which links national economic structures through the extension of corporate organizations across borders, with much intrafirm trade. With the structural interdependence which results, there is increasing policy interdependence and much complex interdependence among governments and firms. Industrial policy endeavours by each national administration are affected by the cooperative or competitive industrial policy measures of other governments and by the positive and negative aspects of strategies implemented by numerous home country and foreign enterprises. There is industrial policy rivalry, with competitive investment bidding, and this rivalry reflects the concerns of governments to enhance relative gains for their economies as deepening integration continues.

The Pacific pattern of deepening integration is assuming larger dimensions while APEC governments interact, distantly and intermittently, over issues of trade and investment liberalization across the Pacific. There is general policy-level interest in reducing administrative barriers to regional commerce, as there would then be increasing gains through efficiencies resulting from the operations of higher-performing firms which would rationalize their operations more comprehensively on a Pacific basis. Apprehensions about changes in the spread of gains from involvement in the regional economy, however, motivate much of the caution evident in displays of commitment to Pacific liberalization.

In East Asia, the basis for caution about the effects of trade and investment liberalization has been related to concepts of structural competitiveness and strategic trade policy, as well as to inequalities in bargaining power when dealing with the USA. There have been active concerns to protect vulnerable home country firms. These concerns have become stronger since the 1997–8 financial crises which disrupted the Indonesian, Thai and South Korean economies. Dependence on adjustment financing from the International Monetary Fund, however, has obliged governments in those distressed states to make their economies more open. At the same time, the USA's bargaining strength on issues of regional economic openness has in effect increased. Yet in the USA the costs of globalization, including those experienced through deepening integration in the Pacific, have become prominent in public debate about foreign economic policy.

The complex trends and issues in the Pacific processes of deepening integration demand close attention from East Asian and North American corporate planners and policy planners. We hope that this volume will assist the development of constructive approaches to the questions of competition and cooperation that are challenging managements and government leaders.

We and our contributors are very grateful to numerous colleagues whose publications and comments have enriched our understanding of the dynamics of deepening integration in the Pacific and of the significance of those dynamics in the larger process of globalization. This work on the Pacific links up with research which several of us have begun on the globalization of the American economy. Our efforts have been greatly encouraged by the enthusiasm of Peter J. Buckley for this project, which has given it a place in his series on New Horizons in International Business. Alan M. Rugman is especially grateful to colleagues who have welcomed him to his new appointment as Thames Water Fellow in Strategic Management at Templeton College, Oxford.

ALAN M. RUGMAN
GAVIN BOYD

1. Pacific integration and globalization

Gavin Boyd

A Pacific pattern of economic relations has been evolving with the rapid growth of large transnational production links and arm's-length trade between East Asian and North American market-economy states. East Asian and US firms have been very active in this pattern, and to a large extent it has been shaped by significant contrasts between those enterprises. Those in East Asia have been influenced by cultures and systems of corporate governance which have motivated much entrepreneurial cooperation and the management of such cooperation in close association with home government policies. American corporations, formed in a very individualistic culture, have operated with a strong emphasis on competition rather than cooperation and on asserting independence from their national administration.

There has been relatively little collaboration between Pacific governments to reduce the administrative barriers that hinder commerce and direct investment. Occasional exchanges occur in the loosely associated consultative Asia Pacific Economic Cooperation (APEC) forum, which includes the East Asian and North American market-economy states plus China. The exchanges have somewhat increased awareness in policy communities that domestic markets in East Asia have been sheltered by fairly high levels of effective protection, in order to assist manufacturing for export, and that the relatively more open US market has greatly encouraged such manufacturing, although its future has been threatened by strong domestic pressures for restraints on imports into the USA. General commitments have been made in APEC to liberalize regional trade and investment, but reservations have been evident, and the USA and Japan, the principal members of the forum, have shown preferences for advancing their interests through bilateral rather than multigroup interactions. Such bilateralism has been possible because of low levels of solidarity between industrializing East Asian states in APEC. The Association of Southeast Asian Nations (ASEAN) is the only subregional grouping with some potential for collective representation of its interests, but this potential has remained weak for many years. Its limitations have been exposed by failures to generate collaborative responses to the disruptions caused by severe financial crises in Thailand and Indonesia during 1997–8.

Commitments made by APEC members to regional trade and investment liberalization had some credibility before the East Asian financial crises, although there were diverging approaches to questions about the negotiations that would be necessary. The financial crises, however, have given prominence to urgent new issues of interdependent adjustment, and have aroused East Asian resentments toward the USA, whose financial institutions were prominent in the speculative attacks on East Asian currencies which caused the crises. Pressures from the International Monetary Fund (IMF) on the distressed governments to make their economies more open to foreign direct investment and to accept the imposition of fiscal discipline were seen as reflections of US influence, and it was clear that US firms were seeking to exploit new opportunities in the disrupted economies, especially in their financial sectors.[1]

. The East Asian financial crises have caused much suffering, especially for the poorer sections of the Thai and Indonesian populations. There has been a large flow of migrant workers from Indonesia's badly affected economy to Malaysia and Singapore; in the latter state, harsh treatment has been intended to discourage further migration. Weak administrative services in Thailand and Indonesia have failed to cope with the unemployment problems that result from contractions of manufacturing and service activities. Economic associations and business networks in both countries, moreover, have failed to respond effectively to the adjustment problems caused by their financial crises. In Indonesia, communal antagonisms have been directed against the Chinese community because of its prominence in the nation's commerce.

Deepening integration is continuing in the stressful conditions which have followed the East Asian crises. Japanese direct investment, the most active process in the regional pattern of deepening integration, has slackened because of both strains in the home economy and the disruptions in East Asian industrializing states. However, it is responding to opportunities resulting from the increased external dependence of those countries, as well as to opportunities for further expansion in the USA, to consolidate market strengths gained initially by exporting. Direct investment by US enterprises, while increasing in the distressed East Asian industrializing states following sharp depreciations of their currencies, has also begun to increase the modest American corporate presence in Japan, especially in its financial sector.

Meanwhile, among industrializing East Asian states substantial direct investment flows remain important secondary features of the regional pattern. The most active participants are Chinese firms based in those states, and among these enterprises those based in Taiwan are advantaged because its economy has not been significantly disrupted by speculative attacks on its currency.

Adjustments by firms and governments are difficult because the pattern of deepening integration has been disrupted. Increased vulnerabilities and uncertainties relating to market, structural and policy changes have strained innovative capabilities in enterprises and national administrations, causing a tendency towards short-term, cautious and experimental decision-making. The interaction of effects, moreover, tends to be dysfunctional, especially because policy-level problems cause firms to focus more on their individual objectives, with greater self-reliance, less confidence in their partners and less responsiveness to home government concerns. All these problems have been evident in the distressed industrializing East Asian states and also, to some degree, in the more integrated and dynamic Japanese political economy, which has superior adaptive capacities.[2]

PACIFIC DYNAMICS

The regional pattern of deepening integration in the Pacific has been shaped by complex processes of reciprocal causality; there have been no overall coordinating functions at the policy level such as those that have been developing in the European Union on a basis of regional community formation that sustains a system of collective management. The principal interactive processes have evolved in the USA–Japan relationship, which has been distinguished by the import-drawing effects of large US fiscal deficits and vigorous Japanese exports of medium and higher technology price-competitive and quality-competitive manufactures to the USA, leading to the growth of a large Japanese production system in the United States.[3] While this has increased in size, with concentrated sectoral effects, notably in the automobile sector, American direct investment in Japan has remained small; however, it has increased in the wake of the East Asian financial crises, especially through entries by US banks and securities firms. Low interest rates in Japan, intended to facilitate growth, have caused Japanese investors to seek opportunities in world financial markets.[4] These opportunities have been opened up by the degree of financial market liberalization which was introduced in 1998 after the failures of some prominent Japanese financial institutions.

Japanese direct investment in manufacturing for the USA from bases in industrializing East Asian states has been linked with production in the United States, which has been growing because of the marketing advantages of such a presence. This direct investment has presented opportunities and problems for firms and governments in industrializing East Asia. There have been some capability for partnerships with the Japanese firms in South Korea and Taiwan, because of national technological capabilities and overall levels of corporate development; but it has been difficult to build on these advantages for more effective cooperation with and competition against the Japanese, especially in South Korea.[5]

For the larger ASEAN members, in particular Thailand and Indonesia, the Japanese presence has been more challenging and has had more fundamental significance, because technological capabilities and levels of corporate development have been lower in these states: the scope for partnership has been quite limited, and business collaboration has developed on less-favourable terms for host country enterprises. Much of the Japanese investment has spread production operations across South-East Asian countries, dispersing assembly-type manufacturing and thus limiting technological transfers. Failures by ASEAN members to develop and coordinate effective structural policies have in effect prolonged their dependence on exports of primary products and low-technology manufactures by their own firms, while preventing any significant improvement in the weak capabilities of their private sector to cooperate with incoming Japanese enterprises.[6]

American direct investment, competing against the Japanese presence in industrializing East Asia, has been structurally less significant because it has been on a smaller scale and is less coherent because it has involved much less extensive entrepreneurial collaboration. Much of this investment is in manufacturing for the home market, Europe and host country markets; rivalry with Japanese competitors is difficult, especially because of the strength of their collaborative networks, but a substantial volume of US investment is in financial services, in which American firms have generally superior competitive advantages.[7] For host country enterprises the American presence offers very important alternatives to collaboration with and competition against the closely linked Japanese firms, and these alternatives provide opportunities for access to the large US market.

The industrializing East Asian states, with the exception of China, have weak capacities for bargaining with transnational enterprises over the terms of direct investment, including related trade issues, and for negotiating with the USA, Japan and the European Union on such matters. Bidding for foreign direct investment, especially by the distressed states, has become very active, and in this regard they compete with each other. Transnational enterprises in the region can thus focus more on the rationalization of production and marketing strategies across the Pacific, and globally, with wider dispersal of operations and greater freedom in the use of transfer prices in intrafirm trade to obtain tax advantages. The ability of host countries to monitor the use of these prices is weak in South-East Asia, and the investment bidding tends to restrain host governments when assessing taxes on foreign firms.

Structural policies have assumed critical importance for East Asian industrializing states in the new regional context of increased investment, trade dependence and altered bargaining strengths. The larger ASEAN states, however, it must be stressed, are seriously disadvantaged because of weak leadership, poor institutional development and limited administrative abilities, as well as because of failures to develop effective partnership links with national firms, many of which have had to function under parasitic official agencies. South Korea and Taiwan, because of institutional development, higher levels of industrialization and technocratic partnerships with organizationally advanced firms, have substantial structural policy capabilities.[8] South Korea's economy, however, has been severely disrupted, while Taiwan, although much less affected by the area's financial crises, has to cope with major problems because of its structural interdependence with distressed neighbours, and because of the discriminatory effects of US and Japanese non-recognition policies. These include exclusion from the World Trade Organization, so there is no recourse against US and other trade and investment measures that adversely affect Taiwan's interests.

The dynamics of the regional political economy, altered drastically by the East Asian financial crises, are tending to increase concentration trends. US multinationals are well positioned to expand operations in East Asia through mergers, acquisitions, and greenfield ventures, because of the area's currency depreciations, the weakened status of its governments and firms, and the strains in the Japanese economy. Increases in East Asian exports to the USA, resulting from the currency depreciations, tend to encourage protectionist demands for changes in US trade policy, but the pressures to shelter affected sectors can be moderated by favourable host country treatment of American direct investment. A considerable volume of this investment is in manufacturing for the home economy. The opportunities for American enterprises have global as well as regional significance, especially because of the scope to enhance world market shares in competition with European firms, and because more active competition against the Japanese presence in industrializing East Asia can limit Japanese entry into other regions, including Latin America.

It is probable that Japanese involvement in the Pacific concentration will become stronger as the distressed East Asian states recover and as growth resumes at home. Japanese firms make intensive use of informal coordination to control their regional and global strategies centrally, while operating with much industry group collaboration. An integrated presence thus develops in each host country, and its linked market strengths facilitate a deepening involvement, increasing the number of subordinate partners and virtually restricting the expansion opportunities of host country firms.[9]

Further changes in relative bargaining strengths associated with regional concentration trends will have implications for policy-level interactions. The USA is becoming more strongly positioned to press for Pacific trade and investment liberalization through bilateral dealings and APEC meetings. Japan, despite its interests in slowing regional liberalization because of the anticipated differential benefits, has the incentive to cooperate cautiously with US initiatives, because of increased dependence on the US market that has resulted from the strains both in its own economy and in industrializing East Asia.

NATIONAL POLICIES AND CORPORATE STRATEGIES

Efforts to promote trade and investment liberalization in the Pacific have restrictive implications for East Asian structural policies: the USA, the main source of pressure for such liberalization, advocates adoption of its tradition of governmental aloofness from industry and commerce. The logic of implementing structural policies, however, has become stronger; it has become clear that their scope will have to be extensive because of the economic stresses that must be overcome through engagement with fundamentals, and because it is imperative to reduce the bargaining inequalities that are otherwise likely to increase.

The functional significance of intensive technocratic-corporate partnerships for outward-orientated growth with increasing technological levels and improvements in bargaining strengths was demonstrated in Japan, South Korea and Taiwan for decades before the East Asian financial crises. Such partnerships, as is illustrated most notably in the Japanese model of alliance capitalism, can generate synergies through the interaction of functionally ordered macro and micro perspectives, on a basis of shared commitments to the common interest. This interaction facilitates learning about the possibilities for coordinating entrepreneurship with projected technological trajectories, while inducing the strong task orientation that is conducive to innovative administrative guidance and strategic planning.[10]

The East Asian financial crises have indicated how efficiencies in administrative–corporate partnerships can be weakened by managerial rent-seeking and the corruption of technocrats, notably in Japan; but they have also indicated how the inability to enter into partnerships has disadvantaged those ASEAN countries at the lower levels of political development, notably Indonesia and Thailand. Advances in political development could have helped those states to develop structural policy capabilities which would have raised their economies to higher levels of industrialization and reduced their vulnerability to destabilizing foreign speculative attacks on their currencies.

Even if the East Asian financial crises had been avoided through better macromanagement in the states which have been seriously affected, the rationale for implementing structural policies would still have become stronger because of fundamentals operating in the regional and global political economies. The intensification of the contest for world market shares, with overall reductions in the number of competing firms and increased concentrations of internationalized market power, make the structural policy capabilities of governments all the more significant in the spread of gains from deepening integration, with its associated costs and vulnerabilities. The strategic orientation of contending firms, together with the strengthening or weakening of their home country ties and of their international alliances, also assumes greater significance as determinants of those gains and with respect to the reach of national structural policies.

The costs of deepening integration, even without major disruptions in national economies, tend to make policy-level acceptance of structural logic essential, qualifying the endorsement of the rationale for a general liberalization of trade and investment policies. The policy reorientation becomes necessary because of the burdens of sheltering and facilitating the adjustment of industrial sectors which are adversely affected by the expanding transnational production and marketing activities of international firms. While these burdens increase, the costs tend to be borne more by labour, which remains immobile, rather than by capital, which has high mobility.[11]

An overall consequence is increasing rivalry for structural competitiveness which in the Pacific has been reflected in the response of

American technology policy initiatives to the rather comprehensive Japanese structural policy capability. Associated with this rivalry, however, is the compulsion to enhance and make more use of bargaining positions, so as to increase national gains by selective import restraints, market-opening leverage and investment bidding. The structural policy rivalry and trade policy activism, together with complex and largely uncoordinated shifts in the strategies of transnational enterprises, contribute to a general increase in uncertainty for governments and for firms. At the policy level, experimental, cautious and disjointed decision-making tends to be the result, especially because of the diversity of demands from affected domestic groups and the complexity of the issues posed by the operations of firms and the measures taken by other governments. The managements of transnational enterprises are less constrained in coping with the uncertainties, because they are able to deal with intraorganizational demands and can spread their operations across national borders, thereby exerting control over multiple environments. Japanese firms are particularly advantaged in these matters by intercorporate solidarity which assists information-sharing and risk-taking.[12]

The rivalry for structural competitiveness raises questions, in the common regional interest, about the potential for structural policy cooperation. US capacity to manage such rivalry is limited by strong pluralism in the national policy process, a tradition of liberal government and negative corporate attitudes towards the US administration. Disadvantages result in the regional rivalry; globally, this tends to be compensated by trade policy activism, but the logic of developing an effective structural policy capability remains basically sound. The benefits that can be gained from the competitive use of such a capability, however, would be less than those that could be gained less stressfully through cooperative methods which could evolve through sustained and constructive interaction with other APEC states, especially Japan. Japanese structural policy rivalry is managed in spite of continuing strains in relations with trade-deficit states, including the USA and most other partners in APEC. Conversion to a policy of structural cooperation, however, would require a considerable change in its strong economic nationalism.

Industrializing East Asian states must anticipate increasing disadvantages in the rivalry for structural competitiveness because relatively their bargaining positions *vis-à-vis* productive cooperation with transnational enterprises have weakened, and they are less able to guide and enlist the collaboration of their national firms, which have received incentives to disperse their operations regionally. Under US and IMF pressure to increase the openness of their economies, moreover, these industrializing states have to accept greater penetration through trade and investment; on balance, this is likely to limit the development of their recovering private sectors. Structural policy cooperation with Japan and the USA, on terms that gave the prospect of greater complementarity, balance and equity, could be striven for if there were encouraging changes in the policies of those two major states.

The regional shifts in bargaining strengths and policy orientation since the East Asian financial crises have made the prospects for the formation of a Pacific community less favourable. Leaders in the USA and Japan have not responded to this problem with initiatives to promote trust, understanding and goodwill. The weaknesses of the Association of Southeast Asian Nations and the developmental problems of its larger members have tended to encourage increased concentration by the US and Japanese administrations on the advancement of their own interests through unequal dealings with ASEAN members and also with South Korea. US transnational enterprises, increasing their competition against Japanese firms in industrializing East Asia, have been exploiting opportunities in distressed states which have had little scope for administrative guidance of the incoming foreign direct investment.

The evolution of the transitional Chinese political economy has assumed more immediate and longer-term significance for the Pacific because of the disruptions of the growth in the market economy East Asian industrializing states. Those disruptions have undoubtedly been seen as warnings that strong formal and informal controls in the financial sector are vital for stable growth and for the promotion of productive rather than rent-seeking activities. The logic of a comprehensive structural policy, moreover, has probably been seen to have greater validity for the promotion of orderly growth with minimal vulnerability to stresses in the regional economy and for effective management of the regime's structural interdependencies. Resistance to external pressures for liberalization must therefore seem to be all the more important. The Chinese policy stance, indeed, suggests that the potential for well-guided and substantially self-reliant growth, without substantial loss of economic sovereignty, is encouraging hopes for the consolidation of a strong and increasingly influential role in regional commerce, with a superior capacity for investment bidding and selective partnerships with foreign enterprises.[13]

The Chinese authorities receive much advice from international economic organizations and from the USA about the efficiency of free market forces; but in their immediate environment they have observed the high levels of growth attained by the Japanese system of guided alliance capitalism. The functional logic of the external advice to liberalize the economy is thus evidently seen as having only partial validity. Questions about political liberalization are associated with foreign economic advice, because of the protests from the USA and other western countries against the regime's hard-line authoritarianism; it appears that the maintenance of strong political controls is considered essential for the preservation of the ruling elite's monopoly of power as well as for effective governance of the economy.

GLOBALIZATION

The APEC region accounts for a large share of world production and trade, principally because of the size and international involvement of the US and Japanese economies. In world higher-technology markets, the leaders are mainly American and Japanese enterprises, which are strengthening their positions while European firms endeavour to cope with technological lags attributable basically to decades of fragmentation in what is now their Single Market.[14] Germany, the leading European exporter to the rest of the world, is internationally competitive predominantly in medium-technology sectors.

Structural interdependencies in the Pacific are assuming global significance as US, Japanese and other APEC enterprises extend their operations in the rest of the world while linking these increasingly to their Pacific activities. In this vast globalization process American international firms are the most active agents of change; however, they usually operate without the intercorporate ties which enable Japanese companies to function in closely united industrial groups. There are related systemic contrasts, as the higher degree of integration in the Japanese political economy tends to ensure greater structural competitiveness in global involvement and more effective control over the evolution of that involvement. The USA, however, has more extensive structural interdependencies in the global economy and, on this account and because of a recent tradition of leadership in the global trading and monetary systems, has the status of a power with major responsibilities for initiating collaborative adjustments as globalization proceeds. Associated with this status are its capacity to contribute to the activities of economic policy communities and corporate associations across the world, especially in Europe. This enables the USA to interact with the European Union in ways which facilitate joint domination of the world trading system and of global monetary relations.

In the evolution of the Pacific's global links, the largest structural interdependencies are between the USA and the European Union, they are expanding principally due to the US corporate presence in Europe. The individualistic pursuits of market opportunities by US firms in Europe are influenced by incentives to collaborate to obtain representation of their common interests in the regional system of collective management, especially through interaction with the European Commission. Cooperative political action is necessary because of the wide range of commercial issues dealt with in that system.[15] European trade, investment and structural policies are responsive to the interests of EU firms, whose positions in the Single Market are challenged by the large US presence. The regional political ties which are becoming necessary between American enterprises in Europe are probably facilitating exchanges which may lead to entrepreneurial collaboration. This could have effects on the strategies of the same and allied firms in the Pacific, where there are no comparable regional pressures to cooperate.

In the global trading system, the USA's influence has been in effect increased by the strains in the Japanese economy since the East Asian financial crises and by Japan's necessarily greater dependence on the US market. Improvements in the European Union's slack growth, moreover, now depend to a greater degree on expansion of its exports to the USA. The United States can thus press more vigorously for trade liberalization at the global level as well as in the Pacific, if decisional problems associated with its system of divided government can be overcome.

The USA's strong role in the international monetary system, however, is being challenged by the formation of the European Monetary Union. The use of the US dollar in international transactions and for reserves will decrease, the European monetary authority will tend to be assertive on behalf of mainly German and French interests, and there will be scope for monetary cooperation between the European authority and Japan, possibly conflicting with US preferences.[16] Impetus has been given to the strong concentration trend in the US financial sector by advances made toward monetary union in Europe, in so far as these seem to have opened the way for more active competition by European financial institutions against American banking and securities firms in their area. A system of monetary cooperation between the USA and Japan, perhaps with other Pacific members, could balance the international role of the European Monetary Union, but such a collaborative arrangement cannot be anticipated.

Japanese attitudes to issues of economic cooperation with the USA at the global level have become less favourable since the East Asian financial crises, due in particular to demands by American policy-makers for Japanese fiscal expansion; this conflicts with warnings from US investment rating firms that such expansion could reduce Japan's international credit status. The involvement of US financial institutions in speculative attacks on East Asian currencies, moreover, has understandably influenced Japanese attitudes, in conjunction with indications that the pressure for fiscal expansion is based on hopes that an increase in Japanese rather than US imports from industrializing East Asian states will assist their economic recovery.

The increased US bargaining strength in the Pacific and in the global political economy, together with the emerging issue of perceived vulnerability to cheaper exports from East Asia, tends to encourage commercial associations to be more assertive in protecting their positions in the domestic US market. American firms exploiting opportunities for entry into the distressed industrializing East Asian states have less reason to discourage protectionism at home, as those states have become more dependent on incoming direct investment. More active pluralism with a stronger protectionist orientation, reflecting concerns not only with East Asia but with apparent rises in the costs of globalization, is thus likely to affect the USA's foreign economic relations.[17]

Japan, while more vulnerable to American pressures for fiscal expansion and for the adoption of liberalizing measures to increase the openness of its economy, is being challenged to make more intensive use of its structural policy capability, to achieve higher growth and to support recovery in its industrializing neighbours. This challenge is being presented at a time when urgent issues relating to its interdependencies with those neighbours and to strains in the domestic economy, especially in its financial sector, are causing stresses in the country's system of consensual macromanagement.[18] The bureaucratic guidance of this system appears to have been weakened by the losses of status caused by publicity about cases of official corruption and by the reactions of business and political groups to the regulatory failures which have contributed to acute instability in the banking system and in securities firms. Administrations in industrializing East Asian states, under pressure to follow IMF advice and US policy suggestions, can look to Japan for collaborative proposals, but it is evidently difficult to generate a Japanese consensus on constructive initiatives.[19]

The opportunities for such initiatives, it must be stressed, are limited because of political uncertainties and administrative weaknesses in Thailand and Indonesia, the two ASEAN countries with the most seriously disrupted economies, and because of long-standing antipathies to Japan in South Korea. The ability of Japan to achieve a sufficient rapport for structural policy cooperation with these and other East Asian states, moreover, is limited by the exclusive nature of Japanese political culture. This sustains the high degree of integration in the Japanese political economy, yet the increased complexities and risks in the nation's foreign economic relations may well cause the management of Japanese multi-nationals which have large foreign investments to concentrate on operations in more stable areas of the world economy, despite the continuing importance of industrializing East Asia. Such a shift of emphasis would tend to induce a change at the policy level.

MANAGING INTERDEPENDENCIES

Structural and policy interdependencies in the Pacific are tending to assume a more hierarchical configuration with the increased scope for expansion by US firms and the strengthening of the USA's bargaining power. This trend will probably continue because Japan's domestic and external difficulties are likely to persist for some years and ASEAN will no doubt remain a loose subregional association with little capacity for structural cooperation among its members or for the collective representation of their interests. Unfavourable asymmetries in financial interdependence overshadow the lack of balance in the production and trade interdependencies of the ASEAN members and other industrial-izing East Asian states.

Complex imbalances in structural interdependence between the USA and Japan pose issues which Japanese policy-makers are facing more comprehensively than are their US counterparts, but difficulties result mainly from inequalities in their bargaining strengths. Changes in the production and trade of manufactures result mainly from the operations of Japanese firms, while financial linkages are shaped principally by the US governmental and the corporate attraction of Japanese investment. Interest rates in Japan have been low, to facilitate growth and to limit the currency appreciation caused by large trade surpluses. Returns to shareholders have also been relatively low because of managerial emphasis on reinvesting profits.

Japanese direct investment in the USA, while ranking next after Britain's, is structurally very significant because it includes the largest foreign manufacturing presence in higher-technology sectors and is linked with the home country intercorporate system in a way which ensures a high degree of control over trade between the two countries. Large favourable balances in Japan's commerce with the USA tend to

increase partly because of imports of capital equipment and intermediate products by Japanese firms in the USA. The smaller American
direct investment position in Japan has contributed at a slower pace and
with overall less technological significance to the growth of transnational
production interdependencies. Japanese direct investment in the US
financial sector, which has been growing with the large presence in
manufacturing and which is more substantial than the corresponding
US presence in Japan, facilitates the expanding operations of the manufacturing presence, and flows of investment from the home country into
US government and corporate bonds. The investment in US government
debt has been higher than that of any European country except Britain,
and, together with the investment in corporate bonds, has been approximating the level of the favourable trade balance. The financial
interdependence, however, has had another dimension: large-scale borrowing in Japan by US institutions, to take advantage of low interest
rates; this is converted into dollars for the purchase of US government
debt and to exploit high-yield investment opportunities in the rest of
the world, using their superior advantages in the management of global
financial services.[20]

In the evolution of this complex interdependence Japanese firms
respond increasingly to incentives to move manufacturing processes
from the high-cost home economy to the lower-cost industrializing
states, to expand exports to the USA and to develop linkages between
those offshore operations and the production activities in the United
States. Increasing high value added production in Japan can absorb
labour displaced by the outward direct investment, but this requires
much coordination between firms – more than is typically motivated by
gains attainable through concerting strategies that yield direct results
from penetrating foreign markets. Because the outward movement of
manufacturing has become a higher-risk process in industrializing East
Asia there is a clear need for more intensive and more integrative
collaboration between the foreign operations of the investing firms, in
order to exploit effectively the opportunities in host countries. It must
be stressed, however, that spontaneous collaboration for this and for
adjustment at home may well decline because of the divisive effects of
increased stresses in the external environment and at home, as well as
because of some weakening of technocratic guidance.

The interdependence between Japan and the USA entails vulnerabilities. Japan, it must be reiterated, has been increasingly exposed to
US leverage for a more balanced trading relationship and for increased
openness in its financial sector. At a more fundamental level, there are
unequally shared dangers due to the risks of a financial crisis in the

USA, because of the destabilizing effects of unsustainable stock market speculation and excessive growth in the money supply.[21] A severe decline in business confidence could trigger a crisis as severe as that in 1987, and this could be more difficult to overcome through releases of credit authorized by the Federal Reserve, as was done in 1987: since that time financial markets have become much more internationalized, and much of the expanded credit could flow into foreign markets. The danger of a crisis may well increase because of rising uncertainties about the international role of the dollar as the European Monetary Union becomes established. In Japanese policy planning the clear need for a strong consultative relationship with the European monetary authority appears to deserve high priority. The US administration will have to work closely with that authority to adjust to the large changes anticipated in the world monetary system, but the desired cooperation may be difficult.

In Japan, intercorporate cooperation facilitates adjustment to stresses in the national economy; but in the USA, the strongly individualistic business culture and the restrictive effects of anti-trust enforcement, together with the distant and distrustful corporate attitudes to the administration, tend to hinder adjustment to and management of economic strains and shocks. Large increases in uncertainties, due to communication problems in a low-trust environment, cause difficulties in assessing and responding to indicators of an impending crisis, and make the dangers of contagion and panic more serious than they would be in a more integrated political economy.

PROBLEMS OF COOPERATION

Deepening integration, with imbalances and strains and with the risk of a serious crisis, is a prospect which makes highly constructive initiatives by governments and corporate managements imperative in the Pacific. Problems of market failure assume cross-border dimensions as deepening integration continues, which are not overcome by increasing market efficiencies in the present regional context. These problems are related to the costs of deepening integration, as its regional and global dimensions increase the costs experienced by communities affected by the externalities of strategies implemented by transnational enterprises.

The market failure problems concern: the growth and use of international oligopoly power; the side-effects of expansion and rationalization decisions by firms acquiring such power or threatened by it; a proliferation of uncertainties and informational deficiencies;

and, fundamentally, the common need for order, balance, stability and growth through coordinated specializations in the regional pattern. Resolution of all these problems through extensive corporate and policy-level collaboration clearly must be striven for: a kind of unplanned equilibrium resulting from competitive and cooperative assertions of perceived interests by corporate groups and governments is not likely.

The emphasis on liberalization in US policy and on guiding market forces in Japan's policy, together with the developmental significance of the Japanese form of alliance capitalism for industrializing East Asia, will have to become subjects of intensive dialogue between Pacific policy communities and economic associations. Dialogue of this kind will be necessary to achieve rapport on issues of interdependent growth and for restraint on the use of bargaining leverage in the pattern of bilateral and regional interactions. The increasing inequalities in this pattern and the related attitudinal changes have set back a process of regional community formation which appeared to have some promise before the East Asian financial crises.

The crises have given new prominence to problems of evolution in political economies. Issues in the development of national political economies become more closely linked with issues in the development of regional political economies as structural interdependencies assume larger dimensions and as policy interdependencies demand greater cooperation. The increasingly extensive independent operations of transnational enterprises, regionally and globally, raise questions about the potential for structural policy cooperation which has been obscured in the literature on rationales for economic liberalization. While it must be recognized that deregulation opens the way for increased efficiencies by widening the scope for entrepreneurship, it also has to be recognized that problems of market failure are likely to become less confined to national economies. In addition, it has to be understood that concerted entrepreneurial endeavours, in the general interest, become more imperative as market forces are given wider freedom; and that, for this to happen, vital guidance functions must be undertaken by cooperating governments.

Regional liberalization opens the way for accelerated structural changes and an internationalization of market failure problems: both demand collaborative management, with policy-level acceptance of extensive cross-border accountability. The deepening integration facilitated by liberalization entails greater exposure to external risk, thus making social insurance increases essential in the more open states. However, developmental logic points to the more fundamental remedy of cooperation between structural policies that engage comprehensively with the tasks of promoting concerted entrepreneurship. The costs of social insurance tend to rise as rationalization strategies are implemented by translational enterprises which gain stronger international oligopoly power and limit tax exposure: hence protectionist pressures tend to increase, threatening the intended benefits of liberalization.

The most serious vulnerabilities to external risk, however, are caused not by the strategies of international manufacturing firms linking and changing national economic structures but by the investment enterprises exploiting opportunities in world financial markets. While these enterprises are provided with opportunities through the macromanagement deficiencies of many governments, they gain from manipulating financial markets in order to cause volatility from which they can profit. If advances could be made toward regional community formation in the Pacific, there would be a basis for productive cooperation with the European Union to impose effective regulation on world financial markets. Engagement with that systemic development task could be more resolute and more comprehensive if the regional community-building process were supporting extensive structural policy cooperation.

NOTES

1. On the IMF pressures see Martin Feldstein, 'Refocusing the IMF', *Foreign Affairs* **77**(2), March/April 1998, 20–33.
2. On Japan's problems, see *World Economic Outlook, Interim Assessment*, New York: IMF, December 1997, pp. 23–8
3. Japanese direct investment in the USA in 1996 included the largest foreign presence in wholesale trade ($36,319 million) and a manufacturing presence in higher-technology sectors larger than that of any European state. See *Survey of Current Business*, **77**(9), September 1997, 88; and Dennis J. Encarnation, *Rivals beyond Trade*, Ithaca, NY: Cornell University Press, 1992, ch. 3.
4. See *International Capital Markets: Developments, Prospects, and Key Policy Issues* New York: IMF, November 1997, ch. 2.
5. On South Korea's problems, see *World Economic Outlook, Interim Assessment*, 1997, and Feldstein, 1998.
6. See studies of ASEAN countries, in Denis Fred Simon (ed.), *The Emerging Technological Trajectory of the Pacific Rim*, Armonk, NY: M.E. Sharpe, 1995, part III.
7. See figures on US investment in *Survey of Current Business*, 1997, 128
8. See *The Developing Economies*, xxxv (4), December 1997: special issue 'Development mechanisms in Korea and Taiwan'.
9. See Richard F. Doner, 'Japan in East Asia: institutions and regional leadership', in Peter J. Katzenstein and Takashi Shiraishi (eds), *Network Power: Japan and Asia*, Ithaca, NY: Cornell University Press, 1997, pp. 197–233
10. See reviews of the dynamics of the Japanese system, in Shumpei Kumon and Henry Rosovsky (eds), *The Political Economy of Japan*, vol. 3, Stanford, Cal.: Stanford University Press, 1992.
11. See Dani Rodrik, *Has Globalization Gone Too Far ?*, Washington, DC: Institute for

International Economics, 1997; and Ethan B. Kapstein, 'Workers and the world economy', *Foreign Affairs*, **75**(3), May/June 1996, 16–37.

12. See Kumon and Rosovsky, 1992.
13. Alternative futures for the Chinese regime are discussed in Dwight H. Perkins, 'China's future: economic and social development scenarios for the twenty-first century', in *China in the 21st Century*, Paris: OECD, 1996, pp. 21–36. The regime's growth strategy is reviewed in Richard Pomfret, 'Growth and transition: why has China's performance been so different?', *Journal of Comparative Economics*, **25**(3), December 1997, 422–40.
14. See Frederique Sachwald (ed.), *European Integration and Competitiveness* Aldershot: Edward Elgar, 1994.
15. See Jack Hayward (ed.), *Industrial Enterprise and European Integration*, Oxford: Oxford University Press, 1995.
16. On basic issues for the USA, see C. Randall Henning, 'Europe's monetary union and the United States', *Foreign Policy*, 102, Spring 1996, 83–104.
17. Increases in lower-cost imports from East Asia have been causing the US trade deficit to rise. The US current account deficit, expected to be $177.5 billion in 1997, was projected to rise to $230.2 billion in 1998. See *World Economic Outlook, Interim Assessment*, 1997, p. 33.
18. See review of the country's political dynamics, in Haruhiro Fukui and Shigeko N. Fukai, 'Japan in 1997', *Asian Survey*, xxxviii (1), January 1998, 24–33.
19. Ibid.
20. See *International Capital Markets*, 1997.
21. *The Economist*, 18–24 April 1998, 67–9.

2. East Asian crises and regional economic integration

Brian K. MacLean, Paul Bowles and Osvaldo Croci*

INTRODUCTION

The collapse of the growth rates of the Asian economies and the financial crisis which has engulfed many of the region's economies is one of the most remarkable, and unforeseen, events in contemporary global economic history. The crisis which has unfolded since July 1997 has come as a major challenge to most of the academic and policy-making communities which had previously focused on two major issues in their analyses of Asia.

The first issue was simply to explain how a significant number of Asian economies had been so successful in their industrialization programmes in the past 30–40 years. The World Bank (1993: 2) estimated that the probability of such a regional concentration of high economic growth performers was about one in ten thousand and the task became one of uncovering the secret of East Asian economic success. The World Bank's famously titled *The East Asian Miracle* provided one explanation with its emphasis on the role of export-orientated industrialization, market-conforming policies and relatively efficient administrations. Others, most notably Wade (1990) and Amsden (1989), placed less emphasis on the market explanation and gave more weight to the role of interventionist industrial policy. Whatever the explanation, the question was the same: how to explain the region's economic success. Even as recently as January 1997, the Asian Development Bank (1997) released its own study entitled *Emerging Asia* complete with projections of how rapidly living standards could rise if the rest of Asia followed the same policies as the East Asian success stories.

The second focus in the academic literature was a growing interest in the region's economic integration. The rapid growth of the econ-

* We wish to acknowledge the outstanding work of Nouriel Roubini of New York University in putting together a website on the East Asian crisis.

omies in the region was paralleled by a rapid growth in assessing the implications of this for regional integration. For some, the motivation was to assess whether the world economy was becoming more regionalized with East Asia emerging as the third part of an increasing triadic world economy. For others, the interest was in promoting the 'Pacific Rim', a region for a new era of trans-Pacific growth and cooperation, the benefits of which would be shared widely by the region's inhabitants. This new region even had its own fledgling regional organization: the Asia Pacific Economic Cooperation forum (APEC).

The economic meltdown since July 1997 has challenged much of this. 'Dynamism' has slipped from the vocabulary describing East Asian economies and the western mass media have painted the Asian crisis as a self-inflicted catastrophe signalling the end of a development path which was lucky that it worked in the first place and is now beset with deep structural problems. Moreover, studies of the region's economic integration that were premised on an extrapolation of pre-1997 trends now seem hopelessly outdated.

The purpose of this chapter is twofold. First, we wish to examine and assess the mainstream view that has been advanced to explain the Asian economic crisis. It has focused on government intervention in the real sector of the economy together with a lack of openness in the financial sector as the causes of catastrophe. These causes are said to be widely applicable across the region's economies and have one main policy conclusion: increased liberalization of financial and real sectors, a conclusion central to the IMF bailouts now in place. We shall examine whether the mainstream view can explain the timing, the severity and the pattern of the Asian crisis and assess the extent to which the policy response is appropriate.

Second, we shall examine the implications of the Asian economic crisis for regional economic integration. The conventional explanation for the crisis and the policy response of liberalization suggest both that Asia will become more integrated into the global economy and that Asian economic structures will move closer to those of western economies. Indeed, it is argued in both popular and academic fora that the current crisis will, to quote Fukuyama (1998: 27), 'puncture the idea of Asian exceptionalism'. With many now pronouncing the end of 'Asian capitalism', we discuss the implications of the crisis for two competing constructions of 'the region' – the 'Pacific Rim' and 'East Asia' – and analyse the implications for regional economic integration.

The chapter is structured as follows. In the next section, we briefly document the spread and severity of the Asian economic crisis and the role of the IMF in it. The subsequent two sections summarize and evaluate two versions of the mainstream view of the crisis and then sketch an alternative view. Following this, as a means of raising relevant scenarios for the future of the East Asian economies in the global economy, we consider implications of the Asian crisis through the lens of the regional economic integration literature. We conclude by summarizing our main points and discussing three issues that arise from rethinking our previous work on East Asian integration in the light of our research into the Asian crisis.

CHRONOLOGY OF THE CRISIS[1]

The Asian crisis was triggered by the decision of the Thai central bank to float the baht on 2 July 1997. In mid-May, the baht and the Philippine peso had come under downward pressure. The central banks had intervened by raising the overnight rate and selling US dollars. In late June, the Thai government had decided to give up supporting Finance One, the largest financial company in the country, which went bankrupt, had suspended the operations of more than a dozen other companies, and ordered them to submit merger and consolidation plans. Despite Prime Minister Chavalit Yongchaiyudh's repeated assurances that the baht would not be devalued, the central bank was unable to defend the currency, and on 2 July it both announced a managed float and called the IMF for 'technical assistance'.

Until this announcement, although some warning signs could be detected, they were not read as an indication of the magnitude of the crisis that was to follow and did not cause much worry among investors. As argued by Radelet and Sachs (1998: 18), 'conditions of vulnerability, and the need for modest adjustments ... can not predict the actual onset of the crisis, since the crisis requires a triggering event that leads short-term creditors to expect the flight of other short-term creditors'. The decision of the Thai government to stop supporting its financial companies and the pegged rate of the baht provided such a trigger. The baht immediately fell by almost 20 per cent (passing from 24.5 to 29.1 baht to the dollar) and contagion spread rapidly to other countries in South-East Asia that were, rightly or wrongly, perceived by investors and speculators to suffer from the same financial problems.

Downward pressures began to mount first on the Philippine peso and the Malaysian ringitt. The central banks immediately intervened to support their currencies. On 11 July the Philippine central bank announced that it would enlarge the fluctuation margins of the peso against the dollar. It was imitated first by the Indonesian central bank and then by the Singapore monetary authority. The Malaysian central bank, on the other hand, decided to let the ringitt float. Malaysian Prime Minister Mahathir Mohamad put the blame for the fate of the ringitt on 'rogue speculators', particularly George Soros. Until the end of July, currency depreciation was still contained, amounting to about 10 per cent for the peso, 7 per cent for the rupiah, 5.5 per cent for the ringitt and a mere 2.2 per cent for the Singapore dollar.

In early August, the crisis hit Indonesia and Hong Kong. The Indonesian rupiah was pushed below the new fluctuation margin set up in July. The central bank first attempted to defend it and then, on 14 August, decided to let it float. It immediately sank by another 14 per cent (to 2970 rupiahs to the dollar compared to the average 2400 where it had hovered during the first six months of the year). In Hong Kong the increase in the overnight rate and the rumour that China was prepared to use US$50 billion to defend the Hong Kong dollar saved it, but the stock market shed almost a quarter of its value.[2] Throughout the month of September, the Philippine peso continued to fall along with the ringitt and the rupiah. On 8 October, when the rupiah had lost another 23 per cent of its value, the Indonesian government announced that it would seek financial assistance from the IMF. Meanwhile the crisis spread to Vietnam and Taiwan. The Vietnamese central bank doubled the permitted fluctuation band of the dong from 5 to 10 per cent, while the Taiwanese devalued their dollar.

In early November the crisis reached Korea. Since the collapse of Hanbo Steel in January, other large conglomerates had also fallen into financial trouble. Compared to the beginning of the year, moreover, the Korean won had progressively shed about 14 per cent of its value while the stock market had declined by 28 per cent. The Korean government blamed press reports which had suggested that the country's financial turmoil might surpass that of Thailand. The central bank hurried to defend the won while officials from the Ministry of Finance and Economy affirmed that they would not alter or abandon their managed system of currency trade and liberalize the market completely. A series of initiatives aimed at cleaning up debt-ridden banks and consolidating supervision of the financial sector into one agency under the finance ministry were also announced. On 17 November, however, the central bank was obliged to abandon the defence of the won when it went through the psychological barrier of 1000 to the dollar. The Korean government was keen to try to solve the crisis on its own. It widened the daily trading band for the won to from 2.25 to 10 per cent, it opened the local bond market to foreign investors, and increased the size of a bank bailout fund. The won kept falling, pulling other South-

East Asian currencies down with it. Having realized that it could not solve the crisis by itself, the Korean government first asked Japan to help persuade its banks to roll over maturing short-term loans to South Korea. On 21 November Finance Minister Lim Chang Yuel announced that the country would seek a rescue package from the IMF.

Currency markets continued to slide in December and January while the IMF negotiated, and renegotiated, with the governments of Thailand, Indonesia and Korea – the so-called IMF-3 – on the terms of the rescue packages. In February 1998, they began to rebound and, with the exception of Indonesia, the feeling was that the situation had stabilized. When the dust had settled, the IMF-3 plus the Philippines and Malaysia had come to be known as the Asian-5: the five economies most seriously affected by the Asian crisis. As of mid-May 1998, the ringitt, the peso and the baht traded at about two-thirds of their value in May 1997. The won had fared worse, having lost three-fifths its value a year earlier. The rupiah, on the other hand, had shed more than three-quarters of its value and was still suffering wild daily swings, due to the political crisis that had followed the economic one.

The Role of the IMF

The IMF entered into action in South-East Asia on 14 July, when it extended and augmented by $1 billion its existing programme for the Philippines. Then, on 20 August, it unveiled a rescue package for Thailand which included loans totalling $17.2 billion. On 5 November, it announced a $40 billion support package for Indonesia and, finally, on 4 December, it organized another rescue package for Korea totalling $57 billion dollars, the largest in the history of the IMF. In all three cases the financial package put together involved loans made also by the World Bank, the Asian Development Bank as well as other countries.

The IMF has intervened in Asia both at the macroeconomic and the structural level.[3] The policies recommended at the macroeconomic level have been, by and large, the traditional ones that have characterized IMF intervention in the past. This approach has been the object of considerable criticism since, unlike the case of Latin American and African countries where the problem was seen as being budget deficits and the level of sovereign debt, the crisis in South-East Asia had its roots in the foreign debt accumulated by the private sector. Moreover, unlike in Latin America where it limited itself to coordinating the action of private banks and acting as a monitor of performance, in South-East Asia the IMF has taken the lead in providing credit. Only in South

Korea has the IMF pushed western and Japanese banks to reschedule some short-term debt owed by Korean institutions.

To stop currency depreciation and to restore confidence, the IMF prescribed its traditional austerity medicine. This involved, first of all, a tight monetary policy, that is, an increase in interest rates and the adoption of strict limits on the growth of money supply. In order to cover the carrying costs of the financial bailout (the full extent of which is obviously spread over many years), the IMF also asked for the curtailment of government budgets (achieved mainly through the reduction of social programmes, the scrapping of large public infrastructure projects and the elimination of subsidies). These fiscal measures have been criticized because none of the countries in question were particularly profligate in their spending. Since 1993, only South Korea had run a deficit – equal to 0.1 per cent of GDP – and this only in 1996. Thailand and Indonesia had run average budget surpluses of 2.3 and 1.2 per cent of GDP, respectively.

Critics argued that the tightening of state budgets would inevitably worsen the recession brought about by the crisis, and it did. The recognition that these policies were not bringing about the desired effects (exchange rates continued to slide, the outflow of capital worsened, and output fell more than had been projected), and the perception that they might trigger social unrest, led the IMF to modify some aspects of its programme. Thus, in all three countries, the original targets of budget surpluses of 1 or 2 per cent of GDP for 1998 were changed to budget deficits of similar magnitude. In Indonesia, the IMF also agreed to let the government continue to subsidize some key food supplies.

The policies undertaken by the IMF at the structural level can be divided in two categories: (a) those designed to reform the financial system, and (b) those aimed at opening up the economies. Under the first category, the IMF has pushed for the closure of insolvent – and, in some cases, even simply illiquid – banks, the enforcement of capital adequacy standards and the adoption of western accounting practices and disclosure rules. The IMF deemed these measures necessary in order to restore confidence in the banking system. Bank closures in the midst of a financial panic, however, invited even greater panic, while the hasty enforcement of capital adequacy standards, in conjunction with the general credit squeeze, contributed to the recession by making it impossible for many companies to obtain even working capital.

Under the second category, the IMF has encouraged the dismantling of national monopolies, the sale of state assets to the private sector, the elimination of tariffs and non-tariff barriers to trade, and the opening up of the financial and insurance sectors to foreign investors. Countries have been pressured into accepting greater foreign ownership even though in the literature on 'firesale FDI', as Bhagwati (1998, p. 9) notes: 'Economists have usually advised the exact opposite in such depressed circumstances: restricting foreign access to a country's assets when its credit, but not that of others, has dried up.' In South Korea, it has also pushed for a change in labour laws to make layoffs easier. It is certainly difficult to argue that these measures are absolutely necessary to solve the current crisis. The violation of national sovereignty involved has been well put by Canadian business columnist David Crane (1998):

> Imagine if the International Monetary Fund came into Canada and said we had to give up our public health-care system, allow foreign takeovers of big Canadian firms and privatize our provincial power utilities. Canadians would be pretty upset. So would Americans if the IMF came in and forced the United States to triple gasoline taxes and let foreigners gain control of General Motors Corp., Microsoft Corp., IBM Corp., or Hewlett-Packard Co. Yet this in effect is what the IMF is doing in Indonesia and South Korea.

Hence, the imposition of these measures has led some observers, even those sympathetic to IMF's past practices, to conclude that the IMF has been 'overdoing it in Asia' (Feldstein 1998).[4]

THE ASIAN CRISIS: AN APPRAISAL OF THE MAINSTREAM VIEW

The Asian crisis took observers by surprise but as it unfolded a mainstream view of the crisis began to spread through the mass media. Briefly put, the mainstream view has been that the Asian crisis represents a defeat for the 'crony capitalism' of East Asia. The basic idea underpinning the mainstream view is that 'incestuous' relationships between the state and business in East Asia led to a bubble, the bursting of which was represented by the collapse of stock markets, real estate markets and currency values in various East Asian countries between July and December of 1997.

This section presents two distinct explanations that support the mainstream view of the Asian crisis. These explanations attribute the crisis to structural features of the East Asian economies that the IMF bailout plans have been designed to alter; they interpret the crisis as a crisis of the 'Asian model'. The explanations are those of Alan Greenspan, Governor of the US Federal Reserve Board, and Paul Krugman, Professor of Economics at MIT.

In the course of examining these explanations we shall consider two

fundamental questions. First, what are the empirically testable hypotheses that have been put forward by the author? Second, what is the
empirical evidence with respect to those hypotheses? Our premise is
that the mainstream view has achieved dominance more because of the
repeated exposure which has been given to explanations supporting it
than because of the strength of the evidence which has been marshalled
in its support. We evaluate the above-mentioned explanations in the
course of describing them and we sketch an alternative perspective in
the section that follows.

Greenspan and the Ascendancy of Market Capitalism

Alan Greenspan, Governor of the US Federal Reserve Board, is responsible for an exceptionally sweeping explanation of the Asian crisis.
In a speech titled 'The Ascendance of Market Capitalism' (Greenspan
1998), he portrays the Asian currency crisis as signalling a second
dramatic stage in the triumph of free market capitalism over alternative
economic systems. The first stage, signalled by the collapse of the Soviet
Union, represented the triumph of capitalism over the central planning
of socialism. The second stage, marked by the Asian crisis, signals the
triumph of free market capitalism over the partial planning of East
Asian mercantilist capitalism. In Greenspan's view, although the East
Asian economies generally relied upon markets and did not engage in
the same pervasive central planning as the Soviet Union, they employed
'elements of central planning in the form of credit allocation, and those
elements . . . turned out to be their Achilles heel'.

In both the Soviet and East Asian cases, planning 'worked for awhile
but then did not'. In the latter case:

> Partial planning of the sort practiced by some East Asian economies can
> look very successful for a time because they started from a low technological
> base and had sufficient flexibility to allow business units to borrow the more
> advanced technology of the fully market economies. But there are limits to
> this process as economies mature.

Greenspan's claim is that, because production in East Asia was 'set
significantly because of government directives', the economies of East
Asia were led to produce goods and services that 'domestic consumers
and export customers apparently no longer want'. The crises in East
Asia were not simply the result of these economies maturing beyond a
technological stage compatible with partial planning. In Greenspan's
words: 'The crises have their roots in the endeavor of some East Asian

countries to open up their economies to world competition, while still mandating a significant portion of their output through government directives.'

Greenspan, of course, is neither the first nor the only person to interpret the Asian crisis as evidence of the ascendance of free market capitalism.[5] The prevalence of similar interpretations in the mass media prompted columnist James Suroweicki (1998) to write, several weeks before Greenspan's speech, that:

> The meaning of the Asia crisis has been self-evident to those who believe that the free market can do no wrong. The collapse of Asian stock markets and banking systems has proven that industrial policy doesn't work, that protectionism is a route to disaster, and state control of credit allocation encourages inefficiency and corruption. In other words, what's happened in Asia is proof that until the rest of the world becomes more like us, it's bound to struggle.

Greenspan, then, constitutes a distinguished exponent of a widely held interpretation.

Greenspan's interpretation raises at least three empirical issues. First, why did the market fail to predict the crisis? This is a particularly difficult question for free marketeers who stress the wisdom of the market. If the markets embody such wisdom, and if the crisis of the East Asian economies was so obviously the result of statist policies, it is odd that the markets took so long to recognize the dangers of such policies.

But it is a difficult question for most commentators, who argue that the crisis arose because of deep-rooted problems in the economies of the region, not just for free marketeers. As Radelet and Sachs (1998) argue, if the crisis was primarily the result of deep-rooted problems, it should not have taken the world by surprise. However, if the crisis was essentially a financial panic, it was an inherently unpredictable event. Careful analysis by Radelet and Sachs demonstrates that up until the third quarter of 1997 optimism about the region was expressed by international bankers (as shown by low and falling risk premiums attached to loans to East Asia), credit rating agencies (as shown by ratings which remained unchanged throughout 1996 and the first half of 1997), securities firms (as shown by published forecasts) and by the IMF itself (as shown, for example, by its published country assessments and its October 1997 *World Economic Outlook*).

A second empirical issue raised by Greenspan's interpretation concerns the timing of the crisis. Greenspan suggests that a partially planned economy will become increasingly vulnerable to crisis as its economy matures and as it opens its economy to international competition. But if this claim is true, the crisis should have hit different East Asian economies at vastly different times in history. Singapore (on which, see Rodan 1989), for example, presumably falls within Greenspan's category of partially planned economies, but it has long been open to international competition – more open than the United States, in fact – and with per capita income on par with the G-7 countries, it is far more economically mature than Indonesia, Malaysia, South Korea and Thailand. According to Greenspan's interpretation, Singapore should have suffered from a crisis long before any of these other countries. In fact, all of these countries experienced the crisis within the space of several months, and Singapore was the least affected.

A third empirical issue regarding Greenspan's interpretation is that there is no obvious parallel between the crisis in East Asia, on the one hand, and the standard explanation for the decline and collapse of the Soviet Union on the other.[6] The standard explanation for the decline of the Soviet Union is that the model of central planning, which had allowed for a few decades of rapid growth, ceased to be an effective model after the initial phase of industrialization had been completed and consumers came to demand more sophisticated products. The maturation of the Soviet economy naturally led to a slowdown in economic growth, but the inability to produce sophisticated products caused not just a slowdown but stagnation and the emergence of a widening gap between living standards in the Soviet Union and those in the countries to which Soviet citizens compared themselves. In addition, the inability to produce sophisticated, high-quality products limited the ability of the Soviet Union to engage in world trade. The collapse of the Soviet Union, in short, was preceded by a long period of stagnation which in turn had its roots in an inability to produce high-quality, sophisticated products.

Many of the East Asian economies, by contrast, owe much of their recent growth to an ability to produce sophisticated manufactured goods for export to high-income countries. These same countries habitually run trade surpluses in manufactured products with countries like the United States, hardly a clear sign of producing goods that 'export customers apparently no longer want'. More importantly, the East Asian economies have over a long period closed the gap between their per capita incomes and those of the United States and they continue to have potential growth rates higher than those of North America and Europe.

To conclude, Greenspan's interpretation of the crisis both fails to explain why the crisis was not widely predicted and why the crisis spread to several countries within the space of a few months. It alludes to parallels between the Asian crisis, on the one hand, and Soviet decline and collapse, on the other, but such parallels remain to be demonstrated.

Krugman on 'Crony Capitalism'

Greenspan's analogy between the decline of the Soviet Union and the crisis in East Asia at least superficially resembles an argument associated with MIT economist Paul Krugman. In a widely cited *Foreign Affairs* article, Krugman (1994) suggested that, like the Soviet Union in its heyday of economic growth, most of East Asia had achieved rapid growth not by utilizing existing resources more efficiently but simply by mobilizing more and more capital and labour for the production process. Asian growth was 'mainly a matter of perspiration rather than inspiration – of working harder, not smarter.' (Krugman 1997c). More precisely, drawing upon empirical work by economist Alwyn Young, Krugman argued that growth in most of East Asia had been achieved as a result of increased inputs, not as a result of increased total factor productivity. Since there are inevitable limits to the achievement of growth by raising savings rates, labour force participation rates, and so on, Krugman suggested that growth rates in Asia would eventually decline.

It was not a particularly bold prediction. Practically all of the academic research on economic growth suggests that the growth rates of economies tend to slow as economies mature. Moreover, it does not appear to have been a particularly well-founded prediction. It now seems that the empirical work by Young on total factor productivity (TFP), upon which Krugman's prediction was based, may have been seriously mistaken. To quote from *The Economist* (1997):

> For instance, a recent report by UBS, a Swiss Bank, repeated Mr Young's analysis using more up-to-date figures for 1970–90, and come to a very different conclusion. In this study, five East Asian countries (Hong Kong, Thailand, Singapore, South Korea and Taiwan) ranked in the top 12 countries (out of 104) for average TFP growth ... In a study of ASEAN countries, Michael Sarel of the IMF also found higher annual TFP growth of 2–2.5% between 1978 and 1996, compared with only 0.3% in America.[7]

Even if the Krugman's prediction had come true, it would have been a dubious achievement. But it has not come true. As Krugman (1997c) himself has admitted, what befell the East Asian countries in the latter half of 1997 was not the slowdown he had predicted, but a sharp downturn: 'The perspiration theory predicts a gradual loss of momentum, not a crash.' Krugman had never predicted that the region's growth would come to an abrupt halt, and had been vehemently opposed to predicting anything more than a slowdown.

Krugman's *post facto* explanation of the crisis in terms of moral hazard associated with bank lending in the context of 'crony capitalism' – which we will henceforth label the 'crony capitalism theory' but which, borrowing from Radelet and Sachs (1998) could equally well be called the 'moral hazard cum bubble theory' – appears to have developed well after the onset of the crisis, probably after the crisis had spread to South Korea in November 1997. Articles by Krugman in 1997 (Krugman 1997a, 1997b) make no mention of the crony capitalism theory, nor do they predict that the crisis would spread beyond South-East Asia. The theory was first formulated in terms of a model by Krugman (1998d) and cautiously described by the author as a preliminary effort that tells 'a story that seems to bear some resemblance' to the Asian crisis. The theory, however, was almost immediately popularized by *The Economist* (1998) as holding the key to understanding the Asian crisis and Krugman himself, apparently without ever engaging in any systematic empirical investigation of the issue, soon set about popularizing the crony capitalism theory (Krugman 1998a) and attempting to argue that it provides a more persuasive explanation of the crisis than the financial panic theory associated with Harvard economist Jeffrey Sachs (Krugman 1998d).

According to Krugman's crony capitalism theory, the Asian crisis represents the bursting of a bubble. What caused the bubble to burst is a minor issue (Krugman 1998a): 'Any little thing can set off an avalanche once the conditions are right.' The problem, according to Krugman, is what caused the bubble in the first place: bad banking. In academic language, Krugman (1998c) described the problem as follows:

> The problem began with financial intermediaries – institutions which were perceived as having an implicit government guarantee, but were essentially unregulated and, therefore, subject to severe moral hazard problems. The excessive risky lending of these institutions created inflation – not of goods, but of asset prices. The overpricing of assets was sustained in part by a sort of circular process, in which the proliferation of risky lending drove up the prices of risky assets, making the financial condition of the intermediaries seem sounder than it was.

In his *Fortune* column, Krugman (1998a) explained this theory in language more evocative of the term 'crony capitalism':

> In all of the countries that are currently in crisis, there was a fuzzy line at best between what was public and what was private; the minister's nephew

or the president's son could open a bank and raise money both from the domestic populace and from foreign lenders, with everyone believing that their money was safe because official connections stood behind the institution ... In Asian countries ... too many people seem to have been granted privilege without responsibility, allowing them to play a game of 'heads I win, tails somebody else loses'.

The bursting of the bubble, according to Krugman, was probably caused by a rise in the value of the US dollar relative to the yen (which would tend to contribute to widening current account deficits in countries with currencies pegged to the US dollar) and to a slump in the semiconductor market. The crisis spread from one bubble economy to another because, as the bubble burst in one economy, investors would wonder whether it would burst in another bubble economy, and in bubble economies pessimism is self-fulfilling.

The crony capitalism theory, then, involves the following claims: first, that the Asian crisis is essentially about the crash of a set of bubble economies, that is, economies that had been growing at rates far exceeding their potential GDP growth rates, second, the key reason that these economies were growing at rates exceeding their potential GDP growth rates is that they had bad banking systems. More precisely, domestic lenders were reckless in lending to those who were viewed as having government backing for their projects. Third, since the economies had been exceeding their potential, it is only natural that they would go through a post-bubble period of very slow, possibly negative, growth. Fourth, both the timing of the Asian crisis and the pattern by which it spread from one country to another were somewhat arbitrary since the bursting of a bubble is triggered by the inherently unpredictable spread of pessimism among market participants. Of the four claims, the first two are the most critical, as the other two are contingent upon them.

The first claim is difficult to prove one way or the other. As illustrated by the debate over whether the US economy in early 1998 is in a soon-to-burst bubble phase, judging whether an economy is in a healthy boom or is experiencing a bubble is a difficult task during the boom phase of the business cycle.

The rise and decline of a stock market index is the typical gauge of bubble activity. Some of the stock markets in the region – specifically those in Thailand and South Korean – had been losing value since early 1996. The Malaysian stock market started losing value in March 1997. Examined on a country-by-country basis, these declines seem quite explicable investor responses to internal problems of corporate bankruptcies, export problems, and so on, in these specific countries. All

East Asian stock markets slumped in the last two quarters of 1997, but what else would anyone expect, given the massive currency collapse and the sense of panic associated with it? In short, the country-by-country pattern of stock market decline does not obviously support the story of a bubble bursting in one economy after another via contagion of investor expectations. A severe contraction makes it easy to convince the public that the preceding period was a bubble phase but, of course, something is not true simply because the public is easily convinced of it.

Rising real-estate prices are presented as additional evidence of an extraordinary bubble that had developed in East Asian economies. This is plausible, but two points should be kept in mind. One is that real-estate speculation is typical of the latter part of the boom phase of a business cycle, and as such requires no special explanation: it is standard market behaviour.[8] The other is that massive capital inflows, as experienced in East Asia during the 1990–6 period, invariably lead to an expansion of the non-tradables sector (including real estate) at the expense of tradables.

The second claim of the crony capitalism theory is that guaranteed lending by banks was critical to the development of the bubble. With respect to the explicit and implicit guarantees, Radelet and Sachs (1998: 31) note that:

> much of the lending was directed to private firms that did not enjoy these guarantees. Approximately half of the loans by international banks and almost all of the portfolio and direct equity investments went to non-bank enterprises for which state guarantees were far from assured. This comes to around three-fifths of the total capital flows to the region.

Furthermore, if these 'bad' banking systems had been jointly implemented in accordance with an East Asian trade and investment agreement in the early 1990s or in response to the 'aggressive unilateralism' of US trade policy, it would be relatively easy to understand how they could give rise to bubbles in several economies a few years later. In fact, however, state-industry–banking linkages have evolved separately in each country over a long time. If such long-standing domestic linkages are at the root of the problem, why were there not domestic or region-wide crashes of similar magnitude in the 1970s and 1980s?

To conclude, Krugman's writings on the Asian crisis (as of May 1998) contain no solid evidence that his crony capitalism theory explains the Asian crisis. His evidence is so weak, in fact, that the popularity of his theory deserves some comment. Our tentative hypotheses are, first, that part of the popularity arises because the crony capitalism theory provides some justification for IMF actions to open up markets and demand structural reforms in East Asia. Various influential people have therefore been inclined to call attention to Krugman's theory. His provocatively phrased, widely debated but essentially banal and ill-founded prediction of an Asian slowdown has been mythologized as a brilliant prediction of the sharp downturn in East Asia, and has been used to confer upon him the status of a prophet.[9]

Second, Krugman is a widely read columnist who has over time created and attracted an audience highly receptive to hypotheses that downplay the significance of the East Asian experience in general and that trumpet the problems of industrial policy. He is writing at a time when US unemployment is at its lowest point in decades, the US stock market is booming and his US readers are probably as prone to feelings of triumphalism as Japanese citizens were during the 'bubble economy' period of the late 1980s. Much of that audience is quite willing to gloss over the differences among faraway economies in a region that contributes to US trade deficits and to assume that in East Asia 'corruption and nepotism ... have flourished on an epic scale' (Krugman 1998d).

Third, a 'bubble cum moral hazard' explanation possesses innate psychological appeal. As Radelet and Sachs (1998) note: 'Financial panic is rarely the favored interpretation of a financial crisis. The essence of a panic is that a "bad" equilibrium occurs that did not have to happen. Market analysts and participants are much more prone to look for weightier explanations than simply a bad accident.' Krugman (1998d) has satisfied the urge for weightier explanation with a morality tale claiming that: 'The crisis ... *was* a punishment for Asian sins, even if the punishment was disproportionate to the crime ... The *specific* sin that pushed Asia to the brink was the problem of moral hazard in lending – mainly domestic lending.' Krugman's explanation also gains psychological appeal from being simple and easy to remember. It is not based upon detailed knowledge of the situation and can be easily comprehended by those lacking such knowledge.

AN ALTERNATIVE VIEW OF THE ASIA CURRENCY CRISIS: FIVE HYPOTHESES

The Asian crisis is still too current to permit more than a tentative evaluation of its causes and potential cures. What follows is a sketch of the alternative view of the crisis that we are in the process of developing.

To keep the sketch succinct, we have formulated it in terms of five hypotheses (plus subsidiary hypotheses where appropriate).

Hypothesis One

The Asian crisis is first and foremost a currency crisis affecting countries with more-or-less fixed exchange rates. The logical first step to explaining the Asian crisis is to ask why East Asian currency values collapsed in the latter half of 1997.

The countries most seriously affected by the crisis had all been pegging their currencies to the US dollar. Thailand had a formal peg for the baht, the Philippines peso was effectively pegged, and Indonesia, Malaysia and South Korea relied upon a crawling peg (Radelet and Sachs 1998: 6). The obvious explanation of the currency collapse is that countries on fixed exchange rates have a far greater potential for currency collapse than currencies with floating rates.[10] Countries with fixed exchange rates can get themselves into situations where there is practically no downside risk to betting against their currencies. As Dornbusch (1998) puts it: 'The average of flat and down is down!'

While this observation is critical to understanding the crisis, it only deals with a proximate cause. For the deeper causes of the crisis, we have to answer questions such as: Why did investors flee from East Asian currencies? Why were some countries much better able than others to withstand currency speculation? Why did several countries experience currency devaluations that by far exceeded what would be deemed appropriate by any economic models in vogue at the time of the crisis?

Hypothesis Two

Investors fled from the East Asian currencies because the currencies came to be seen as being overvalued and likely to be floated. The indicators of currency overvaluation they looked to were current account and trade deficits. As Thurow (1998) has observed: 'The Asian countries whose economies have recently been collapsing were all running large trade deficits – $8 billion in Indonesia, $4 billion in Malaysia, $10 billion in Thailand, $4 billion in the Philippines, and $19 billion in Korea.'

The literature suggests at least five possible causes of deteriorating trade balances in East Asia. The most often cited reason for rising trade deficits is the rise in value of the US dollar since late 1995, particularly against the Japanese yen. The yen–dollar exchange rate went from approximately 85 yen to the dollar in autumn 1995 to approximately 130 yen to the dollar by late 1997. The strengthened US dollar has brought about increased trade deficits for the United States; not surprisingly, it has also brought about increased trade deficits for countries who pegged their currencies to it.

A second reason focuses on the import side. The rapid growth of imports in many East Asian countries was linked to the stage of the business cycle which many of them had reached. It has long been observed that in the latter part of a boom phase of a business cycle, imports will tend to grow more rapidly than exports, in part because of rising consumer incomes, in part because domestic supply constraints will lead some domestic purchasers to turn to foreign suppliers.[11]

A third reason for deteriorating trade balances in East Asian countries was an excessive allocation of investment to the real-estate sector. Real-estate speculation does little for productivity growth and competitiveness. It would not have become as much of a problem if the East Asian countries had followed more closely (like Japan in the 1950s and 1960s; see MacLean 1990) the traditional industrial policy of channelling funds to industry. As Stiglitz (1998) notes:

> Thailand, for instance, used to restrict bank lending to real estate, both because it realized the danger of such lending, and because it wanted to direct credit to what it viewed as more growth-enhancing investments. But again, partly under pressure from those who claimed that such restrictions interfered with economic efficiency, it liberalized, eliminating the restrictions with the predictable consequences we have seen.

A fourth reason for rising trade deficits is the emergence of China as a major trading power. China, which for decades operated a highly autarkic economic policy, has evolved into the world's tenth largest trading nation. While China has provided an expanding market for exports from other East Asian countries, it has run larger and larger trade surpluses with them (in the context of China's global trade surpluses) and has been encroaching on their market share in third countries such as the US and Japan.

A final reason for deteriorating trade balances (or, more precisely, current account balances) in East Asia, and the most fundamental one, relates to rising investment levels in the context of stable domestic savings rates (see Park 1996). By definition, a current account deficit is equal in magnitude to the amount by which domestic investment exceeds domestic savings. All else being equal, a surge in investment will manifest itself in an increased current account deficit.[12] East Asia witnessed extraordinary investment levels in the 1990s; they were made possible, and in some sense driven, by massive capital inflows. According to IMF statistics, the East Asian countries (excluding Japan) experienced a net inflow of $261 billion during the period 1990–4, an amount that accounted for 50 per cent of total capital inflows to developing countries. Wolf (1998), citing statistics from the Institute for International Finance, notes that: 'The five countries that have been most damaged by the crisis – Indonesia, Malaysia, South Korea, Thailand, and the Philippines – had net private inflows of $41bn in 1994. By 1996, this had jumped to $93bn.'

Hypothesis Three

Although current account and trade deficits were the primary indicators to which investors turned in deciding to flee from East Asian currencies, the use of those indicators was less than rational, and the collapse itself was wildly incommensurate with any deterioration in fundamentals that preceded it. The collapse had all the markings of what is known in the literature as a 'currency panic' or, more generally, as a 'self-fulfilling attack'.

For the region as a whole (as opposed to Thailand in 1997), current account deficits were ambiguous indicators of currency overvaluation. They were primarily associated, as noted above, not with borrowing to finance overconsumption, which has provided the historical case for their use as an indicator of overvaluation, but with borrowing to finance investment. Provided that high rates of investment result in growth, and in particular in export growth, they provide the basis for ready repayment and a rational basis even for exchange rate *appreciation*. Yet the markets are accustomed to thinking of a current account deficit as a sign of trouble; it is a rule of thumb traditionally used by traders, who may have no inkling of its origins, to predict exchange rate *depreciation*. So, as Park (1996: 362) astutely observed:

> The increase in the current account deficit . . . alarms the foreign investors, even though the deficit will help to expand export capacities in the long run. If, for whatever reasons, foreign investors believe that the deficit is unsustainable and that a currency devaluation is imminent, they may pull out of their investments en masse, precipitating a major financial crisis that could be contagious.

This, of course, is precisely what happened in the Asian crisis.

What happened in Asia was a classic currency panic. The empirical literature on currency panics has three major implications, as summarized by Wyplosz (1998: 2), which explain: (a) why the *possibility* of a financial meltdown in Asia could be foreseen (by someone familiar with the literature); (b) why it should not be surprising that the panic resulted in speculative attacks even on the currencies of economies in the region which had exhibited almost no indications (rule of thumb or more rational) of deteriorating fundamentals; and (c) why it could not be predicted that the crisis would hit in the last two quarters of 1997:

> First, financial market liberalization is the best predictor of currency crises. This has been true in Latin America in the 1980s, in Europe in the early 1990s and in Asia in 1997. The channels are capital inflows which pose delicate policy problems, exposure to currency risk, and heightened volatility.
>
> Second, crises seem to spread contagiously. Once one country comes under attack, 'similar' countries follow. What 'similarity' exactly means remains an open research question. There are clear geographical aspects (Latin America, Europe, South East Asia) but structural aspects, such as banking structure or external debt levels, also seem to matter.
>
> Third, crises often occur without warning signals and come as big surprises.

The impossibility of predicting the timing of currency panics, it should be noted, arises because outcomes in currency markets are subject to self-fulfilling expectations: 'expectations that are *ex ante* unjustified are validated *ex post* by the outcome that they have provoked' (ibid.: 9).

The Asian collapse has prompted efforts, most notably by Krugman, to develop new theories of crisis. But the broad features of the Asian crisis are perfectly explicable in terms of the previously available theoretical and empirical literature and were foreseen by certain economists familiar with that literature. Indeed, it seems safe to say that the Asian crisis provides such a resounding confirmation of the dangers of capital mobility identified by the existing literature that it was inevitable, in an era of globalization, that public attention would be diverted away from obvious but inconvenient explanations and towards new and irrelevant ones.

Hypothesis Four

What made the Asian crisis a good possibility, then, was massive capital inflows in the years leading up to the crisis, particularly inflows of short-term capital, that were used to finance high investment levels but that turned into massive capital outflows when panic struck. A number of factors explain the inflows, but the key factor was financial liberalization.

The Asian-5, as mentioned above, are estimated to have received net capital inflows of $93 billion in 1996. In 1997 they experienced an estimated capital outflow of $12 billion. Wolf (1998) has pointed out that this swing of $105 billion amounts to 'a staggering 10 per cent of the combined pre-crisis gross domestic product of the five economies'.

The volatility of capital flows has varied greatly according to their type. Foreign direct investment flows have been fairly stable, as have flows from non-bank private creditors. Portfolio investment, by contrast, shifted from a net inflow of $12 billion in 1996 to an outflow of similar magnitude in 1997. Most significant of all was the dramatic shift by commercial banks from $56 billion of net lending in 1996 to net repayment of $21 billion in 1997.

Massive capital inflows to East Asia date from about 1990. One approach to explaining these flows is to divide causal factors into those external to the economies receiving the capital inflows and those internal to the economies. Calvo *et al.* (1996) identify a number of external factors explaining capital inflows to both East Asia and Latin America in the 1990s, the most important of which appears to be a sustained decline in interest rates in the developed nations that prompted investors to seek high yields in rapidly growing developing economies. For East Asia, others have emphasized internal factors such as the extremely rapid real GDP growth rates, healthy government budget balances and stable nominal exchange rates.

Such explanations are quite reasonable so far as they go. But in explaining why various people have walked through an open door, the fact should not be overlooked that they are only able to walk through it if someone has unlocked it for them. As Bello (1997) mentions, in East Asia various countries followed policies of financial liberalization:

> the elimination of foreign exchange and other restrictions to the inflow and outflow of capital, fully opening up stock exchanges to the participation of foreign portfolio investors, allowing foreign banks to participate more fully in domestic banking operations, and opening up other financial sectors, like the insurance industry, to foreign players.

Some countries had their own reasons for engaging in financial liberalization, most notably to keep up foreign investment flows after the flow of Japanese direct investment began to taper off at the beginning of the 1990s.[13] In general, however, the East Asian economies were strongly encouraged to pursue financial liberalization policies by the United States and by the IMF (and, as we noted on p. 23, the IMF-3 have been obliged to engage in further liberalization as a condition of receiving bailout funds).

Hypothesis Five

Of the Mexican crisis of December 1994, it has been said (Calvo *et al.* 1996: 37) that the severity 'would have been lessened had the [capital] inflows (which became outflows) been smaller' and 'had their maturity been longer'. The same is true of the Asian crisis. And it points to differences in policies and practices with respect to capital flows as a key determinant of the differences in the extent to which various East Asian countries were affected by the Asian crisis.

Countries potentially have access to measures to regulate both capital flows and their composition. One way to regulate capital flows is simply to retain traditional capital controls. Countries such as China, Vietnam and Taiwan have retained such controls to a greater degree than the Asian-5 and this apparently provided them with some insulation from the Asian crisis (though, as noted below, massive foreign reserves at least partially explain the resilience of China and Taiwan to speculative currency attacks).

Policies with respect to the composition of capital flows seem to help explain why, for example, Malaysia has so far emerged from the Asian crisis a bit less battered than the IMF-3 despite having foresworn the tens of billions of dollars that would have been forthcoming if it too had agreed to accept IMF tutelage. Much has been made about the possibly damaging effects of Malaysian Prime Minister Mahathirs's remarks about 'villainous' currency speculators on jittery markets. What was less commented upon is that Mahathir's remarks were an extreme expression of an apparently sensible policy to discourage short-term capital inflows. In a survey of capital inflows to developing countries, Calvo *et al.* (1996: 137) rated Malaysia alongside Chile as two examples of sophistication in managing capital flows. Dornbusch (1998) has observed that: 'Malaysia ... was financed predominantly by direct investment and for that reason avoided the more extreme meltdown experienced in countries where capital flight was a multiple of reserves.'

Another variable associated with an economy's capacity to resist speculative attacks is the extent of its foreign exchange reserves. As Feldstein (1998), for example, pointed out: 'A clear lesson of 1997 was that countries with large reserves could not be successfully attacked by financial markets. Hong Kong, Singapore, Taiwan, and China all have very large reserves, and all emerge relatively unscathed.' As of October 1997, China had reserves of $141 billion, Taiwan $83 billion, Hong Kong $79 billion, and Singapore $74 billion. As Feldstein recognizes, these large reserves are related to capital flows. The countries accumulated their reserves by running trade surpluses and saving the resulting foreign exchange. In essence, they accepted capital inflows but channelled them into reserves. Or as Wolf (1998) put it: 'The view of capital flows taken by these successful governments was just like President Bill Clinton's of marijuana: it's fine to smoke, so long as one does not inhale.'

In short, for financial markets to succeed in 'speculative attacks' they require effective mechanisms to carry out those attacks. If a country has engaged in limited financial liberalization, it is less vulnerable. It is also less vulnerable to the extent that the foreign capital it has attracted takes the form of foreign direct investment as opposed to portfolio investment, and to the extent that it accumulates foreign reserves.

Conclusion

Our five hypotheses do not deal with the intricacies of the unfolding of the Asian crisis. A solid account that touches upon Asian-5 policy mistakes, IMF blunders and other important details has already been provided in Radelet and Sachs (1998). Neither do we regard these hypotheses as being definitively proven by the evidence and arguments we have provided. Indeed, part of the reason for formulating our view of the crisis in terms of explicitly stated hypotheses is to lay the ground for rigorous empirical testing. Nevertheless, we believe that in laying out these five hypotheses we have made a strong case for an alternative view of the Asian crisis, a case that is considerably stronger than has been made for the 'crony capitalism' theory.

THE POST-CRISIS FUTURE THROUGH THE LENS OF THE REGIONAL INTEGRATION LITERATURE

In the analysis that follows we look at three different types of 'economic integration' – trade integration, business practice integration and institutional integration – and examine the implications of the Asian economic crisis for each of them. Since in some circles economic integration has the narrow meaning of 'a state of affairs or a process which involves the amalgamation of separate economies into larger free trade regions' (El-Agraa 1997: 1), we should emphasize that we employ the term in its broader sense.

This section is offered as an exercise in scenario-building. There are too many factors at play for anyone to be able to predict the future of economic integration as it involves the countries of East Asia. One way to try to grasp the situation is to consider factors identified in the literature on regional economic integration. This approach at least provides us with plausible scenarios or relevant dimensions for consideration. In the final section of the chapter we shall add own our hypotheses about regional integration and link them to our view of the causes of the Asian crisis.

In examining the post-crisis future through the lens of the regional integration literature, we concentrate on scenarios involving two competing constructions of the 'region', namely, the (Greater) East Asian region and the Pacific Rim. These two 'regions' have dominated the literature on integration for the past decade and therefore provide the focus for the discussion here.

Trade integration

Trade integration refers to the process of deepening trade ties among a set of countries. It is a process typically investigated by neoclassical trade theorists to address the issue of regional trade 'bloc' formation. This type of neoclassical integration analysis has been common over the past ten years and seeks to analyse the extent to which trade patterns display a regional bias. By using gravity models, trade flows are examined to test whether countries in a particular region trade disproportionately with each other; that is, whether countries trade with each other more than would be expected on the basis of the characteristics of each country such as its economic size and level of per capita income and the distance between countries. If countries in a particular region do trade disproportionately with each other in this sense, then countries are said to form a 'natural trade bloc'. This trade bloc may, or may not, form the basis of an actual regional trading agreement; the purpose of the adjective 'natural' is to permit an analysis of economic data and an identification of regions without the necessity to refer directly to states as political actors and to regional economic integration as requiring a political superstructure.

The motive for many of these types of studies has been to shed light on the question of whether the world economy is becoming more regionalized, a concern most evident before the conclusion of the Uruguay Round when the fear of a world of rival trade blocs was at its highest. The issue of regional economic integration in Asia was therefore framed within the wider debate concerning regionalism and multilateralism as alternative trade policies and their welfare implications. This analysis was applied to 'Asia' – typically the countries of East and South-East Asia – to examine the extent to which trade displayed a regional bias and how any such bias was changing over time. This allowed assessment of the extent to which Asia was indeed already, or becoming, an integrated 'region'.

If regional economic integration is seen in these terms, how might it be affected by the Asian economic crisis since mid-1997? The collapse in Asia's growth rates will have the effect of reducing the share of intraregional trade to total trade within the region. Measures of trade integration should therefore fall and the region will appear less integrated than before. To the extent that the region's governments are successful in targeting the now faster growing extraregional markets for their products in the face of low domestic demand and slow regional growth, then this trend will be more noticeable. The fact that the regions' currencies have depreciated to a greater degree against extraregional currencies than against each other means that the growth of extraregional exports should be further stimulated. Furthermore, if Asian countries are able to target the now seemingly dynamic US market for a greater share of their exports, then these types of trade integration measurements will reinforce the position of those who view the Pacific Rim as a natural, and integrating, economic region.

Business Practice Integration

Economic integration in the Asian region has also been attributed to the particular forms which business practices take, that is, to business practice integration. This can be captured under the general heading of 'network capitalism', which Stubbs (1995) has argued constitutes a 'third form of capitalism' and is distinctive to the Asian region. The focus of this approach is the argument that dense networks of personal relations and supplier relations characterize Asian businesses and that they form the basis for integrating the region's economies. These networks are also said to be distinctive to Asia and to differentiate the region from both North America and Europe; the forms of business practice also link therefore with the analysis of an emerging triadic global economy: this time, with economies based on differentiated business practices rather than by intraregional trade flows (although it is possible that the two may be linked).

The characterization of Asian economies as 'network economies' rests, according to Stubbs, on the activities of two types of firms. The first is the overseas Chinese firm. The expanding Chinese diaspora has received much academic interest, with overseas Chinese firms being characterized as being organized on patriarchal lines and operating on the basis of personal connections. The increasing importance of these firms in the regional economy is widely recognized, as is their role in facilitating cross-border trade and investment flows. Hong Kong and Taiwanese firms have dominated investment in China, particularly in southern China where the cultural affinities between Hong Kong and Guangdong and between Taiwan and Fujian have shaped investment flows. While such regional integration based on personalistic networks is generally accepted as a valid characterization, there is debate on how such networks should be assessed. Some view them as a demonstrably vibrant economic force and refer to such connections as 'network capital'; others, such as Fukuyama (1995), view the Chinese family firm as an indicator of a lack of 'trust' or 'social capital' in the region since societal trust is a necessary precondition for the development of the modern corporation, an enterprise form which relies on cooperation between unrelated individuals and which is the engine of economic growth.

The second type of firm identified by Stubbs is the Japanese multinational corporation. These multinationals are argued to be integrating the region through their extensive network of suppliers operating in many different countries. This regional network has both socio-technological and economic origins. The socio-technological origins lie in the adoption of post-Fordist production techniques by Japanese firms based on just-in-time supply systems. The economic origins lie in the rapid spread of Japanese corporations overseas following the appreciation of the yen after the Plaza Accord in 1985, which is seen by many as constructing a regional hierarchy and division of labour often referred to as the 'Flying Geese' model.

What might be the implications for these two types of firms, and regional integration, of the Asian economic crisis? The view that the crisis has been caused by excessive government interventionism has led to policy prescriptions favouring economic liberalization and the opening up of domestic markets to foreign ownership; these form a core part of the policy conditions attached to IMF loans, as indicated above (pp. 23–5). The opening of domestic industries to foreign ownership, together with the acquisition of assets at fire-sale prices, suggests that the ownership composition of many economies in the region might change significantly, the trend being increased foreign ownership. Given the continued weakness of the Japanese economy and the financial weakness of Japanese banks, the major actors in this trend would probably be European and, especially, US firms. In this case, the importance of the Chinese diaspora might diminish somewhat and the importance of Japanese FDI in the region similarly recede from the heights which it reached from the mid-1980s to early 1990s in the wake of the Plaza Accord. If this were to be the case, then the role of overseas Chinese firms and Japanese multinationals in creating an integrated regional economy based upon a dense network of interfirm relations would diminish in importance. The regional economy could be thought of as replacing Japanese economic hegemony (and the 'flying Geese' model) with US economic hegemony (in what many in Asia now fear to be US neo-colonialism), and the 'Pacific region' increasing in importance as an integrative force over the 'East Asian region'.

However, all the evidence is not in this direction. First, as an empirical point, the expected surge in inflows of US investment into Asia has not as yet materialized. Certainly, there are examples of increased investment in specific well-managed firms; however, it has not been a widespread increase affecting whole industries (Lutterbeck 1998). While Japanese multinationals may decrease in importance somewhat, it would be too soon to suggest their eclipse by marauding US investors. Despite the potential for ethnic conflict associated with the practices of Chinese firms in societies which are not predominantly Chinese, a potential that became an unpleasant reality with the torching of Chinese businesses during the Indonesian riots, a case can be made for the continued importance of the overseas Chinese firm. It has been argued that their success has relied on their ability to reduce risks through networks of personal and reciprocal connections in a region where contract enforcement mechanisms through legal means are generally weak (by Anglo-American standards), and legal systems in the region are likely to change slowly. In this case, the shift to an integrating Pacific region is much less likely to happen and the regional integration through business practice is likely to retain a strong East Asian flavour.

Institutional Integration

The competing constructions of the region are perhaps most evident in the sphere of formal institutional integration. While the main actors in the two previous dimensions of integration are economic, it is states which are the important actors in attempts at regional institutional integration. Here, the past decade has witnessed two main state groupings, namely, the East Asian Economic Caucus (EAEC), and the Asia Pacific Economic Cooperation (APEC). At present, the EAEC exists as a sub-group of APEC, although the two groupings were originally conceived of as representing quite different views of the 'region' (Higgott and Stubbs 1995). Both institutions owe their origins to the same temporal phenomenon: the push for more-integrated economic blocs in both Europe (represented by the 'Single Market' initiative and the Maastricht Treaty) and North America (represented by the

Canada–US Free Trade Agreement and, subsequently, the North American Free Trade Agreement – NAFTA). The question of how the countries in East Asia should respond to this met with various answers; some, most notably Malaysia's Prime Minister Mahathir, argued for an 'Asian' response which would include only nations found on the Asian side of the Pacific, while others pushed for a trans-Pacific approach. Since it was the latter, in the form of APEC, which has become the more prominent of the two responses, we concentrate here on the implications of the Asian economic crisis for this particular vision of regional economic integration.

Because APEC includes both developed and developing countries and because it was formed in 1989 in response to rising fears of continental protectionism – fears which have gradually subsided with the conclusion of the Uruguay Round – APEC has typically been long on generalities and short on specifics. To provide itself with a clearer sense of purpose and direction an Eminent Persons Group (EPG), chaired by US economist Fred Bergsten, was set up in 1993. This coincided with the United States' assuming the chair of APEC and upgrading the annual meeting to a Summit of Heads of State, thereby raising APEC's political profile. APEC's economic significance resulted from the EPG's vision for the organization, which was based on free trade. The EPG's recommendations culminated in the commitment by APEC leaders, at their 1994 summit in Bogor, Indonesia, to achieve free trade and investment in the region by 2010 for developed countries and by 2020 for developing countries. These targets are to be achieved through each country's 'individual action plan', which form the basis of APEC's 'collective action plan' and which inform sectoral liberalization initiatives.

How will the Asian crisis affect APEC and its vision of regional economic integration? At first sight, one might expect APEC's vision to be enhanced as a result of the economic crisis. The economic ideology underlying APEC since its adoption of the '2010/2020' agenda has been neoliberal in orientation and in accord with IMF thinking on the need for Asian economies to adopt widespread liberalization measures to get out of the crisis on a longer-term basis. APEC's working groups on trade and investment, trade promotion, investment and technology transfer, human resources development, regional energy cooperation and telecommunications might all be thought of as fora in which this agenda could be pursued. APEC's close links with the business community, through the APEC Business Advisory Committee set up in 1997, might be another forum in which liberalization initiatives could be pursued on a trans-Pacific basis.

Liberalization and integration across the Pacific, with the policy agendas of APEC and the IMF reinforcing each other, is one possibility, but is not the only one, or even the most likely one. APEC's vision of regional integration is, in fact, highly problematic for a number of reasons. First, APEC itself has been sidelined throughout the Asian economic crisis. Even though APEC's 1997 summit was held in November as the extent of the Asian crisis was becoming fully known, the summit produced general remarks but no specific action. It provided a forum for leaders to discuss the problems, but APEC, as an organization, has played no role in the solution.

Second, APEC's liberalization agenda has been controversial within APEC; it only exists as an agreement because it is non-binding on member countries. There has always been concern among developing-country members that APEC does not pay sufficient attention to their interests, and among East Asian countries that APEC promotes a non-interventionist economic strategy at variance with the growth record of East Asian economies, a concern to which we return in the conclusion below.

There is even a possibility that the crisis may lead to a reaction by some Asian countries against the 'Pacific Rim' idea in favour of a more 'East Asian' regional identity. For example, in a televised speech, Malaysian Prime Minister Mahathir warned about the 'great danger of recolonization'. Indeed, most of the countries hit by the crisis seem to regard the policies enforced by the IMF not as a necessary, although bitter, medicine but as a potion concocted by the American administration to sap the strength of their economies. These feelings are not always publicly manifested, especially by government officials in Korea and Thailand, but they seem to simmer below a more compliant surface.

It is evident that, in order to be of any significance, any Asian bloc would have to include Japan. So far, however, there is little evidence that Japan regards the Asian crisis as an occasion to spur the formation of such a bloc. At the annual IMF/World Bank Conference held in Hong Kong in September 1997, Japan did sponsor the idea of setting up a kind of Asian Monetary Fund (with a permanent secretariat of its own and funding amounting to $100 billion) aimed specifically at dealing with the Asian economies. The IMF, the US and other G7 countries, however, were able to push the idea aside, arguing that there was no need for an addendum to the IMF. After this initiative Japan has limited itself to making money available in emergency loans (about twice the amount provided by the US), but the rescue plan was hammered out in Washington by the US Treasury Department and the IMF. American government officials, nevertheless, have lost no opportunity to cast

Japan in the role of the villain, denouncing in particular what they perceive as that country's failure to play the role of locomotive for the Asian economies hit by the crisis. Faced with constant American criticism and attacks, it would not be unthinkable for the Japanese government eventually to organize, as it were, mounting Asian resentment in order to counter more effectively continued American 'aggressive unilateralism'.

Since institutional integration requires state action, the motives and forces acting upon states must be considered when examining the prospects for institutional integration. Although the ideological free market basis of APEC may appear at first sight more compatible with the 'end of Asian exceptionalism' thesis, we would argue that such a view significantly underestimates the strength of opposition in Asian government and policy-making circles to a US agenda and the continued appeal of some kind of 'Asian bloc'.

CONCLUSION

The mainstream view of the Asian crisis, we have argued, portrays it as a self-inflicted catastrophe rooted in the 'crony capitalism' practised in Asian countries. It points to the increased liberalization of financial and real sectors as a sensible policy direction that will permit the Asian-5 to overcome their problems.

In the preceding pages we have developed an alternative view of the crisis that emphasizes the importance of capital flows. Succinctly put, our view is that the Asian crisis is best viewed as primarily a currency crisis affecting countries that had pursued fixed or heavily managed exchange rates. The Asian-5 ran large trade deficits which were used in a rule-of-thumb fashion by currency traders in deciding to flee currencies. Once the trigger was provided by deteriorating economic circumstances in Thailand, speculative attacks were waged with greater and greater ferocity against the currencies of the region. Those countries which had accepted large capital inflows, especially short-term inflows, and had given up all or most of their capital controls, were ill-prepared to deal with the attacks. The countries that had maintained capital controls, avoided short-term inflows and accumulated large foreign exchange reserves were better able to resist.

Having developed an alternative view of the causes of the Asian crisis, we then examined the implications of the crisis for regional economic integration. In so doing, we examined two competing constructions of 'the region', namely, the 'Pacific Rim' and the 'East Asian' regions, both of which have been important foci for academics and policy-makers during the past decade. We argued that, although the crisis might be regarded as strengthening the position of the 'Pacific Rim' as the basis for regional economic integration, such a view may be too simplistic. This argument was made by considering three different types of integration: trade, business practice and institutional integration.

In concluding this chapter, we would like to highlight a few issues that arise from rethinking our previous work on East Asian integration (Bowles and MacLean 1996a, 1996b) in the light of our research into the Asian crisis. Bowles and MacLean (1996a: 410) stressed that 'states are key actors in the process and that economic variables, such as aggregate trade trends, are insufficient for the discussion of bloc forma-tion'. The Asian crisis reconfirms the relevance of this claim but it also points to the importance in discussions of regional economic integration of considering international financial institutions like the IMF, a matter we had not given adequate consideration. It is noteworthy that the crisis has stimulated greater interest in the political economy of the IMF, with even fairly mainstream economists (Bhagwati 1998; Wade and Veneroso 1998) emphasizing the relevance of the 'IMF–Treasury complex' as an analytical concept.

In Bowles and MacLean (1996b: 166), we also stressed that studies of East Asian economic integration need to recognize that 'a key ideo-logical division in the world economy of the 1990s appears to be between the free-trade ideology of the advanced capitalist economies and the interventionist-development ideology of most newly industrial-izing economies'. The Asian crisis has reconfirmed the relevance of this observation as well, with much of elite opinion in the West interpreting the Asian crisis as being rooted in the interventionist-development ideology of the East Asian countries, and with the IMF using the crisis as an opportunity to impose its free-market ideology on Thailand, Indonesia and South Korea.

As our analysis of the causes of the Asian crisis has shown, the free-market interpretation of the crisis is poorly grounded. It is not sur-prising, therefore, that the developmentalist paradigm is still considered relevant to many countries in the region. For example, interviews with senior economists in China's State Planning Commission in February 1998 revealed that South Korea's economy still holds much appeal as a development model for China's leadership.[14] Even though South Korea's economy has suffered serious financial weakness and has been subject to a massive IMF bailout, its industrialization record over the previous 30 years continues to capture the attention of policy-makers elsewhere. In reforming China's state-owned enterprises, the enterprise group model followed in South Korea has a significant following in Beijing policy circles; the lesson learned in Beijing from the South Korean crisis has been that financial institutions and enterprises should be more autonomous from each other, not that the state should not intervene to fashion an enterprise system. Thus, powerful groups within East Asian economies still regard 'developmentalism' as a viable economic strategy and reject significant elements of the IMF (and APEC) liberalization agenda.

Continued interest in the developmentalist paradigm and recognition of the factors (outlined above, pp. 39–40) that allowed some countries to emerge from the Asian crisis relatively unscathed suggest another reason for the East Asian countries to reject the liberalization agenda of the IMF and APEC. Governments in the region need to be able to implement measures to control the volume and composition of capital inflows. As Park (1996: 364–5) has argued, there are 'dangers in imposing such controls unilaterally,' so 'serious consideration should be given to multilateral efforts to control speculative short-term capital movements, rather than leaving the problem to individual countries'. Given the movement to amend the IMF articles of agreement to promote capital mobility and the related attempt at the OECD to bring about a Multilateral Agreement on Investment, it appears that the only realistic option for East Asian countries which would like to impose stricter capital controls without doing it unilaterally would be to enter into an agreement with other East Asian countries. A more general version of this option was raised in Bowles and MacLean (1996a: 167) where it is pointed out that:

> whereas EC integration is interesting for thinking about bloc formation with common minimum social standards and NAFTA has raised the issue of bloc formation with common minimum environmental standards, an East Asian economic grouping may be significant for showing how bloc formation might proceed while allowing states the necessary degree of leeway for industrial and macroeconomic strategies.

Finally, in our earlier work on East Asian economic integration, we implicitly assumed societies characterized by a high degree of social consensus or at least societies where the overthrow of elites could be treated as a remote possibility. In the light of the Asian crisis, such assumptions are no longer necessarily valid, in part because East Asian elites preside over countries with strongly nationalist populations and have become vulnerable to the charge of kowtowing to the West, but also because several countries in East Asia appear to be on the verge of an unemployment crisis. The most optimistic forecasts expect unemployment, which hovered around the 2 per cent mark in the early 1990s, to rise in 1998 to between 6 and 7 per cent in Thailand and South Korea, and to 10 per cent in Indonesia. Large-scale dismissals, moreover, have yet to come. In South Korea, changes in the labour legislation to allow layoffs were passed only in March 1998, and since firms are required to give 60 days' notice, the full impact of the crisis has yet to manifest itself.

The prospects are particularly grim since governments in the region have traditionally relied on a combination of high growth rates and long-term, if not lifetime, employment to provide social security for their citizens. Indonesia and Thailand have no unemployment insurance plans. To cope with the emergency, the Indonesian government has tried to defuse the situation by encouraging rural immigrants to return to their villages by reducing the price of train tickets from the cities to the countryside and increasing the fares in the opposite direction. The Thai government has hurriedly passed a law which obliges firms to increase severance pay. In South Korea, the government has upgraded its unemployment insurance programme (first established in 1995) by increasing the basic compensation from 50 per cent to 70 per cent of the minimum wage, payable for a maximum period of seven months. This improvement, however, is simply the price that the government has paid to receive the consent of trade unions to change labour legislation in order to make it easier for firms to carry out layoffs.

The situation is likely to get worse before it begins to improve. J.P. Morgan, an American investment bank, has forecast that GDP will fall by around 10 per cent in Indonesia this year and by about 4 per cent in South Korea and Thailand. Growth is expected to resume in 1999 but to reach only 3 or 4 per cent, less than half the average rate in the early 1990s. An extensive process of corporate restructuring has also just begun. Firms, in other words, are switching from the goal of increasing their market shares, and hence creating jobs, to that of maximizing profits. The restructuring of the financial sector will make it more difficult to invest in less than very profitable ventures. Finally, large-scale public projects are being cancelled or scaled down.

Layoffs and the rise in food prices caused by the depreciation of the local currencies and the end of government subsidies have already led to some episodes of social unrest. These have been particularly severe in Indonesia because of both the absence of a social safety net and existing ethnic tensions. For the moment they have only led to the resignation of President Suharto, but more profound political changes could follow.

NOTES

1. This chronology is based on reports that appeared in the *Wall Street Journal*, the *New York Times* and *The Financial Times*.
2. Unless otherwise indicated, references to dollars throughout this chapter are to US dollars.
3. A detailed list of the measures enforced by the IMF in Asia can be found at http://www.imf.org/External/np/exr/facts/Asia.HTM
4. In this chapter we employ numerous documents downloaded from internet sites. Some of these documents are formated in a way that does not allow us to give page numbers for quotations. This is the explanation for page numbers being given for some of our quoted material (specifically, printed sources and sources in PDF format) but not for all of it.
5. Krugman (1998b) refers to four schools of economic thought on the Asian crisis, the first of which consists of 'free market enthusiasts'.
6. Note that our concern is not with the veracity of the standard interpretation of Soviet decline and collapse but rather with the accuracy of Greenspan's suggestion of a parallel between the Soviet crisis and the East Asian crisis.
7. See also the explanation in Stiglitz (1998) on why the results of Young 'are simply not very robust'.
8. See, for example, Sharpe (1996: esp. 173) on the behaviour of Canadian (Ontario) real-estate markets in the 1980s. Stiglitz (1998) provides a US comparison: 'Even the overbuilding in East Asia needs to be put in perspective. The commercial vacancy rates in Bangkok and Jakarta have been around 15 percent and are expected to rise to 20 percent – comparable to Dallas and Houston today, and well below the vacancy rates of 30 percent or higher seen in several major American cities in the 1980s.'
9. See, for example, Frankel (1998). For an analysis of the Asian situation that genuinely warrants description as prophetic, see Park (1996).
10. Part of the reason for this relates to forces identified by the macroeconomic principle known as the 'inconsistent trinity': 'that we can only have two of the three following features: a fixed exchange rate, full capital mobility and monetary policy independence. Any pair is possible but attempts at achieving all three inevitably results in a currency crisis' (Wyplosz 1998: 4).
11. See Ito (1992: 82–4) for an analysis of this in the case of Japan under the Bretton Woods system.
12. See, for example, Lincoln (1988) for an example of this sort of analysis applied to the evolution of US and Japanese current account balances. Wolf (1998) makes the relevant points very succinctly:

> Yet remember that the greatest benefit of large-scale international lending should be the opportunity to invest more than a country can itself save; that this can only happen if there is a current account deficit; that a real appreciation is how such a current account deficit is produced; that the appreciation works by reducing the relative incentive to invest in production of exports and import substitutes; and that, under a fixed exchange rate, a rise in the domestic price of non-tradables, including property, is how this change in incentives takes place.

13. A proper analysis of the causes of financial liberalization in East Asia is not possible here. The complexity of the issue is illustrated by the discussion of Wade and Veneroso (1998), who note that: 'In Korea key people were bribed by Japanese and western financial institutions, thanks to which they did something that was counter to the whole thrust of Korean development policy for decades past. Bribery aside, the government placed great emphasis on joining the OECD, and the OECD made financial openness a condition of membership.'

14. Personal interviews by Paul Bowles, Beijing, February 1998.

REFERENCES

Amsden, Alice H. (1989), *Asia's Next Giant: South Korea and Late Industrialization*, New York: Oxford University Press.

Asian Development Bank (1997), *Emerging Asia: Changes and Challenges*, Manila: Asian Development Bank.

Bello, Walden (1997), 'Asia–Europe Relations in the light of the Southeast Asian financial crisis', ASEM Seminar, Transnational Institute, Amsterdam, October.
http://www.worldcom.nl/tni/archives/bello/essen.htm

Bhagwati, Jagdish (1998), 'The capital myth', *Foreign Affairs*, May/June, 7–12.

Bowles, Paul and Brian MacLean (1996a), 'Regional blocs: can Japan be the leader?', in Robert Boyer and Daniel Drache (eds), *States Against Markets: The Limits of Globalization*, London and New York: Routledge, pp. 155–69.

Bowles, Paul and Brian MacLean (1996b), 'Regional trading blocs: will East Asia be next?', *Cambridge Journal of Economics*, **20**, 393–412.

Calvo, Guillermo, Leonardo Leiderman and Carmen Reinhart (1996), 'Inflows of capital to developing countries in the 1990s', *Journal of Economic Perspectives*, Spring, 123–39.

Crane, David (1998), 'IMF's intrusive policy raises criticism', *Toronto Star*, 10 March.

Dornbusch, Rudi (1998), 'Asian crisis themes', February.
http://web.mit.edu/rudi/www/asianc.html

The Economist (1997), 'Is it over?', 1 March.
http://www.stern.nyu.edu/~nroubini/asia/sf0839.html

The Economist (1998), 'Economics focus: why did Asia crash?', 10–16 January.

El-Agraa, Ali M. (1997), *Economic Integration Worldwide*, New York: St Martin's Press.

Feldstein, Martin (1998), 'Refocusing the IMF', *Foreign Affairs*, March–April.

Frankel, Jeffrey (1998), 'The Asian model, the miracle, the crisis, and the Fund', paper delivered at the US International Trade Commission, 16 April.
http://www.stern.nyu.edu/~nroubini/asia/EACRITC.pdf

Fukuyama, Francis (1995), *Trust: The Social Virtues and the Creation of Prosperity*, New York: Free Press.

Fukuyama, Francis (1998), 'Asian values and the Asian crisis', *Commentary*, February, 23–7.

Greenspan, Alan (1998), 'The ascendance of market capitalism', speech to the Annual Convention of the American Society of Newspaper Editors, Washington, DC, 2 April.
http://www.bog.frb.fed.us/boarddocs/speeches/19980402.htm

Higgott, Richard and Richard Stubbs (1995), 'Competing conceptions of economic regionalism: APEC versus EAEC in the Asia Pacific', *Review of International Political Economy*, **2**(3), 516–35.

Ito, Takatoshi (1992), *The Japanese Economy*, Cambridge, Mass.: MIT Press.

Krugman, Paul (1994), 'The myth of Asia's miracle', *Foreign Affairs*, November/December.

http://web.mit.edu/krugman/www/myth.html

Krugman, Paul (1997a), 'Bahtulism: who poisoned Asia's currency markets?', *Slate*, 14 August.
http://www.slate.com/Dismal/97–08–14/Dismal.asp

Krugman, Paul (1997b), 'Currency crises', paper prepared for NBER conference, October.
http://web.mit.edu/krugman/www/crises.html

Krugman, Paul (1997c), 'What ever happened to the Asian miracle?', *Fortune*, 18 August.
http://web.mit.edu/krugman/www/perspire.htm

Krugman, Paul (1998a), 'Asia: what went wrong?', *Fortune*, 2 March.
http://www.pathfinder.com/fortune/1998/980302/fst8.html

Krugman, Paul (1998b), 'I told you so',
http://web.mit.edu/krugman/www/I-told-you-so.html

Krugman, Paul (1998c), 'Will Asia bounce back?', speech for Credit Suisse First Boston, Hong Kong, March.
http://web.mit.edu/krugman/www/suisse.html

Krugman, Paul (1998d), 'What happened to Asia?', paper prepared for a conference in Japan, January.
http://web.mit.edu/krugman/www/DISINTER.html

Lincoln, Edward (1988), *Japan: Facing Economic Maturity*, Washington, DC: Brookings Institution.

Lutterbeck, D. (1998), 'Softly, softly: a predicted tidal wave of investment is only a ripple so far', *Far Eastern Economic Review*, 9 April, 40–2.

MacLean, Brian (1990), 'Have low housing investment levels been a cause of high Japanese growth rates?', unpublished PhD dissertation, York University.

Park, Yung Chul (1996), 'East Asian liberalization, bubbles, and the challenge from China', *Brookings Papers on Economic Activity*, **2**, 357–71.

Radelet, Steven and Jeffrey Sachs (1998), 'The onset of the East Asian financial crisis', paper prepared for the National Bureau of Economic Research Currency Crises Conference, 6–7 February.
http://www.hiid.harvard.edu/pub/other/eaonset.pdf

Rodan, Gary (1989), *The Political Economy of Singapore's Industrialization*, London: Macmillan.

Sharpe, Andrew (1996), 'The rise of unemployment in Ontario', in Brian K. MacLean and Lars Osberg (eds), *The Unemployment Crisis: All for Naught?*, Montreal and Kingston: McGill-Queen's University Press, pp. 153–76.

Stiglitz, Joseph (1998), 'Sound finance and sustainable development in Asia', keynote address to the Asia Development Forum, Manila, 12 March.
http://www.worldbank.org/html/extdr/extme/jssp031298.htm

Stubbs, Richard (1995), 'Asia-Pacific regionalisation and the global economy: a third form of capitalism?', *Asian Survey*, September, 785–97.

Surowiecki, James (1998), 'The Asian about-face', *Slate*, 22 January.
http://www.slate.com/motleyfool/98-01-22/motleyfool.asp

Thurow, Lester (1998), 'Asia: the collapse and the cure', *New York Review of Books*, 5 February.
http://www.nybooks.com

Wade, Robert (1990), *Governing the Market: Economic Theory and the Role of Government in East Asian Industrialization*, Princeton, NJ: Princeton University Press.

Wade, Robert and Frank Veneroso (1998), 'The Asian crisis: the high debt model vs. the Wall Street–Treasury–IMF complex', New York: Russell Sage Foundation, March.
http://epn.org/sage/imf24.html
Wolf, Martin (1998), 'Flows and blows', *The Financial Times*, 3 March.
http://www.stern.nyu.edu/~nroubini/asia/CapitalFlows-IIF-Wolf-FT398.html
World Bank (1993), *The East Asian Miracle: Economic Growth and Public Policy*, New York: Oxford University Press.
Wyplosz, Charles (1998), 'Globalized financial markets and financial crises', paper prepared for the Coping with Financial Crises in Developing and Transition Countries Conference, Amsterdam, 16–17 March.
http://heiwww unige.ch/~wyplosz/fondad.pdf

3. Pacific economic integration and the 'flying geese' paradigm

Terutomo Ozawa

Ten East Asian economies – Japan, the NIEs South Korea, Taiwan, Hong Kong and Singapore, the ASEAN-4 Indonesia, Malaysia, the Philippines, Thailand and China – have recorded miraculous growth since the mid-1950s. Japan was the first Asian economy that succeeded in catching up with – and surpassing in some industrial activities – the West in the post-Second World War period. The Japanese economy in its emulative growth period (1950–73) grew annually at about 10 per cent until the first oil crisis of 1974. Japan's phenomenal growth soon began to be replicated by the new industrializing economies (NIEs) in the 1960s (the average annual growth rate was 7.6 per cent in South Korea, 9.1 per cent in Taiwan and 8.7 per cent in both Hong Kong and Singapore), and their growth continued unabated into the 1970s (9.3 per cent, 10.2 per cent, 8.9 per cent, and 9.4 per cent in these economies, respectively) and the 1980s (8.0 per cent, 8.0 per cent, 7.1 per cent, and 7.2 per cent, respectively).[1] It is no wonder, then, that such regionally clustered growth came to be identified as 'the East Asian miracle' (World Bank, 1993). In fact, it is comprised of a string of miracles.

What is more, such a succession of clustered economic expansions has resulted in an ever-expanding and ever-integrating intraAsian market. It is largely *de facto* economic integration, since such a phenomenon of rapid growth was brought about by way of concatenated agglomeration – that is, Japan's successful structural transformation imparted growth stimuli to other Asian economies, first to the NIEs, then to the ASEAN-4, and currently to China and Vietnam, each in turn transmitting stimuli to others. In this process of tandem growth, cross-border business activities of multinational corporations (MNCs), such as trade, foreign direct investment (FDI), licensing and sub-contracting, have been serving as catalysts for structural upgrading. In order to attract trade-orientated, especially export-driven forms of MNCs' activity, these Asian economies have all been pursuing an outer-focused strategy of catching-up development. A sub-regional *de jure* integration pursued among the ASEAN-4 is an additional impetus in this direction.

Although in the context of the East Asian miracle Japan is often considered to be the 'lead goose' (in terms of the 'flying geese' paradigm explained below), the very success of its catch-up growth was made possible under the aegis of the *Pax Americana*. During the Cold War, the United States opted for a foreign policy in favour of security, even at some cost to its own economic interests. This policy allowed Asian economies, beginning with Japan, the opportunity to harvest benefits from the liberal trade regime set up by the *Pax Americana* for the free world. The oft-quoted statement, 'The Cold War is over, Japan has won', captures the outcome of America's post-Second World War foreign policy in a nutshell.[2] For reasons which will be explored below, it is even more appropriate to paraphrase that as 'East Asia has won.'

As will be stressed below, even though the Cold War has ended, the dynamics of trade expansion and economic growth set in motion by the *Pax Americana* is still vibrantly at work throughout the Pacific Rim, because the United States has been keeping its market relatively open to imports and continues to absorb manufactures from export-orientated developing countries. The East Asian economic miracle is an unfolding epic of global capitalism whose *modus operandi* was moulded by the requirements of the *Pax Americana* against the backdrop of its confrontation with Soviet-led communism.

The themes of this chapter are as follows: (a) a so-called 'flying geese' paradigm of economic development provides an appropriate metaphoric frame of analysis to capture the intra-Asia-Pacific dynamism of tandem growth and economic integration; (b) the United States, Japan and the Asian NIEs have so far effectively played their role as the lead goose, the second goose (Asia's lead goose), the third-ranking geese (Asia's second geese), respectively, in sequential transmissions of growth impulses further down the regional hierarchy of economies, inducting first the ASEAN-4, and then China (and most recently Vietnam) into global capitalism; but (c) the manner in which the United States, Japan and the NIEs have each played their respective roles is considerably different and distinct. The United States has pursued a hegemony-compelled, Cold War driven policy of liberalism, Japan a catch-up focused, self-reliant strategy of techno-protectionism, and the NIEs a demonstration-triggered, trade-pushed path of neo-mercantilism (except *laissez-faire* Hong Kong). On the other hand, the ASEAN-4 have been resorting to an MNC-dependent, export-pulled strategy of industrialization (that is, pro-transnationalism), while China has an ethno-centripetal, 'open-door' policy for economic modernization.

Although these divergent approaches reflect each regime's mandates, they are nevertheless the outcomes of strategic interactions among themselves, culminating in an ever-deeper integration of the Asia Pacific economies. In short, the sequential appearance of Cold War induced liberalism (US) → catch-up focused techno-protectionism (Japan) → demonstration-triggered neo-mercantilism (Korea, Taiwan and Singapore) → MNC-dependent pro-transnationalism (the ASEAN-4) → ethno-centripetal modernization (China) has been the essential locus of the evolving political economy of the Pacific Rim.[3] Now, however,

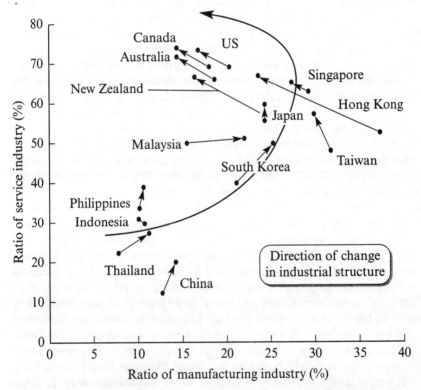

Note: Machinery products represent SITC section 7 (machinery and transport equipment); light industry products represent SITC section 6 (manufactured goods classified chiefly by material) and section 8 (miscellaneous manufactured articles).

Source: Asian Development Bank, 'Key indicators of developing Asian and Pacific countries', as presented in JETRO (1995: 36).

Figure 3.1 Changes in industrial structures of Asia Pacific countries and areas, 1982–92

the US is shaping a new post-Cold War policy, and so is Japan in its effort to mould a post-catch-up phase of strategy. These themes will be elaborated, after we have taken a brief look at the overall dynamics of East Asia.

STRUCTURAL DYNAMISM

East Asia is in the midst of rapid structural change. At the most funda-mental level, structural dynamism is reflected in the rapid transformation from the primary sector into the secondary sector in the region's rapidly developing economies such as the ASEAN-4 and China, and the swift transformation from the secondary sector to the tertiary sector, along with a deepening sophistication within both sectors, in Japan and the NIEs. These patterns of structural change underlie the dynamics of the Asia Pacific region. These changes are what is expected from a rapidly growing economy, as predicted by the stages theory of growth (Clark 1935). This type of structural change is illustrated in Figure 3.1. The advanced economies are all moving in a north-westerly direction and clustering in the upper left-hand side of the diagram, whereas the ASEAN-4 and China are moving in a north-easterly direc-tion and are situated on the lower left-hand side.

In addition to the intersectoral changes, export-driven structural transformation involves rapid capital intensification in the secondary sector. This is demonstrated in Figure 3.2. Structural upgrading has been occurring within the manufacturing sector from light industry goods (such as apparel and sundries) to heavy industry goods (such as steel and electrical/electronics goods), as revealed in their shifting export compositions. Korea and Hong Kong have graduated from being light-industry orientated and become, respectively, a more capital-inten-sive manufacturer and a service provider; whereas Indonesia, Thailand, the Philippines and China have been developing labour-intensive manu-facturing. Interestingly, both Singapore and Malaysia have been moving 'vertically' and have become sharply more capital-intensive in their manufactured exports – without following the 'normal' pattern of round-about growth. Their uniqueness reflects a relatively small popu-lation base and their governments' active involvement with structural upgrading.

Furthermore, each sector goes through the stages of upgrading from low-end (low value-added) to higher-end (higher value-added) varieties of goods and services, along with the process of capital intensification. In short, structural dynamism stems from the three basic types of

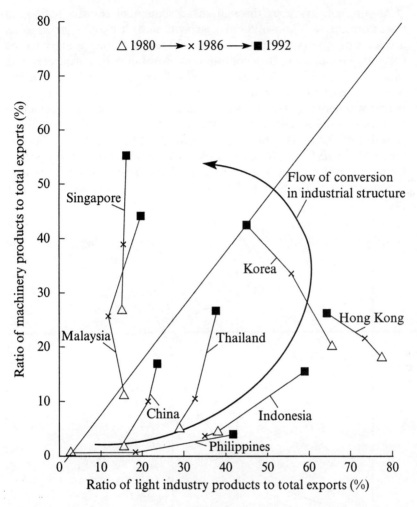

Note: This is merely a schematic presentation for illustrative purposes only; each economy is on its own growth curve.

Figure 3.2 Ratio of machinery and light industry products to total exports from countries and areas in East Asia

restructuring: (a) intersectoral restructuring *à la* Colin Clark (primary → secondary → tertiary sector); (b) interindustry restructuring with capital deepening (light industry → heavy and chemical industry → assembly-based industry → innovation-driven industry); and (c) intra-industry product upgrading (low-end products → high-end products).

As an economy goes through these sequential transformations, it traces out the well-known S-curve growth path. It initially grows at an accelerating rate (when resources are shifted from the primary to the secondary sector), and then continues to grow but only at a decelerating rate – that is, with an inflection in growth rates. Rapid growth occurs when the economy is around the inflection point, and this particular period will hereafter be called the 'inflection growth period'. Advanced countries are all in a growth-decelerating phase (close to the top of the growth curve), the NIEs have been approaching the end of the inflection phase, the ASEAN-4 are in the middle of the inflection-growth period. China has just entered such a period. The relative positions of these economies along the S-shaped growth curve are schematically shown in Figure 3.3.

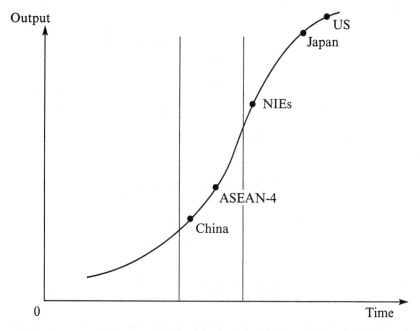

Note: In the period before the Second World War, Japan had already succeeded in building tier IV and tier III industries. However, these phases of industrialization were reworked for export competitiveness in the postwar period, providing new momentum to build upper-echelon industries.

Source: Ozawa (1995: 220).

Figure 3.3 Riding on an S-shaped growth curve

It may be wondered, why therefore, there, is this string of concatenated periods of growth spurt. In this regard, Robert Aliber (1993) stressed the historical fact that when any economy industrializes, it goes through a period of rapid growth at least once (with an exception of a war-devastated economy which may repeat rapid growth twice, as Germany and Japan did after the Second World War). He identified such a growth spurt as a period during which the share of its manufacturing in national incomes rises, its export competitiveness develops, initially in unskilled labour-intensive industries – usually under the favourable influence of an undervalued home currency and foreign capital inflows, both FDI and portfolio. Aliber then explained the sources of rapid growth in terms of (a) the movement of labour from agriculture to industry; (b) increased participation in the world economy via exports; (c) a sharp decline in the average age of labour and physical capital stock (plant and equipment) – hence, increased competitiveness by way of low-cost flexible labour and the advanced technologies embodied in capital goods; and (d) a rise in the infrastructural investment necessitated by industrial growth and its accompanying urbanization.

Indeed, this rapid growth period is identical with the first phase of transition from the primary to the secondary sector *à la* Colin Clark, as well as with Rostow's 'take-off' period (Rostow 1960), although these associations are not specifically mentioned in Aliber's work. Aliber regards the period of rapid growth that occurs at least once in any country's lifetime experience of industrialization as a *key* determinant of inward investment, both FDI and portfolio. In this respect, his model is quite relevant to East Asia where inflection growth is now sequentially observed. In other words, we can witness the phenomenon of concatenated inflection growth in the region. Yet a question still remains unanswered: Why does such rapid growth occur – and more importantly, why in succession (country after country) and in a regionally clustered fashion as it does in East Asia?

It needs to be stressed here that merely being near or at that particular juncture of economic development characterized by rapid inflection growth does not automatically guarantee a growth spurt. The fact that East Asian economies are able to translate this growth potential so successfully into actual reality has much to do with the current particular evolutionary phase of global capitalism. This is a phase in which Japan has luckily been able to participate effectively, transforming itself into Asia's first fully industrialized nation, and has, in that process, capitalized on, moulded in its own ways and then trans-grafted global capitalism on to the Asia Pacific through its cross-border business activities. In this intra-Asian spread of capitalist development, MNCs from the West and Japan – and most recently from the NIEs and even from the ASEAN-4 themselves – are serving as the providers of industrial technology, management and organizational skills, finance, intermediate goods and access to markets in the advanced countries. Indeed, MNCs, a major instrument of present-day global capitalism, have been the vital catalysts for strengthening and upgrading East Asia's industrial structure and export capacity.

Moreover, the governments of these East Asian economies play an equally critical role as promoters of economic development by way of their policies for macroeconomic stabilization, human resource development, infrastructural development, trade, FDI and industrial restructuring. In other words, East Asia is pursuing the MNC cum host-government assisted path of growth.

THE 'FLYING GEESE' PARADIGM

The structural dynamism of the Asia Pacific, outlined above, can be nicely placed within the framework of the so-called 'flying geese' (FG) paradigm of economic development, a paradigm originally conceptualized by Kaname Akamatsu in the 1930s (*inter alia*, Akamatsu 1935). This metaphor of a regionally clustered flock of economies advancing together in a FG formation has become popular both inside and outside Japan as a way of depicting the current pattern of tandem growth in the region.

Akamatsu's FG-formation model can be described as an evolutionary paradigm of sequential catch-up growth along the stages of industrialization by exploiting the external economies of hierarchical concatenation. It is based on a dynamic perspective of interactive industrial upgrading and growth, a view that the global economy goes through structural renovations because of mutual interactions between leader ('lead goose') and emulator/challenger ('follower geese'). As Akamatsu (1962: 1) put it: 'It is impossible to study the economic growth of the developing countries in modern times without considering the mutual interactions between these economies and those of the advanced countries.'

The basic idea implicit in his paradigm is that any developing country in an open-economy context can industrialize step by step, if it is capable of capitalizing on the learning opportunities made available in its external relations with the advanced world. Economic development is essentially looked upon as a learning-by-emulating or knowledge-absorption process, a process facilitated by, and derived from interactions with, the more advanced economies – instead of being an autonomously self-propelled discrete phenomenon. Put simply, it is a derived development. Looked in this light, East Asia's tandem growth is nothing but an interconnected series of derived developments. In this process of knowledge transmission and learning, MNCs do play a vital role, since they are generators and transmitters of industrial technology and organizational skills ('created assets').[4]

JAPAN AS ASIA'S LEAD GOOSE

The East Asian miracle began only after the Second World War. The high degree of export competitiveness exhibited first by Japan and later by other Asian economies in tandem can be best explained in terms of the FG paradigm of catch-up economic growth.

The postwar high-growth environment (during the 1950–74 period which is now identified as the Golden Age of Capitalism[5]) was an important contributory factor to Japan's rise as an economic super-power. The premise here is that Japan's postwar economic miracle as demonstrated by rapid structural upgrading – and now other Asian economies' miracles – has emanated from the internal logic of the *Pax Americana*. This logic worked itself out in a series of events that can be summarized as follows (Ozawa 1995):

1. As a byproduct of the war-induced economic mobilization, the United States came to dominate the world in practically every industry at the end of World War II. It had come to possess a full set of *all* manufacturing industries, ranging from the most techno-logically sophisticated to the most labour-intensive standardized industries. It was an unprecedented situation, indeed, in which one nation was so totally self-sufficient, so enviably affluent and so dominantly powerful in every respect.
2. Ironically, this very dominance contained a built-in mechanism to foster challengers. For analytical purposes, America's industrial co-lossus in the immediate postwar years can be divided vertically into four basic tiers, which are distinguishable in declining order of capital intensity and technological sophistication (Figure 3.4):

    Tier I: innovation-driven, R&D-intensive industries, such as air-craft, computers and pharmaceuticals;
    Tier II: assembly-driven, component-intensive industries, such as cars, televisions and household electric appliances;

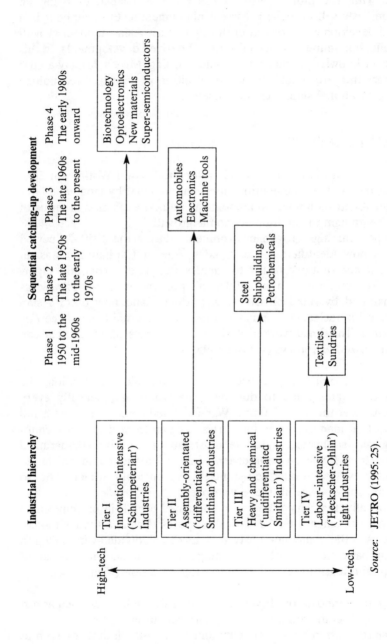

Industrial hierarchy

Sequential catching-up development

Phase 1	Phase 2	Phase 3	Phase 4
1950 to the mid-1960s	The late 1950s to the early 1970s	The late 1960s to the present	The early 1980s onward

Tier I
Innovation-intensive ('Schumpeterian') Industries

Tier II
Assembly-orientated ('differentiated' Smithian') Industries

Tier III
Heavy and chemical ('undifferentiated' Smithian') Industries

Tier IV
Labour-intensive ('Heckscher-Ohlin') light Industries

Biotechnology
Optoelectronics
New materials
Super-semiconductors

Automobiles
Electronics
Machine tools

Steel
Shipbuilding
Petrochemicals

Textiles
Sundries

High-tech

Low-tech

Source: JETRO (1995: 25).

Figure 3.4 Sequence of postwar structural upgrading under the aegis of the Pax Americana

Tier III: heavy and chemical industries, such as steel, heavy machinery and basic chemicals;

Tier IV: labour-intensive light industries, such as apparel, shoes, and sundries.

At the start of the postwar period, the United States had 'everything' and stood on top of the world, enjoying absolute advantage, superiority and competitiveness in every single manufacturing industry – as well as in agriculture, forestry and mining (including oil). Yet the United States could not afford to remain a secluded colossus. As the leader of the free world, it had to take the initiative in revitalizing Europe and Japan by promoting freer trade and investment in order to stem the rising tide of communism.

Freer trade, however, led ineluctably to the gradual loss of the markets for goods in successive lower-tier industries in which the United States had comparative disadvantages. Tier IV industries comprised the first segment that was quickly lost to imports. This was indeed the first sign of the self-transformative logic of the *Pax Americana*.

3. Nevertheless, the United States still had dominance in higher-tier industries. In fact, in the early 1960s George Meany, president of the American Federation of Labor and Congress of Industrial Organizations (AFL-CIO), declared that it was in the interests of the United States to import freely small Volkswagens from Germany and toys from Japan so that the Germans and Japanese could in turn purchase American goods. He strongly supported the Trade Expansion Act of 1962. In those days, therefore, the doctrine of comparative advantage and free trade was strongly espoused and put into practice and was even strongly endorsed by the labour unions. The logic was that, even though the United States might lose some import-competing industries, it would gain even more in its export industries; trade was therefore considered a positive-sum game and mutually beneficial (Evans 1967).

4. Japan was clearly among the foremost beneficiaries of America's postwar trade policy. Early on, for example, the United States encouraged Japan to manufacture and export textiles by using as raw materials the cotton supplied by the US government on generous credit (Arisawa 1967). (The United States was obviously interested in turning Japan into a major importer of American cotton then in surplus, given the favourable attitude shown by its labour unions towards manufactured imports.) Initially, in order to earn precious foreign exchange, Japan eagerly exported textiles and

other light industry goods such as toys and sundries that its low-wage labour was able to produce. During the 1952–4 period, for example, Japan's hourly wage rate was only 10 per cent of that of the United States (Kenen 1960).

STRUCTURAL UPGRADING AND OUTWARD FDI

Japan, however, did not remain a happy toy-maker for long. It soon began to climb the ladder of industrialization by proceeding to tier III and then on to tier II, and most recently it has finally reached the start of tier I (as illustrated in Figure 3.4):

Stage I: Labour-driven (tier IV 'Heckscher–Ohlin') manufacturing of textiles, sundries and other light industrial goods as the leading export sector (from 1950 to the mid-1960s).

Stage II: Scale-driven (tier III 'undifferentiated Smithian') heavy and chemical industrialization in steel, aluminium, shipbuilding, petro-chemicals and synthetic fibres (from the late 1950s to the early 1970s).

Stage III: Assembly-based, subcontracting-dependent (components-intensive) (tier II 'differentiated Smithian') industries, such as automobiles and electrical/electronics goods as the dominant sector (from the late 1960s to the present).

Stage IV: Innovation-driven (tier I 'Schumpeterian') industries, such as high-definition TVs, new materials, fine chemicals, advanced microchips and digital electronics (from the late-1980s onwards).

Japan thus has successfully moved from textiles to heavy machinery and chemicals, to automobiles and computers, and most recently to biotechnology, microelectronics, new materials and other knowledge-based industries: that is, from low value-added to higher value-added sectors consistent with the rising level of technological sophistication and factor endowments (greater capital accumulation per capita) which necessarily culminated in wage hikes and higher standards of living. In other words, Japan has effectively generated and exploited dynamic comparative advantages.

But what has Japan done with those comparatively disadvantaged industries? Interestingly enough, they have been transplanted abroad by way of FDI and other forms of cross-border business operations of Japanese MNCs (Kojima 1978, 1990; Kojima and Ozawa 1984, 1985; Ozawa 1979a, 1979b, 1992). In fact, Japan's overseas investment so far has gone through three different phases. The first phase of overseas

expansion via FDI (from the mid-1960s to the mid-1970s) was dominated by labour-intensive light industries (textiles and sundries) and
resource-seeking ventures (exploration and extraction of oil, natural
gas, iron and copper ores and the like); the second phase (from the
mid-1970s to the early-1980s) was joined by more capital-intensive
industries such as chemicals, metal products and machinery; and the
third phase (from the early 1980s onward), in which Japanese industry
has most recently been involved, entails the transplantation of component-intensive, assembly-based industries, notably automobiles and
electronics goods (both consumer electronics and related parts). Japan's
outward FDI has thus been the outcome of its structural transformation
and the changing dynamic comparative advantages, closely corresponding to the four stages of structural upgrading described above.

In particular, the sharp appreciation of the yen after the Plaza Accord
of 1985 contributed to the dramatic increase of Japan's outward FDI.
The high yen abruptly reduced the price competitiveness of Japanese
firms' home-based production and exports. Consequently, they were
compelled to seek lower-cost production locations overseas, particularly
in the nearby Asian economies which happened to be quite eager to
attract investment from foreign MNCs as the catalyst for economic
development. In the 1970s, the NIEs used to be the most popular hosts
for Japanese firms, but during the latter half of the 1980s they were
overtaken by the ASEAN-4, which were in turn superseded by China
in 1993 (Figure 3.5).

The rush of Japanese manufacturers setting up offshore production
is causing some concern about a possible hollowing-out of Japanese
industry. Yet this is certainly a plus factor for other East Asian economies, since FDI is potentially an effective mechanism for knowledge
transfer and learning (depending on the absorptive capacities of the
host economies).

JAPAN'S CATCH-UP FOCUSED TECHNO-PROTECTIONISM

In the early years following the Second World War, Japan adopted a
neomercantilist policy of fostering 'infant industries', as it had done
before in the prewar days. Even before the war, Japan had already
succeeded in building tier IV (for examples, cotton and then rayon
textiles) and tier III industries (iron and steel, shipbuilding, industrial
machinery, chemicals) – all as part and parcel of its imperialist policy
of *fukoku, kyohei*, or 'wealthy country, strong army' – step by step,

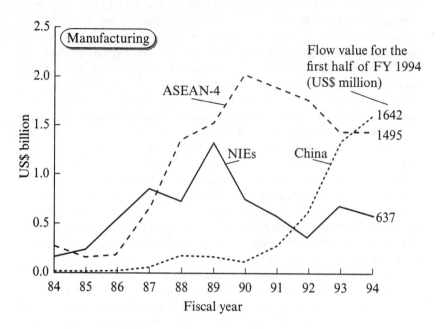

Source: Japan's Science and Technology Agency (1996: 142).

Figure 3.5 Trends in Japan's foreign direct investment in East Asia

through the state-guided process of import substitution and export
promotion (Akamatsu 1962; Arisawa 1967; Lockwood 1954; Nakamura
1983; Smith 1955).

This 'techno-protectionism' has been Japan's national developmental
ideology, an ideology 'that technology is a fundamental element in
national security, that it must be indigenized (*kokusanka*), diffused
(*hakyu*), and nurtured (*ikusei*) in order to make a nation rich and
strong' (Samuels 1994: x). This triple-note chord of Japan's techno-
nationalism springs from a pervasive anxiety and insecurity (*fuan*) Japan
as a nation constantly feels as a result of 'its special vulnerabilities in a
Hobbesian world' (ibid.: x).

Indeed, the absorption (adoption, adaptation and assimilation) of
advanced western technologies has been a crucial driving force of
Japan's modernization effort. Early on (during the Meiji period of
1868–1912), Japan absorbed industrial knowledge from the West
through the hiring of western engineers and technicians (Lockwood
1954; Smith 1955). In fact, there once occurred an inward FDI boom

during 1888–1930, when joint ventures with western firms (such as GM, Ford, GE, Western Electric, Otis Elevator, B.F. Goodrich Rubber and Siemens) were the popular way of acquiring advanced technologies and managerial skills. This brief period of Japan's liberal policy for foreign investment, however, came to an end with the rise of militarism in Japan.

During the catch-up phase after the Second World War, however, absorption was mainly through licensing agreements rather than inward FDI (Ozawa 1974; Peck and Tamura 1976; Moritani 1982). After the war, Japan devoted practically all its national energy and resources (since it no longer needed to spend for military purposes) to catching up with the West in commercial industrial endeavours by making best use of its huge technology gap *vis-à-vis* the West, a gap that had in fact widened during the war. Luckily, Japan could concentrate its industrial efforts under the benign tutelage of the United States in the context of the deepening Cold War. The United States largely tolerated Japan's protectionism, enabling the latter to build up industries by importing technology mostly through licensing agreements and limiting inward FDI to a minimum.

As a consequence, Japan's balance of technology trade initially recorded a huge deficit. In 1963, for instance, it 'imported' $136 million-worth of technology, measured in terms of royalty payments, while 'exporting' a relatively small $7 million – an export–import ratio of 5 to 100, or 0.05.[6] Yet Japan was not merely becoming dependent on foreign technology. Japanese firms were making their own efforts to improve significantly on imported technologies. In many cases, imported technologies were not fully commercialized ones but 'seeds' that required further adaptive R&D on the part of the Japanese licensees. As a result, even though Japan continued to increase technology imports, it also began to develop and export its own versions at a much faster pace; in consequence, the gap was closing (that is, there was a continual deficit reduction on the technology trade balance).

Therefore, the technology export–import ratio rose continually, reaching 0.14 in 1970, 0.27 in 1980 and 0.47 in 1991. Yet aggregate statistics of this sort miss the vital changes that have been occurring in Japan's technology trade partners and in the technological levels of different industrial sectors.

As may be expected, for example, Japan has been exporting a substantial amount of technology to the developing countries. In fact, Asian countries as a whole are Japan's largest customers for technology sales, accounting for 47 per cent (in 1994). Korea, Taiwan, Singapore, Thailand, China and Indonesia are the major Asian recipients, absorbing as much as 83.3 per cent of Japan's technology exports to Asia (Science and Technology Agency 1996).

Some technologies have begun to be imported from other Asian countries in the recent past, but such imports are still insignificant in value. Japan thus runs a totally one-sided surplus in technology trade with the developing countries. But this is not surprising, since it has been importing technologies as 'raw materials', just like any other industrial raw material, to be processed, assimilated, synthesized with local industrial knowledge, transformed into 'finished technologies' and exported back to the rest of the world, especially to the developing countries. Here, Japan serves as a vital *intermediary* in technology processing and transfer. This is one of the key mechanisms through which the rest of Asia is integrated with Japanese industry.

Japan likewise exports technologies to other advanced countries. In fact, Japan began to experience a surplus in technology trade with the United Kingdom in 1987, and technology export receipts were more than three times the payments in 1994 (Figure 3.6). Japan still registers technology trade deficits with other major countries, notably Germany (with a balance ratio of 0.43), the United States (0.53) and France (0.58).

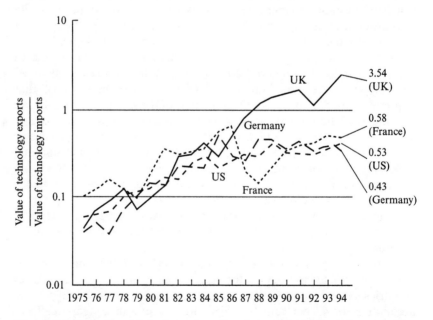

Figure 3.6 Japan's trade balance in technology with other major countries

Similarly, disaggregation of Japan's technology trade balance by industry reveals the differences in its sectoral patterns. Japan's top net technology exporters are the construction industry (for example, technologies related to earthquake-resistant buildings, tunnel-making and so on) which had a balance ratio of 8.35 in 1994, followed by the steel industry (5.48), the transport equipment industry (4.61) and the stone, clay and glass industry (4.58). Japan's manufacturing sector as a whole has begun to enjoy a surplus in its technology trade since 1993 (with a balance ratio of 1.23 in 1994). The chemical industry is near parity, oscillating around the balance line. The appearance of these industries as net technology exporters occurred in that order. As seen earlier, Japan went through tier III industrialization, starting in the late 1950s and continuing throughout the 1960s: the very period of Japan's postwar inflection growth when infrastructural investment (to rebuild the war-worn industrial base and infrastructure) and heavy and chemical industrialization proceeded, resulting in ever-rising demands for construction services, steel and products of the stone, clay and glass industry, mostly as construction materials. The rapid reconstruction and further expansion of these industries were the ideal conditions under which advanced foreign technologies were imported under license and new technologies were simultaneously developed mostly as byproducts of technological absorption (via adaptive R&D).

By any measure, indeed, Japan's techno-protectionism has succeeded in attaining its own stock of technological knowledge, thanks in large part to America's postwar liberalism influenced by the Cold War. As we have already hinted above, and as we shall explain below, Japan's very successful pursuit of techno-protectionism and high economic growth has made it possible for Japanese industry to pass on growth impulses of its own to the rest of the Asian flock of follower geese. These impulses are mostly in the form of 'processed technologies' which Japanese firms transplant by way of their cross-border business activities such as trade, FDI, licensing and other forms of operations. In other words, it would not be amiss to claim that, without Japan's neomercantilist techno-nationalism, Japan would never have emerged as Asia's lead goose, and neither would the East Asian Miracle have occurred.

THE NIEs' DEMONSTRATION-TRIGGERED, TRADE-PUSHED STRATEGY

Korea, Taiwan and Singapore were quite effectively *dirigiste* in managing their spectacular process of industrialization in the recent past

(Hofheinz and Calder 1982; Amsden 1989; Wade 1990). In fact, their cases are often presented as evidence of the important role a state can play in facilitating economic development within the framework of a free-enterprise market economy. In fact, it is widely recognized that these three NIEs, Korea in particular, have learned from and emulated many of the Japanese experiences with regard to catch-up policy-making and institution-building. Japan's economic success no doubt had a strong *demonstration* effect on the rest of East Asia, and the NIEs' success in turn added to the Asian fever for emulation (Linder 1986). The NIEs' approaches are often considered even more favourably than Japanese *dirigisme*, since the latter severely discriminated against inward FDI in the early years following the Second World War. On the whole, Korea and Taiwan have been relatively more MNC-friendly and open to inward FDI. In many instances, the Korean firms even willingly served as 'apprentices' to foreign MNCs in learning new skills and technologies (Amsden 1989). For that matter, the other two NIEs, Hong Kong and Singapore, adopted an even more open policy, almost *laissez-faire*, towards foreign MNCs' operations. All the NIEs have capitalized on foreign MNCs as providers of industrial knowledge and skills and for access to markets in the advanced countries.

In the early years, as shown in Table 3.1, the United States was the major FDI investor in the NIEs, but Japan in particular soon emerged as another significant industrial transplanter. In Taiwan, for example:

> The size of Japanese FDI flows [rose] from US$179 million during the second half of the 1970s to no less than US$1.9 billion during the second half of the 1980s. As a result, their share in total inward investment flows grew from 18.4 per cent in 1976–80 to 27.6 per cent in the next five years and even 31.5 per cent in 1986–90.   (Van Hoesel 1996: 286)

It is interesting to note how the United States dominated the NIEs as the major FDI investor until the first half of the 1980s, but it was joined by Japan and Europe by the end of the decade (Table 3.1). The US share steadily declined from 44.8 per cent in 1984 to 33.6 per cent in 1992, while Japan's share expanded considerably, overtaking the US in the latter half of the 1980s (mainly because of the precipitous appreciation of the yen which led to a gush of Japan's outward FDI after the Plaza Accord). The EU's share also increased, from 17.2 per cent to 19.2 per cent over the same period. Thus, the multinationals from the Triad are the major providers of 'created assets'.

So far as market access for the NIEs' exports is concerned, however, the United States still continues to be the single most important market,

Table 3.1 Recent patterns of inward FDI into and exports from the NIEs

Year	Top FDI investors in production base ($ million and (%))			Top export market for the NIEs ($ million and (%))		
1984	1. US	763	(44.8)	1. US	39 655	(35.4)
	2. Japan	381	(22.3)	2. EU	12 594	(11.2)
	3. EU	293	(17.2)	3. Japan	9733	(8.7)
	4. Others	268	(15.7)	4. NIEs	9733	(8.7)
	Total	1705	(100.0)	5. Others	40 450	(36.1)
				Total	112 165	(100.0)
1986	1. Japan	649	(35.8)	1. US	50 546	(37.4)
	2. US	555	(30.6)	2. EU	16 292	(12.1)
	3. EU	280	(15.5)	3. Japan	13 858	(10.3)
	4. Others	328	(18.1)	4. NIEs	12 065	(8.9)
	Total	1812	(100.0)	5. Others	42 423	(31.4)
				Total	135 184	(100.0)
1989	1. Japan	1460	(32.4)	1. US	73 334	(29.9)
	2. US	1065	(23.6)	2. EU	34 001	(13.9)
	3. EU	789	(17.5)	3. Japan	30 671	(12.5)
	4. Others	1194	(26.5)	4. NIEs	28 145	(11.5)
	Total	4508	(100.0)	5. Others	79 014	(32.2)
				Total	245 165	(100.0)
1992	1. US	1374	(33.6)	1. US	83 462	(24.7)
	2. Japan	1214	(29.7)	2. EU	49 951	(14.8)
	3. EU	784	(19.2)	3. NIEs	48 391	(14.3)
	4. Others	713	(17.5)	4. Japan	31 968	(9.4)
	Total	4085	(100.0)	5. Others	124 626	(36.8)
				Total	338 398	(100.0)

Source: Compiled from data in JETRO (1995: 34–5)

although its share declined from 35.4 per cent in 1984 to 24.7 per cent in 1992. Interestingly, the share of Europe as the second most important market for the NIEs rose steadily from 11.2 per cent to 14.8 per cent over the same period. In contrast, Japan's share hovered around 9–10 per cent in 1992, while the NIEs themselves became significant export markets for each other, the share rising from 8.7 per cent in 1984 to as much as 14.3 per cent in 1992. Intra-NIE exports themselves have thus become much larger in value than the NIEs' exports to Japan. Besides, the 'others' category (constituting the largest share) includes export markets such as the Middle East, Latin America, Central and Eastern

Europe (the former Soviet bloc) and Africa, but most importantly, ASEAN and China themselves probably account for a major and increasing component of this category. In other words, intra-East Asian trade is sharply on the rise.

As the NIEs initially succeeded in implementing labour-driven industrialization, wages began to rise at home, thereby destroying the price competitiveness of their exports. Still fresh is our memory that Korea used to be the major exporter of wigs; Hong Kong of artificial flowers; and Taiwan of beach sandals and sports shoes; and that all of them were competitive manufacturers of apparel and textiles. They soon lost comparative advantages in all those labour-intensive standardized manufactures – as Japan had earlier experienced towards the end of tier IV industrialization. The currencies of all the NIEs also appreciated against the dollar, further weakening their export competitiveness in price-sensitive light industrial goods.

Suddenly, the NIEs began to make overseas investments in the 1980s, especially in the latter half of the decade. This phenomenon caught the attention of some observers, who identified it as the birth of Third World multinationals (Wells 1983). Thus, they in turn became active FDI investors, although they continued to be net FDI recipients. Their overseas investments have so far been principally in labour-intensive manufacturing (tier III industries), and in resource-related industries (especially Korea and Taiwan).

With rising wages and per capita incomes, all the NIEs pushed for higher-tier industries. Korea and Taiwan followed the Japanese steps; first, they moved into tier III heavy and chemical industrialization and have only recently succeeded in entering tier II assembly-based industries, notably automobiles, auto-parts and electronics. As they climb the ladder of industrialization to these component-intensive tier II industries, they have become increasingly dependent on imports of capital goods (parts, components and equipment), technology and organizational know-how from Japan. This is the inevitable result of these NIEs' strategy of initially taking up low-end assembly operations in high-technology industries by importing all the necessary inputs, equipment and knowledge, which they intend to replace eventually by their domestic counterparts when they acquire the skills and technologies. In other words, the growth of new industries in the NIEs thus has become driven by both exports and input-imports, that is, truly *trade-driven*.

This development resulted in two new patterns of trade during the 1980s: a growth of intra-industry trade in manufactures between the NIEs and Japan and the rise in triangular trade. With respect to the growth in intra-industry trade, Yung Chul Park and Won-Am Park made an insightful observation:

> It is generally accepted that intra-industry trade tends to be prevalent between countries with similar factor endowments and skill levels and when scale economies and product differentiation are significant. That is, intra-industry trade will expand between economies at similar levels of economic development. Much of the trade among industrialized countries is character-ized by the dominance of intra-industry trade, of which volume is largely influenced by factors on the demand side. In contrast, intra-industry trade between advanced and developing countries includes mostly exchanges of manufactured goods differentiated by different processing stages in the same industry. This type of trade is likely to be determined by comparative advan-tage based on differences in technology, endowments of research and development (R&D) stock and human capital; that is, factors on the supply side.
>
> The growth of intra-industry trade in capital-intensive manufactures between Japan and the [NIEs] has been led by two categories of products. The first is made up of products *differentiated by quality and price*; this is the case in the consumer electronics trade, where Japan exchanges more sophisticated and high-quality products for cheaper, lower-quality electronics from the [NIEs]. The other category consists of products at *different pro-duction stages in the same industry.*   (Park and Park 1991: 101; italics added)

Even when the NIEs produce quality/price-differentiated manufac-tures in capital-intensive industries, such as electronics and automobiles, they are often dependent on some key inputs and technologies imported from Japan. Similarly, when they specialize in parts and components (differentiated by production stages), most of these are produced by Japanese subsidiaries and affiliates in the NIEs with Japanese manage-ment skills and technology.

In the context of America's hegemony-compelled trade liberalism, this new type of trade also led to an expansion of triangular trade among the NIEs, the United States and Japan: Japan exports capital goods and technology to the NIEs, which in turn export finished/ assembled goods to the United States. This type of roundabout trade was already observable in the early 1970s, although it increased drasti-cally after the Plaza Accord of 1985.

So far as Hong Kong and Singapore are concerned, these space-confined 'city economies', because of their geographical constraints, skipped tier III and moved up to some specialized segments, notably electronics, of tier II industries; but they quickly became highly service-orientated.

In sum, the NIEs have succeeded in graduating from labour-driven industrialization. With a considerable accumulation of human capital

and industrial knowledge, they have emerged as world-class manufacturers. Notable are Korea's semiconductor and automobile industries
and Taiwan's personal computer industry. Both Korea and Taiwan have
consolidated tier III heavy and chemical industries and are now building
up tier II assembly-based industries.

THE ASEAN-4's MNC-DEPENDENT INDUSTRIALIZATION

In contrast to the geographically confined, high population density
'small' economies of the NIEs, the ASEAN-4 have a relatively large
expanse of land and rich natural resources. In the early years, they all
depended mainly on primary exports to earn foreign exchange; but
during the past two decades, they have actively promoted manufacturing
– and have succeeded in doing so – via inward FDI, thereby diversifying
their industrial bases and exports.

One unique feature of the ASEAN-4's economies is that their industrial, financial and commercial sectors have been – and still are –
dominated by overseas Chinese, despite their minority ethnic status.
They constitute approximately 2 per cent of the local population of the
Philippines, 3 per cent in Indonesia, 9 per cent in Thailand, and 35 per
cent in Malaysia; they dominate their local economies by 50 per cent,
70 per cent, 80 per cent, and 70 per cent, respectively.[7]

This is in part a legacy of western colonialism. Although before the
arrival of Europeans a large number of Chinese had emigrated from
the poverty-stricken and overpopulated south-eastern provinces of
China (notably, Guangdong, Fujian and Guangxi) into the West Pacific
Rim, it was only during the European colonial period that the number
of overseas Chinese swelled considerably in the local economies, since
the European colonizers eagerly recruited Chinese workers for their
mines, plantations and administrative works.[8]

The colonial experience of South-East Asia began with the Portu-
guese seizure of Malacca in 1511; this was followed by the Spanish
arrival in the Philippines in 1565; the establishment of the Dutch East
India Company in Jakarta in 1619; the British East India Company in
Penang in 1786; Singapore in 1819; Hong Kong in 1841; the French
control of the south of Vietnam in 1860; America's acquisition of control
of the Philippines after the Spanish–American war of 1898; and finally
Japan's colonialism that started prior to and continued during the
Second World War (Hodder 1992: 27).

Interestingly enough, all the ASEAN-4 can be characterized as 'patrimonial states' (Yasuba 1996). This thesis posits that the patrimony and politics of the authority are intermingled with foreign economic interests:

> The ruling authority from time to time sold off part of their power to minority groups, usually Europeans and overseas Chinese, to make the best use of patrimony. 'Tax farming' in which the authority sold off the right to tax, is the typical patrimonial way to run the state. Similarly, the ruling authority sold off various monopoly rights, the right to produce and sell a certain product, the right to organize gambling, and the right to dig a canal and to sell the land along it . . .
>
> Even today, it may be argued that the ASEAN states are still patrimonial states. Much of the industrialization before 1970 can be explained in terms of patrimonialism. Direct foreign investment for import substitution can be explained away as giving investment privileges and protection to foreigners in exchange for positions and shares in joint ventures and other gifts. (Yasuba 1996: 424)

In addition to Thailand, upon which the above observation is largely based, Indonesia is another prime example. Golkar, the ruling party of Indonesian President Suharto, has sold off lucrative monopolies to Indonesia's ethnic Chinese businessmen:

> Of the 140 major business conglomerates that account for the bulk of Indonesia's gross national product, 110 of them are controlled by ethnic-Chinese families . . . Most of the others are connected to close friends or relatives, including several children, of Mr Suharto. But they, too, maintain close ties to their Chinese-owned counterparts.   (Waldman and Solomon 1997)

No doubt, all the current rapid growth of the ASEAN-4 derives from their MNC-assisted strategy of industrialization. They are surely more dependent on foreign MNCs for technology, skills, management and access to global markets than the NIEs have been in their industrialization effort.

In the late 1980s, which saw a rebound in growth among the ASEAN-4 following brief stagnation in the mid-1980s, Japan and the NIEs were two major investors, together accounting for almost 60 per cent of total FDI inflows in these West Pacific Rim hosts (Table 3.2). But the US and EU also became major FDI players in the early 1990s. In 1992, therefore, EU, Japan, the NIEs and the US came to form the quadropoles of FDI suppliers responsible for 70 per cent of total FDI inflows.

So far as the export markets for the ASEAN-4 are concerned, it was initially Japan (in 1989) and then the NIEs (in 1992) that provided the largest markets. This is, indeed, in sharp contrast with the NIEs' exports, of which the United States has been number one absorber, as seen in

Table 3.2 Recent patterns of inward FDI into and exports from ASEAN-4

Year	Top FDI investors in production base ($ million and (%))			Top export market for ASEAN-4 ($ million and (%))		
1989	1. Japan	5594	(31.2)	1. Japan	18 271	(24.4)
	2. NIEs	4899	(27.3)	2. US	15 451	(20.6)
	3. EU	2773	(15.5)	3. NIEs	15 158	(20.4)
	4. US	966	(5.4)	4. EU	11 338	(15.1)
	5. Others	3681	(20.6)	5. Others	14 696	(19.6)
	Total	17 913	(100.0)	Total	74 914	(100.0)
1992	1. EU	6886	(25.0)	1. NIEs	27 815	(23.8)
	2. Japan	4596	(16.7)	2. Japan	23 593	(20.2)
	3. NIEs	4488	(16.3)	3. US	23 159	(19.8)
	4. US	3512	(12.7)	4. EU	19 142	(16.4)
	5. Others	8093	(29.3)	5. Others	23 278	(19.9)
	6. Total	27 575	(100.0)	6. Total	116 987	(100.0)

Source: As Table 3.1.

Table 3.1. This contrast is, however, not surprising, since Japan and the NIEs are basically the exporters of manufactures which have long been targeted mostly at the western markets, whereas the ASEAN-4 have been primarily the exporters of industrial raw materials and fuels, although they now export manufactures in increasing amounts. Being exiguous in natural resources, Japan and the NIEs have been of the 'workshop' type of economy, importing industrial resources and processing them into finished goods for export. Hence, they eagerly purchase industrial resources from the ASEAN-4. Thus a quadruple channel of trade – that is, the ASEAN-4's resource exports → Japan's and the NIEs's manufactured exports → the US and Europe – has been established.

Moreover, Japan and the NIEs have also emerged as the new markets for light industrial goods from the ASEAN-4, the labour-intensive goods that the MNCs from Japan and the NIEs outsource and import back home – in addition to exporting to third-country markets (again, mostly to the West). Once again, the quadrapoles of the market (the NIEs, Japan, the US and EU) for labour-intensive manufactures have come into existence, absorbing as much as 80 per cent of the ASEAN-4's exports.

CHINA'S ETHNO-CENTRIPETAL MODERNIZATION

China's miraculous growth ever since it opened its doors to the global economy has been propelled by inward FDI and other forms of activity by foreign MNCs. It is a well-known fact that, so far as overall FDI in China is concerned, the major investors are not from the advanced countries but mainly from the ethnic-Chinese NIEs (Hong Kong, Taiwan and Singapore) and the overseas Chinese diasporas in the ASEAN-4 and other countries. In 1992, for example, no less than 80 per cent of FDI came from the NIEs, as shown in Table 3.3, since the 'others' category (9.0 per cent), whose FDI is larger than that of the US. (5.4 per cent), Japan (3.7 per cent) and EU (0.9 per cent), actually includes those FDIs made by the overseas Chinese businessmen from the ASEAN-4. Hence, China's inward FDI is clearly driven by its ethnic ties with the rest of East Asia at this stage of economic development. None the less, FDIs from the US, Japan and the EU are generally in higher-technology production, and as China moves up the ladder of industrialization, these FDIs are expected to grow in importance.

The bulk of China's exports is already manufactured goods, and their share has risen to 85 per cent of total exports from 50 per cent over the past decade; and to this growth in manufactured exports, so-called 'foreign-funded enterprises' have been making a considerable contribution: in 1995, they accounted for about 28 per cent of China's total trade value: 'Of the 235,000 foreign-funded enterprises approved to the end of 1995, more than 110,000 have begun operations, employing 15 million workers. Industrial products accounted for 90 per cent of total exports' (Asian Development Bank 1996: 59). The more approved FDI projects that come on stream, the further will their export contribution expand.

The same thing can be said about China's export markets. The NIEs are the predominant market (49.9 per cent) for Chinese goods, followed by the 'others' (again, most importantly the ASEAN-4). Thus, China's FDI-linked growth and trade expansion may be most appropriately characterized as 'ethno-centripetal' industrialization. Indeed, a new prosperous economic zone is in the making, a subregion that connects Southern China (in particular, Guangdong and Fujian) to Hong Kong and Taiwan, or what may be called 'Greater South China Economic Sphere'. A study of the Asian Development Bank (Thant *et al.* 1994) identified it as one of the so-called 'growth triangles' in Asia. The statistics in Table 3.3 attest to the emergence of Southern China as an emerging growth triangle driven by inward FDI and trade.

Table 3.3 Recent patterns of inward FDI into and exports from China

Year	Top FDI investors in production base ($ million and (%))			Top export markets for China ($ million and (%))		
1992	1. NIEs	47 001	(80.9)	1. NIEs	42 677	(49.9)
	2. US	3121	(5.4)	2. Japan	11 699	(13.7)
	3. Japan	2173	(3.7)	3. US	8599	(10.1)
	4. EU	575	(0.9)	4. EU	7627	(8.9)
	5. Others	5253	(9.0)	5. Others	14 890	(17.4)
	6. Total	58 123	(100.0)	6. Total	85 492	(100.0)

Source: As Table 3.1.

It is widely known that first Japan's economic miracle and then the NIEs' had a great impact on China's development policy, which now emphasizes the virtues of a combination of import substitution and export-led growth or 'outward-looking import-substitution'. No doubt, China emulates the experiences of both Japan and the NIEs and accepts the role of foreign MNCs as facilitators of industrialization. China's industrial development plan, *Outline for Industrial Policy in the 1990s*, approved by the State Council in March 1994, for example, emphasizes the development of basic industries through privatization with infusions of foreign capital. In addition, reminiscent of the early postwar industrial policy of Japan's Ministry of International Trade and Industry (MITI), China has designated as 'pillar industries' electronics, machinery, petrochemicals, automobiles and construction (Taylor 1996: 39). These are the higher-tier industries that China strives to develop by way of capitalizing on the resources of foreign MNCs, as well as creating its own MNCs as procurers of state-of-the-art technologies and new ideas abroad.

In this respect, China and overseas Chinese diasporas in East Asia are creating and consolidating new diasporas in the advanced countries, especially in North America. These are developing into new skill reservoirs for China's efforts to build up high-tech industries. In this respect, it is following in the footsteps of the NIEs, which have drawn heavily upon their expatriate engineers, research scientists and business managers who were educated abroad and had plenty of experience in high-tech industries abroad. The World Bank, for example, emphasized this important route of knowledge transfer:

Drawn partly by the high wages made possible by exports, many residents of Korea and Taiwan, China, trained abroad, particularly in new sectors such as electronics and computing, have returned home to work. Many returning nationals have received education in OECD economies and then worked for OECD economy firms. Their return has provided significant transfer of best-practice methods. For example, foreign-educated nationals account for *all* the postgraduates employed in the industry of Taiwan, China. *This source of knowledge of international best practices becomes more important as changing factor prices dictate a shift to more capital- and technology-intensive sectors in which higher-level skills are needed to unlock knowledge that may be embodied in patents, licenses, or the use of specialized nontraded equipment.* (World Bank 1993: 320; italics added)

To catch up with the advanced world, it is not sufficient just to invite foreign MNCs which can bring the latest industrial knowledge by way of FDI, licensing, subcontracting and other means of local production. The nationals of a catching-up country need to be educated and trained in the advanced countries. This is the most effective way of enhancing a developing country's learning capacity, thereby securing best-practice methods. There is no superior substitute for this. And being fully aware of the NIEs' success in this regard, China is intent on exploiting it. Besides, China can indeed rely on its growing disaporas in North America and Europe.

Furthermore, China is emulating *keiretsu*-style, or rather *chaebol*-style, business conglomerates. The Korean *chaebol* seems to have a greater appeal to China, since it is much more closely linked to the state in its financial control than is the Japanese *keiretsu*.[9] CITIC Pacific (which has interests in 'power stations, toll roads, airlines, and shopping malls'), Beijing Enterprises (with interests in 'a hotel, a toll road, and a chunk of the Great Wall') and Shanghai Automobile Industry Corp (with interests in two car-making joint ventures, one with Germany's Volkswagen, the other with America's General Motors, and two electrical goods firms) are said to be the prime examples of nascent *chaebol*-like conglomerates in China (*The Economist*, 7 June 1997: 61).

In addition to China's strategy of following in the footsteps of its successful neighbours, that is to say, being an efficient follower goose of the Asian flock, it is organizing its own internal – ethnicity-based – version of FG formation within its sphere of influence. Hong Kong, Taiwan and Singapore are the ethnic-Chinese lead geese for the southern provinces of China, forming the Greater South China Economic Sphere which in turn will serve as a domestic lead goose for the interior of China, notably in labour-intensive manufacturing. Here, ethno-centripetal forces are clearly at work. Yet, as China strives to develop higher-tier industries, the multinationals from Japan and the

West are increasingly courted – and often pitted against each other – as suppliers of technical and organizational skills.

Instead of just letting China's hinterland wait for the centrifugal growth impulses transmitted from the southern-coastal growth pole, the Chinese government is trying to create a preferential industrial zone in its remote region. In early 1997, the government placed, Chongquing in Sichuan Province, a laggard central region, on its select list, which already includes Beijing, Shanghai and Tianjin, so that industrialization would also flourish in the poverty-stricken interior as well (Yuasa 1997). Chongquing is a former military industrial complex, situated south-west of Shanghai and upstream on the Yangtze River where the Three Gorges Dam is under construction. The city is now being encouraged to transform itself into a modern civilian manufacturing centre based on the production of motor cycles and other vehicles. Its two major manufacturers, Changan Automobile Co. and Jialing Industry United Corp., have been reorganizing themselves from military to civilian production in joint ventures with Japan's Suzuki Motor for subcompact cars (since 1996) and with Japan's Honda Motor for motor cycles (since 1993), respectively.

In terms of the stages theory of industrial upgrading, these are tier II assembly-based industries which are skill-intensive in organization and production. China is thus turning for help to multinationals from the advanced countries rather than from its ethnic-Chinese NIEs. In this respect, the future modernization strategy of China will change increasingly from the ethno-centripetal phase to the demonstration-triggered neomercantilism path trodden by the NIEs (minus Hong Kong).

Another sign of this development strategy is that China has most recently succeeded in attracting Japan's NEC to build a $1 billion chip-making factory in Shanghai, a facility which will make China a world-class chip-maker in early 1999 – despite the fact that IBM, Rockwell, Texas Instruments and Siemens had all turned down the Chinese government's invitation to bid for the business because of China's poor record in intellectual property and their own governments' reluctance to grant export approval for the advanced chip-making equipment. Reportedly, through this joint venture with NEC (who has an only 28.6 per cent minority interest), China will secure some of the best semiconductor manufacturing know-how around. NEC has recently developed a new technology 'to cram more DRAM (dynamic random access memory) devices on to a wafer of silicon than any of its leading rivals' (*The Economist*, 7 June 1997: 62).[10]

A NEW ERA OF INFORMATION REVOLUTION

As the East Asian economies have successfully started to go through the stages of growth previously pioneered by the West since the Industrial Revolution, the overall hierarchical structure of the industries itself (a structure illustrated in Figure 3.4) has been continuously upgraded, both technologically and organizationally. Above all, it is becoming increasingly information-intensive and knowledge-driven. Intangible or created assets have become proportionately more important than natural or endowed assets. At the vanguard of this information revolution is the United States, which is generating a new wave of technologies, especially in the area of multimedia and cyberspace communications.

As the advanced countries (including Japan) are pushed up to the tier I innovation-driven growth phase, information (in the form of human knowledge and ideas) is thus the most critical factor of production – as well as the major output. Information-driven activities (most importantly, innovations resulting from R&D) not only build up tier I industries *per se*, but also create spillovers and a demonstration effect to lower-tier industries. In other words, dynamic feedback effects are exerted on, and absorbed by, the latter. In fact, firms in lower-tier industries are even diversifying into higher-tier industries (for example, many manufacturers of chemicals, steel and automobiles enter electronics and informatics), an activity stimulated by the demonstration effect of tier I industrial growth.

Consequently, lower-tier (conventional) industries themselves are all induced to overhaul the way they organize and manage production and marketing, as well as upgrading the quality and range of goods/services they produce. For example, super-fibres are manufactured by the textile industry (tier IV) in highly automated and cybernated factories; super-steel, super-ships and super-materials are made in the heavy and chemical industries (tier III); and super-clean engines and super-fuel-efficient cars are manufactured in the assembly-based industries (tier II). Above all, technological advances in communications and transportation, as well as the recent trend toward market liberalization world wide, have reduced the transaction costs of trade and overseas investments. As a result, market competition is rapidly being globalized and intensified (that is, the emergence of 'megacompetition').

This means that the stages of growth are no longer linear and monotonic, in the sense that different sequences of stages are now possible – instead of the monotonic sequence running from tier IV to tier I. Although tier IV labour-driven industrialization ought still to be the basic starting point, the development of tier II industries (such as cars and electronics) may be promoted simultaneously with, or even given priority as a stimulus to, that of tier II industries (such as steel and basic chemicals as inputs). Modern telecommunications, a tier I industry, now needs to be established as infrastructure even if a country is still in the labour-driven stage. This possibility of stages realignment presents both opportunities and dangers, however. For instance, latecomers are tempted to join the bandwagon of structural upgrading by jumping on to higher-tier industries instead of, and in addition to, starting at the bottom of the industrial hierarchy. They are tempted to do so, because MNCs from the advanced world can provide all the necessary ingredients (created assets) of industrial development (production technologies, key inputs, management and marketing skills and access to markets), without regard to the developing countries' absorptive capacities. In this regard, with the help of MNCs, the NIEs have been able to move successfully into higher-tier industries, notably in electronics and telecommunications, particularly because of their absorptive capacities that are built with the effective accumulation of indigenous human capital.

But such an opportunity also creates problems for some developing countries, because they may not yet be prepared to avail themselves of it effectively in terms of their indigenous factor supplies and infrastructural and technological sophistication. In other words, they encounter bottlenecks in the input market and infrastructural provision. At the moment, these problems appear to be the major concern for the ASEAN-4, which are rapidly losing competitiveness in labour-intensive production and hence need to move up to higher-tier industries.

In fact, fully aware of such bottlenecks and their needs for structural upgrading, Malaysia, Thailand and the Philippines have recently initiated state-led projects designed to usher them into the new age of the information revolution. Malaysia is building a Multimedia Super Corridor; Thailand is working on IT (information technology) enhancement; and the Philippines is striving to implement its National Information Technology Plan 2000. They all focus on infrastructural and human resource development in the area of communications infrastructure and software specialists. Indeed, not only the ASEAN-4 but also the NIEs have huge developmental gaps *vis-à-vis* Japan in information-related activities.[11]

The ASEAN-4 – and for that matter, China and other late latecomers – in particular, are seeking the participation of MNCs from the advanced countries as partners in this modern infrastructure building. The traditional type of infrastructure, such as sea ports, railways, bridges and roads, used to be a 'non-tradable' good constructed and operated by the local government. Modern infrastructure such as telecommunications and transportation facilities has increasingly become intangible and more knowledge-intensive, instead of tangible and physical-capital-based. It is now a 'tradable' good which is frequently financed, constructed and managed as joint ventures with foreign MNCs.[12]

PRESENT QUANDARIES AND FUTURE PROSPECTS

Despite the miraculous expansion of the region and its continued high growth relative to that of other regions, there have recently appeared several signs of economic weakness in East Asia. As if in accordance with the FG ranking itself, Japan, Korea and Thailand – in that order – have become financially the most troubled economies in tandem.

Japan's banking sector is still struggling to recover from its excessive lending for speculative investment in real estate and stocks during the bubble economy (1986–90).[13] Although the banking industry's health has considerably recovered from the bad loan syndrome, thanks to unprecedentedly low interest rates, it most recently experienced political and managerial scandals as well.

Japan is also suffering from the rigidities and increasing incompatibility of its prevailing system of political economy, a so-called '*1955-taisei*', which was established in the early 1950s – and was once quite effective – as a set of institutions, regulations and practices designed to catch up with the West. Its regulatory regime has surely outlived its usefulness, now that Japan is an economic superpower and can no longer pursue its catch-up focused techno-protectionism. Japan has been deregulating itself in hitherto protected industries such as banking and finance, distribution, transportation, and medical and health services. And it is also intent on reforming its political and administrative systems. Now that Japan's structural reforms have gathered momentum, a new Japan will emerge sooner or later. In fact, therefore, Japanese policy-makers are by and large sanguine about the future prospects of the Japanese economy as an Asian lead goose.[14] Overall, a new Japanese industrial thrust, which may be called 'post-catch-up, Pacific-based globalization', seems in the making.[15]

Korea has also had similar problems in its financial sector, involving the insolvencies of three *chaebols* (the Hanbo, Sammi and Jinro groups) and several management scandals. It is also struggling to reform its over-regulated economic system.[16] Moreover, Korea is faced with a ballooning current account deficit (over $23 billion in 1996), caused mostly by a deterioration in its terms of trade with sharp declines in its major export prices such as memory chips, steel, petrochemicals and automobiles; the recent depreciation of the Japanese yen (from mid-1995 to the present) has also eroded Korea's price competitiveness in the world market.

Thailand, too, has experienced a wobbly banking industry under the weight of bad loans and a deteriorating current account deficit (8 per cent of GDP in 1996), the same size as Mexico's prior to its financial meltdown in 1994. So far (at the time of writing), the Thai government has managed to avert the Mexican-style collapse by 'a mixture of foreign-exchange intervention, somewhat higher interest rates and selective capital controls' (*The Economist*, 24 May 1997: 15). Similar concerns have been expressed about Malaysia, Indonesia and the Philippines.

Indeed, a debate is in the making as to whether the East Asian miracle is over. 'Pessimists' attribute the current quandary to its structural weakness; their growth (except Japan's) has been achieved merely with massive mobilization of physical inputs (capital and labour) but without gains in efficiency (total factor productivity or TFP) (Krugman 1994). In contrast, 'optimists' explain the current malaise in terms of cyclical factors such as the recessions in Europe and Japan, the appreciation of the dollar (to which many Asian currencies are tied) and the slump in the world semiconductor market. The causes are no doubt both cyclical and structural.

The Asian flock of flying geese is at a critical point: since many of them are bumped against the next higher tier, each must climb up but it is a struggle to do so. Japan's deregulations and institutional reforms may help to revitalize it as the Asian goose by successfully entering upon tier I information-driven industries. So it is with Korea, in its effort to consolidate tier II assembly-based industries. The ASEAN-4's task is to graduate from labour-driven industrialization and begin to develop indigenous human resources for higher-tier industries. This need is now even greater, since they accepted three new members in July 1996: Cambodia, Laos and Myanmar, whose per capita incomes and labour costs are much lower than theirs and whose industrial activities will hence soon centre on labour-intensive production.

Regionally, America's trade policy is inclined towards forcing other countries to open up their markets, especially to purchase US goods and services, rather than adopt protectionism. This recently emerged policy of insisting on market-opening reciprocity makes perfect sense, since it enables the US finally to exploit, on a 'level playing-field', the commercial opportunities developed in East Asia under its erstwhile

Cold War-driven trade liberalism. In response, and because of their structural necessities, all the East Asian economies are liberalizing their trade and investment regimes. This augers well for the MNCs, whose role as catalysts for structural upgrading is now widely acknowledged and eagerly sought after.

NOTES

1. Growth statistics are from Economic Planning Agency (1996).
2. The statement, 'The Cold War is over, Japan has won', is attributed to Chalmer Johnson, a political scientist at the University of California, San Diego. The US foreign policy that prioritized security over economic interests was examined in Krasner (1987: 2–3), in which he argued: 'The extraordinary political, military, and economic dominance it was bequeathed by the consequences of World War II made it possible for the United States to adopt a very long time-horizon and pursue generous policies. Japan and Western Europe could act as free risers on the liberal economic regime without incurring the wrath of the United States, which was more concerned with political and economic stability than with strict adherence to liberal rules.'
3. It should be noted that the United States is currently in the post-Cold War phase of reformulating its global economic strategy. Similarly, Japan is in the midst of searching for a new post-catch-up macro-developmental policy.
4. Akamatsu, however, did not foresee this key role of MNCs. The FG paradigm was, therefore, further elaborated by Kiyoshi Kojima (1973, 1978) in terms of the role of FDI, and additionally expanded by Kojima and Ozawa (1984 and 1985). More recently, Ozawa (1992, 1993, 1996) inquired into the impact of Japan's structural change and FDI on other East Asian economies, thereby further developing the FG paradigm into a theory of MNC-assisted regional growth. Kojima (1996) explicitly recognizes the pedigree of 'Akamatsu–Kojima–Ozawa' (in Kojima's phrase) in the on-going development (*dénouement*) of the paradigm.
5. See, for example, Marglin and Schor (1990).
6. Statistics on technology trade cited in this section are from various issues of Science and Technology Agency, *Kagaku Gijutsu Hakusho* [White Paper on Science and Technology], Tokyo.
7. Estimated by Ichikawa (1996: 62–3). Hodder (1992) provides another similar set of statistics: 1.5 per cent in the Philippines; 2.8 per cent in Indonesia; 30.9 per cent in Malaysia; 75.9 per cent in Singapore; and 28.0 per cent in Brunei. He explains the problem of estimation: 'One difficulty is the definition of "Chinese". In the Philippines, for example, many Chinese, both ethnic Chinese (pure Chinese) and *mestizos* (a mixture of Chinese and some other race) have adopted Filipino names and Catholicism... and taken on Filipino nationality... To a lesser extent the same problem arises in [Malaysia's *Baba* Chinese in its southwest]... Another complicating factor is that the Chinese are not a clearly defined and homogeneous group. The Overseas Chinese come from many different parts of China, though mostly from southeastern China. They speak different dialects, most of which are mutually unintelligible, and they have different beliefs, values and predilections. The Hokkien, Cantonese, Hakka, Teochew, Hainanese and many other groups do not always operate together as one might expect; and they often specialise in their economic activities' (Hodder 1992: 44).
8. 'Overseas Chinese communities were used by the colonial powers deliberately to suppress the indigenous populations and to link the populations and the resources of their countries into a growing and insatiable world capitalist system. The Chinese

formed the middlemen – a link, or a channel of exploitation – between the indigenous populations and the colonial rulers. Whatever the truth of this matter, the Chinese were undoubtedly regarded as a real asset by the Europeans in their colonising process' (Hodder 1992: 46).

9. 'The relatively greater role of government policy in the formation and growth of chaebol is obvious in a key organizational difference from Japan's financial keiretsu: Commercial banks in Korea by law are not allowed to be a part of chaebol groups. To a large extent, therefore, the government has been the main conduit of finance to chaebol firms. For example, until the early 1980s, the government was the majority share holder (25 to 35 per cent) of all major commercial banks in Korea and effectively controlled all significant lending decisions. Due to the dominant role of the Korean government in the allocation of credit, banks have had less discretion and relatively little incentive to monitor lending compared to main banks in Japan's financial keiretsu' (Huh and Kim 1993: 3).

10. It is further reported: 'the company is well into the fourth "shrink" of its basic 16-megabit DRAM design, getting upwards of 700 chips on to a standard eight-inch wafer. Firms still using third-shrink designs have to make do with around 450 chips per wafer . . . China bought some $7 billion worth of semiconductors last year for its surging computer and telecoms industries . . . the figure will be $17 billion by 2000' (*The Economist*, 7 June 1997: 62).

11. One estimate shows that the 1995 output of the information industry (both hardware and software) stood at $57.6 billion in Japan; $3.3 billion in Korea; $1.3 billion in Taiwan; $1.1 billion in Singapore; $230 million in the Philippines; $210 million in Thailand; and $200 million in Malaysia (that is, in terms of relatives, 100 in Japan; 5.7 in Korea; 2.3 in Taiwan; 1.9 in Singapore; 0.39 in the Philippines; 0.36 in Thailand; and 0.35 in Malaysia). Computed from data shown in 'ASEAN rushes into technology, offers hosts of handouts', *Nikkei Weekly*, 16 June 1997: 24.

12. This multinationalized approach to building up a developing country's infrastructure will certainly lead to a greater dependency on inward FDI during the inflection growth period. This will have an important implication for the so-called 'investment-development-path (IDP)' theory (Dunning 1981; Dunning and Narula 1996); the IDP waves are all the more amplified.

13. The bubble economy experienced the 1.9-fold (nearly double) rise of stock prices from 1986 (3rd quarter) to 1989 (4th quarter) and the 2.2-fold increase of land prices from 1989 (3rd quarter) to 1990 (3rd quarter). Capital gains alone in 1989 exceeded that year's GDP by 27 per cent. The post-bubble declines in land and stock prices were equally precipitous; stock prices declined 63.1 per cent over the 33-month period up to August 1992, while land prices dropped more than half from 1990 to 1994. These capital losses amounted to 86.9 per cent of GDP in 1992 (Hashimoto 1995: 219–22).

14. Optimism as to how effectively Japan will come out of the present doldrums with demanding reforms is expressed, for example, by Eisuke Sakakibara (1997: 90): 'As we have done for the 130 years since the Meiji Restoration, we will quickly absorb what needs to be absorbed and become fully competitive with the Anglo-Saxon and other systems.'

15. As seen above, Japanese industry has been integrating with the neighbouring economies at a rapid pace, especially through the networks of MNCs. The competitiveness of Japan's manufactures increasingly depends on its outsourced intermediate goods in East Asia, and vice verse. Japan's production will be mostly based on Asia, while its marketing will be global.

16. Korea's Ambassador to the US, Seung-Soo Han, for example, officially admits the over-regulated status of the Korean economy: 'despite the government's determined efforts to pursue deregulation, I have to admit that there are still far too many regulations that restrict and hamper corporate activity' (Han 1997: p. 2). These regulations are contributing to Korea's high costs of transportation and industrial sites.

REFERENCES

Akamatsu, Kaname (1935), 'Wagakuni Yomo Kogyohin no Boeki Suisei' [The trend of Japan's foreign trade in woollen manufactures], *Shogyo Keizai Ronso* (Journal of Nagoya Higher Commercial School), 129 ff.

Akamatsu, Kaname (1962), 'A historical pattern of economic growth in developing countries', *Developing Economies*, preliminary issue, No. 1 (March–August): 1–23.

Aliber, Robert Z. (1993), *The Multinational Paradigm*, Cambridge, Mass.: MIT Press.

Amsden, Alice H. (1989), *Asia's Next Giant: South Korea and Late Industrialization*, New York and Oxford: Oxford University Press.

Arisawa, H. (ed.) (1967), *Nihon Sangyo Hyakunenshi* [A 100-year History of Japanese Industry], vols 1 and 2, Tokyo: Nihon Keizai.

Asian Development Bank (1996), *Asian Development Outlook 1996 and 1997*, New York: Oxford University Press.

Clark, Colin (1935), *The Conditions of Economic Progress*, London: Macmillan.

Dunning, John H. (1981), 'Explaining the international direct investment position of countries: towards a dynamic or development approach', *Weltwirtschaftliches Archiv*, **119**, 30–64.

Dunning, John H. and Rajneesh Narula (1996), 'The investment development path revisited: some emerging issues', in John Dunning and Rajneesh Narula (eds), *Foreign Direct Investment and Governments: Catalysts for Economic Restructuring*, London and New York: Routledge, pp. 1–41.

Economic Planning Agency (1996), *Azia Keizai 1996* [Asian Economy 1996], Tokyo: Ministry of Finance Printing Office.

Evans, John W. (1967), *U.S. Trade Policy: New Legislation for the Next Round*, New York: Harper.

Han, Seung-Soo (1997), 'The challenges and choices facing the Korean economy', *Korea Economic Update* (newsletter), Korea Economic Institute of America, **8**(2), 1–4.

Hashimoto, Juro (1995), *Sengo no Nihon Keizai* [Postwar Japanese Economy], Tokyo: Iwanami Shinsho.

Hodder, Rupert (1992), *The West Pacific Rim: An Introduction*, London: Belhaven Press.

Hofheinz, Roy Jr and Kent E. Calder (1982), *The Eastasia Edge*, New York: Basic Books.

Huh, Chan Guk and Sun Bae Kim (1993), 'Japan's keiretsu and Korea's chaebol', *FRBSF Weekly Letter*, no. 93–25, 16 July.

Ichikawa, Shu (1996), *Hazusareru Nihon: Asia Keizai no Koso* [Japan Excluded: The Design of the Asian Economy], Tokyo: NHK Books.

JETRO (Japan External Trade Organization) (1995), *White Paper on International Trade Japan in 1995*, Tokyo: JETRO.

Kenen, Peter B. (1960), *Giant Among Nations: Problems in United States Foreign Economic Policy*, New York: Rand McNally.

Kojima, Kiyoshi (1973), 'A macroeconomic approach to foreign direct investment', *Hitotsubashi Journal of Economics*, **14** (1), 1–21.

Kojima, Kiyoshi (1978), *Foreign Direct Investment: A Japanese Model of Multinational Business Operations*, London: Croom Helm.

Kojima, Kiyoshi (1990), *Japanese Direct Investment Abroad*, Monograph Series

1, Social Science Research Institute, Tokyo: International Christian University.

Kojima Kiyoshi (1996), 'Shuyu no Bi: Zoku: Waga Gakumon Henro' [The beauty of ending: my academic career], *Surugadai Keizai Ronshu*, **6** (1), 103–460.

Kojima, Kiyoshi and Terutomo Ozawa (1984), 'Micro- and macro-economic models of direct foreign investment: toward a synthesis', *Hitotsubashi Journal of Economics*, **25** (1), 1–20.

Kojima, Kyoshi and Terutomo Ozawa (1985), 'Toward a theory of industrial restructuring and dynamic comparative advantage', *Hitotsubashi Journal of Economics*, **26** (2), 1–35.

Krasner, Stephen D. (1987), *Asymmetries in Japanese–American Trade: The Case for Specific Reciprocity*, Berkeley, Cal.: Institute of International Studies, University of California.

Krugman, Paul R. (1994), 'The myth of Asia's miracle', *Foreign Affairs*, **73** (6), 62–93.

Linder, Burenstam Staffan (1986), *The Pacific Century: Economic and Political Consequences of Asian-Pacific Dynamism*, Stanford, Cal.: Stanford University Press.

Lockwood, William W. (1954), *The Economic Development of Japan: Growth and Structural Change 1868–1938*, Princeton, NJ: Princeton University Press.

Marglin, Stephen A. and Juliet B. Schor (1990), *The Golden Age of Capitalism: Reinterpreting the Postwar Experience*, Oxford: Oxford University Press.

Moritani, Masanori (1982), *Japanese Technology: Getting the Best from the Least*, Tokyo: Simul Press.

Nakamura, Takafusa (1983), *Economic Growth in Prewar Japan*, New Haven, Conn.: Yale University Press.

Ozawa, Terutomo (1974), *Japan's Technological Challenge to the West, 1950–1974: Motivation and Accomplishment*, Cambridge, Mass.: MIT Press.

Ozawa, Terutomo (1979a), 'International investment and industrial structure: new theoretical implications from the Japanese experience', *Oxford Economic Papers*, **31**, 72–91.

Ozawa, Terutomo (1979b), *Multinationalism, Japanese-style: The Political Economy of Outward Dependency*, Princeton, NJ: Princeton University Press.

Ozawa, Terutomo (1992), 'Foreign direct investment and economic development', *Transnational Corporations*, **1** (1), 27–54.

Ozawa, Terutomo (1993), 'Foreign direct investment and structural transformation: Japan as a recycler of market and industry', *Business and the Contemporary World*, **5** (2), 129–50.

Ozawa, Terutomo (1995), 'Structural upgrading and concatenated integration: the vicissitudes of the Pax Americana in tandem industrialization of the Pacific Rim', in Denis Simon (ed.), *Corporate Strategies in the Pacific Rim: Global versus Regional Trends*, London and New York: Routlege, pp. 215–46.

Ozawa, Terutomo (1996), 'Professor Kojima's "trade augmentation" principle and the "flying-geese" paradigm of tandem growth', *Surugadai Economic Studies*, **5** (2), 269–96.

Park, Yung Chul and Won-Am Park (1991), 'Changing Japanese trade patterns and East Asian NICs', in Paul Krugman (ed.), *Trade with Japan: Has the Door Opened Wider?*, Chicago: University of Chicago Press, pp. 85–120.

Peck, Merton J. and Shuji Tamura (1976), 'Technology', in Hugh Patrick and

Henry Rosovsky (eds), *Asia's New Giant: How the Japanese Economy Works*, Washington, DC: Brookings Institution, pp. 525–85.

Rostow, W.W. (1960), *The Stages of Economic Growth: A Non-Communist Manifesto*, Cambridge: Cambridge University Press.

Samuels, Richard J. (1994), *'Rich Nations, Strong Army': National Security and the Technological Transformation of Japan*, Ithaca, NY: Cornell University Press.

Sakakibara, Eisuke (1997), 'Reforming Japan: the once and future boom', *Economist*, **343**, 22 March, 89–90.

Science and Technology Agency (1996), *Kagaku Gijutsu Hakusho* [White Paper on Science and Technology], Tokyo: Ministry of Finance Printing Office.

Smith, Thomas C. (1955), *Political Change and Industrial Development in Japan's Government and Enterprise, 1868–1880*, Stanford, Cal.: Stanford University Press.

Taylor, Robert (1996), *Greater China and Japan: Prospects for an Economic Partnership in East Asia*, London and New York: Routledge.

Thant, Myo, Min Tang and Hiroshi Kakazu (1994), *Growth Triangles in Asia: A New Approach to Regional Economic Cooperation*, Hong Kong: Oxford University Press.

Van Hoesel, Roger (1996), 'Taiwan: foreign direct investment and the transformation of the economy', in John Dunning and Rajneesh Narula (eds), *Foreign Direct Investment and Government: Catalysts for Economic Restructuring*, London and New York: Routledge, pp. 280–315.

Wade, Robert (1990), *Governing the Market: Economic Theory and the Role of Government in East Asian Industrialization*, Princeton, NJ: Princeton University Press.

Waldman, Peter and Jay Solomon (1997), 'As good times roll: Indonesia's Chinese fear for their future', *Wall Street Journal*, 6 June, A18.

Wells, Louise T. (1983), 'Foreign investors from the Third World', in K. Kumar and M.G. Mcleod (eds), *Multinationals from Developing Countries*, New York: Lexington Books.

World Bank (1993), *The East Asian Miracle: Economic Growth and Public Policy*, New York: Oxford University Press.

Yasuba, Yasukichi (1996), 'The rise of East Asia and recent external shocks', in John Kuark (ed.), *Comparative Asian Economies*, Greenwich, Conn.: JAI Press, pp. 421–32.

Yuasa, Kenji (1997), 'Chinese government wants Chongqing to lead central region', and 'Japanese tie-ups key elements in change', *Nikkei Weekly*, 9 June, 20.

4. Pacific market integration: firms and governments

Terry Ursacki and Ilan Vertinsky

Economic integration, though much discussed, is seldom explicitly defined. It is generally taken to imply some form of interconnectedness of economies, but there are at least three possible ways in which this might manifest itself: by the existence of institutions for economic coordination, by the volume and nature of transactions occurring across borders; or by the tendency of movements in economic variables (such as price and output levels) to follow one another in the economies in question, the latter indicating 'high sensitivity to developments elsewhere in the region' even if cross-border transactions are few (Cooper 1994: 12).

A full understanding of the extent of and trends in integration within a region thus requires consideration of several different measures of the density of linkages and of the degree of interdependence and coordination among them. The volume of trade flows is the most common measure used but can be misleading if variations in economic growth rates and their impact on the volume of transactions are not taken into account. The nature of trade flows is also significant; in particular, the share of trade accounted for by intrafirm transactions is an indicator of the degree to which production processes have been coordinated across borders by private-sector actors. Apart from merchandise trade, linkages may also take the form of flows of factors of production such as investment or migrant or expatriate labour.

Since some degree of linkage exists between almost all economies, how are we to tell whether these networks of ties are 'dense', or are becoming 'denser'? For example, economies which double in size may have twice the volume of flows between them as before, but this implies no real increase in the degree of integration. One standard for comparison is simply the density of trade or other flows relative to what would be expected if flows were spread evenly across countries based on their shares in the world economy. This implies normalization by share of world trade or GDP (excluding the reference country). Comparison may also be made of changes in density relative to those developing with other regions in order to evaluate the pace of the integration process relative to other regions or to the rest of the world as a whole. A more sophisticated comparison would also allow for the fact that some countries are closer (or even contiguous) and hence likely to trade more than average. This is what economists refer to as a 'gravity' model. By adding a series of dummy variables to a gravity model, any tendency or 'bias' to trade with groups of countries more than would be expected based on their size, level of development and proximity can be discerned.

Such analysis shows that the Asian-Pacific Economic Cooperation network (APEC) appears to be building on a firm foundation of existing 'supranormal' trade flows. It is, perhaps, not so surprising that APEC should show a higher degree of trade integration than a purely Asian grouping. In Asia it encompasses a collection of states with, as noted above, a strong propensity to trade with one another, while in North America it includes the Canada–USA dyad, perhaps the two most tightly integrated major economies in the world. Trans-Pacific links also have a strong historical basis due to the targeting of the relatively rich and open North American markets by East Asian economies during their periods of export-based growth. As each developed and lost competitiveness in low-end labour-intensive manufacturing, there was always another to take its place. Indeed, in recent years Japanese firms have actively developed production in lower-wage Asian countries for the export to North America of goods in which Japan is no longer competitive (Dobson 1993). APEC thus encompasses three trading relationships, each of which has, for diverse reasons, denser networks of linkages than might be expected based on purely intrinsic characteristics.

In view of frequent reports of the re-emergence of a *de facto* 'Greater East Asia Co-prosperity Sphere' centred on Japan, it is perhaps surprising that a gravity model analysis indicates that there was no increase in the degree of intraregional trade 'bias' in East Asia during the 1980s, nor any evidence that trading patterns were centred on Japan. Intraregional trade within East Asia did increase from 23 per cent of total trade in 1980 to 39 per cent in 1990, and East Asian nations were likely to trade on average about 80 per cent more with one another than might be expected based on their economic and geographical characteristics, but this pattern showed no change over the decade (Frankel 1993). The bulk of the growth in intraregional trade in the 1980s could, in other words, be explained by the simple fact that these neighbouring economies were growing more quickly than the rest of the world.

These levels of trade 'bias' are, in fact, less than those found on the other side of the Pacific or among the countries of the Pacific region as a whole. Western hemisphere nations trade approximately twice as much with one another as would be expected based on a gravity model, while APEC (which includes Canada and the United States) shows the highest propensity of all to trade intraregionally: 'two APEC countries trade three times as much as two otherwise similar countries' (Frankel 1993: 234).

The 1990s have seen a continuation of these patterns. Overall, the conclusion which emerges from the analysis of Asia is that, in quantitative terms (value of international transactions per dollar of GDP), integration may not be changing all that much, though there are some exceptions where, as in China, policy change is resulting in a catch-up phase of increased integration with the world economy as a whole. Such policy changes also result in increased subregional economic integration as they allow penetration of the international market economy further and further into the hinterland from beach-heads in coastal zones or major urban centres. In North America, however, there is clear evidence of rapid quantitative increases in market integration.

Qualitatively, however, a transformation is underway throughout the Pacific as multinational corporations (MNCs) increase their direct role in the economic linkages among economies in the region. This development is perhaps most advanced within North America, but is also clearly evident in trans-Pacific linkages. The figures suggest that integration across the North Pacific has come largely at the initiative of Asian firms, mostly Japanese but also Korean. Within the western hemisphere integration has been largely driven by US firms. American corporations have shared the leadership role with Japanese firms in integration across the South Pacific, where there is a nascent corporate presence from Asia involved as well.

These trends are likely to strengthen as incomes in Asia Pacific increase and as local MNCs acquire the requisite sophistication to undertake a more aggressive international posture. In the more advanced Asian economies there has already been an evolution in corporate strategies from resource-seeking to knowledge-seeking to market-seeking. These qualitative changes will lead to a shift from trade based on resource complementarity (cheap, labour-intensive goods in exchange for technology) to trade based on similarity (intraindustry trade in differentiated manufactures).

In the following sections we examine the trans-Pacific economic relationship and then subregional patterns in Asia and in North America to identify key characteristics of Pacific market integration.

We then consider the factors which have led governments throughout the region to pursue economic integration as well as those affecting whether they chose to do so solely through market mechanisms or to supplement these with formal institutional structures. After a review of corporate responses to these policy choices, we conclude by sketching the implications for the future of market integration in the Pacific.

TRANS-PACIFIC ECONOMIC LINKAGES[1]

The first step in understanding how governments and firms have interacted in the Pacific market integration process must be to identify what is actually happening in the region. A review of the data on trade, intrafirm trade and investment flows leads to the following conclusions:

1.   *The principal pattern in the North American Free Trade Agreement (NAFTA) – Asia relationship has been slower integration with the richer Asian economies than with the lower-income ones; the latter are increasingly taking over the production of products previously manufactured in the higher-income Asian economies for export to North America.*

At first glance, US trade with the western Pacific Rim in aggregate terms appears to have grown rapidly in recent years: from 1990 to 1995 exports to the ten main East Asian economies (Japan, China, Korea, Hong Kong, Taiwan, Singapore, Malaysia, Indonesia, the Philippines and Thailand, hereafter referred to as the EA-10) rose 66.9 per cent from $105.0 billion to $174.2 billion,[2] about half again as fast as US exports to the rest of the world (ROW) excluding the EA-10. The latter rose 41.7 per cent from $288.1 billion to $408.3 billion. Imports from the EA-10 rose 60.0 per cent from $191.0 billion to $305.6 billion, again about half again as quickly as imports from the ROW (excluding the EA-10), which grew 42.8 per cent from $326.0 billion to $465.4 billion. As a result, the share of the EA-10 in US exports rose from 26.7 per cent to 29.9 per cent, and in imports from 36.9 per cent to 39.6 per cent.

This 'extra' trade volume, however, is easily explained by the rapid growth of the East Asian economies. While US GDP rose a cumulative total of 31.2 per cent from 1990 to 1995 (in current dollars), the EA-10's total GDP rose by 76.3 per cent (in current US dollars). By themselves these trade figures suggest no significant increase in integration between the US and the EA-10 as a whole.

The aggregate figures hide an important contrast, however: while trade grew relatively slowly with Japan (a cumulative total of 35.2 per cent), Taiwan (39.4 per cent), Hong Kong (48.7 per cent) and Korea

(49.3 per cent), it rose much more rapidly with Malaysia (200.4 per cent), China (185.6 per cent), Thailand (112.8 per cent), Philippines (107.7 per cent) and Indonesia (103.5 per cent). (Singapore was in between these groups at 88.9 per cent). Thus, in terms of sheer dollar value of trade, integration seems to be proceeding at about the same pace with the higher-income countries of the western Pacific as with the rest of the world, but more rapidly with the lower-income western Pacific economies. This appears to reflect the 'flying geese' pattern of industrialization, through which successively lower-income countries take over the production and export of labour-intensive manufactures (Kojima 1995; Fukusaku 1992; Fukushima and Kwan 1995). Ohta *et al.* (1995) have also referred to this shift as a 'billiard ball' pattern.

2.   *The principal actors driving these changes have been Japanese firms in the North Pacific, though US firms play a large role in the South Pacific.*

Japanese firms have dominated the integration process in the North Pacific. Although Japan was the host with the largest single increase in FDI by US firms among the EA-10, with US FDI rising 73.5 per cent from $22.60 billion to $39.20 billion, it accounted for only 5.9 per cent of the increase in US FDI in the world as a whole and 5.5 per cent of the accumulated stock at historical cost. These figures compare with Japan's 24.7 per cent of world GDP (excluding the United States) and 9.8 per cent of world exports (excluding the United States). Thus US investment in Japan is much lower than might be expected based on the country's economic weight. Although there once were regulatory issues which limited inward investment, Lawrence (1993) argues that today the principal reason for the low rate of inward investment by foreign companies of all nationalities is the difficulty of making acquisitions in Japan due to cross-shareholdings among *keiretsu* members (see also Weinstein and Yafeh 1995).

On the other hand, while Japanese FDI in North America rose dramatically during the bubble era of the late 1980s and represented a major integrating force during that period, between 1990 and 1995 it rose only 30.0 per cent in the USA, from $83.5 billion to $108.6 billion. This was slightly slower than US GDP, which increased 31.2 per cent. However, Japan's FDI in the USA is both larger and growing in larger increments than US investment in Japan.

Intrafirm trade data confirm the dominant role of Japanese firms in bridging the North Pacific (see Zeile 1997). They show that US trade with Japan is dominated by intrafirm trade to a greater extent than trade with any other partner except Switzerland: fully 70 per cent of

US exports to Japan and 71 per cent of imports from Japan consisted of trade between related firms in 1992, the most recent year for which comprehensive data by country are available. Of this trade, over three-quarters of the exports were from Japanese affiliates in the USA shipping goods to their parents, while 97 per cent of intrafirm imports into the United States from Japan were goods shipped by Japanese parents to affiliates in the USA. Japanese firms are thus clearly playing the leading role in determining the extent and nature of trade across the North Pacific.

US firms have played a more active role in the relationship across the South Pacific. The stock of US FDI in the EA-10 excluding Japan (China, Hong Kong, Indonesia, Korea, Malaysia, the Philippines, Singapore, Taiwan and Thailand, hereafter called the EA-9) showed impressive growth in the first half of the 1990s, but still falls short of matching the weight of the region in world trade or GDP. From 1990 to 1995 US FDI almost doubled in the Philippines (up 95.4 per cent from $1.36 billion to $2.65 billion), Taiwan (up 97.3 per cent from $2.23 billion to $4.39 billion), and Korea (up 97.5 per cent from $2.70 billion to $5.32 billion). It more than doubled in Indonesia (up 119.8 per cent from $3.21 billion to $7.05 billion), Hong Kong (up 127.6 per cent from $6.06 billion to $13.78 billion), Malaysia (up 149.2 per cent from $1.47 billion to $3.65 billion) and Thailand (up 156.8 per cent from $1.79 billion to $4.60 billion). It more than tripled in Singapore (up 216.2 per cent from $3.98 billion to $12.57 billion) and more than quintupled from a low base in China (up 464.1 per cent from $354 million to $2.00 billion). These impressive growth rates are somewhat misleading, however: the EA-9 accounted for 11.7 per cent of the increase in US FDI and 7.9 per cent of the stock while contributing 9.7 per cent of ROW GDP (excluding the United States) and 17.1 per cent of ROW exports (and higher percentages of the growth in these aggregates). Put in this light, the pace of US firm-driven integration with Asia seems roughly in line with other regions.

If we compare this activity to that of firms from the EA-9, it is clear that EA-9 firms' eastward advance into the USA, while growing, is still a much smaller factor than the westward expansion of US firms. Firms from several other East Asian economies appear to have begun to expand aggressively into the USA during the 1990s: FDI in the USA from Korea rose from –$0.85 billion in 1990 (reflecting debt financing of investments) to $1.91 billion in 1995, while Taiwanese investment more than doubled (up 128.1 per cent from $0.93 million to $2.12 billion), and Malaysian FDI increased almost fourteen-fold from $31 million to $429 million. Investment from other East Asian economies showed much lower rates of growth, probably due to a lack of local firms capable of international expansion apart from moving offshore to offset rising labour costs: Singaporean FDI in the United States rose 18.5 per cent from $1.13 billion to $1.34 billion, while Hong Kong's rose 11.9 per cent from $1.24 billion to $1.39 billion and that of the Philippines 7.8 per cent from $77 million to $83 million. While these relationships are still small, they do suggest that a qualitative change in the nature of firm activities may have begun in the relationship between the United States and some EA-9 economies as well.

With two notable exceptions, the dominance of US firms is also evident from data on intrafirm trade. Among Asian partners other than Japan, only US trade with Singapore (32.2 per cent) and Hong Kong (37.0 per cent) has an intrafirm trade share of exports of over 30 per cent, but in most cases US firms export the majority (often 80 per cent or more) of the intrafirm goods. The exceptions are China (only 10 per cent of intrafirm exports controlled by US firms) and Korea (only 32 per cent controlled by US firms). In all three cases (Japan, Korea and China) where foreign firms control the bulk of the intrafirm exports, trading companies play a prominent role in sourcing goods for the importing economy. This is reflected in high ratios of wholesale trade to manufacturing trade for these countries. In the case of US exports, these ratios range from 33:1 for China to 32:1 for Korea (compared to 10:1 for Japan).

Turning to US imports from Asia Pacific, Singapore (66.9 per cent) and Hong Kong (49.2 per cent) have the highest intrafirm shares after Japan, with Korea (32.2 per cent) the only other to exceed one-quarter. Some 93 per cent of US intrafirm imports from Korea are controlled by non-US parents. In every other case US parents control from 44 per cent (Taiwan) to 80 per cent (Hong Kong and Singapore) of intrafirm imports. Thus, with the exception of Korea, in trans-Pacific integration between the USA and the EA-9 it is US firms that are playing the leading role. Data from the 1990s therefore seem consistent with earlier analysis of the 1980s, which demonstrated that 'the ASEAN countries (with the notable exception of Indonesia) had the highest level of IIT [intra-industry trade] with North America', with a 'high degree of "intra-firm and inter-processed" trade between the United States and ASEAN' as a 'consequence of the globalization of corporate activities along the Pacific Rim' (Fukusaku 1992: 30). Since there is a strong tendency for the proportion of US trade accounted for by intrafirm transactions to be higher the richer the trading partner (Zeile 1997), the rising incomes of Pacific Asia are likely to lead to further strengthening of this trans-Pacific intrafirm trading relationship.

3.   *Changes in the relationships between the NAFTA countries and the richer Asian economies have been more qualitative than quantitative in nature. While FDI totals have risen only at rates approximating overall economic growth, there has been a notable qualitative shift, as Japanese firms, driven by dramatic changes in exchange rates that have eroded their cost advantage at home, have begun to use the United States as an export platform.*

Additional details on intrafirm trade with Japanese companies support the conclusion that Japanese FDI is fostering closer integration of the US and Japanese economies through the export of US-made products produced in Japanese-owned plants, often using some Japanese components. This trend was identified in the 1980s data by Anderson and Noguchi (1995), and is consistent with a finding by Menon (1997) that all the growth in trade between the USA and Japan from 1986 to 1991 was intra-industry trade (which is often intrafirm). Exports by US affiliates of Japanese firms to their foreign parent groups jumped 107.8 per cent from $14.5 billion in 1988 to $30.0 billion in 1994, rising from 4.5 per cent to 5.9 per cent of total US exports. While wholesale trade exports rose 92.9 per cent from $13.6 billion to $26.7 billion, manufacturing exports more than quadrupled from a low base, rising 305.1 per cent from $786 million in 1988 to $3.2 billion in 1994. While imports climbed only 35.5 per cent from $63.9 billion to $86.7 billion, manufacturing affiliate imports rose 181.6 per cent from $5.1 billion to $14.5 billion, eight times as fast as the 22.9 per cent growth in imports by wholesale trade affiliates (from $58.6 billion to $72.0 billion). While it has been argued that 'almost all Japanese FDI in US manufacturing has been motivated, at least in part, by the desire to overcome protectionist trade barriers such as the anti-dumping dispute mechanism and voluntary export restraints (VERs)' (Kojima 1995: 98), this pattern suggests an evolution towards the United States becoming a manufacturing platform for Japanese companies. This may be a result of the substantial shift in relative costs between the two countries (Daly 1997), or perhaps a political tactic to appease widespread US calls for Japanese action to reduce the trade imbalance between them (Choate 1990).

4.   *Trade between Asia and Latin America shows a clear difference between NAFTA member Mexico and the rest of the western hemisphere. While the weight of trade with the EA-10 has increased noticeably in western hemisphere countries that are not part of NAFTA, the EA-10's share of total trade has actually dropped in Mexico. Structural changes in trade, however, suggest increasing use of Mexico as an export platform*

by Asian firms seeking to penetrate the rich markets of the northern members of NAFTA.

Mexico's trade with the EA-10 shows a very mixed pattern over the 1990–5 period. Total trade with the EA-10 grew somewhat more slowly than ROW total trade (133.6 per cent versus 168.6 per cent), but exports and imports followed widely divergent trends. Exports to the EA-10 rose from $1.77 billion to $1.84 billion, an increase of just 3.8 per cent compared to the 207.1 per cent increase in ROW exports (excluding the EA-10) from $25.4 billion to $78.0 billion, while imports from the EA-10 grew much more quickly than ROW imports, rising from $2.03 billion to $7.11 billion, a 250.6 per cent increase versus the 133.6 per cent rise in ROW imports from $28.0 billion to $65.4 billion. This contrast between export and import performance appears to reflect Asian manufacturers' use of Mexico as a vehicle to penetrate NAFTA markets by exporting parts and components there for assembly and subsequent export northwards.

The EA-10's share of the total trade (exports plus imports) of the non-NAFTA countries in the western hemisphere rose from 12.1 per cent to 15.6 per cent from 1990 to 1995, but the pattern was the opposite of Mexico's: exports to the EA-10 have grown much more quickly than ROW exports, while the opposite was true for imports. Exports to the EA-10 by the non-NAFTA countries in the western hemisphere during the 1990–5 period rose from $13.8 billion to $35.2 billion (155.5 per cent), outpacing the 44.1 per cent growth in the region's exports to the ROW (from $91.8 billion to $132.2 billion). The 19.1 per cent growth in imports from the EA-10 from $14.4 billion to $17.2 billion, on the other hand, lagged behind ROW import growth of 33.9 per cent (from $127.5 billion to $168.6 billion). This pattern appears to reflect differences in growth rates, with the rapid growth of Asia pulling in imports faster than the Latin American economies.

5. *Canada appears to have been left largely on the sidelines in these developments.*

Canada's centre of gravity in trade appears to be drifting away from Asia. Trade with the EA 10 rose only 36.9 per cent from $28.5 billion to $39.0 billion between 1990 and 1995, versus 44.5 per cent (from $217.6 billion to $314.5 billion) for the ROW – despite Asia's much more rapid growth. As a result, the EA-10's share of Canada's total trade dropped from 11.6 per cent to 11.0 per cent. Within this overall structure, however, the same pattern was evident as for the United States: trade with the richer countries of Japan, Taiwan, Hong Kong and Korea grew only half as fast as ROW trade growth (20.2 per cent from $22.9 billion to $27.6 billion), while trade with the lower-income countries of China, Indonesia, Malaysia, the Philippines and Thailand grew almost twice as fast as Canadian trade as a whole, rising 82.5 per cent from $5.5 billion to $10.1 billion (again, Singapore came in the middle, rising 61.7 per cent). This pattern seems driven by the shift of production out of Japan and into South-East Asia: it results in the EA-9 purchasing more raw materials from Canada and in turn displacing Japan as a source of consumer goods such as electronics (Ursacki and Vertinsky 1996).

Canada reports significant FDI relationships with only two of the EA-10, Japan and Hong Kong. The former relationship is larger, but growing slowly: Japanese investment in Canada rose 28.5 per cent from C$5.2 billion to C$6.7 billion between 1990 and 1995. In US dollar terms this was only a 9.3 per cent increase, much less than the overall growth of Japanese investment, though faster than the growth of the Canadian economy. Canadian investment in Japan grew more rapidly, rising 250.3 per cent from C$0.9 billion to C$3.5 billion, but the bulk of this increase resulted from the statistical reclassification of existing investments of US subsidiaries of Canadian firms rather than fresh investment (*CJTC* 1992: 6). The relationship with Hong Kong became much closer in the first half of the 1990s: inbound investment into Canada rose 131.9 per cent from C$1.4 billion to C$3.2 billion, while Canadian direct investment in Hong Kong, based largely on its roles as a gateway to China and as a major international financial centre, more than quadrupled from C$0.6 billion to C$2.5 billion. Investment flows to and from the the other EA-10 economies for which figures are reported separately have been quite modest. South Korea's investment in Canada actually dropped 39.7 per cent from C$312 million to C$188 million, while the combined total for Singapore, Taiwan and Malaysia more than tripled from C$150 million in 1990, but still amounted to less than half a billion Canadian dollars in 1995 (C$479 million). Outbound investment by Canadians in Singapore grew 11.5 per cent from C$1.8 billion to C$2.0 billion and exceeded the combined total for Indonesia, Taiwan, Malaysia and Korea (C$1.2 billion in 1990 and C$1.8 billion in 1995). The stock of investment from 'Other Pacific Rim' (including China) grew just 13.4 per cent from C$454 million to C$515 million, but outbound investment in the remainder of the region (mostly China) rose six-fold from C$350 million to C$2.2 billion. With the exception of ties to Hong Kong, which have been strongly encouraged by the flow of immigrants into Canada, direct investment has done little to integrate the Canadian economy into the Pacific region. While it is common to suggest that 'Canada's lack of significant presence in Asia reflects fear or laziness on the part of Canadian firms', Head and Ries (1995: 31) suggest instead that 'the relative lack of Canadian business presence points to the absence of profitable opportunities. The homogeneous, resource-based products that Canada sells to East Asia are unlikely sources of rents. Nor is it probable that Canadian firms would need to establish a local market presence in Asia to better sell these kinds of goods.'

ECONOMIC LINKAGES WITHIN EAST ASIA

On the Asian side of the Pacific, data on trade and investment patterns suggest the following conclusions:

1. *Increases in intraregional trade seem largely to reflect overall growth in these countries' economies.*

Between 1990 and 1995 intraregional exports as a share of total EA-10 exports increased from 39.5 per cent to 47.5 per cent. Intraregional exports rose 123.4 per cent from $278.3 billion to $623.0 billion, almost exactly twice as fast as exports to the rest of the world, which rose 61.8 per cent from $425.7 billion to $688.6 billion. While this may seem striking, it should be recalled that the EA-10's GDP in US dollar terms rose 76.3 per cent from $4.1 trillion to $7.3 trillion over this period, while the rest of the world's output rose just 15.3 per cent from $18.9 trillion to $21.8 trillion.[3] With output (and hence total income) rising five times faster than in the rest of the world, it should not be surprising that intraregional trade has increased. Indeed, if anything, it might be wondered why it has not increased more rapidly. This is not to suggest that the increased weight of intraregional trade is unimportant: Watanabe (1997:40), for example, argues that 'East Asia is becoming a resilient, self-reliant regional unit subject to limited influence from the large economies outside the region.' The conclusion is rather that this trend, whatever its implications, is a natural product of economic growth and not the outcome of preferential treatment or grand strategy by governments or corporations to create a *de facto* trading bloc.

2. *Quantitatively Japan's role in East Asia seems no larger than warranted by the respective sizes of the Japanese and EA-9 economies, except in China, where a catch-up from a long period of economic isolation is underway. Firms from the EA-9 are also vigorously involved in integrating China and other countries which have recently adopted more FDI-friendly approaches to the world economy.*

The EA-10's total exports and imports rose by 80.4 per cent and 86.3 per cent between 1990 and 1995, reaching $1,311.7 billion and $1,181.5 billion respectively. In dollar terms, Japan's exports to the EA-9 rose by 112.9 per cent from $85.2 billion to $181.4 billion, while its imports from them rose 84.7 per cent from $62.5 billion to $115.5 billion. The growth in trade with China was substantially more rapid than that with the other EA-9 countries. Japanese exports to China rose 256.9 per cent (from $6.1 billion to $21.9 billion) and imports 197.9 per cent (from $12.1 billion to $35.9 billion). This was two-and-a-half to three times as fast as trade with the other EA-9 countries. Exports to them were up from $79.0 billion to $159.5 billion (101.7 per cent) and imports from $50.5 billion to $79.6 billion (57.7 per cent). This more rapid growth suggests that there may have been some increase in the level of integration between China and Japan as part of a catch-up phase of greater integration with the world economy as a whole after a long period of isolation, and that there was little change with other Asian trading partners in volume terms.

Japanese FDI (JFDI) outflows are roughly triple the total for all the rest of Asia combined, and hence must be the focus of any consideration of FDI as an integrating force in the Pacific. Japan's FDI outflow to the EA-9 grew from $6.95 billion in Fiscal Year (FY) 1990 (ending 31 March 1991) to $12.15 billion in FY1995, and now represents 23.1 per cent of Japan's total FDI outflow.[4] This figure exceeds the 8.7 per cent weight of the other EA-9 economies in ROW GDP and their 18.7 per cent share of ROW exports. The bulk of the difference, however, is again accounted for by China, which took 8.7 per cent ($8.1 billion) of Japanese FDI in FY1995 but contributed only 2.5 per cent of ROW GDP and 3.2 per cent of ROW exports. This represents a substantial shift, since in 1990 China received only 0.6 per cent ($349 million) of total JFDI outflows and the other eight countries 9.8 per cent of the Japanese outflow ($6.60 billion). To put this in perspective, however, China alone took 11.3 per cent of total world FDI outflows in 1995, indicating that its integration with the rest of the world is, if anything, proceeding even faster than that with Japan. A prominent role in this process belongs to firms from the EA-9, particularly Hong Kong, Macau and Taiwan, which were responsible for 70 per cent of the $33.9 billion in investment implemented in China in 1994 (Watanabe 1997: 48). In recent years Chinese firms have also been moving into Hong Kong to open a window on the capitalist world (Chen and Wong 1995). Korean, Hong Kong and Taiwan firms have also been active in integrating other less-developed South-East Asian nations into the world economy by establishing plants in countries such as Indonesia to produce for export, taking advantage of the reputation with buyers gained by the parent firm over the years (Wells 1993). Fukushima and Kwan (1995: 10), however, caution that some of this investment, particularly in China and Malaysia, may actually be 'round-trip investment ... domestic investment under the guise of foreign investment to take advantage of fiscal and other benefits given to foreign investors'.

The seven East Asian economies reported in the IMF's *Balance of Payments Yearbook* (the EA-9 – Taiwan and Hong Kong) were the recipients of an 18.0 per cent share of world FDI outflows in 1995, a fraction very close to their share of JFDI and of ROW exports. Although the increase in Japanese investment in East Asia may thus not be extraordinary in volume terms, it has nevertheless played an important part in the industrialization of the region by nurturing infant industries and then gradually moving into more sophisticated and diversified activities (Kojima 1995).

NORTH AMERICAN ECONOMIC INTEGRATION

Intra-NAFTA patterns of trade and investment suggest one strong conclusion: there has been a substantial increase in intraregional trade among the NAFTA partners which cannot be explained solely by market growth, and in which US firms are playing the leading role.

Within North America, economic integration among the NAFTA economies appears to be proceeding rapidly, building on already substantial historical trading relationships with the United States. Canada's exports to the United States rose 60.2 per cent from $95.4 billion to $152.9 billion between 1990 and 1995 (from 75.4 per cent to 80.4 per cent of total Canadian exports), while imports rose 44.8 per cent from $75.3 billion to $109.0 billion (from 62.4 per cent to 66.7 per cent of total imports). Mexico's shift was even more dramatic, with exports to the United States up 254.4 per cent from $18.8 billion to $66.8 billion (rising from 69.3 per cent of Mexican exports in 1990 to 83.6 per cent in 1995) and imports up 172.2 per cent from $19.8 billion to $54.0 billion (from 66.1 per cent of total imports to 74.5 per cent). Exports to Canada rose 775.7 per cent from $226 million to $2.0 billion, tripling their share of total exports from 0.8 per cent to 2.5 per cent, while imports grew 251.4 per cent from $391 million to $1.4 billion, rising from 1.3 per cent to 1.9 per cent of total Mexican imports. As all these increases vastly exceed both the increases in overall trade (as shown by the increases in share figures) and the changes in current US dollar GDP over the period of –1.4 per cent for Canada, +1.2 per cent for Mexico and +31.2

per cent for the United States. The trade figures provide unambiguous evidence of an increase in economic integration within North America.

Within the western hemisphere both Canada and Mexico show moderately high levels of intrafirm trade with the USA: 41.4 per cent of US exports to Canada and 26.3 per cent of those to Mexico were intrafirm, with US firms controlling 90 per cent of the intrafirm exports to Canada and 95 per cent of those to Mexico. The situation with imports was similar: 46.7 per cent of US imports from Canada and 34.7 per cent of those from Mexico were intrafirm, with 80 per cent of intrafirm imports from Canada and 88 per cent of those from Mexico controlled by US firms. US firms are thus the dominant players in the North American integration process.

Figures on FDI show strong increases in the level of North American integration. From 1990 to 1995, US FDI in Mexico rose from $10.3 billion to $14.0 billion (36.1 per cent) and US FDI in Canada rose from $69.5 billion to $81.4 billion (17.1 per cent). While both these increases were slower than total US FDI growth of 65 per cent over the period (and hence these countries' share of US FDI dropped), the increases were much faster than host GDP growth, resulting in a rise in US FDI as a share of host country GDP. Canadian FDI in the United States rose from $27.7 billion to $46.0 billion (65.9 per cent), while Mexican FDI in the United States rose from $554 million to $1.9 billion (252.3 per cent). In short, the FDI figures again suggest a strong rise in the level of integration on the North American side of the Pacific.

To summarize, market integration appears to be most advanced on the North American side of the Pacific, where both quantitative and qualitative changes are occurring. While the numbers on standard measures of integration such as trade, when carefully analysed, show few quantitative changes within Asia or across the Pacific, qualitative changes are occurring through the activities of MNCs, where the long-dominant role of US and Japanese firms is now being supplemented by rapidly growing firms from the rest of the EA-10.

THE IMPETUS FOR MARKET LIBERALIZATION IN EAST ASIA

Economic integration, as we have defined it, is concerned with the intensity of interconnectedness of economies. For such interconnectedness to evolve requires both that the obstacles to such ties be surmountable and that economic agents find it worthwhile to pursue such linkages, that is, to expand the economic borders of their home countries.

One of the key obstacles to the integration of economies has long been government intervention. The desire to preserve sovereignty both for its own sake and as a means for the accomplishment of national goals has led governments to impose measures which have restricted trade either directly (via tariffs, quotas and the like) or indirectly (via subsidies, procurement policies, administrative procedures and so on). The economic and political borders of nation-states have thus often coincided, hemming in their own firms and keeping foreigners out, except on a carefully prescribed basis.

Not long ago, the Asian side of the Pacific could be viewed as a region of numerous such small, highly segmented economies with coincident economic and political borders. Today, many of its economies are singled out as examples of, if not pure free trade, at least a pragmatic openness widely held to have made a substantial contribution to the region's economic growth (*World Development Report* 1987). Meanwhile, the second-tier economies on the eastern rim of the Pacific, Canada and Mexico, have dropped many of the barriers that separated them from the United States. What has led to these shifts in orientation?

Considerable liberalization of international economic exchange has occurred on both sides of the Pacific, but the degree of maturity of the integration processes and the specific methods by which the liberalization of international economic exchange has occurred have differed substantially. Understanding this process requires, first, an examination of the forces which have led to greater integration, and second, an analysis of the factors which have differentiated the specific approaches pursued on the eastern and western rims of the Pacific.

The reforms which have expanded the economic borders of states in the Pacific have been fostered by four main developments:

1. the recognition that the state was overextended and its activities needed to be rolled back;
2. the demonstration effect of successful open economies;
3. geopolitical factors which have narrowed the range of options available to nations on the periphery; and
4. the increase in the cross-border flow of information.

The geographical reach of economic agents within a country and the ability and interest of economic agents outside the country to be engaged in its economy depend on a variety of factors. One important element is the size, extent and type of intervention by the government in its economy. For example, a large government with a hands-on style of economic management and an autarkic ideology may limit both the scale and scope of interaction of domestic economic agents with foreigners and provide little scope or motive for outsiders to become engaged in its economy (an extreme example is North Korea and its *juche* ideology). A smaller government with a hands-on economic management style subscribing to neomercantilistic policies may promote exports and the strategic outflow of foreign direct investment while creating hurdles for outsiders to engage in its economy (Japan and the Republic of Korea during their economic take-off phases provide examples). In this case, the asymmetries that are created in the reach of domestic and foreign agents tend to induce retaliation by foreign states and create demands for bilateral or multilateral intergovernmental coordination of policies to resolve conflicts. Small governments with economic *laissez-faire* regimes provide opportunities for both domestic and foreign agents to engage in cross-border economic transactions. In this case economic integration will reflect market forces shaped by economic, technological and geographical factors.

The causes, scale and specifics of the roll-back of government activities have varied, but throughout the Pacific governments have found they needed to withdraw from certain spheres of activity. In North America, the pressure of chronic deficits has led to a sharp ideological shift which has pushed governments to abandon activities to the market, sometimes with little but free-market ideology as a guide to predict the consequences. In Latin America, the debt crisis ushered in a new era of modesty in government as it became recognized that the challenge of development was beyond the scope of any government unless it harnessed market forces to the fullest (*World Development Report* 1991). If this lesson was not learned directly, it was sometimes imposed by adjustment programmes drawn up by international financial institutions. The more advanced Asian states found that their economies had become so complex that the bureaucratic guidance of the developmental state had become counterproductive. Asset quality problems of monumental scale emerged throughout the banking sectors of Japan and Korea as an expensive legacy of the over-regulated financial systems which had been used to promote economic development. Overly close relations between business, politicians and bureaucrats, which had earlier contributed to the implementation of national economic plans, were found to have fostered massive corruption. The resulting ever-widening series of scandals has also shaken the public's faith in the infallibility of government economic management and discredited even such venerable institutions as Japan's Ministry of Finance. Democratization in Korea and the end of one-party rule in Japan (due, at least in part, to these scandals) have constrained governments' freedom to manouevre. The economic shocks which rocked much of South-East Asia, particularly Thailand, in mid-1997 are likely to lead to further rethinking of the role of the state in the economy.

In the less-advanced economies of Asia, perhaps a more potent factor to date has been the demonstration effect of the Four Tigers. While two of these (Hong Kong and Singapore) have had indisputably open economies, there is considerable controversy over the openness of Taiwan and Korea, at least during the take-off phases of their development (Amsden 1989; Wade 1990). Nevertheless, it seems clear that they were more outward orientated than many of their neighbours, a point which has not been lost on the latter as they have searched for a development model. Multilateral liberalization also contributed to the recognition that nations which isolated themselves from economic integration risked being left behind by more favourable investment environments.

For some of the most recent converts (such as Vietnam), communism's collapse in the USSR and *de facto* abandonment by China have deprived their former allies and clients of alternatives as cuts in aid revealed the true economic costs of forgoing economic integration with the capitalist world.

Migration and the resulting 'overseas' communities have always been vehicles for the transmission of information which facilitates the breaching of economic borders. Throughout history expatriate communities have acted to facilitate economic integration through trading activities based on family or ethnic ties. Today, however, the spread of travel and the influence of mass media have meant that such information about potential trading opportunities is much more widely held. Producers and consumers alike are more aware of opportunities elsewhere and hence more likely to agitate for changes in regulations or procedures which they see as blocking them from the pursuit of their self-interest. They are also able to pursue such opportunities at lower cost due to widespread familiarity with western 'universal' business culture (often adopted as a cultural lingua franca even among non-western traders).

The shift to a more open relationship with the world economy thus seems to have been principally a reaction to the perceived failure of economic models which were either explicitly based on opposing concepts or were incompatible with integration to varying degrees.

POLICY CHOICES FOR ECONOMIC INTEGRATION: MARKETS OR MANDARINS?

It has often been observed that economic integration in Asia Pacific is a market-led rather than a policy-led process, in contrast with North America, where NAFTA has provided a formal institution for the promotion of freer trade. To a certain extent this might be considered an artificial distinction that ignores the degree of maturity of the integration process. Integration is often brought about by market forces. These create both the derived demand for liberalization and the domestic political forces that promote and sustain market opening. Nations respond by acting unilaterally and/or attempting to negotiate new specific arrangements for trade and foreign direct investment. As the economic relationships deepen and mature and their scope and scale expands, the complexities involved in cross-border transactions lead partner governments to negotiate a more comprehensive trade regime.

While it is tempting, for example, to attribute the higher rates of market integration in North America to the policy initiatives associated with the FTA in 1989 and NAFTA in 1994, closer examination of the data reveals that processes of integration had already picked up considerable momentum prior to the negotiations leading to the agreements. Thus, for example, shifts in domestic policies in Mexico in response to potential threats and opportunities faced by its economy created momentum for an integration process that eventually led to formalization through the NAFTA. In Asia, a mix of domestic policy shifts and market forces combined to create an economic integration process. For example, Japanese foreign direct investment, often considered the engine of market-led economic integration in Asia, would not have been possible without the liberalization of outbound investment by Japan and inbound investment by the host nations.

The key distinction between these integration processes is that informal integration in the western rim is a result of policy change at the national level, with the liberalizing government retaining control of the pace of change – or even its continuance. Often the international effects of such policy changes may even be incidental to their main, domestic objectives. Use of the term 'market-led' may perhaps not be inappropriate in such cases. In other cases, the policy may be intended to make the form of interaction with the outside world conform to specific national objectives, by encouraging exports and limiting imports, for example (though once firms are exposed to the external market they often develop in ways which undermine the original intent of the policy). This might be termed a 'government-led' integration process.

Formal integration, on the other hand, implies relinquishing some measure of discretion through binding external commitments. This may sometimes be unappealing due to authoritarian habits, nationalism, fear of domination by regional hegemons, potential loss of illicit income from the sale of influence, and so on. Integration promoted by participating in international agreements might be referred to as being 'intergovernmentally led'.

Within Asia, even when transnational institutions are established, they are typically of a more informal nature than elsewhere. For example, Roberto Romulo, head of the APEC Business Advisory Council, says that APEC:

> recognizes that the work of economic development is done by business and markets, while the role of government is to lower trade and other barriers that interfere with the ability of corporations and individuals to compete and cooperate across borders. Compare this core philosophy with that of the European Union, which relies on an increasingly complex system of bureaucratic structures, seemingly designed more to appease domestic political constituencies than to facilitate a freer flow of goods, capital and technologies across today's global economy. (*Asiaweek*, 6 December 1996, 14)

Indeed, APEC has been referred to as 'a Trade Facilitation and Business Promotion Association – a new form of regional cooperation concentrating on unilateral trade liberalization, serious trade facilitation (through harmonization of standards and customs procedures as well as other policies), and a commitment to business promotion' (Fayé 1996: 183).

North American integration, on the other hand, has proceeded on a more formal, 'intergovernmentally led' basis in recent years, as the Canada–USA FTA which came into effect in 1989 was soon followed by NAFTA, which was approved by the member governments in 1993 and implemented in 1994.

These differences in the specifics of the integration process on the two sides of the Pacific Rim reflect:

1. the maturity and scope of intraregional economic relationships;
2. the degree of complementarity in regional comparative advantage profiles;
3. the maturity and size of local economies;
4. the size, management styles and ideologies of governments;
5. patterns in historical security interrelationships;
6. domestic political regimes; and

7. business and political cultures.

The eastern Pacific Rim is dominated by the mature USA–Canada trading relationship. The large number of firms with operations on both sides of the border created a strong constituency for the removal of obstacles to the seamless integration of operations as well as a derived demand for the reduction of uncertainties created by the political border, such as the threat of anti-dumping or countervailing duty suits. Further south, the *maquiladora* programme had shown US firms the advantages of having a low-wage neighbour as a production base, but asymmetries in market access meant many marketing opportunities there remained beyond their reach. The hope that trade-induced growth in Mexico would reduce the pressure of illegal migration was a further motivation for the USA to pursue a formal agreement. When Mexico opened up its economy to cope with economic stagnation, reversing decades of economic policy, its leaders recognized that some means of ensuring that these reforms could not be rolled back by a future administration was necessary if MNCs were to have the confidence to make long-term investments. Thus, in all three economies market-led integration was approaching the limits of the existing institutional framework and further formal, intergovernmental agreements became necessary for the integration process to continue.

Elsewhere in Latin America, with the exception of Chile, the preconditions for further formal institutions of economic integration with North America do not yet appear to exist. The history of high trade barriers in the region has left considerable scope for further market-led integration to occur now that a more free-market approach has been adopted throughout most of the region. Most firms still have ample room to expand within such structures as Mercosur, and hence are not yet running up against the growth constraints that would push them to call for freer trade with the United States at the expense of the loss of protection of their domestic markets (hence the slow progress of the initiative for a Free Trade Area of the Americas).

Within the western Pacific Rim, the relatively recent opening up of many economies has left a similarly rich supply of regional opportunities and meant there is little call for formal institution building. Moreover, Japan's *sogo shosha* (general trading companies), with their vast information networks and risk-spreading abilities, have proved capable of moving into emerging markets at a very early stage and laying the groundwork for further investment by their *keiretsu* (industrial group) sister companies, thereby largely obviating the need for formal institutions as confidence builders.

The degree of complementarity of economies on the two sides of the Pacific has also influenced the nature of the integration process. As long as North American integration was built upon the complementarity of goods made with inexpensive Mexican labour and abundant Canadian resources feeding into the US manufacturing hub, an adequate trade framework resulted simply from each party pursuing its own interests. However, as these relationships, particularly that between the United States and Canada, matured and became dominated by intra-industry trade based on the similarity of tastes and incomes, the need arose for some type of formal harmonization to ensure standards, regulations and other measures that indirectly affected trade flows did not block the further development of trade ties.

Among the EA-10, on the other hand, there has been an evolution from a strictly competitive pattern of comparative advantage based on inexpensive labour. Differences in the timing of the adoption of pro-market policies have resulted in considerable gaps in wealth across nations (for example, Singapore and Indonesia). Thus, integration is still able to occur without formal institution building as the richer states shed the more labour-intensive parts of industries, which move to the less-advanced economies. In the mid-1990s, however, several of the more developed economies experienced the typical slowdown in growth that accompanies rich-nation status, and the poorer ones encountered adjustment difficulties such as banking collapses and currency crises. If these warning signs signal the end of the general prosperity which had previously allowed intraregional economic tensions to be glossed over, the need for coordination at the intergovernmental level to cope with economic conflict may become more urgent.

The size and nature of government intervention in the economy has also led to differences in the integration processes. On the eastern Pacific Rim, while the level of intentional government intervention in international trade is relatively low, the complexities of running a sophisticated, modern industrial economy have resulted in a proliferation of micro-level regulations for the pursuit of social goals (such as higher environmental quality and a more equitable distribution of income) which can have profound indirect effects on trade. Removing these obstacles requires detailed intergovernmental coordination and the ability to make complex trade-offs, and hence is greatly facilitated by formal institutional structures.

On the western rim of the Pacific, most of the economies (with the notable exception of Hong Kong) have been managed by small, activist governments pursuing neomercantilist policies. Such policies create asymmetries in market access with trading partners and eventually lead to a need for coordination to resolve conflicts (especially across the Pacific). At the same time, they make it difficult initially to cooperate and integrate within the region.

There are also sharp differences in the nature of international relations on the two sides of the Pacific. On the eastern rim, the dominant relationship has been the very close one between Canada and the United States. Close partners may feel more comfortable about giving up their individual discretion and relying on rule-based trading regimes because the 'complex interdependence' which has evolved between them limits opportunistic exploitation of the rules (Keohane and Nye 1989). In the western Pacific, however, there is a long history of mutual suspicion. The major players in Asia, Japan and China, are political rivals, and there is a large number of countries involved; both these factors make agreement on anything substantial difficult to achieve (Panagariya 1994: 831–2).

Leaders throughout Asia are often young enough to recall at firsthand Japan's harsh wartime colonial rule, and hence they harbour lingering suspicions over how Japan will wield its economic clout, let alone how it might act if it were to undertake a more activist military role in the region. China still smarts from the unequal treaties imposed on it by colonial powers and sees the temptations of its vast potential market as a source of bargaining leverage it is unwilling to see constrained by commitments to act within standardized international rules. China also represents both military and economic threats to many countries in the region. It has shown little reluctance to use force or the threat of it to resolve disputes, ranging from jurisdiction over the Spratly Islands to reunification with Taiwan. At the same time, China's size, growth rate and instability threaten to swamp many of the smaller economies around the region: its exports exceed the combined total of Malaysia, Thailand and the Philippines, and current Chinese overcapacity has driven down export prices in key sectors such as electronics and textiles, contributing to the region's painful slowdown of 1996–7. In 1996, President Suharto of Indonesia observed: 'We are afraid that China will dominate the world market with an economic might that enables it to produce low-priced products' (*Nikkei Weekly*, 19 August 1996: 21). Scarcely a year later, his fears appear to have materialized, as Michael Taylor of brokerage firm W.I. Carr observed that 'it's not just a coincidence that China's exports are surging [while others are hurting] ... on its own, Southeast Asia would have only a moderate capacity problem. With China, they have a big one' (*Globe and Mail*, 14 July 1997: B4).

Given this background of potential and actual conflict, a case-by-case approach allows leaders to cooperate quietly while still reserving the option of appealing to xenophobic sentiment to mobilize public support. Thus, for example, for a time both Taiwan and the PRC turned a blind eye to growing trade and investment so as to allow both sides to maintain their politically expedient hostile public postures towards one another while quietly reaping economic gains from collaboration (Clough 1993). An informal approach also allows the reluctant to experiment cautiously since if a strategy reversal is later required exit costs are lower than would be the case if reforms were locked in by international commitments. A further consideration is that the ability to offer (or extract) special deals and favouritism is preserved due to the lack of transparency of an informal relaxation of restrictions on international economic exchange, which are less vulnerable to challenges on most-favoured nation (MFN) grounds. Such flexibility may be viewed as necessary to prevent domination by regional hegemons.

The domestic political environments in Asia also reinforce the preference for more informal trading frameworks. While most Asian nations are now democracies, the 'Asian values' debate has made it clear that among many Asian elites there is a preference for a somewhat firmer brand of democracy than that practised in the individualistic West (Zakaria 1994; Kim 1994). The informal approach fits well with this philosophy because it preserves the discretion of those in positions of power. Those with influence tend to prefer a less rule-based approach since it allows them to benefit from their leverage with decision-makers and skill in manipulating a non-transparent process (Haley 1991).

Asia has a long history of informal, market-led integration, particularly through networks of overseas Chinese traders (Brown 1995). These networks have evolved to substitute kinship or ethnic ties for contract law where the legal infrastructure to support trade was weak or absent (Landa 1981) and to facilitate the collective action necessary for development by overcoming free-riding problems in the absence of a state capable of doing so (Grabowski 1997). Such networks not only served as a safety valve for excessively autarkic nationalist economic policies in some non-Chinese states, but also allowed the exceptions to remain dependent on the sufferance of indigenous political leaders. This preserved the leverage of the latter in the face of the economic power of Chinese business elites (Parker 1993), while at the same time preventing a broader local constituency from developing in favour of less-restrictive policies and undermining central control.

The region's largest economy, Japan, has a further reason for preferring informal arrangements: given its current domestic political weakness, it finds it difficult to undertake any controversial initiative.

It is thus easier to make small, incremental deals than sweeping agreements that would threaten the fragile domestic political equilibrium.

Differences in culture across the Pacific have provided a further source of divergence in approaches to integration. Both Canada and the United States are strongly 'universalistic' in culture. Trompenaars (1993) found that the United States was the most universalistic country in his sample of 23; given their similarity, both might thus be expected to evince a preference for contracts and formalized commitments. While Mexico was found to be notably more particularistic, it was basically signing up to a process the parameters of which were already well established. Moreover, the leaders who initiated the process had been educated in the United States.

Cultural traits such as particularism and pragmatism, on the other hand, further reinforce the tendency of Asian business and political leaders to prefer informal approaches. Particularism, that is, favouring case-by-case decisions rather than broad, inflexible principles, is strongly ingrained in most Asian cultures, particularly those influenced by Confucianism. Trompenaars (1993), for example, found that four of the six most particularistic cultures in his sample of 23 were Asian; all of the five Asian countries included were in the more particularistic half. A particularistic outlook, with its tolerance of special deals and exceptions in order to adapt to individual circumstances, is advantageous when sweeping agreements would be difficult due to the heterogeneity of the region in ethnic, linguistic, religious and ideological terms.

From a purely pragmatic standpoint an informal approach also offers advantages. For political leaders whose commitment to the free market is instrumental rather than ideological, the principal objective is to find the best vehicle for the pursuit of their vision for the economy. Internationalization of the economy is thus simply one possible means to that end and not, in itself, something to be either pursued or avoided. An informal approach to integration allows step-by-step relaxation of restrictions, with a binding principle established only when all the ramifications are known in practice – if such a principle is established at all.

Given these factors, it is clear that the Asian preference for informal integration should not be seen as a failure of policy but rather as a policy in itself, a means of making policy via trial and error which is particularly suited to Asian circumstances at present. The outcome of such a policy, however, depends critically on the response of the private sector to the opportunities created.

THE CORPORATE RESPONSE

MNCs have always been an integrating force, arbitraging capital, technology, managerial skills and intellectual property across borders. In earlier times, this was often a source of conflict as nation-states attempted to control the activities of their own MNCs abroad and foreign MNCs at home, to preserve 'sovereignty' and protect domestically orientated companies.

Today, however, companies are better positioned than ever to take advantage of opportunities presented by the weakening of economic borders. This is due to:

1.   the maturing of large companies in several of the major economies in the region;
2.   changes in technology, particularly communications, which have made it easier for even small firms to operate overseas;
3.   the opening up of numerous markets around the world, which offers even non-state-of-the art firms possibilities to take advantage of their technology and management skills.

Control over debt financing has been one of the key forms of leverage East Asian economic bureaucrats have used to coax private industry in the directions they thought best. Today, however, Japanese companies have largely outgrown their dependence on debt finance and have either accumulated large hoards of cash or at least established sufficient access to international credit markets that they need no longer respond to the dictates of their government to ensure their access to capital. Korea's *chaebol*, while less financially stable as a whole, have grown so large that they are almost beyond disciplining. Harming any one of them can have a measurable adverse impact on macroeconomic performance, as became clear when the Korean government had to relent in its punishment of *chaebol* leaders for political interference due to the negative impact these punishments had on exports, and hence on the crucial balance of trade.

Greater maturity has also led to changes in the type of economic regulation preferred by large corporations in several East Asian nations, both domestically and in the international sphere. Once the firm is past the stage where government assistance is critical to its survival, *ad hoc* 'guidance' by the home government becomes perceived as interference, leading to a preference for a transparent, rule-based domestic economic regime. Such a shift tends to erode economic borders by eliminating the higher transactions costs incurred by foreign firms when they attempt to deal with the often opaque decision processes of informally regulated economies. Internationally, while firms may prosper for a time under the shelter of protectionist policies, as they grow in size and sophistication they begin to chafe under the accompanying restrictions on their freedom of action, particularly where, as in Korea, the protection was arbitrary and contingent on close adherence to state economic plans (Amsden 1989). Development thus almost inevitably pushes MNCs to become active proponents of domestic and international policies that favour economic integration. Initially, they may see their overseas involvement principally as a means to obtain scarce natural resources or technology, but eventually the need to achieve economies of scale pulls them towards full-scale internationalization.

Technology has made it easier than ever to enter the international market place. Improved telecommunications have lowered the cost of operating at a distance and, through the use of cellular phones, made it possible to overcome deficiencies in local communications infrastructure. Flexible, computer-controlled production has allowed firms to integrate their production systems with those of their customers, facilitating design and marketing feedback. For example, it is now within the means of firms of quite modest size for their salespeople, equipped with laptop computers, to work at a customer's desk on another continent in order to customize product features and transmit the required specifications directly into the computer which controls the order generation and production process. Thus, the imperative to locate production near markets has weakened, allowing small, nimble firms to locate their production where comparative advantage leads to minimum costs.

The transition of the formerly centrally planned economies to capitalism and the adoption of more market-orientated policies by many less-developed countries, often at the insistence of international financial institutions, has provided opportunities for firms with less than leading-edge expertise to move abroad – if they are prepared to live with higher risks. Korean firms, for example, have aggressively pursued a strategy based on exploiting often second-hand technology in markets where it still represents a considerable advance over local practices (Lee 1995). An example in the EA-9 region is Kia's collaboration in the national car project in Indonesia.

To gain access to complementary assets (for example, technologies and marketing skills) of western MNCs, Asian companies will seek to increase their participation in trans-Pacific alliances and consortia. Technology acquisition has, for example, been a prime motivation for foreign investment by the Samsung Group (Kim 1997), and its growing participation in North American research consortia indicates that this is still an important objective.

Increases in the scale and scope of MNC activities are likely to continue to play a leading role in the Pacific integration process. Technological change which permits value chains to be broken apart and globalized, while still reaping economies of scale and allowing product customization through flexible manufacturing, will propel further increases in the sizes of MNCs, and lead to further rationalization and globalization of markets. This will in turn create incentives for strengthening the coordination of production across international boundaries, whether through *keiretsu* or *chaebol*-type structures or less-formal interfirm vertical or horizontal cooperative arrangements. In some cases such developments will be actively promoted by governments which perceive a need to have their own corporate players on the world stage (for example, China's state-controlled 'Red Chip' conglomerates).

IMPLICATIONS: THE FUTURE OF MNC–GOVERNMENT INTERACTION IN THE PACIFIC

The emergence of business networks has tended to diminish the power of states *vis-à-vis* corporate actors. Governments have often been constrained in their efforts to reestablish tighter controls over MNCs and internationalized business networks by:

1. the risk of impairing home firms' competitiveness;
2. the international mobility of assets held by companies, particularly those in information-based sectors;
3. the increasing role of intrafirm trade, which reduces the credibility of governmental threats to restrict trade due to the potential for retaliation created by interdependence; and
4. the political power wielded by multinational corporations and networks to affect domestic policies as well as shape the international economic policy agenda.

Throughout the region, MNCs are exploiting the resultant weakening of economic borders to rationalize their operations and undertake new forms of cooperation. Along with this new freedom, however, have come the challenges of operating in an environment of considerable cultural complexity. The experiences of both Japanese and, more recently, Korean expatriate managers have provided ample demonstration of the fact that, for example, dysfunctional cultural insensitivity is by no means a western monopoly. Overall, however, the trend towards greater openness and less regulation has been a highly favourable one for the development of international business operations. Cyberspace offers them the even more tantalizing prospect of near-total escape from government control – and more importantly, perhaps, taxes. To date, nation-states have reluctantly allowed the balance of control to swing towards MNCs, as the economic progress they have brought has seemed adequate compensation.

This corporate freedom is not without its perils, however. When no clear formal restrictions exist to constrain socially harmful side-effects of business operations, even the most conscientious manager will feel pressure to push the limits of the acceptable. Over time, such incremental decisions can cause a substantial drift away from socially desirable behaviour and lead to public calls for greater corporate accountability: calls which governments will be hard put to ignore. The international dimensions of issues such as environmental preservation also become increasingly apparent as industrialization proceeds, and will create pressure for cross-border coordination. Moreover, the same technologies which promote the globalization of enterprise can also be used by non-governmental organizations to promote their causes. Environmental, labour and human rights issues can now lead to strong pressures through coordinated global private actions such as boycotts and staged media events. This, in turn, will generate pressures for MNCs to manage social issues globally, and perhaps even lead to greater corporate receptivity to calls for common international ground rules.

Thus, while a policy of 'market-led' integration may be most appropriate for the Asian side of the Pacific at present, this very process will result in the longer run in pressures to reassert control over internationalized business networks and a need for governments to coordinate their policies and enforcement measures with others. This will require the harmonization of policies and the emergence of a rule-based international regime and institutional structures to implement, monitor and enforce the rules. The probable result will be long-run pressures for a deepening of the formal institutions of APEC and other intergovernmental economic institutions in the Pacific.

NOTES

1. Unless otherwise stated, figures for imports and exports are derived from *IMF Direction of Trade Statistics*, and GDP and exchange rate data are from *IMF International Financial Statistics*. Where these sources lack figures for Taiwan, they have been supplemented by *Financial Statistics; Taiwan District, The Republic of China* and *Taiwan Statistical Data Book*. Missing data for Hong Kong were taken from *Europa World Yearbook*. US figures on FDI and intraindustry trade are from *Survey of Current Business*. Canadian FDI figures are from *Canada's International Investment Position*, Japanese FDI figures are from Ministry of Finance press releases, and Korean FDI data are from *Republic of Korea Economic Bulletin*. Other FDI data are from *IMF Balance of Payments Yearbook*.
2. All dollar amounts relate to US dollars, unless otherwise stated.
3. World output figures from *IMF World Economic Outlook*, May 1997, 131.
4. Stock figures are no longer reported by the Japanese Ministry of Finance: they recently began reporting data in yen and historical figures were in US dollars.

REFERENCES

Amsden, Alice H. (1989), *Asia's Next Giant: South Korea and Late Industrialization*, New York: Oxford University Press.
Anderson, Andrew D.M. and Kazuo Noguchi (1995), 'An analysis of the intrafirm sales activities of Japanese multinational enterprises in the United States: 1977 to 1989', *Asia Pacific Journal of Management*, **12** (1), 69–89.
Asiaweek (1996), 'The way ahead: how APEC can become the standard bearer of world trade', 6 December, 12–14.
Brown, Rajeswary Ampalavanar (1995), 'Chinese business in an institutional and historical perspective', in Rajeswary Amapalavanar Brown (ed.), *Chinese Business Enterprise in Asia*, New York: Routledge.
Canada–Japan Trade Council Newsletter (*CJTC*) (1992), 'Foreign direct investment in Japan', July–August, 6–10.
Canada's International Investment Position (various issues), Catalogue Number 67–202XPB, Ottawa: Statistics Canada.
Chen, Edward K.Y. and Teresa Y.C. Wong (1995), 'Economic synergy: a study of two-way foreign direct investment flow between Hong Kong and mainland China', in Nomura Research Institute, *The New Wave of Foreign Direct Investment in Asia*, Singapore: Institute of Southeast Asian Studies.
Choate, Pat (1990), *Agents of Influence*, New York: Alfred A. Knopf.
Clough, Ralph N. (1993), 'The PRC, Taiwan and the overseas Chinese', *Journal of Northeast Asian Studies*, XII (3), 34–48.
Cooper, Richard (1994), 'World-wide regional integration: is there an optimal size of the integrated area?', in Ross Garnaut and Peter Drysdale (eds), *Asia Pacific Regionalism: Readings in International Economic Relations*, Prymble, Australia: Harper Educational
Daly, Donald J. (1997), 'Japanese imports of manufactured products: recent developments in perspective', paper presented at the Association of Japanese Business Studies Annual Meeting, Washington, DC, 13 June.
Dobson, Wendy (1993), *Japan in East Asia*, Singapore: Institute of Southeast Asian Studies.

Europa World Yearbook (various years), London: Europa Publications.

Fayé, Andrew A. (1996), 'APEC and the new regionalism: GATT compliance and prescriptions for the WTO', *Law and Policy in International Business*, **28**(1), 175–215.

Financial Statistics, Taiwan District, The Republic of China (various issues), Taipei: The Central Bank of China.

Frankel, Jeffrey A. (1993), 'Is Japan creating a yen bloc in East Asia and the Pacific?', in Ross Garnaut and Peter Drysdale (eds), *Asia Pacific Regionalism: Readings in International Economic Relations*, Prymble, Australia: Harper Educational; reprinted, with deletions, from Jeffrey A. Frankel and Miles Kahler (eds), *Regionalism and Rivalry: Japan and the United States in Pacific Asia*, Chicago: University of Chicago Press, 1993, pp. 53–85.

Fukusaku, Kiichiro (1992), 'Economic regionalization and intra-industry trade: Pacific Asian perspectives', OECD Development Centre Technical Paper no. 53, Paris: OECD.

Fukushima, Kiyohiko and C.H. Kwan (1995), 'Foreign direct investment and regional industrial restructuring in Asia', in Nomura Research Institute, *The New Wave of Foreign Direct Investment in Asia*, Singapore: Institute of Southeast Asian Studies.

Globe and Mail (Toronto), various issues.

Grabowski, Richard (1997), 'Developmental states and entrepreneurial groups: Asian experiences', *Journal of Asian Business*, **13** (1), 25–44.

Haley, John Owen (1991), *Authority Without Power: Law and the Japanese Paradox*, New York: Oxford University Press.

Head, Keith and John Ries (1995), 'Canada's business presence in East Asia: overview and strategic options', in Albert Edward Safarian and Wendy Dobson (eds), *Benchmarking the Canadian Business Presence in East Asia*, Toronto: University of Toronto, Centre for International Business.

International Monetary Fund (IMF), *Balance of Payments Yearbook* (various years), Washington, DC: IMF.

International Monetary Fund (IMF), *Direction of Trade Statistics* (various years), Washington, DC: IMF.

International Monetary Fund (IMF), *International Financial Statistics* (various years), Washington, DC: IMF.

International Monetary Fund (IMF) (1997), *World Economic Outlook*, May, Washington, DC: IMF.

James, William E. (1994), 'Changing patterns of trade in goods and services in the Pacific region: market-driven economic integration', *Business Economics*, xxix (2), 14–20.

Keohane, Robert O. and Joseph S. Nye (1989), *Power and Interdependence*, 2nd edn, New York: HarperCollins.

Kim, Dae Jung (1994), 'Is culture destiny? The myth of Asia's anti-democratic values. A response to Lee Kuan Yew', *Foreign Affairs*, **73** (6), 189–94.

Kim, Youngsoo (1997), 'Technological capabilities and Samsung Electric International Production network in Asia', BRIE Working Paper 106, University of California, Berkeley.

Kojima, Kiyoshi (1995), 'Dynamics of Japanese direct investment in East Asia', *Hitotsubashi Journal of Economics*, **36**, December, 93–124.

Landa, Janet T. (1981), 'A theory of the ethnically homogeneous middleman group: an institutional alternative to contract law', *Journal of Legal Studies*, x, 349–62.

Lawrence, Robert Z. (1993), 'Japan's low level of inward investment: the role of inhibitions on acquisitions', in Kenneth A. Froot (ed.), *Foreign Direct Investment*, Chicago: University of Chicago Press.

Lee, Honggue (1995), 'Globalization, foreign direct investment, and competitive strategies of Korean electronics companies', in Nomura Research Institute, *The New Wave of Foreign Direct Investment in Asia*, Singapore: Institute of Southeast Asian Studies.

Lodge, George C. and Ezra F. Vogel (1987), *Ideology and National Competitiveness: An Analysis of Nine Countries*, Boston, Mass. Harvard Business School Press.

Menon, Jayant (1997), 'Japan's intraindustry trade dynamics', *Journal of the Japanese and International Economies*, **11**, 123–42.

Nikkei Weekly, various issues.

Ohta, Hideaki, Akihiro Tokuno and Ritsuko Takeuchi (1995), 'Evolving foreign investment strategies of Japanese firms in Asia', in Nomura Research Institute, *The New Wave of Foreign Direct Investment in Asia*, Singapore: Institute of Southeast Asian Studies.

Panagariya, Arvind (1994), 'East Asia and the new regionalism in world trade', *World Economy*, **17** (6), 817–39.

Parker, Stephen (1993), 'Trade and Investment in Southeast Asian Development', *Journal of Northeast Asian Studies*, XII (3), 49–65.

Republic of Korea Economic Bulletin (various issues), Seoul: Ministry of Finance and Economy, Korea Development Institute.

Survey of Current Business (various issues), Washington, DC: US Department of Commerce.

Taiwan Statistical Data Book (various issues), Taipei: Council for Economic Planning and Development, Republic of China.

Trompenaars, Fons (1993), *Riding the Waves of Culture*, London: The Economist Books.

Ursacki, Terry and Ilan Vertinsky (1996), 'Canada–Japan trade in an Asia-Pacific context', *Pacific Affairs*, **69** (2), 157–84.

Wade, Robert (1990), *Governing the Market: Economic Theory and the Role of Government in East Asian Industrialization*, Princeton, NJ: Princeton University Press.

Watanabe, Toshio (1997), 'The new shape of East Asian economic development: from dependency to self-reliance', *Japan Review of International Affairs*, **11** (1), 40–51.

Weinstein, David E. and Yishay Yafeh (1995), 'Japan's corporate groups: collusive or competitive? An empirical investigation of *keiretsu* behavior', *Journal of Industrial Economics*, XLIII (4), 359–76.

Wells, Louis T. (1993), 'Mobile exporters: new foreign investors in East Asia', in Kenneth A. Froot (ed.), *Foreign Direct Investment*, Chicago: University of Chicago Press.

World Development Report (various issues), Washington, DC: World Bank/ Oxford University Press.

Zakaria, Fareed (1994), 'Culture is destiny: a conversation with Lee Kuan Yew', *Foreign Affairs*, **73** (2), 109–26.

Zeile, William E. (1997), 'US intrafirm trade in goods', *Survey of Current Business*, February, 23–38.

5. Multinational enterprises in APEC

Alan M. Rugman and Cecilia Brain

The key themes of this chapter are developed from the data on APEC multinational enterprises (MNEs) reported in Tables 5.1–5.6. These reveal that 90 per cent of the 320 MNEs in APEC from the list of the world's 500 largest MNEs are from two of the eighteen APEC economies (that is, the United States and Japan) and that eight of the APEC economies do not have any of these 500 very large MNEs. This role of the large market 'triad' in the strategies of MNEs and foreign direct investment (FDI) decisions is vital to any understanding of the role of MNEs in Asia in general and APEC in particular.

Within APEC there are four types of MNEs that need to be analysed: (a) North American 'networks'; (b) Japanese *keiretsus*; (c) Korean *chaebols*; and (d) Chinese 'clans'. The strategies of APEC-based MNEs vary by the home base of these four types of business systems. Within APEC, Asian business networks depend on social structures that differ from North American networks. For example, in North America, key sectors have MNEs as 'flagships', for example, auto, chemicals, electronics. In the other large APEC-based MNE systems there are different types of business networks, as is discussed below.

The Asia-Pacific Economic Cooperation (APEC) group has evolved into an international institution with an important trade and investment liberalizing agenda since its founding meeting in Canberra, Australia, in 1989. The membership of APEC is unique in that it involves the three economies of China (the People's Republic of China, Hong Kong and Taiwan), two of the world's economic superpowers (the United States and Japan), as well as all the other important economic countries bordering the Pacific Ocean. The 18 members of APEC are: Australia, Brunei Darussalam, Canada, Chile, the People's Republic of China, Hong Kong, Indonesia, Japan, the Republic of Korea, Malaysia, Mexico, New Zealand, Papua New Guinea, the Republic of the Philippines, Singapore, Chinese Taipei, Thailand and the United States of America.

The APEC has also evolved in political importance. Since 1993 at the Seattle meeting, there have been annual meetings of the heads of government in addition to the on-going meetings of trade and finance ministers. The heads of government also met in 1994 in Bogor (Jakarta), Indonesia; in 1995 in Osaka, Japan; in 1996 in Subic Bay (Manila), the Philippines; and in 1997 in Vancouver, Canada. The 1997 meeting was the fifth APEC summit meeting of heads of government and the ninth APEC ministerial meeting.

With the participation of heads of government, APEC has been transformed from an informal technical meeting group into a quasi-institution in which the 18 member countries are becoming increasingly committed to economic cooperation and free trade. While not a formally constituted institution with a permanent secretariat, like the World Trade Organization (WTO), APEC has a consultative process which helps to overcome its small, roving secretariat and light institutional framework. Economic substance is being added through the recent development of an ongoing trade and investment agenda carried out by committees which report to leaders who are subject to peer group pressure. In particular, there is an effective process of trade liberalization and some prospect of investment liberalization. This process reflects the consultative style of Asian trade and business negotiations, rather than a western rules-based style. APEC, in short, is an evolving western-style international institution with an Asian shape.

There is now a formal statement by APEC dealing with the liberalization of FDI: this is the Bogor declaration of 1994 for free and open trade and investment. While this was a path-breaking statement, there was little of immediate value since the process to achieve FDI liberalization was not spelled out. Indeed, some APEC members, especially Malaysia, have been opposed to the inclusion of investment rules in APEC. Despite this, there are some signs of an emerging investment agenda at APEC (Rugman 1997). The majority of APEC members are recipients of strong inward FDI flows and they do not yet see the need to stabilize the climate for investment, whereas the wealthier countries have MNEs which need secure access for FDI. It is inevitable that these initial tensions over rules for investment will be replaced by a greater sensitivity to the leading role of MNEs in Asian development, and this will lead to pressure for an investment code. In the remainder of this chapter, we shall explore the APEC MNEs and their corporate strategies in order to examine how liberalization of FDI measures can be incorporated into APEC.

DATA ON MNEs IN APEC

The 500 largest MNEs in the world account for over 90 per cent of all the world's FDI and also for about half the world's trade, much of this being intrafirm (Rugman 1981; Rugman and Hodgetts 1995). In Table 5.1 the MNEs listed in the latest available *Fortune* Global 500 are reported for the 18 members of APEC. The United States is the home base for 162 MNEs, closely followed by Japan with 126. Together these two large triad economies account for 90 per cent of all the large MNEs in APEC. The only other country in double figures with large MNEs is South Korea with 13. Canada has six; Australia has five; China has three; Hong Kong has two; and there is one from each of Mexico, Taiwan and Malaysia. The other eight APEC countries do not have any MNEs in the top 500.

Table 5.1 Multinational enterprises in APEC countries, 1996

Home country	No. of MNEs	Average revenue of MNEs (million US$)	% of MNEs/ APEC MNEs	% of MNEs/ all 500 MNEs
United States	162	21 884.1	50.6	32.4
Japan	126	26 329.0	39.4	25.2
South Korea	13	25 126.3	4.1	2.6
Canada	6	12 276.1	1.9	1.2
Australia	5	12 329.5	1.6	1.0
PR China	3	16 797.0	0.9	0.6
Mexico	1	28 429.5	0.3	0.2
Hong Kong	2	17 149.6	0.6	0.4
Taiwan	1	9 816.2	0.3	0.2
Malaysia	1	11 553.6	0.3	0.2
Total	320		100.0	64.0

Source: *Fortune*, 'The *Fortune* Global 500', 4 August 1997.

These data are not at all surprising to scholars of international business. Across the *Fortune* 500, well over 80 per cent of the MNEs have been based in the triad economies of the United States, Japan and the EC (now the EU) for at least the last 20 years, (Rugman 1987). Although the United Nations Conference on Trade and Development World Investment Report (1996) identifies as many as 33 000 MNEs, the largest 500 account for 90 per cent of the FDI, and many of the small MNEs identified by the United Nations are actually associated with one or other of the largest MNEs in business networks, or clusters. Thus the MNEs in APEC reflect the asymmetry of MNEs globally, and it is no surprise that virtually all the APEC MNEs came from North America and Japan–Korea.

Table 5.2 reports the largest 20 APEC MNEs. Of these, eleven are from Japan, eight are from the United States and one is South Korean. Here again, another size asymmetry is apparent, since General Motors is nearly three times as large (in total sales) as is the number 20 MNE, Daewoo.

Table 5.2 The 20 largest APEC MNEs, 1996

Rank in the Global 500	Company name and country	Revenues (US$ millions)
1	General Motors (USA)	168 369.0
2	Ford Motors (USA)	146 991.0
3	Mitsui (Japan)	144 942.8
4	Mitsubishi (Japan)	140 203.7
5	Itochu (Japan)	135 542.1
7	Marubeni (Japan)	124 026.9
8	Exxon (US)	119 434.0
9	Sumitomo (Japan)	119 281.3
10	Toyota Motor (Japan)	108 702.0
11	Wal-Mart (USA)	106 147.0
12	General Electric (USA)	79 179.0
13	Nissho Iwai (Japan)	78 921.2
14	Nippon Tel. & T. (Japan)	78 320.7
15	Int'l Business Machines (IBM) (USA)	75 947.0
16	Hitachi (Japan)	75 669.0
17	AT&T (Japan)	74 525.0
18	Nippon Life Insurance (Japan)	72 575.0
19	Mobil (USA)	72 267.0
22	Matsushita Electric Ind. (Japan)	68 147.5
24	Daewoo (Korea)	65 160.2

Source: As Table 5.1

The 20 largest US MNEs are identified in Table 5.3. These include the large auto assemblers, GM and Ford, the major oil companies such as Exxon and Mobil, and other manufacturers such as IBM and GE. It also includes service-based organizations such as Wal-Mart and large insurance companies.

In addition to the 11 Japanese MNEs identified in Table 5.2, in Table 5.4 the next largest nine Japanese MNEs are listed, completing the largest 20 Japanese-based MNEs. As is well known, these Japanese MNEs are grouped together in *keiretsus* (Gerlach 1992). Each of these 20 very large Japanese MNEs now operates relatively autonomously in highly competitive global industries. For example, while Toyota (6) and

Table 5.3: The 20 largest US MNEs, 1996

Rank in US	MNE name	Revenues (US$ millions)
1	General Motors	168 369
2	Ford Motors	146 991
3	Exxon	119 434
4	Wal-Mart	106 147
5	General Electric	79 179
6	International Business Machines (IBM)	75 947
7	AT&T	74 525
8	Mobil	72 267
9	Chrysler	61 397
10	US Postal Service	56 402
11	Philip Morris	54 553
12	Texaco	44 561
13	State Farm Insurances Cos	42 781
14	Prudential Ins. Co. of America	40 175
15	E.I. Du Pont de Nemours	39 689
16	Chevron	38 691
17	Hewlett-Packard	38 420
18	Sears Roebuck	38 236
19	Procter & Gamble	35 284
20	Amoco	32 726

Source: As Table 5.1

Toshiba (15) are both in the Mitsui *keiretsu*, each of these MNEs operates with independent strategies, rather than as being dependent on the Mitsui trading company. Toyota does its own sales and marketing and owns foreign subsidiaries to ensure market access; it does not rely on Mitsui to find export markets for it. This, we argue, reflects the maturing of Japanese MNEs and the globalization of world business. It allows us to analyse these 20 large Japanese MNEs and independent firms on a par with US MNEs. While there will still be Japanese 'cultural' factors at work, we do not believe that analysis at *keiretsu* level is required when examining the strategies of these large Japanese MNEs.

Table 5.5 lists the 13 largest South Korean MNEs to make the *Fortune* Global 500 list. The large *chaebols* have grown remarkably in the last decade and are also moving from exporting to FDI, where overseas subsidiaries in North America and the EU are now being established to ensure market presence. Again, these 13 Korean MNEs can be examined as independent MNEs, in relationship to their US and Japanese competitors.

Table 5.4 The 20 largest Japanese MNEs, 1996

Rank in Japan	MNE Name	Revenues (US$ millions)
1	Mitsui	144 942.8
2	Mitsubishi	140 203.7
3	Itochu	135 542.1
4	Marubeni	124 026.9
5	Sumitomo	119 281.3
6	Toyota Motor	108 702.0
7	Nissho Iwai	78 921.2
8	Nippon Telegraph & Telephone	79 320.7
9	Hitachi	75 669.0
10	Nippon Life Insurance	72 575.0
11	Matsushita Electric Industrial	68 147.5
12	Nissan Motor	59 118.2
13	Sony	50 277.9
14	Dai-Ichi Mutual Life Insurance	49 144.7
15	Toshiba	48 415.8
16	Honda Motor	46 994.5
17	Tomen	46 506.3
18	Bank of Tokyo-Mitsubishi	46 451.0
19	Tokyo Electric Power	44 735.0
20	Sumitomo Life Insurance	44 063.3

Source: As Table 5.1

Table 5.5 The 13 largest South Korean MNEs, 1996

Rank in Korea	MNE name	Revenues (US$ millions)
1	Daewoo	65 160.2
2	Sunkyong	44 031.0
3	Samsung	34 286.5
4	Ssangyong	30 530.8
5	Hyundai	27 278.5
6	Samsung Electronics	24 710.3
7	Samsung Life Insurance	17 530.0
8	LG International	17 311.1
9	LG Electronics	14 765.5
10	Hyundai Motor	14 491.2
11	Korea Electric Power	14 393.7
12	Pohang Iron & Steel	11 990.0
13	Kyobo Life Insurance	10 163.3

Source: As Table 5.1

Table 5.6 lists the 19 MNEs from all other APEC economies besides the United States, Japan and South Korea. Canada has six MNEs, of which three are chartered banks and one is in distribution (George Weston). The largest, BCE, is a holding company with links to Nortel, whose own sales are too low to put it into the *Fortune* Global 500 listing. Australia has five MNEs, and Hong Kong has the trading house Jardine Matheson and Peregrine Investment Holdings. The Mexican state-owned oil firm, PEMEX is listed, as is one Taiwanese oil firm and a Malaysian oil firm. The other eight APEC members do not have any MNEs in the top 500.

Table 5.6 MNEs from other APEC economies, 1996

Country	Rank	MNE name	Revenues (US millions)
Canada	1	BCE	20 658.0
	2	Royal Bank of Canada	12 065.6
	3	Seagram	11 194.0
	4	Canadian Imperial Bank of Commerce	10 896.7
	5	Bank of Montreal	9 521.2
	6	George Weston	9 320.9
Australia	1	Broken Hill Proprietary	14 923.1
	2	Coles Myer	14 418.1
	3	National Australia Bank	11 516.3
	4	Woolworths	10 854.4
	5	News Corp	9 935.8
China	1	Bank of China	20 416.0
	2	Sinochem	17 953.0
	3	Cofco	12 021.9
Hong Kong	1	Peregrine Investment Holdings	22 694.1
	2	Jardine Matheson	11 605.0
Mexico	1	PEMEX (Petroleos Mexicanos)	28 429.5
Malaysia	1	Petronas	11 553.6
Taiwan	1	Chinese Petroleum	9 816.2

Source: As Table 5.1

STRATEGIES OF MNEs IN APEC

North American Business Networks

The MNEs from the United States and Canada are usually 'flagship' firms at the hub of a much larger business network or cluster. The large MNEs, such as General Motors, Ford, IBM, DuPont and so on, are examples of flagships in these sectors; indeed, all US MNEs in Table 5.3 can be examined as flagship firms. Business networks are becoming increasingly common in industries such as autos, electronics, chemicals, where globalization is advanced. In a business network a set of companies interact and cooperate with each other from the manufacture of basic raw materials to final consumption. Conventional business relationships are characterized by arm's-length competition between firms as they buy and sell. Such relationships, which are the basis of Michael Porter's (1980) five forces model of competitive advantage, are based to a large extent on the development and exercise of market power. They tend to foster a short-term orientation among participants, each participant being concerned primarily with its own profitability.

The Rugman and D'Cruz (1996, 1997) flagship model is based on the development of collaborative relationships among major players in a business system. Its focus is on strategies that are mutually reinforcing. By their very nature, such relationships tend to foster and depend upon a collective long-term orientation among the parties concerned. Hence, they form an important facilitating mechanism for the development of long-term competitiveness.

There are two key features of such a system: first, the presence of a flagship firm which pulls the network together and provides leadership for the strategic management of the network as a whole; and second, the existence of firms that have established key relationships with that flagship. These relational contracts cross organizational boundaries, symbolizing the nature of interfirm collaboration. In contrast, conventional arm's-length relationships stop at organizational boundaries.

The five partners business network consists of a group of firms and non-business institutions which compete globally and are linked together by close interfirm organizational linkages (D'Cruz and Rugman 1992, 1993, 1994). There are five partners in the business network: the flagship firm (which is an MNE), key suppliers, key customers, competitors and the non-business infrastructure. The latter partner includes the service-related sectors, educational and training institutions, the various levels of government, and other organizations such as trade associations, non-governmental organizations and unions.

The strategic management aspects of this flagship model are now developed in detail.

The relationship between the modern theory of the MNE and the flagship model, with its implication for some de-internalization (when successful network relationships are developed) has been discussed by Rugman, *et al.* (1995). They argue that the internalization decision for an MNE takes into account concepts of business policy and competitive strategy and that proprietary firm specific advantages yield potential economic profits when exploited on a worldwide basis. Yet the MNE finds these potential profits dissipated by the internal governance costs of its organizational structure and the difficulty of timing and sustaining its FDI activities. This leads to de-internalization when the benefits of internalization are outweighed by its costs. De-internalization usually occurs within a business network when successful partnerships are found, as in the flagship model. The movement from internalization to business network requires analysis of parent–subsidiary relationships and the governance costs of running an MNE versus managing relationships in a business network.

A fundamental feature of these relationships is their focus on collaborative rather than competitive behaviour. Thus, in transactions based on a network alliance relationship, the parties are motivated to work closely with each other to further the aims of the network which they regard as compatible with their own welfare. This can be contrasted with the competitive behaviour described in the five forces model by Porter (1980). The latter model encourages firms to behave in competition with their suppliers and customers for a share of the profits in transactions with each other. It focuses on the development and exercise of a market power in business systems, with managerial attention devoted to optimizing results on a transaction-by-transaction basis – a short-run orientation. On the other hand, the network mode of collaboration requires that both parties to a relationship apply the calculus of the benefits they hope to obtain and the costs they will incur across an indefinite stream of transactions rather than on one transaction at a time. It encourages the sharing of market intelligence and intellectual property without recourse to formal contracting to protect the self-interest of either party. In sum, these relationships are collaborative and long-term in orientation.

The large auto makers are often cited as examples of firms that have adopted the flagship mode of operations. Thus Ford, for example, has developed close collaborative relationships with its key suppliers, who are often encouraged to establish their own plants close to its assembly plants. These relationships are of a collaborative nature with both sides operating on the assumption that the relationships will continue indefinitely. This facilitates the making of highly specialized capital investments by both parties in order to optimize their joint operations. Similarly, Ford develops close long-term relationships with its dealers, who operate as an integral part of the overall system which is directed by the auto maker. The entire chain – suppliers, auto maker, dealers – is managed as a single system whose strategic direction comes almost exclusively from the auto maker who functions as its flagship. The amount and nature of the coordination necessary for effective functioning of this system can best be appreciated by considering what occurs when a new platform is created. Decisions about positioning and timing, for example, are the exclusive preserve of the auto maker. The introduction of a new platform also involves the adoption of new process technology. On the other hand, there is a myriad of operational issues which are the responsibility of the network partners, who are frequently required to make considerable investments in new equipment and training.

As a second example, let us examine the role of Nortel as the flagship of BCE's Canadian-based telecommunications system (D'Cruz and Rugman 1994). Its strategic role is to provide the vision and direction for the technological choices and associated commercial initiatives for the system. Thus, Bell Canada/Stentor developed a system that was at the leading edge in such technologies as fibre optics and digitalization. It required its suppliers and distributors to devote resources to developing their own capabilities in these areas. Equally important, it provided strategic leadership to a network of government-funded research centres on telecommunications to coordinate the development of technology in these areas. It also directed the country's training institutions in telecommunications to make appropriate changes to their curricula in order to ensure the availability of a workforce skilled in these technologies. What has emerged is an advanced telecommunications system with a highly centralized process for strategic decision-making coupled with decentralized operational capability. The key features of a flagship network – strategic asymmetry and collaborative relationships – are abundantly evident.

Japanese *Keiretsus*

A related type of flagship business network with a strong MNE presence is that created by the Japanese. Known as vertical *keiretsu*, these networks have succeeded in building formidable global competitive positions in such diverse fields as consumer electronics (Sony,

Matsushita), automobiles (Toyota, Nissan) and computers (NEC, Toshiba). The strategies and structures of a vertical *keiretsu* are significantly different from those of the traditional Japanese horizontal *keiretsu*, which is a family of broadly diversified companies with a bank/ trading company at its centre: Mitsui, Mitsubishi, Sumitomo, Fuyo, Sanwa and Dai-Ichi Kangyo. For a discussion of the latter Japanese business networks see Fruin (1992, 1997) and Gerlach (1992).

Michael Gerlach (1992) argues that distinct economic, political and social pressures determine the business system. For instance, while the United States and other western capitalist economies have firm relationships that resemble Japanese alliances, the structure of these alliances in Japan's economy is more stringent. The different environments under which enterprises have evolved provide a way to understand the differences between business networks. The United States created impediments, such as anti-trust laws and the restriction of shareholding of industrial firms stocks by banks, so the kinds of alliances that exist in Japan are illegal in the United States. While this prevented Japanese-type alliances, it led to the creation of other corporate structures to reduce transaction costs (Gerlach 1992). The large, hierarchical command-centred corporation of the United States is a result. Additionally, the preferences of individuals, and of society in general, must have repercussions on the kind of business system that evolves. Country-specific degrees of risk aversion, social penalties from non-cooperative behaviour, altruism, are all determinants of the business system. Furthermore, these preferences are likely to propel the country-specific regulations that shape the business system.

Gerlach (1992) calls the Japanese system 'alliance capitalism' characterized by reciprocal cooperation between members of group alliances, *keiretsus*. There are three major advantages for members:

1. a reduction in transaction costs as relationships are solidified and transactions become more routine. This is partly a result of a reduction of moral hazard and information asymmetries due to long-term relationships that result in less opportunism;
2. risk-sharing among members. With a system of life-long employment, the losses from company failure are high. Members of vertical and horizontal *keiretsus* insure themselves with other group members, creating a trade-off between stability and flexibility that is based on mutual loyalty;
3. information sharing between members reduce costs of research and development (R&D).

As Japan opens up its domestic market, the future existence of Japanese *keiretsus* is uncertain. Helper and Sako's (1995) analysis of Japanese and US firms is based on a survey of auto manufacturers that attempts to determine how supplier–customer relations are evolving in both countries. While these are two countries where supplier–customer relationship have been at extremes, the survey indicates (a) a clear belief on the part of US suppliers that their customers are more willing to cooperate with them than in the past; and (b) that Japanese suppliers no longer feel as certain about their customers' long-term plans for cooperation.

Nonaka and Takeuchi (1995) attribute Japan's *keiretsu* success to its cultural homogeneity. The global environment with its cultural diversity could be more hostile and it might put pressure on *keiretsu* members to behave more competitively. The new opportunities for both suppliers and customers to deal with non-*keiretsu* partners, who might have specific advantages, and the increased competition in the domestic and foreign market poses serious challenges to the traditional *keiretsu*.

The *keiretsu* introduced a set of informal trade barriers through its domestic distribution system; this is being restructured because of international pressure and might imply market share losses for the *keiretsu* (Encarnation 1992). Gerlach (1992) acknowledges the existence of these pressures and argues that while *keiretsus* will not continue in their present form, they have the potential to adapt to the new global environment. He recognizes that the Japanese economy is undergoing structural changes; however, he also provides examples of cases in which foreigners have had to adapt to the *keiretsu* system in both the domestic market (IBM Japan) and the foreign market (Canon US).

The extreme forms of western and Japanese capitalism have benefits and costs. While short-term contractual behaviour that pits one supplier against another can increase competition, reducing prices and possibly promoting innovation, there are negative effects from non-cooperative behaviour. The costs of bargaining might be large and both suppliers and customers might be opportunistic; this would lead to wasteful and costly behaviour. Additionally, suppliers might not be willing to make necessary long-term investments due to uncertainty. 'Alliance capitalism', in theory, could lead to less effort on the part of the supplier because the costs of not delivering are reduced. To have some insurance might lead to lower average supplier profits than not having insurance (Helper and Sako 1995). However, this does not necessarily mean that customers receive the surplus from cooperation. The supplier is provided with insurance and pays a premium for it. Meanwhile, the customer is less flexible to exchange suppliers, can look forward to a long-term collaboration, and has purchased additional risk. An optimal amount of supplier certainty, where some degree of competition is achieved that does not outweight the cost of friction, should be followed by customers.

In the next section we shall examine the strategies of Japan's six largest *keiretsus*. The leading companies in Japan (Table 5.4) are all based in at least one of these intramarket *keiretsus*. Quasi-affiliates and joint ventures between the groups have been a part of the success of the large multinationals that are prevalent in the Japanese economy.

Sumitomo

Sumitomo ranks as the fifth largest company in Japan with revenues of $119 281.3 million. It is the head of the Sumitomo *keiretsu* which is a descendant of the oldest *zaibatsu* (the pre-Second World War predecessor of a *keiretsu*), founded in 1590. After the US occupation, the heads of the companies were dismissed, the Sumitomo family's holdings frozen, and the firms forbidden to use their names. This was also the case with Mitsui and Mitsubishi. However, the new officials continued to maintain ties with the old *zaibatsu* members and eventually reunited under their original name. Sumitomo works as an intermarket *keiretsu*. It owns 63.9 per cent of the shares issued by the group. Most affiliated companies have shares in the bank, and the bank has shares of most of the members. When there is no connection between the bank and the firm, they connect through other firms' holdings.

Mitsui

The Mitsui group (founded in 1615) contains the largest firm in Japan (see Table 5.4) and the third largest in the world. Toyota Motors (the sixth largest MNE in Japan) is a member of the group, and Toshiba (the fifteenth largest MNE in Japan) is also a member. Toyota and Toshiba both have their own vertical *keiretsu* of suppliers.

Mitsubishi

The Mitsubishi group (founded in 1871) is another of the three survivors of the major *zaibatsus*. Its members include Mitsubishi, the fourth largest company in the world with revenues of $140 203.7. Unlike Mitsui and Sumitomo, it also has directors from other groups (Sumitomo and Dai-ichi Kangyo Bank), making it the most open of the three oldest *keiretsus*.

Fuyo
The Fuyo Group is one of the bank groups (non-*zaibatsu*), with 38.1 per cent of all equity inside the group. It is the most open firm to outside directors, including directors from Mitsui, Sumitomo, Sanwa and Dai-Ichi Kangyo Bank. Its members include the trade and commerce company Marubeni, fourth largest in Japan and seventh largest in the world, Nissan Motor and Hitachi. The latter MNE is also a member of the two other major bank groups (Sanwa and Dai-Ichi Kangyo).

Sanwa
Sanwa Group is the company with least inside share ownership, at 28 per cent. It is highly affiliated to the Dai-ichi Kangyo Bank group (DKB), as this group owns 10.2 per cent of DKB and DKB owns 12.8 per cent of Sanwa. Furthermore, there is a high rate of exchange of directors between the two groups as well as a variety of joint projects, including the seventh largest company in Japan, Nissho Iwai, and Hitachi (Fuyo is also involved). It is also the exclusive owner of Nippon Life, the tenth largest company in Japan.

Dai-Ichi Kangyo Bank
Dai-Ichi Kangyo Bank group owns 31.6 per cent of its stock, while it owns 12.8 per cent of Sanwa's stock. Its group exchanges 38.7 per cent of its directors and it also receives directors from Mitsubishi (which owns 5.3 per cent of DKB stock) and Sanwa. DKB bank is the main lender in most areas, supplemented by Asahi Mutual Life. There is a wide range of directorship exchange. The Bank has sent directors to all but two of the companies. Its main companies are all joint projects with Sanwa (Nissho Iwai and Hitachi). Fujitsu, one of the largest high-tech manufacturing companies, is a clear example of a firm that works within the *keiretsu* and follows an independent path towards globalization (Kondo 1995).

In this section we also examine the strategies of two Japanese MNEs, separate from their *keiretsu* linkages.

Fujitsu
Fujitsu, a latecomer in the high-technology business, presently ranks as the largest computer company in Japan and it has become a leading contender in technology innovation around the globe with revenues of $36 billion in 1996. Major investments in high-value technology have made Fujitsu grow faster than IBM or NEC, allowing it to catch up to its largest competitors (Kondo 1995). The Fujitsu group has more than

440 firms worldwide; it produces computers, telecommunication equipment, semiconductors and other electronic devices. Protectionism during the 1980s and limits on foreign investment led the company to adopt a global philosophy. Kondo lists the three restructuring goals set up by the company in 1985:

1. harmony with local communities;
2. partnership with customers;
3. cooperation and co-prosperity.

Fujitsu aims to become a global and not a Japanese firm. The company has global manufacturing networks encompassing firms in Europe, Asia, North America, Australia, New Zealand and Africa. Fujitsu believes that to be able to work in local communities, it must have a cross-cultural mindset; to do this, it integrates local managers into the company. It not only acquires technology by acquiring local companies or by joint ventures, it also acquires access to the market through the local company's knowledge of its domestic market.

. Cooperation and prosperity have come about by interlinkages with its main competitors. Fujitsu has cross-licensing agreements with Intel, IBM, AT&T in the United States and with its Japanese competitors. This and other forms of interlinkages has created networks between international firms. These interlinkages do more than provide for an exchange of technology, they also reduce individual firm's risk during R&D. Additionally, Fujitsu has aimed at friendly acquisitions by purchasing controlling shares in firms that possess key technological know-how, such as International Computers Ltd of Britain, and Amadahl Corporation and Ascom Nexion Inc. of the United States. Each of these firms had innovated in an area that Fujitsu wanted to incorporate.

NEC
NEC is the most global of the high-technology Japanese MNEs, with 20 per cent of production in overseas plants (Kondo 1995). According to the *Fortune* Global 500 (1996), NEC was the forty-seventh largest company in the world with revenues of $43.9 billion. NEC's globalization plans include 'optimum location' of production in world markets. With firms in North America, Brazil, Europe, Asia and Australia, NEC maintains access to technology and to human and natural resources while assuring a market share in developing markets. To facilitate decision-making, the Value Added Network (VAN) was created to provide information on logistics and resource allocation (Kondo 1995). VAN connects NEC's international purchasing offices (IPOs) around

the globe to facilitate decision-making on the purchasing of materials and the location of production. IPOs provide information on quality, price and inventory of parts and materials locally available (ibid.).

NEC is not as active on mergers and acquisitions with foreign companies as is Fujitsu. None the less, NEC is constantly embarking on joint ventures with companies such as: AT&T and Synopsys Inc. of the United States; ATI Technologies Inc. of Canada; and Hitachi and Fujitsu of Japan; for R&D and marketing purposes. When NEC, like Fujitsu, is looking for linkages to other companies, the aim is technology sharing and access to markets. The sense of cooperation in dealing with other companies, as well as the perception of a need to become culturally global, favours Fujitsu over NEC. Fujitsu's strategy resembles the new mentality of the Korean companies which we will now discuss.

Korean *Chaebols*

Unlike the bank-centred Japanese *keiretsu*, during its early formation the South Korean *chaebol* was dependent on a government-run banking system. Thus, the Korean government controlled the flow of funds and foreign exchange, exercising a greater level of power over its industries than did its Japanese counterpart. It is the government policies that are credited with the rapid growth of the Korean economy. Some of these policies included the protection of the home market, incentives for exports, law on arbitration instead of strikes, and subsidies to key industries (Kim 1997).

Chaebols are run by the founding families, something which was eradicated in Japan during the Allied occupation. Member firms are grouped together by the family links of the shareholders. A hierarchical structure in which decision-making is concentrated at the top and middle management is lean and stripped of decision-making authority has been the norm. Authors generally explain this phenomenon by the relatively young age of the enterprises (see Yoo and Lee 1987; Ungson *et al.* 1997).

The era of globalization has brought a new set of demands to the Korean economy. Faced with internal social pressures, as well as external demands for the liberalization of the economy, the Korean government is striving to find ways to increase the international competitiveness of its *chaebols* while liberalizing the protectionist structure that put them in the international arena in the first place. The government has concentrated on the following goals: (a) price stability; (b) market liberalization; and (c) balanced economic growth. Some of the most radical changes include: the selling of commercial banks to private shareholders; reductions in subsidies; increases in interest rates; and attempts at liberalizing trade (Ungson *et al.* 1997). Additionally, the government has been pressuring the largest *chaebols* to select a few core industries and to specialize.

Most *chaebols* are seeking to attract trained professionals from the countries they do business with. This is an understandable trend as the Korean labour market has the very low unemployment rate of 2.4 per cent. Small businesses in particular have problems meeting standards because the *chaebols* attract the most skilled workers. *Chaebols* themselves are now restructuring to adjust to higher labour costs and more competition from R&D-intensive firms in the West and Japan, and the low labour-cost firms of other developing countries in Asia. From 1984 to 1994, average monthly wages more than tripled. Yet there remains concern that the structure of the *chaebols* might be an obstacle to internationalization. We shall now discuss the recent restructuring initiatives of the major *chaebols*.

Samsung

Samsung is the second largest of the 'big four' *chaebols* (Daewoo, LG Group and Hyundai are the others). Samsung is an example of a company which relied heavily on its domestic market, low labour costs and preferential treatment by the government. It is now faced with the challenge of globalizing. To respond to a variety of domestic economic and political circumstances, the *chaebol* has adapted by increasing its FDI. Initially, as the government imposed an export-orientated policy, Samsung's aim was to create foreign centres from which to market its products; thus it opened offices in New York, Tokyo and Frankfurt (Lee 1995). When the company needed stable natural resources, it created a linkage to a country that possessed them. Trade barriers led to FDI in the United States, Great Britain and Portugal in the early 1980s. Increased domestic labour costs led to subsidiaries in developing nations (ibid.).

Faced with the end of a protected home market and higher labour costs, Samsung needs to secure a strong hold internationally. It can no longer compete on cheap labour and government subsidies in a protected home market. International markets and suppliers must also be available if the company is to continue as a world leader. For this, it must secure access to foreign natural, technological and human resources. Additionally, it must secure access to international markets and to suppliers (ibid.). The lack of technological superiority compared to its competitors, particularly the Japanese, has led the company to opt for a higher degree of R&D. Presently they are a leading manufacturer and innovator of semiconductors, holding a large part of the US market (Abbeglen 1994).

Chairman Lee of Samsung reduced working hours in the expectation of increased productivity, and encouraged managers to be more independent, analytical and innovative (Ungson *et al.* 1997). The company has made a variety of efforts to build a global mindset in management. These include the assembly, in 1997, of a Global Strategist Group (a multinational panel of experts from Europe and the United States) to provide consultancy and guidance to 36 different Samsung companies. Furthermore, Samsung is sending its young managers to US universities in order to understand North American corporate strategy, middle management initiatives and the US market. Also, the *chaebol* has created an Institute of International Education in which executives are trained in how to compete internationally, and in languages and foreign cultures. Internationalization also comes with the hiring of non-Koreans, the aim of Samsung being to have all its international headquarters managed by host-country nationals.

Daewoo
Established in 1967, in less than 30 years Daewoo has become the largest company in South Korea. Daewoo has a unique strategy for the future: manufacturing, rather than innovation, will drive it to internationalization. It is more decentralized than the average Korean *chaebol*. Unlike the other *chaebols*, the president is not a family member but a professional manager. Member companies enjoy a high degree of autonomy. Yet it resembles the Japanese *keiretsu* in that the different firms have interlocking investments with each other. Unlike Samsung, Daewoo is concentrating its efforts in developing countries. As Unger *et al.* (1997) point out, the objective of Daewoo is to increase its technological capabilities, enter new markets and have access to low-cost inputs.

LG Group
LG Group, formerly Lucky-Goldstar Group, plans to become international through alliances with foreign companies. Zenith Electronics, GE Appliances, Oracle Corporation and IBM, from the United States, as well as Hitachi and Sharp from Japan, all have ongoing projects with LG. Additionally, they are seeking the advice of McKinsey & Company about applying western management techniques to the company (Ungson *et al.* 1997).

Chinese Clan Systems

Chinese business systems are controlled by a group of people who are connected through kinship, school ties, place of origin or age. Members of the clan share reciprocal obligations for the welfare of the group These are *guanxi*-type networks; *guanxi* is a Chinese word referring to the concept of drawing on personal connections and family networks in order to secure help and favour in business relations (Shenkar 1990, Luo 1997). The networks take a variety of forms, from largely diversified firms to vertical networks, and from capitalist Hong Kong to the communist People's Republic of China (PR China).

PR China

One major difference between the PR China and other Asian-Pacific countries studied in this chapter is the communist legacy. The reforms that led to the opening up of the Chinese economy have attempted to differentiate between the free market and capitalism, embracing the first and being wary of the second. These reforms include a restructuring of management, which could become an interesting experiment in the diversification of ownership. Professional managers are now in charge of autonomous companies that are owned by the Chinese government. While companies still experience losses, success stories have emerged, as is the case of the Sanjiu Group, Shougang (Capital and Steel Company) and the DongFeng Motor Group (Nolan and Xiaoqiang 1997; Nolan 1995, Qiaosheng 1997).

Some of the reforms that contribute to the success of these government companies (see Gao 1996) are:

1. the power to plan production: now plans can utilize market input to decide on the production mix;
2. the purchasing and marketing power of the products: enterprises can purchase directly from suppliers without having to depend on government allocating agencies; they are also more independent with respect to distribution;
3. power to fix prices: enterprises can set prices to reflect costs and quality;
4. the right to utilize funds: the enterprises are allowed to retain a greater degree of funds to reinvest;
5. the allocation of wages and bonuses: the government has provided a scale of compensation, and the enterprise can place its employees on that scale;
6. the right to develop lateral economic associations: a variety of

cooperative relations are being formed, from supplier relations to horizontal relations to joint ventures;
7. the right to control employment: although there is a great degree of job security, companies are now directly responsible for hiring employees.

Wage differentials, as well as a form of mortgage fund that is accessed to make up for lack of profits, have increased the incentives for individuals in companies. While the rewards are not nearly as high as in other free market economies and the wage differences are less drastic, the new incentives have contributed to the efficiency of the new enterprise.

The Chinese business network is still in its early stage. This is a result of the previous inability to associate with other groups unless through a government agency. With the restructuring of the system, successful companies have been forced to have linkages with suppliers and distributors through share control (Gao 1996) or full mergers. These linkages lead to: (a) a decrease in information costs as well as an alignment of the actors in the production process; (b) horizontal relationships with similar domestic and foreign companies to share and develop technology; and (c) relationships with companies the government wants to save by making them subsidiaries of well-managed companies (Nolan and Xiaoqiang 1997). The particular environment under which these enterprises exist might produce a different kind of network from any previously studied.

Sanjiu Group   This group is wholly owned by the Chinese army. Its core firm, Nanfang Pharmaceuticals, established in 1985, is currently the second largest pharmaceutical company in China and one of the 100 largest companies in China. Its production increased by over one hundred and fifty times from 1987 to 1994, while its profits increased from 1.65 million yuan in 1987 to 382.0 million yuan in 1994. In 1992, the structure of the group was as follows: companies manufacturing medicines (13); plants producing health-care products (3); research institutes (2); import–export companies (1); advertising companies (2); international offices (8); trading companies (2). Such groups cover all aspects of manufacturing and distribution. Additionally, it had various unrelated firms, including six real-estate companies; three tourism companies; two printing companies; and three automobile companies. The core company is expanding into the West, and it recently won approval from the US Federal Drugs Administration to sell in the United States. Furthermore, it is modernizing by purchasing both Chinese and foreign equipment. The company now has joint ventures with companies in Thailand, Hong Kong and the United States, and it has a biotechnology research company in Singapore (Nolan 1997).

The DongFeng Group (DFG)   Before the reforms, DFG was dependent on the state for all its inputs. In 1986 a set of recommendations led DFG to become an experimental site for enterprise groups (Qiaosheng 1997). Firms that contributed to the production process were to be directly controlled by DFG, creating a vertically integrated network. Additionally, the group was allowed to build up its own financial company. By 1992 DFG had control of 79 firms through majority ownership of the shares, non-controlling shares of 143 companies and 264 co-ordinated companies (ibid.). The company is acquiring technology through joint ventures, the latest being with Cummins (USA) and Volkswagen (Germany).

Taiwan

Taiwan's networks consist of a variety of firms with common owners and directors. However, companies are not necessarily family owned, as in the Korean form. This type of Chinese networks evolves as a pyramid. A business leader aids a trusted employee in the pursuit of a new and independent business. The employee–employer relationship turns into a junior–senior partner relationship in which the senior partner is usually a silent partner. The junior partner might do the same for another employee and create a further enterprise. This creates overlapping ownership of the firms. Thus the Taiwanese system is a derivative of the broader Chinese-type clan system of business networks (Numazaki 1993).

Acer   This is the fourth largest manufacturer of personal computers in the world (Dobson 1997) and one of Taiwan's most successful MNEs. It has 70 branch offices worldwide and distribution networks in 100 countries (Yue and Dobson 1997). It began operations as a producer for other labels, and is now trying to establish its brand name internationally. Acer continues to produce under other brand names, such as Hitachi and Siemens (Dobson 1997). A very flexible company, it can adapt quickly to a changing environment. It functions as a top coordinator with a variety of groups that have the flexibility to implement the goals of its headquarters. Ownership of Acer was diversified by dividing the company into 21 public companies to be traded in foreign markets. It is hoped that this plan will provide incentives for local employees and customers in foreign subsidiaries (ibid.).

Acer's globalization strategy was to switch towards its own brand name and enter the developed countries' markets. Additionally, Acer bought technology through purchasing Counterpoint Computers in 1987, a US maker of multiuser systems; Altos, a US maker of desktop workstations, was purchased in 1990. In the same year Acer bought Kangaroo Computer, a Dutch producer of personal computers. Joint ventures with high-technology producers in foreign markets were also pursued, leading to partnerships with Smith Corona of the United States, International Computers Limited in the UK, Hitachi of Japan and Messerchmitt in Germany (ibid.). The company is also looking for the cross-licensing of patents with foreign companies such as IBM.

CONCLUSIONS

In this chapter we have provided a review of the published data on the nature and extent of large MNEs in APEC. We have also used published research to analyse the major types of US, Japanese, Korean and Chinese MNEs and network business systems. Of the 320 MNEs in APEC listed in the *Fortune* Global 500 as the world's largest MNEs, the biggest set comes from North America (USA: 162, Canada: 6 and Mexico: 1). These 169 MNEs operate as flagships in clusters of business networks. Their production networks cross borders and have been facilitated by the rules-based market access provisions of the NAFTA regime. In its turn, NAFTA was built upon previous investment liberalizing agreements, such as the Canada–USA auto pact of the 1960s, which led to the integration of the automobile sector and accounts for about one-third of Canada's bilateral trade with the United States. The Asia-Pacific members of APEC, including Japan with 126 MNEs and South Korea with 13 MNEs, would benefit from a similar set of investment liberalization methods in APEC. China and the fast-growing economies of South-East Asia, including the ASEAN members, have been mainly recipients of inward FDI, but in the future they may start to develop large home-based MNEs conducting outward FDI.

The role of FDI and the MNE as an engine for APEC economic integration is likely to continue to increase, so the more attention APEC can pay to establishing well-known procedures for open FDI the better. In the future, APEC should consider much more seriously the NAFTA experience with respect to investment. NAFTA demonstrates the need for an integrated approach to international investment issues, in the form of strong rules for FDI. The investment provisions of NAFTA could provide a guide for similar provisions in APEC (Rugman 1997).

This would extend the benefits of the liberalization of investment beyond North America to all member economies of APEC. While the APEC agenda has not yet endorsed a rules-based approach to investment liberalization, it is inevitable that APEC members will need to consider a deeper form of FDI integration and a rules-based system well before 2020.

The implications of this chapter are somewhat limited by the broad coverage of all the large MNEs in APEC. The strategies and performance of US, Japanese and Korean MNEs are well known. The challenge for future research is to investigate fully the strategies and performance of the rapidly growing MNEs from South-East Asia, especially in ASEAN countries and in China. Here we can still only speculate about the manner in which Chinese *guanxi* family networks may (or may not) lead to the development of long-run strategic firm-specific advantages (FSAs) and/or core competencies. It may be that excessive reliance on *guanxi* could even delay the development of MNEs with technological and/or managerial FSAs. In contrast, Japanese MNEs did not have *guanxi* networks but have been very successful in extending their FSAs in technology throughout Asia and globally. The *guanxi* networks may help growth within parts of Asia, but will it be a non-location-bound FSA, such as the Japanese and Koreans have developed to compete with US MNEs? This type of research is for future papers.

REFERENCES

Abegglen, James C. (1994), *Sea Change: Pacific Asia as the New World Industrial Center*, New York: Free Press.
Boisot, Max and John Child (1996), 'From fiefs to clans and network capitalism: explaining China's emerging order', *Administrative Science Quarterly*, **41**, 628–660.
D'Cruz, Joseph R. and Alan M. Rugman (1992), *New Compacts for Canadian Competitiveness*, Toronto: Kodak Canada.
—— and —— (1993), 'Developing international competitiveness: the five partners model', *Business Quarterly* **58**(2), 101–7.
—— and —— (1994), 'Business network theory and the Canadian telecommunications industry', *International Business Review*, **3**(3), 275–88.
Dobson, Wendy (1997), 'East Asian integration: synergies between firm strategies and government policies', in Wendy Dobson and Chia Siow Yue (eds), *Multinationals and East Asia Integration*, Ottawa: International Development Research Centre, pp. 3–27.
Encarnation, Dennis J. (1992), *Rivals Beyond Trade: America versus Japan in Global Competition*, Ithaca, NY: Cornell University Press.
'The *Fortune* Global 500' (1997), *Fortune*, 4 August.

Fruin, W. Mark (1992), *The Japanese Enterprise System: Competitive Strategies and Cooperative Structures*, Oxford: Oxford University Press.
—— (1997), *Knowledge Works: Managing Intellectual Capital at Toshiba*, Oxford: Oxford University Press.
Gao, Shangquan (1996), *China's Economic Reform*, London: Macmillan.
Gerlach, Michael L. (1992), *Alliance Capitalism: The Social Organization of Japanese Business*, Berkeley, Cal.: University of California Press.
Helper, Susan R. and Mari Sako (1995), 'Supplier relations in Japan and the United States: are they converging?', *Sloan Management Review*, **36**(3), 77–84.
Kim, Eun Mee (1997), *Big Business Strong State: Collusion and Conflict in South Korean Development, 1960–1990*, Albany, NY: State University of New York Press.
Kondo, Katsuto (1995), 'The globalization of Fujitsu', in Denis Fred Simon (ed.), *Corporate Strategies in the Pacific Rim*, New York: Routledge, pp. 249–66.
Lee, Chol (1995), 'Globalization of a Korean firm', in Denis Fred Simon (ed.), *Corporate Strategies in the Pacific Rim*, New York: Routledge, pp. 249–66.
Luo, Yadong (1997), 'Guanxi and performance of foreign-invested enterprises in China: an empirical inquiry', *Management International Review*, **37**(1), 51–70.
Nolan, Peter (1995), 'Large firms and industrial reform in former planned economies: the case of China', DAE Working Paper no. 9516; Cambridge University.
—— and Wang Xiaoqiang (1997), 'The Chinese army's firm in business: the Sanjiu Group', DAE Working Paper no. 9702, Cambridge University.
Nonaka, Ikujiro and Hirotaka Takeuchi (1995), *The Knowledge-creating Company: How Japanese Companies Create the Dynamics of Innovation*, New York: Oxford University Press.
Numazaki, Ichiro (1993), 'The Tainanbang: the rise and growth of a banana-bunch-shaped business group in Taiwan', *Developing Economies*, **31**(4), 486–510.
Porter, Michael E. (1980), *Competitive Strategy: Techniques for Analyzing Industries and Competitors*, New York: The Free Press.
Qiaosheng, Chen (1997) 'On the adjustment of China's industrial structure: the lateral unification of automobile industries', in Fumio Itoh (ed.), *China in the Twenty-first Century: Politics, Economy, and Society*, Tokyo: United Nations Univesity Press.
Republic of Korea, National Statistical Office, *Korea Statistical Yearbook, 1995*.
Rhee, Jong-Chang (1994), *The State and Industry in South Korea: The Limits of the Authoritarian State*, London: Routledge.
Rugman, Alan M. (1981), *Inside the Multinationals: The Economics of Internal Markets*, New York: Columbia University Press.
—— (1997), 'Towards an investment agenda for APEC', *Transnational Corporations*, **6**(2), 115–27.
—— and Joseph D'Cruz (1996), 'Partners across borders: the five partners business network model', *International Management* **1**(1), 15–26.
—— and —— (1997), 'The theory of the flagship firm', *European Management Journal*, **15**(4), 403–12.
——, —— and Alain Verbeke (1995), 'Internalization and de-internalization: will business networks replace multinationals?', in Gavin Boyd (ed.), *Com-*

petitive and Cooperative Macromanagement: The Challenge of Structural Interdependences, Aldershot, UK: Edward Elgar, pp. 107–28.

—— and Richard Hodgetts (1995), *International Business: A Strategic Management Approach*, San Francisco: McGraw-Hill.

Shenkar, Oded (1990), 'International joint ventures' problems in China: risks and remedies', *Long Range Planning*, **23**(3), 82–90.

Simon, Denis Fred (1995), *Corporate Strategies in the Pacific Rim: Global versus Regional Trade*, New York: Routledge.

Ungson, Gerardo R., Richard M. Steers and Seung-Ho Park (1997), *Korean Enterprise: The Quest of Globalization*, Boston, Mass.: Harvard Business School Press.

Yiu, Chia Siow and Wendy Dobson (1997), 'Harnessing diversity', in Wendy Dobson and Chia Sow Yui (eds), *Multinationals and East Asia Integration*, Ottawa: International Development Research Centre, pp. 249–65.

Yoo, Sangji and Sang M. Lee (1987), 'Management style and practice of Korean chaebols', *California Management Review*, **29** (4), 95–110.

6. Corporate–government relations in the Pacific

Gavin Boyd

The East Asian and North American market economy states, together with the transitional Chinese economy, are being linked structurally and through policy interdependencies by a vast pattern of dynamic corporate activities and a more restricted and a less productive pattern of inter-actions between governments. The corporate pattern is dominated by Japanese and American firms in a rivalry which has effects throughout the pattern. In the configuration of policy-level interactions the US and Japanese administrations are especially prominent and can exert considerable influence because ties between the other East Asian and North American states are weak, and their governments have to cope with weak bargaining positions in their relations with the USA and Japan.

In the deepening regional integration which results from corporate activities, firms which are expanding their transnational production and trading operations are relating to an often increasing number of govern-ments. The interactions are tending to become more substantial as corporate managements seek increasing policy-level cooperation on issues of taxation, regulation, infrastructure, trade, technology and competition, and as national administrations seek corporate cooperation to enhance growth and employment. The location and production decisions of firms are influenced by national policy mixes, and oppor-tunities to exploit investment bidding by governments increase as foreign production operations become more extensive. Symmetries and asymmetries in complex structural interdependence are assuming larger regional dimensions as the interactions between firms and governments multiply. The effects are evident in technological levels, financial flows, market efficiencies and failures, the overall spread of gains, bargaining strengths, and degrees of control over the region's sectoral and cross-sectoral linkages.

The processes of reciprocal causality in corporate–government relations across the Pacific are similar to those in other parts of the world, especially in the European Union. They necessitate analysis which combines the study of firms with research into intercorporate systems and into the interdependencies between firms, intercorporate systems and governments. In the Pacific, it must be stressed, analytical perspectives must take into account forms of corporate–government cooperation in East Asia that have made possible high levels of outward-orientated growth. Attention must also be given to problems in corporate–government relations in the USA that have had adverse effects on structural competitiveness. Imbalances in the spread of gains from deepening regional integration are attributable in varying degrees to the contrasts at and between the corporate and government levels across the region.

Competitive pressures in deepening integration can force convergence in corporate strategies and national policies. Firms can make similar optimizing choices about structures and operations, and governments can make similar endeavours to optimize their structural policies. The dynamics of corporate and policy-level decision-making in political economies on each side of the Pacific, however, are much less conducive to convergence than the corresponding processes in Europe, where social distances are shorter and cultural affinities are more significant. The dimensions of success in raising Japan's structural competitiveness tend to reinforce the established processes of corporate–government cooperation in that country, while adaptation to the demonstration effect is virtually impossible in the USA because of the influence of strong individualism in its intercorporate system and its form of government.

The demonstration effects of Japan's achievements have encouraged administrative efforts to promote similar growth in the industrializing East Asian states. The endeavours in South Korea and Taiwan have had very impressive results, attributable to corporate dynamism and sound structural policies, but in most of the South-East Asian states the necessary technocratic capabilities have been lacking. These deficiencies have been related to larger problems of political development which were dramatized in 1997 by crises in the financial systems of Thailand, Indonesia, Malaysia and the Philippines. These crises revealed flaws in financial administration, deficiencies in fiscal, monetary, trade and structural policies, and insufficiently productive interactions between corporate groups and governments.

CORPORATE–GOVERNMENT INTERDEPENDENCIES

As national economies become more complex, with multiplying inter-related manufacturing and service specializations linked across borders through trade and transnational production, interdependencies between firms and governments assume larger dimensions. Governments, seeking to raise levels of structural competitiveness in the rivalries associated with deepening integration, seek to provide more attractive environ-ments for corporate operations. Public management extends beyond the maintenance of law and order and the development of infrastruc-tures into financial, trade, technology, competition and other measures designed to enhance the efficiencies of national and favoured foreign firms. Consultations with enterprises and industry groups seek to promote functional alignments between their strategies and evolving structural policies.[1] There may be elements of tacit policy collusion on competition issues, which are of benefit to international oligopolistic interests that appreciate discretionary cooperation. Firms coping with competitive pressures in world markets seek to optimize advantages derived from home and host government policy mixes, especially by encouraging and exploiting the investment bidding of those adminis-trations.[2]

Interactions between the corporate and government levels, motivated by varying compatibilities of interest, evolve in contexts with differing processes of systemic development or decline. Market-seeking logic drives corporate international expansion in which relations with numerous governments have to be managed. Ranges of choice relating to investment, production and marketing issues widen; bargaining strength is increased; and the trade, financial, technological, transaction cost and information cost advantages secured through dealings with host administrations tend to become more substantial and more relevant to planning than those obtained through links with the home govern-ment.[3] Meanwhile, involvement in international corporate alliances becomes more rewarding and more absorbing, especially because of technology sharing and market sharing benefits.[4] Governments, however, remain national, with concerns about structural competitive-ness that focus on enhancing the efficiencies of industrial capacity at home. There may be nominal recognition that general benefits will result from the free movement of capital between countries in response to market opportunities, but the common practical consideration is that national growth and employment must have priority.[5]

Policy-level concentration on growth and employment issues tends to increase as the vulnerabilities and costs of deepening integration become more evident and demonstrate the uncertainties posed by shifts in the strategies of transnational enterprises.[6] Structural policies that can secure the cooperation of national firms and foreign corporations assume greater significance for governments; but, it must be stressed, they have to reckon with the increasing interests of international firms in optimizing the advantages gained from bargaining with numerous host governments.

In a highly integrated national political economy, however, the benefits of active home country ties can dominate the strategies of its international firms, while enabling them to interact advantageously with foreign governments and enterprises. Comprehensive partnerships between the administrative and corporate levels, based on community values which are strengthened in this process, can make it possible for the integrated political economy to expand internationally *as a system*, instead of being fragmented by the independent strategies of its firms as they extend their foreign operations.[7]

Japanese corporations have derived very substantial advantages from relational links with their home administration and from the solidarity of their national intercorporate system. Through consultative interactions with their Ministry of International Trade and Industry (MITI) and other economic agencies they have contributed significantly to the development and implementation of trade, structural, technological and other policies that have aided their international expansion.[8] The interactions have been productive, in terms of community building, policy learning and managerial learning, because of shared responsiveness and the strength of cooperative orientations based on the traditional culture. For Japanese firms, large favourable bargaining asymmetries have thus facilitated advantageous dealings with enterprises and governments in the industrializing East Asian states which have hosted Japanese direct investment and received Japanese exports.[9] Smaller asymmetries have also been useful in relations with American corporations and the US administration.

For US firms, however, the advantages of their home country intercorporate affiliations and of their domestic political action capabilities tend to become less significant as their interactions with foreign governments become more numerous, especially those relating to direct investment issues. Relations with the US administration remain distant and rather distrustful, while corporate contributions to policy-making have to work through narrowly focused interest groups, a fragmented pattern of business associations and strongly pluralistic legislative as well as executive processes.[10] The incentives to devote resources to productive interactions with host governments tend to become stronger as foreign direct investment activities increase; they may also become stronger because of strains in the US economy associated with its problems of governance.

The contrasts are significant regarding the dynamics of planning. Japanese enterprises are able to make bolder foreign direct investment decisions and with long-term perspectives because of the solidarity of their integrated political economy. US firms, obliged to operate with much greater self-reliance, have to rely on careful calculations about the expected returns from foreign ventures over shorter time periods.[11] In the Pacific, moreover, estimates of cooperation from enterprises and governments have to reckon with a gradual strengthening of the Japanese presence in the industrializing East Asian states, due to the systemic dynamism of that presence.

Japan's achievements in implementing a systemic approach to international competitiveness have had strong demonstration effects in industrializing East Asian states, resulting partly from the large outflows of Japanese direct investment. Problems of political development, however, especially in South-East Asian countries, have made adaptive replication difficult. At leadership levels, commitments and competence have been lacking, elements of personal rule have been expressed in patrimonial practices drawing support from secondary elites, technocratic capabilities have been weak, the treatment of many national firms has been predatory and restrictive, and official favours extended to firms with high-level connections have limited opportunities for other enterprises. All these deficiencies have been very serious in Indonesia's authoritarian regime and in the military regimes which have ruled Thailand.[12] Higher levels of institutional development and performance, however, have been attained in Malaysia.

In North-East Asia, South Korea has been a very impressive example of administrative corporate partnership for rapid outward-orientated industrialization at rising technological levels, but this began under authoritarian regimes and with bias in favour of large conglomerates. Subsequent problems of political development under a system of representative government have limited the productive potential of the partnership, which in principle is now more inclusive. The trade, technological, financial and other benefits for South Korean firms have been significant but modest compared with those enjoyed by their Japanese rivals. Hence there have been imperatives to develop highly innovative strategies and to maximize the utility of links with the administration. The innovative strategies that have been adopted have included ambitious foreign production ventures, notably in the USA and Europe.[13]

REGIONAL PATTERN

The various types of corporate–government interactions are evolving in a regional pattern of market-driven integration which may be given more scope through trade and investment liberalization endeavours within the Asia Pacific Economic Cooperation (APEC) forum.[14] The developing pattern of integration has contrasts in market penetration, degrees of outward orientation, and dimensions of cross-border market efficiencies and failures, which are related to asymmetries in the spread of gains and in degrees of control over structural interdependencies.

Market Penetration

The contrasts in market penetration, attributable to the interacting effects of corporate activities and national policies, are most evident in the USA–Japan relationship, which has drawn much attention in the research literature. The principal achievement of the corporate–government partnership in Japan has been the substantial penetration of higher-technology sectors into the large US markets, notably in electronics and automobiles, through price and quality competition and with leads in applied innovation. The systemic logic of this, which virtually amounts to a strategic trade policy and opens the way for a strategic foreign direct investment policy, has entailed a high degree of internalization in the home economy, limiting entries through trade and foreign direct investment.

Questions of efficiency and equity in the asymmetric structural interdependence have become extremely complex and have been viewed by some observers with the idea that degrees of market penetration through trade and transnational production should be balanced bilaterally. Concerns with the overall dimensions of the relationship, however, have been at the appropriate policy level rather than corporate considerations in Japan. Yet at both levels there has been the understanding that the nation has to finance imports of food, energy and manufacturing inputs through surpluses in the service of foreign markets for industrial products, in the course of multicountry commerce. It is also understood that the USA, while it is the largest foreign market, is maintaining large fiscal deficits which sustain strong internal demand, and that its balance of payments deficits are attributable in large measure to the service of foreign markets through international production at volumes roughly five times greater than its exports.[15]

The Japanese corporate–government partnership, conditioned by the need to deal with an unfriendly immediate environment, is basically a closed system, relating distantly to the pluralistic authority structure and to the loosely aggregated processes of corporate representation in the USA. Attempts at rapport on basic issues of structural interdependence are not encouraged; US trade diplomacy has resorted to abrasive methods; and there has been no scope for dialogue about US fiscal policy or the balance of payments effects of high-volume US foreign production. In this setting, active concerns about American market-opening leverage tend to motivate Japanese concentration on service of the US market through higher volume manufacturing in the USA. Shifts in relative bargaining strengths can be anticipated because the financing of US fiscal deficits depends, to a significant degree, on the confidence of Japanese investors.[16]

Corporate–government relations in the USA show an inability to achieve coordinated responses to the asymmetries in structural interdependence with Japan. The absence of strong peak business associations, the institutional weaknesses of the major political parties, and the difficulties of consensus-building in the system of divided government tend to perpetuate problems of advanced political development. These, in conjunction with the costs of aiding sectors and communities adversely affected by imbalances in deepening integration, add to the incentives that motivate outward direct investment by US manufacturing firms.[17] The main destination for this investment continues to be the European Union, which appears to have received more attention since the 1997 financial crises in South-East Asia that have caused lower growth in the larger ASEAN members. Virtually complete market integration in and enlargement of the European Union have encouraged regional rationalization of the operations of US firms in Europe, in order to service that market with less reliance on exports from the USA. European penetration of the US market, through exports and direct investment, is on a smaller scale and strategically is less significant than the Japanese penetration, which is more focused in sectors where US export competitiveness has been lost.[18]

Market penetration in industrializing East Asian states reflects differences in the functional significance of their forms of corporate–government interaction. The South Korean partnering has ensured considerable control over entries into the national economy by Japanese and US firms. The principal objective has been to protect the domestic market positions of major national firms striving to make technological gains and acquire strengths in foreign markets through collaboration with and competition against Japanese and US rivals, notably in the electronics and automobile sectors.[19] In the larger ASEAN countries the generally less functional processes of corporate subordination to government domination, which have been related to attempts at import substituting industrialization, have allowed market penetration following openness to foreign direct investment which has been accepted without effective structural policies.

Outward Orientation

Outward orientation in manufacturing has developed in concert with a striving for structural competitiveness in Japan, but less so in the USA. In Japan, administrative guidance and corporate learning have been responsible for sectorally concentrated export-directed production, principally in electrical and non-electrical machinery, transportation equipment, and instruments and related products. Between 20 per cent and 30 per cent of production in these sectors is externally orientated, while import penetration in these industries and in manufacturing as a whole is low compared with other advanced countries.[20] Imported input shares, moreover, are low and have been declining, with a movement of assembly-type manufacturing into industrializing East Asian states. The outward-orientated manufacturing is related primarily to production in the USA, where direct investment ($118, 116 million in 1996, on a historical cost basis) included $29,454 million in manufacturing and $38,021 million in trading. The latter figure reflected the distribution of operations on a scale far greater than those of European firms in the USA.[21]

Export-oriented manufacturing by US firms accounts for about 13 per cent of national manufacturing output, but the proportions are larger for industrial machinery and equipment (25.8 per cent), electronic equipment (24.2 per cent), chemicals (15.8 per cent), transportation equipment (17.8 per cent) and instruments and related products (21.3 per cent). The outward-directed production is related more to manufacturing by US firms in Europe than to their operations in East Asia, where US exports are lower than those of Japan.[22] A further contrast with the Japanese pattern of outward-orientated manufacturing is that there are substantial degrees of import penetration in the sectors with significant proportions of production for export. These include industrial machinery and equipment (27.8 per cent), electronic equipment (32.5 per cent), transportation equipment (24.3 per cent) and several low-technology industries.[23] Japanese exports account for high proportions of the import penetration figures.

The general effects of the technological orientation in Japan's administrative–corporate partnership have been evident in the proportion of manufactured products in the country's exports to the USA (about 82 per cent in 1993, mostly in mature and high-technology sectors). Of Japan's imports from the USA in 1993 about 59 per cent were manufactured products and the remainder were foods and raw materials; all these imports from the USA constituted about 23 per cent of the nation's total imports, while Japan's exports to the USA were about 29 per cent of its foreign sales. In world high-technology trade the comparisons have further significance: in 1987–90 Japan had a 23 per cent share of trade in high-technology electronics and a trade balance of 19.4 per cent of total world trade, while the USA had a 17.8 per cent world market share and a balance representing –4.7 per cent of world trade. For the same period, in high-technology machinery Japan's share of world trade 16.8 per cent (about 1 per cent higher than the USA's) and Japan's trade balance was 14.3 per cent of world trade in those sectors, compared with a US balance of –4.1 per cent. The Japanese share of world trade in high-technology chemicals, however, was only 5.4 per cent, while the USA's was 13 per cent, and the balance, as a proportion of world trade in that sector, was only 0.3 per cent, while the USA's was 5.5 per cent. The largest asymmetries were in high-technology aerospace, in which the US world market share was 43.3 per cent, while Japan's was 0.8 per cent.[24]

In the larger ASEAN countries, outward-orientated manufacturing, except at low-technology levels, has developed mainly through Japanese and American direct investment. Japanese direct investment has been higher than that by US firms and in 1993 amounted to 20.6 per cent of the total foreign stock in Indonesia, 22.3 per cent in Malaysia, and 23.8 per cent in Thailand; the corresponding figures for the USA were 5.5 per cent, 11.2 per cent and 14 per cent. In the Philippines, however, the Japanese share was only 15.5 per cent, while the USA's was 50.2 per cent. In South Korea and Taiwan, direct investment by Japanese firms during 1993 was also higher than that of the USA as a share of the total: in South Korea it amounted to 41 per cent, while the USA's was 29.3 per cent. In both cases the Japanese and US direct investment was mostly outward-orientated, but industrialization in these two states had developed with only modest inward direct investment, and the outward orientation of their medium and higher-technology manufacturing firms was relatively high.[25]

Regional Market Efficiences

Regional market efficiences are assuming cross-border dimensions with the proliferation of trading and transnational production activities in various national policy environments. Allocative efficiencies are facilitated by international competition, principally between Japanese and US firms, depending on information flows and the extent to which problems of market failure are increased or overcome by corporate strategies and national policies. Dynamic efficiencies, as multiplying transactions provide opportunities for innovative productive entre-preneurship, depend increasingly on coordination functions, degrees of intercorporate trust and the extent to which managements can work autonomously, on a stable basis and with long-term perspectives.

Allocative efficiencies are relatively higher in the USA than else-where in the Pacific, mainly because of intense competition between national firms and between these and Japanese enterprises. Prices tend to be uniform across the large integrated domestic market. The involve-ment of Japanese firms is the main external contribution to the internationalization of allocative efficiencies in the US market, and operates in conjunction with European corporate involvement. The combined result is a degree of domestic market penetration somewhat below that in major European states, but the allocative efficiencies in the USA are linked more closely with those in the European Union than with those in East Asia.[26] The exposure of the US market to foreign products through trade and direct investment is about 15 per cent, that is, closer to the British, French and German levels and much higher than Japan's. Import shares in several US industries, including industrial machinery and equipment, electronic and electrical equip-ment, and transportation equipment, are above 20 per cent of internal consumption.[27]

Allocative efficiencies in Japan's much less internationalized market depend heavily on its distribution system, which has evolved under administrative guidance that is opposed to excessive competition and committed to support of the domestic market positions of major firms. Concerns with outward-orientated dynamic efficiencies have been more active in Japanese structural policy, which, it must be stressed, has evolved in response to spontaneous order in the national intercorporate system. The achievements in structural competitiveness that have resulted have tended to sustain policy emphasis on the promotion of dynamic efficiencies, while allocative efficiencies have remained lower.[28] Requests by US administrations for liberalization of the Japanese distri-bution system, which would increase the openness of the economy to American products, have been seen as forms of foreign interference which would threaten dynamic efficiencies that have to be maintained for effective performance in world markets.

Dynamic efficiencies in the USA tend to be limited by relatively low levels of intercorporate trust and cooperation, and by pressures for short-term profits that derive from the system of corporate governance. Coordination problems, to which solutions are necessary in the interests of systemic development, have cumulative negative effects.[29] The costs of these tend to increase as complex specializations multiply in the American economy and as adjustments fail to be made to the vulnerabilities caused by deepening integration. Partial solutions to the problems affecting dynamic efficiencies are sought at the policy level through attempts to manage high-technology trade with Japan, depending on the leverage that can be used for intervention in the allocative functions of its market.[30] Bargaining strength that can be used for this purpose is based on a capacity to alter allocative efficiencies in the USA's own market, but it must be stressed that dependence on Japanese investor confidence, in the context of asymmetric macroeconomic interdependence, is a major restraint.

Market Failure

Problems of market failure in the USA are created first of all by oligopoly power used in tacit collusion to avoid anti-trust enforcement. This oligopoly power, based in the home market, has developed mainly in medium and high-technology sectors, is linked especially with market strengths acquired by US firms in Europe, and is active in global oligopolistic rivalries. Expansion into East Asia, while hindered by the larger and faster-growing Japanese corporate presence, responds to opportunities that are less significant than those in Europe, where the competing Japanese presence is smaller and encounters more policy-level and corporate resistance than in the USA. In the home economy a relaxation of anti-trust enforcement over the past decade, motivated in part by concerns about structural competitiveness, has encouraged increases in concentration through mergers and acquisitions.[31] This trend does not appear to have aided the development of stronger US corporate involvement in the Pacific, but it may well continue because of a balance of political forces favouring continued relaxation. The European Commission is the only external organization with the potential to challenge the trend where it may threaten European enterprises.

Oligopoly power affects allocative efficiencies in the USA, but this is considerably less than would otherwise be the case because of substantial Japanese and European market penetration. The active rivalry of Japanese oligopolistic firms is increasing, with gains in market strengths that overall may become greater than those acquired by US firms through mergers and acquisitions in the sectors in which Japanese enterprises are especially active and in which US loss of competitiveness has been associated with substantial import penetration.³² Dynamic efficiencies in the USA are affected by the oligopoly power of its large firms because of the pervasive problem of coordination failure, and because the entry barriers set by those firms hinder the establishment of potentially innovative new firms which could develop complementary operations.

Externalities that constitute market failure problems in the USA are attributable mainly to restructuring by large national firms which shift operations to foreign locations or to alternative domestic sites without taking account of the adaptive measures necessary for affected industries and communities. The strongly individualistic culture allows restructuring with little regard for the adverse consequences it may have for local labour markets and related enterprises. Major business associations, because of their organizational weaknesses, do not expect of their members significant degrees of informal accountability for the social consequences of restructuring, and usually do not sponsor collaborative schemes for sectoral adjustment.³³ At the policy level, the problems of governance that prevent the development of an effective structural policy are responsible for the inaction that invites only market solutions. The basis for optimism about these, however, is weak, and in general tends to become weaker because of the strengthening corporate trend towards optimizing the use of foreign location advantages on a global basis. This trend underlies observations about the rising costs of globalization for the USA.³⁴

Orderly development of sectoral interdependencies, with dynamic efficiencies, is the most important underproduced public good. This problem is attributable to coordination failures which tend to become more serious as US international firms focus individually on rationalizing their global operations. The result of this coordination deficiency, it must be stressed, is not recognized as a policy challenge, because of the liberal political tradition. The public good of orderly growth in the USA, however, is an increasingly urgent systemic imperative and assumes increasing transnational dimensions as deepening integration continues. Informational market failure problems are related to the coordination deficiency and result from low levels of trust and cooperation.

Market Failure in Japan

Market failure problems in Japan due to the oligopoly power of national firms are moderated by spontaneous restraints on destructive competition and by customary respect for the interests of smaller firms and those experiencing difficulties. A general effect is a sustained diffusion of domestic market strengths, maintained in part by wide-ranging cooperation in the penetration of foreign markets.[35] Externalities associated with shifts of industrial capacity to overseas locations are not significantly disruptive because of collaborative intercorporate adaptations. Technocratic encouragement of these adaptations promotes restructuring at home into capital- and research-intensive outward-orientated manufacturing. This is a major achievement in cooperation between the corporate and government levels, and to a considerable extent it is self-sustaining. The collaboration is part of a larger public good: the coordinated development of sectoral interdependencies at rising technological levels, linked in an orderly pattern with the building of an integrated production system in industrializing East Asian states and with a similar one in the USA. Informational problems are kept relatively small through active communication flows that facilitate concerted entrepreneurship throughout this outward expansion of the intercorporate system.[36]

Mixes of efficiencies and failures in the more nationally confined markets of industrializing East Asian states provide scope for the expansion of the dynamic efficiencies in the Japanese system. Allocative efficiencies in the ASEAN countries, except Singapore, are quite low because of the interacting effects of weaknesses in their distribution systems, communal and other cleavages in their intercorporate systems, and problems of governance, especially where administrations are not only corrupt and incompetent but also predatory, notably in Indonesia and Thailand. The development of national firms in these states has been hindered by protectionist policies which have sheltered their markets from each other as well as from outside enterprises. Entrepreneurial ventures which have been successful despite all these problems have tended to invite administrative predation.[37]

The allocative deficiencies have had negative implications for dynamic efficiency because, while there have been many uncertainties about market trends, policy shifts and administrative practices, possibilities for entrepreneurial collaboration, especially on a long-term basis, have been affected by the divisive consequences of bureaucratic patronage and exploitation. Pressure on the policy levels for improved performance has come from American and Japanese firms, but improvements have tended to favour those enterprises. The Japanese firms are the most active foreign corporations in the larger ASEAN members, except the Philippines; and prospects for higher dynamic efficiencies in those members have depended mainly on opportunities for national enterprises to collaborate with the Japanese companies, mostly as suppliers.

Assessments of the allocative and dynamic efficiencies have been difficult because of the poor quality of statistics on the performance of the larger ASEAN economies, due to the weaknesses of their economic bureaucracies. The domestically based growth that has been achieved in these countries has been due mainly to the vigour of their Chinese business communities, operating in generally difficult circumstances and with few opportunities to contribute to reform at the policy level.[38]

EAST ASIAN FIRMS AND GOVERNMENTS

Shared understanding of functional complementarities and community obligations have strongly influenced the development of corporate–government relations in Japan, South Korea and Taiwan, because of the emphasis on social obligations in their traditional cultures and because the imperatives for collaborative national growth were recognized in their experiences of western imperial aggression and exploitation. In most of South-East Asia, however, the cultures of majority ethnic groups have been less orientated towards community values, and western aggression and exploitation contributed much less to the solidarity-building that could sustain corporate–government partnerships. Problems of political development, moreover, have been very serious: ruling elites have had much weaker macromanagement capabilities, and their policies have been implemented through technocratic structures with low levels of competence.

Japanese Alliance Capitalism

Japanese alliance capitalism, as a form of applied systemic logic, has become a dynamic response to intensifying international performance pressures on firms, intercorporate systems and governments. Partnership between firms and the administration to continue penetration of foreign markets, has evolved through the interest – aggregating and consensus – forming activities of multiple intercorporate linkages and associations under the sponsorship of dedicated technocratic expertise. Intensive task – orientated communication flows in this system facilitate wide-ranging entrepreneurial coordination and continuing interactive learning at the corporate and bureaucratic levels. The cumulative effects of all this collaboration have been substantial because of institutional stability and highly professional technocratic functions on the government side and much organizational stability in the nation's firms, industry groups and in its intercorporate system as a whole.[39]

At the corporate level, systemic logic is expressed organizationally and functionally with emphasis on the synergies of partnership between innovative integrated work teams and with managements providing guidance rather than direction. Quite high X efficiencies are thus generated, the scope for organizational manipulation in the middle management layers is very limited; there is little reliance on bureaucratic discipline; there are constant advances in applied technology; managerial concentration on innovative entrepreneurship is facilitated; and there is virtually no pressure to adopt alternative structures. There are no powerful compulsions to internalize production functions on a larger scale, through absorbing other firms, as the pervasive relational contracting perpetuates a vast pattern of autonomous innovative specializations.[40]

Systemic logic is concentrated on core functions, and accordingly there is extensive subcontracting, the relational basis of which ensures stability in production networks. Numerous cross-holding arrangements among principal manufacturing firms constitute other applications of systemic logic, providing further stability and encouraging information sharing for entrepreneurial coordination. The cross-holding sustains diffuse reciprocal monitoring, in a context in which there is more substantial monitoring by the main bank with which each principal manufacturing firm is usually linked.[41] Continual improvements in performance are encouraged by this monitoring and are aided by the secure long-term financing commonly obtained from the main bank. Much informal accountability is associated with the cross-holdings and the relationships with main banks. The stable shareholding is maintained with the informal cooperation of securities firms, which are linked relationally, like the main banks, with many principal manufacturing enterprises. Stock market expansion thus brings with it limited volatility, which however could be increased by the intrusion of foreign securities firms.[42]

A highly functional dimension of the system of corporate governance is the substantial long-term funding of industry, which is sustained by a broad consensus on the vital harmony between corporate interests and policy-level preferences. The level of bank financing is slightly more than twice as high as in the USA and is the main supplement to internal financing (a ratio of about 27 per cent to 70 per cent). The volume, stability and relatively low cost of bank funding encourages strong investment competition against American and European firms.[43] The technological advantages gained through leads in applied frontier research assist in the continuing penetration of foreign markets, that is in conjunction with entrepreneurial cooperation in Japanese industry groups and in the entire intercorporate system. US enterprises are the main rivals, and their strategies are affected by financial market constraints.

The financial sector is recovering from serious weaknesses in the banking industry which developed at the beginning of the 1990s due to the collapse of large-scale property speculation. The sector's problems have not significantly affected the funding of industry and the related functions of advising and monitoring manufacturing firms. There has been small-scale but increasing foreign financing of these firms, aided by a deregulatory trend which began in 1995.[44] This trend has been a response to American pressures for financial liberalization which would open up opportunities in Japan comparable with those available for Japanese financial institutions in the USA. The practical significance of the deregulatory trend, however, has been determined more by increases in bureaucratic regulatory discretion than by formal administrative measures.[45] The relational bonds between Japanese manufacturing and financial interests and their administration must be expected to continue to protect the system of industrial funding.

The rationale for liberalization in the implementation of financial deregulatory measures has referred to potential efficiencies, through increased access for Japanese firms to foreign funding. The South-East Asian financial crises in 1997, however, which have posed major issues for large numbers of Japanese firms, have made increased regulatory powers all the more necessary for the Ministry of Finance's surveillance, advisory and control functions. The context of corporate dialogue with that ministry regarding the benefits of access to external funding by Japanese firms operating abroad has been changed by South-East Asia's financial problems. These have tended to strengthen the logic of close corporate–government collaboration to maintain a high degree of integration in the national political economy.[46] A factor in the political dynamics of corporate dialogue with the administration is the negative aspect of deregulation, in so far as it is identified as an accommodation to American pressures.

At the policy level, interactions between major corporate groups, peak economic associations and the leading economic ministries (Finance and International Trade and Industry) are the dominant factors in macromanagement. The direct representation of labour interests is weak: most unions are company organizations and the main socialist party is a secondary political force, with only moderate appeal, which has shown a willingness to cooperate with conservative political groups. The most important of these is the Liberal Democratic Party, with which all the major firms and industry groups have strong connections. This party has recovered from a severe drop in public support caused by corruption scandals and intra-elite conflicts during the early 1990s. Like other Japanese political organizations, it has a factionalized leadership and relates to a public that has become somewhat disenchanted with the political system; but for the present its degree of cohesion encourages continued unity in the intercorporate system.[47] If the party were to experience serious internal conflicts and lose status there could be some fragmentation in the intercorporate system. Japanese managements could increasingly focus on their opportunities to build networks and alliances with foreign firms and develop ties with host governments. External networks and alliances are managed instrumentally, rather than relationally, and substantial advantages are derived from solidarity within and among Japanese industry groups. A decline in that solidarity could force concentration on strategies which would seek compensating advantages through international operations that would involve increased external partnerships.

South Korea and Taiwan

These two East Asian political economies have achieved high levels of outward-orientated growth through corporate–administrative cooperation, basically similar to that in Japan. In each case, resource deficiencies and difficult security problems have had strong motivating effects, together with emphasis on community values in the traditional cultures. In the formative stages of the partnerships, each country's technocratic authorities were much more assertive than those in Japan, and they have been operating under representative administrations only in the 1990s. Corporate representation of interests to the policy levels, while freer under those administrations, have become more urgent because of the increased need for official support. This has become more necessary in their unequal contest against Japanese and American firms for world market shares. A critical requirement is collaboration to increase investments in new technology, resources for which are not as substantial as those available for major Japanese and American enterprises.[48]

In South Korea, under democratic government, the corporate–administrative partnership has been affected by intercorporate cleavages and by strains in government interactions with firms and with a highly politicized public. A number of large conglomerates which were very active in the industrialization programmes of former authoritarian administrations were favoured by those governments, while the interests of many small and medium-sized firms were neglected. The policies of representative governments have been influenced by antipathies towards the conglomerates but also by respect for their achievements as internationally prominent exporters of mature and high-technology products.[49]

Interactions between the administration, the conglomerates and the smaller enterprises occur in a conflictual environment not only because of intercorporate cleavages but also because of contests for power between several political parties. These contend for the support of a population that has been strongly politicized, especially in the urban areas, by agitation against systems of authoritarian rule and then by labour union demands on distributional issues. In this environment the large conglomerates have strong incentives to extend their international operations, to ensure increased security against adverse developments at home, more effective bargaining with their administration, and more productive dealings with foreign governments, as well as to be able to compete more vigorously in external markets. Intercorporate solidarity appears to be below Japanese levels, especially because of the divisive effects of structural policies implemented by former authoritarian administrations. Their power was used forcefully in separate dealings with each of the large conglomerates, thus discouraging the formation of an integrated intercorporate system. Under representative government, clientelist ties with members of the ruling elite have evidently become vital for each conglomerate's interests; but the changing fortunes of members of this elite necessitate greater self-reliance, which can be attained by building up international production systems to service foreign markets.[50]

The administration has strong technocratic capabilities, but these and its foreign commercial intelligence system are weaker than those in Japan and have a history of less productive interactions with the corporate level. Technological lags behind Japanese and American firms have to be overcome by major Korean enterprises through government-supported innovations, which are used to achieve improved performance in alliances with foreign corporations, while the gains made in managing those alliances become more significant in the technological rivalry.[51] Such gains are especially important because, while the South Korean administration's capacity to provide supportive market-opening leverage is relatively weak, it also has only moderate bargaining power to protect the domestic market positions of national firms. US pressure for trade liberalization necessitate accommodative measures more substantial than those adopted under such pressures in Japan. The lower level of solidarity in the South Korean intercorporate system, moreover, limits the possibilities for informal business cooperation to control foreign intrusion.

In Taiwan, intercorporate relations have been more harmonious, partly because the industrial establishment has comprised a large number of small and medium-sized firms, few of which appear to have received special administrative favours. Government dealings with all these firms have been more impartial, more respectful of their autonomy and thus more conducive to responsive cooperation. In the wider political context, the representative administration relates to a less-politicized public. Corporate interests have reflected narrower sectoral development than in Korea, as its diversified pattern of advanced industrialization has not been feasible because of the combination of dispersed, modest-scale industrial capacities and the absence of an ambitious and forcefully implemented structural policy. The principal achievements in export-led growth have been in the electronics sector.[52]

The administration's support for trade policy has been vital for the outward-orientated firms, especially because of heavy dependence on access to the American market. Securing trade policy cooperation from the US administration has been difficult for the Taiwan government, because of the USA's non-recognition policy, the prominence of its interests in trade with the transitional Chinese communist regime, and its great bargaining strength. Taiwanese firms have increasingly sought opportunities for commerce with and production in the mainland economy, in advance of facilitating shifts in their administration's policy. A related strategy for expansion has been the development of trade and transnational production links with South-East Asian states, especially through bonds with the Chinese communities which dominate their economies.[53]

Larger ASEAN Political Economies

Those larger ASEAN political economies which are at lower levels of political and economic development than South Korea and Taiwan have not evolved comparable systems of corporate–government partnership, primarily because of administrative deficiencies. These deficiencies in Indonesia have been the failings of soft authoritarianism, where a ruling military elite has implemented economic policies with weaker techno-cratic capabilities than those in former South Korean regimes, and through more forceful and less functional interactions with the national business community, which has been mainly Chinese. In Thailand, under much less stable military regimes, the pattern has been similar; under subsequent representative governments, which have been unstable coalitions, institutional development and policy learning have been hindered by weak leadership and pervasive clientelism. Such problems have also been acute in the Philippines. Malaysia, at a significantly higher level of institutional development, has achieved advances in outward-orientated industrialization under a structural policy which favours the politically dominant Malay community. State power has been used to impose a system of corporate–government partnership in line with that policy.

The Malaysian system of corporate–government relations is distinctive in the ASEAN context because it has developed in a stable democratic structure in which significant technocratic capabilities have been used to promote the formation of a predominantly Malay economic elite, working in relative harmony with Chinese business groups under pressure to collaborate. The degree of communal bias in this structural endeavour has been moderated, in recognition of the entrepreneurial talents of Chinese managers, while most of the Chinese community has adapted to the imperatives for cooperation. Pressures for efficiency, in the interests of export performance, forced changes in the late 1980s which put Chinese and foreign management personnel in charge of state-sponsored enterprises which had been under Malay control. Business ventures undertaken by the ruling United Malays National Organization, however, continued, and benefited from official favouritism when contracts were awarded for infrastructure projects.[54]

Malaysian structural policy has sought to promote outward-orientated industrialization at higher technological levels mainly by attracting foreign direct investment into assembly-type manufacturing for export. The scope for related technology transfers has been modest because of the splitting up and dispersal of foreign production processes and the lack of an effective policy that would raise levels of technological competence. The Malay political elite's communal concerns have tended to divert attention from requirements for a vigorous technology policy, and initiatives for the development of such a policy do not appear to have been forthcoming from within the Chinese community: its entrepreneurial talents have been given limited scope, with discouraging effects, despite the moderation of the communal bias in structural policy.[55]

Chinese commercial and industrial interests have understandably focused on the use of clientelist ties with influential Malay political figures. The main Chinese political organization, the Malaysian Chinese Association, has to function as a subordinate ally of the dominant Malay party. Securing favourable treatment in the implementation of the administration's structural policy, however, is a process that has to be linked increasingly by Chinese managements with direct investment in other ASEAN members and in Taiwan. Such expansion is necessary because of the small size of the Malaysian economy, the need to spread risks and gain strength through overseas operations, and the pressing requirement to compete against Japanese and American penetration of the ASEAN economies. Business links with Chinese firms in Singapore have been useful for this regional expansion, although the scope for local enterprises in that small state has been limited by its openness to foreign direct investment from industrialized countries, which has resulted in an overwhelming foreign presence.[56]

Indonesia has a less stable pattern of corporate–government relations which has evolved under the opportunities and constraints determined by high-level preferences into a system which combines elements of personal rule with bureaucratic authoritarianism. The ruling military elite is committed to outward-orientated industrialization, in which there is considerable high-level personal and family involvement, but without communal bias against the Chinese business community, which has substantial entrepreneurial freedom but must maintain clientelist ties with prominent officials. Chinese and Indonesian commercial groups have to operate mainly within the government-sponsored political party, Golkar, which is intended to function as an encompassing organization. In this context and in their dealings with the economic ministries, the representation of business interests focuses on firm-specific trading, production and financial issues in order to secure bureaucratic cooperation. The aggregation of corporate interests and the formation of consensus for inputs into policy is on a modest scale because of the limited scope for organizational autonomy.[57]

Uncertainties about the outcome of rivalries in the military elite and about shifts in policy and in clientelist patterns add to the normal economic incentives which motivate expansion into foreign production and trade. Such expansion is also given impetus by Japanese, American and European direct investment, which is attracted into manufacturing for export but which challenges the domestic market positions of Indonesian firms. The foreign involvement is mainly in assembly-type production and, as elsewhere in South-East Asia, this reflects the regional dispersal of production functions by Japanese and western enterprises and their recognition of the relatively low levels of technological competence in the host country.

A technology policy implemented by the administration has had limited scope, and this is evidenced in functional deficiencies in the interactions between firms and the administration. The scope for the development and exercise of technocratic competence has been somewhat restricted by the concentration of power at the top of the Indonesian system and by problems of institutional development in the bureaucracy, attributable especially to the elements of personal rule and the toleration of corruption in the regime.[58] In recent years the orientation of economic policy has been influenced by a trend in high-level thinking which has emphasized the efficiencies of market forces, in line with much advice from external sources, including international lending agencies. The 1997 South-East Asian currency and stock market crises, however, have posed macromanagement, structural and regulatory issues which highlight the requirement for more productive corporate–government interactions in order to cope with problems of market failure and government failure.

Overall allocative efficiency is lower than in Malaysia's more developed economy, where stable institutions provide a more market-friendly environment for national firms and a relatively larger foreign commercial presence. Dynamic efficiency also appears to be lower than in Malaysia, because of weak competitive pressures and the negative effects of administrative deficiencies. Allocative and dynamic efficiencies are affected by the oligopoly power of officially favoured national firms, especially large conglomerates, and of state enterprises which dominate the chemicals, cement and rubber products sectors. There is insufficient coordination of corporate strategies because of the divisive effects of the regime's authoritarian involvement in the economy, which discourages autonomous activities by business associations.[59]

Improved macromanagement has become all the more necessary since the 1997 financial crises, especially in so far as these have dramatized structural imperatives. Fiscal discipline has been relatively weak, the level of public debt has been higher than in Malaysia (37.4 per cent of GDP in 1991–5, compared with Malaysia's 22.2 per cent); and gross external debt, minus foreign exchange reserves, as a proportion of exports and non-factor services, has been high – 176.7 per cent, compared with 8.8 per cent in Malaysia. Exports as a percentage of GDP have been low – 26.1 per cent, compared with 88 per cent in Malaysia. Inflation had averaged 8.9 per cent during 1991–5, slightly more than double the rate in Malaysia.[60] Debt service obligations entail vulnerabilities to decreases in exports and in foreign investor confidence. To achieve the necessary changes in fundamentals, increased fiscal discipline must be accompanied by a sound structural policy to promote outward-orientated industrialization at higher technological levels with balanced diversity. For the necessary policy learning, more productive and less unequal interaction between firms and the national administration would be desirable, but in the present authoritarian context such initiatives would have to come from the policy level.

The administrative deficiencies which limit the utility of corporate–government interactions have assumed greater prominence since the 1997 financial crises, thus tending to reduce the confidence of national firms and encouraging capital flight. The administration's capacity to promote the development of the financial sector and regulate it, with the emphasis on the funding of industry, is clearly in doubt because of problems of competence and commitment at the highest level and throughout the economic bureaucracy. These problems, it must be stresed, may well become more serious in the context of intra-elite rivalries for control of the regime.

Thailand, the first South-East Asian country to be seriously affected by the 1997 financial crises, has experienced the effects of prolonged political instability on institutional development, macromanagement and processes of corporate–government interaction. Successive military regimes and factionalized representative governments threatened by military takeovers have prevented the development of effective institutions, perpetuated low levels of administrative performance and discouraged the formation of strong economic associations to which policy-makers might become informally accountable. Corporate managements have been heavily dependent on favours obtained through clientelist ties with ruling and secondary elites, and corporate groups have formed on the basis of family and other personal bonds, while firms in these groups have tended to engage in excessive diversification, partly for enhanced security. Such tendencies have been evident in the Indonesian and Malaysian business communities, where a common effect has been to limit concentration on core organizational capabilities and thus on the requirement for investment in new technology.[61]

An effective structural policy has been virtually impossible in Thailand, because of the administrative deficiencies associated with acute political instability, but one has become all the more necessary since the 1997 financial crises. These revealed serious macromanagement failures, inadequate development and regulation of the financial sector, and neglect of the requirements to promote industrialization that would reduce dependence on exports of primary products and low-technology manufactures. External public debt as a proportion of GDP during 1991–5 at 11.4 per cent was about half Malaysia's, but exports as a percentage of GDP were 29.3 per cent, compared with Malaysia's 88 per cent, and gross external debt minus foreign exchange reserves as a proportion of exports of goods and non-factor services was 59.5 per cent: almost eight times higher than Malaysia's.[62]

Slack growth and many economic and political uncertainties since the 1997 financial problems appear to have encouraged individual corporate endeavours to adapt through more intensive use of clientelist ties, concentration on short-term business opportunities and the movement of resources into foreign operations. Capital flight is facilitated by lax financial controls and tends to be motivated by lack of confidence in the potential for broadly collaborative business adjustment and for administrative improvement. Meanwhile, as in Mexico, increased acquisitions of national firms by US, Japanese and European enterprises are tending to make the business community more international, diversifying networks and alliances in which family and other personal bonds persist but in which the development of encompassing national economic associations will become less likely. Advances in political development, to provide substantially improved macromanagement, must thus be expected to depend very much on the administrative capabilities of the leaderships in power during the current period of economic recovery. If those capabilities are slight, in line with the country's recent history, weak allocative efficiencies and weak dynamic efficiencies, while hampering economic recovery, will tend to perpetuate fragmentation in the pattern of intercorporate relations and clientelist links between that pattern and the authority structure.

The Philippines, following recovery from gross mismanagement under the Marcos regime, has a clientelist configuration of corporate–government relations similar to Thailand's. A fragmented intercorporate system is the source of multiple interactions with an authority structure which is at a low level of institutional development, but which has a higher degree of legitimacy as a form of representative government. Outward-orientated industrialization has been lagging behind Thailand, and a high level of public debt (43 per cent of GDP during 1991–5) has been reflected in a high level (150.6 per cent) of gross external debt, minus foreign exchange reserves, as a percentage of exports of goods and non-factor services during the same period. Exports are low ($17,502 million in 1995), compared with Thailand's ($56,662 million in 1995) and have been increasing at a modest pace, which suggests that they will continue to lag for many years.[63]

The need for an effective structural policy is more urgent than it is in Thailand, but there is no prospect of the constructive interactions that would be necessary between the corporate and the policy levels. Low economic growth and weak trade performance must be expected to keep the Philippines on the periphery of ASEAN's intrazonal commerce and on the periphery of the Pacific pattern of deepening integration. Within the projected ASEAN Free Trade Area, the Philippines is likely to remain the most disadvantaged of the larger members, attracting relatively less of the direct investment flowing between Chinese communities in South-East Asia and the Greater China area. These flows are introducing regional links into the patterns of corporate–government relations in Malaysia, Indonesia and Thailand which may gradually alter policies and entrepreneurial choices through changes in bargaining strengths and learning processes. Structural changes resulting from the expanding Japanese presence may be larger, and are evidently more strategically significant, but they are associated with a more distant involvement in relations between the corporate and government levels.

China

China is prominent in the regional pattern as a transitional political economy in which corporate–government interactions have been on a restricted scale, under a system of hard authoritarianism, exercised through an administration that has tended to multiply bureaucratic controls. Despite these controls and uncertainties about the evolution of economic policy, a private sector with limited scope has functioned vigorously. Elite opinion, reflected in the controlled media, has evidenced gradual acceptance of the logic of extending the process of economic liberalization, and this has indicated the probability of shifts towards openness to representations of corporate interests. Hong Kong, incorporated into the regime in 1997 with considerable local autonomy, has become a strong source of corporate influence on official thinking, especially because of its importance as a centre for the spread of mature and higher-technology manufacturing into nearby coastal areas.

Political change associated with economic liberalization is altering the context of corporate–government relations. The liberalization is having de-radicalizing effects, weakening the credibility of the ideology by virtually encouraging capitalist development and by allowing extensive contacts with foreign societies. While the intended social role of the Communist Party is becoming less effective, its importance as a control apparatus linked with the economic bureaucracy is being reduced. Meanwhile the military establishment appears to be gaining political influence while sharing in the benefits of economic growth through involvement with defence-related state enterprises. The armed forces have a vital internal security function, and the influence of their leaders on overall economic policy may well favour further reductions of the Communist Party's role in the economic bureaucracy, in order to allow more scope for professional technocratic capabilities.[64] In the type of bureaucratic authoritarianism which might thus emerge, corporate representation of interests could become more active.

NORTH AMERICAN FIRMS AND GOVERNMENTS

The productive and unproductive effects of differing East Asian patterns of corporate–government interactions are regionally active mainly in rivalry with the American presence. In the Pacific this is constituted by US firms which engage in extremely competitive rather than cooperative activities, while relating distantly and distrustfully to their home government. Corporate representation of interests to that administration tend to be fragmented into a proliferation of sector-specific demands, related principally to trade and taxation issues. Structural policy initiatives by the administration are not favoured because of a common lack of confidence in official competence and integrity. On the policy side, moreover, such initiatives are virtually precluded by a well-established tradition of limited government.

The typical American firm is structured by formal arm's-length contracting; its risks from moral hazard, opportunism and adverse selection are larger than those in Japanese enterprises. The dangers of X inefficiencies are greater and are reflected in weaker efficiencies at the intercorporate level, where interactions are intensely competitive rather than cooperative. The business culture is extremely individualistic, and anti-trust legislation, despite relaxations in recent years, discourages collaboration on the basis of explicit agreements.[65] Responsibilities for organizational performance are concentrated at the top levels; the downward exercise of authority, with only moderate trust at the working levels, tends to result in excessive middle-management expansion. Hence there are dangers of organizational manipulation, which can impose influence costs.

American corporate strategies respond to several developmental imperatives. The compulsion to grow through applications of internalization logic are strong, because of transaction costs and risks in a society with low levels of trust which discourage expectations of relational contracting. Intensifying competitive pressures in the home and foreign markets, however, necessitates concentration on core capabilities. At the same time, there are pressures to expand internationally, with an emphasis on organizational self reliance.

With such expansion, however, the formation of international corporate alliances becomes advisable, especially for higher-technology firms. These alliances are managed instrumentally, rather than relationally, with changes in bargaining strengths and strategies and in mixes of cooperation and competition.[66] The main foreign market in contest is the European Union, but successes in that area depend increasingly on gains in rivalries with Japanese enterprises in the Pacific and the rest of the world.

Increasing ventures into international production and reduced dependence on arm's-length exporting lower regulatory exposure to the home administration, augment bargaining strength in interactions with it, and make possible productive interactions with an increasing number of host administrations. As the transnational production expands, the pattern of business associations in the USA remains fragmented; it may well be tending to become more fragmented, thus limiting possibilities for interest aggregation and consensus formation in a highly pluralistic system of corporate–government interactions. The activities of numerous narrowly focused business groups seeking trade, taxation and other favours continue to expand, but overall they are evidently of declining utility for American enterprises with large-scale foreign operations.[67]

The international orientation of corporate strategies is difficult to measure but is clearly quite strong and is becoming increasingly significant in relations between US firms and their administration. While the export share of US manufacturing industries is only 13.4 per cent of their output, the foreign production of US firms is several times greater and, although this includes inputs from the USA which are counted as exports, the estimated volume suggests that the external manufacturing plus the export-orientated manufacturing at home reflect a very substantial outward focus. This is evidently tending to increase significantly, relative to domestically orientated operations, as outward direct investment is growing much faster than increases in GDP,[68] and as US involvement in international corporate alliances is also expanding substantially.

With the strong outward focus, US firms can be seen to have incentives to secure support from their home government for the establishment of a favourably designed international direct investment accord and for numerous forms of beneficial leverage against host governments. For these endeavours, however, there is evidently no willingness to work for the formation of strong peak economic associations: the intense individualism of the business culture would make that very difficult; a common preference is to work within specialized interest groups that can relate effectively to legislators and bureaucrats. Yet the importance of this type of activity, it must be stressed, is diminishing because of the bargaining strength that corporations gain while expanding their international operations, and also because they can exploit investment bidding by actual and prospective host governments.

The system of corporate governance, as shaped by legislation and the national culture, tends to perpetuate fragmentation in the intercorporate system and to strengthen the international emphasis in entrepreneurial strategies. Managements have to respond to shareholder pressures for high short-term performance which are felt through stock markets constantly manipulated by speculators seeking profit from volatility. Legislative restrictions limit the scope for cross-holdings and for bank and other institutional holdings that could provide degrees of stability. Continuity in corporate identity is uncertain because of vulnerability to takeovers, and managerial roles tend to be threatened by shareholder activism.[69] Initiatives to generate broad support for change in the system of corporate governance are discouraged by the spirit of aggressive self-reliance in the national culture and by the difficulties of securing legislative approval, which are very serious in the US system of divided government.

By expanding international production, American firms can operate with fewer of the restraints and vulnerabilities of the national system of corporate governance. There is greater scope for managerial discretion in the development of investment, production and marketing strategies, and reduced exposure to monitoring by or on behalf of shareholders. Overseas operations are more profitable and thus facilitate satisfaction of home country demands for high short-term profits. Risks, moreover, can be spread widely, while the exploitation of foreign location advantages can be optimized. Further, tax advantages can be gained through the reinvestment of profits earned abroad. This, together with the opportunities for income-shifting to limit tax burdens, is especially significant because of the rising costs of government in the USA due to deficit spending and increasing allocations for the sheltering or relief of communities and sectors adversely affected by globalization.[70]

US firms producing abroad can use protectionist and market-opening demands from special interest groups at home as a means of leverage against host governments. When substantial market positions are gained in host countries, however, there can be little interest in facilitating entries by other American enterprises, especially if satisfactory working relationships have been established with the host administrations, and if favourable treatment by those administrations would be expected to diminish after strong US market-opening pressures. American international companies support trade policy activism directed mainly against Japan and industrializing East Asian states, but apparently with reservations because of interests in host country goodwill and adversarial attitudes toward their home administration. There is little support for trade policy activism directed against the European Union, where the largest concentration of US foreign direct investment receives favourable treatment.

Protectionist demands influencing US trade policy come, first, from low- and medium-technology firms that have lost international competitiveness and experience substantial import penetration: leather products, textiles and wood products. Trade policy activism is also demanded by higher-technology firms threatened by exports from other industrialized states, including especially Japan. The sectors from which these demands come are automobiles, electronics and industrial machinery. US administrations have been particularly responsive to demands from the automobile and electronics sectors. Regarding the former, there have been high-priority employment concerns, activated by Japanese penetration of a market experiencing excess capacity and stagnant demand.[71] An unacknowledged threat of import restrictions induced restraint by Japanese automobile exporters, in effect extending limitations imposed under a Voluntary Export Restraint (VER) agreement which has lapsed. Under World Trade Organization rules, such agreements are no longer allowed, but of course may be replaced by confidential understandings.

The US administration's interest in responding to demands for trade policy activism tends to be stronger than its concern with corporate requests in other areas. Displays of vigorous engagement with foreign trade issues can secure immediate political benefits because of media emphasis on the disruptive effects of imports from unfair trading partners and because of popular perceptions that leverage against such partners is vital for many US industries. On taxation, foreign direct investment, technology and finance issues of importance to US corporations, public interest is usually not aroused and the domestic political benefits from administrative attention given to these are small. The complexities and uncertainties of these issues, moreover, in the highly pluralistic dynamics of American economic policy-making, tend to discourage high-level involvement.

The fragmentation of corporate interests partly reflects the organizational weaknesses of the major political parties in the USA, which allow strong pluralism in its policy processes. It also reflects problems of entrepreneurial coordination in the system of intercorporate relations. There is a secretive oligarchical process of interest representation by large corporations through the Business Roundtable, which admits top executives by invitation and which interacts on a confidential basis with government agencies. There is an apparent preference to stand apart from the numerous associations identified with small enterprises and from the large, loosely organized National Association of Manufacturers and the confederally constituted United States Chamber of Commerce.[72] The major political parties have not evolved strong interest-aggregating capabilities that would encourage the formation of peak economic associations; indeed, the structural weaknesses of these parties, together with the intense pluralism which perpetuates those weaknesses, invites political action by specialized interest groups operating generally as rivals.

Oligarchic entrepreneurial coordination without the risks of anti-trust enforcement may develop informally in the Business Roundtable, but coordination of corporate strategies on a broader scale is difficult to achieve because of the intense competitiveness and the low levels of trust in the intercorporate system, and also because of the inhibiting effects of anti-trust restraints, which derive from judicial decisions as well as from the work of regulatory agencies. Policy-level concerns with structural competitiveness have relaxed anti-trust enforcement through guidelines for regulatory agencies that recognize the efficiencies of collaboration between firms, notably in pre-competitive technological development. Cooperation between firms, specialized interest groups, legislators and the bureaucracy for the implementation of a substantial technology policy, however, is very difficult to promote. Corporate rivalries, competition between specialized interest groups, changing political contracting by legislators and bureaucratic pluralism all encourage complex bargaining in which the public interest is relativized.[73]

Cutting across the problem of intercorporate cooperation and corporate–government cooperation is the problem of high-volume rent-seeking in relation to productive activity. The potentially most destabilizing form of rent-seeking is stock market manipulation, in which large-scale speculators exploit volatility, affecting what may be called market efficiency in ways that harm small investors and precipitate rises and falls in confidence that can lead to a financial crisis. High-volume manipulation is increasing as stock markets become more internationalized and is increasingly linked with speculative operations in money markets. All this rent-seeking diverts talents and resources from productive entrepreneurship: hence there is a fundamental problem of corporate ethics which defies regulatory solutions.[74]

The danger of instability in stock and currency markets is especially serious because of the accumulation of US government debt, which is becoming unsustainable, and the persistence of adverse balances of

payments, due mainly to trade deficits. These sources of strain must be
expected to become more serious as some form of monetary union is
established in Europe. The new role likely to be assumed by the European currency could no doubt lead to massive shifts in official reserves
and private portfolios, which would reduce the international value of
the US dollar, perhaps rapidly.[75] Attempts at Atlantic cooperation for
a smooth transition might not be adequate, and accordingly the burdens
of adjustment for the US administration and for US firms could be
heavy.

Imperatives for extensive corporate–government cooperation can be
seen as the dimensions of national macromanagement issues become
more evident and as those issues become more urgent. The imperatives
for collaboration have been obscured in the adversarial political processes which have evolved on the basis of the liberal political tradition,
and in these processes there is a constant danger of pluralistic stagnation
which, with related inefficiencies and costs, increases the incentives for
US enterprises to focus on expanding their systems of transnational
production. The major advantage of reduced vulnerability to volatility
in internationalizing US financial markets, it must be stressed, is clearly
more significant than the uncertain potential for concerted corporate
efforts to work with the administration for greater market stability. Yet
this is a basic requirement and, together with the fiscal and balance of
payments problems, it is a challenge which necessitates the building
of strong peak economic associations committed to constructive interactions with the administration.[76]

The problems of corporate governance and of advanced political
development are challenging American firms and policy-makers.
Reform of the system of corporate governance, through change in its
culture and regulatory structure, is necessary for a reorientation towards
more productive and cooperative activity, with restraints on rent-
seeking and destructive competition. Greater stability and extensive
entrepreneurial collaboration is required, with rises in the levels of
intercorporate trust and in responsiveness to the common good.
Reformed corporate governance could aid the development of peak
economic associations with capacities for broad consensus building, and
thus for contributing to greater order and productive deliberation in
policy communities. Political reform, which would help in this way, will
depend on efforts by leading figures to inspire an increasing zeal for the
public interest and to construct stronger organizations for consensus-
building. Concerted political entrepreneurship for the general welfare
could interact productively with a concerting of corporate strategies for
complementary specializations, higher growth and greater equity.

Canada and Mexico

Partners of the USA in the North America Free Trade Area (NAFTA), Canada and Mexico have minor roles in the Pacific pattern of deepening integration, and their systems of corporate–government relations have evolved under the strong influence of heavy dependence on the large US market and of openness to the expansion of direct investment by US firms, especially those with strong positions in the home economy. Increased diversification in foreign economic relations has been advisable for Canada and Mexico, but the main direction of structural change has been the development of complex asymmetric production and marketing linkages with the USA. These are evolving in a context of regional liberalization for which common institutions have not been planned. A collaborative competition policy is not in prospect. Scope for the assertion of American preferences on regional issues tends to increase as the asymmetric structural changes continue, while economic links between Canada and Mexico evolve on a much smaller scale.

The Canadian pattern of business associations is fragmented, like that in the USA. A Business Council on National Issues functions as an elite group for informal high-level interactions with policy-makers, similar to the Business Roundtable in the USA; there are no organizational links with other corporate organizations. These are mostly loose associations which confine themselves to making representations on special issues, without seeking opportunities for partnership in policy processes.[77] As the structural interdependencies with the USA increase, with large direct investment flows each way, the fragmentation of the pattern of business associations will probably become greater. This trend, moreover, may well be given impetus by uncertainties about the future of Quebec, where there is strong support for separation from Canada.

Corporate attitudes to the Canadian administration have developed in a system of adversarial politics, like those in the USA and Britain. In this system, uncertainties about the fortunes of major political parties, and about the dynamics of Canadian federalism, have tended to limit interest in structural policy initiatives, although productivity growth has been lagging behind that of the USA and there is considerable stagnation in industrial sectors. Levels of investment in advanced technology are low compared with other industrialized countries, and degrees of import penetration in high-technology sectors have been increasing. High levels of protection, until recent decades, had in effect encouraged excessive diversification in Canadian industries. The number of small firms, while declining under the competitive pressures of liberalized commerce, is still very large, and they invest very little in new technology.[78]

Mexico's corporate associations have evolved through a long history of soft authoritarian rule by a revolutionary regime which promoted ideological hostility to the private sector and set up large state enterprises. The ruling revolutionary party has been well entrenched, but has been tolerating gradual democratization while implementing privatization policies. These have expanded opportunities for independent firms, but the regime's administrative capabilities and high-level leadership capacities have been inadequate to manage the transitional economy. The country is recovering gradually from a severe financial crisis which began in late 1994 after large outflows of portfolio investment which had entered in anticipation of rapid growth following the formation of NAFTA. The severe recession which followed this crisis drastically reduced business confidence and intensified awareness of dependence on opportunities to collaborate with US firms.

The ruling party, while in effect obliged to take much guidance from the International Monetary Fund, the World Bank and the US administration, is not able to offer credible prospects of partnership with the private sector for renewed growth on a more secure basis. Meanwhile, the severe stresses in the economy appear to have increased fragmentation in the representation of business concerns, especially by causing managements to focus more intently on the advancement of their own interests through clientelist links with the administration. The stresses since 1994 have evidently had divisive effects because their intensity has been experienced after a succession of earlier macromanagement failures, notably during the 1980s.[79]

INTERACTING ISSUES AND TRENDS

The patterns of corporate–government relations in Japan and the USA dominate the Pacific configuration of change and continuity in the cross-border linking of markets and economic structures and the evolution of policy interdependencies. Systemic logic in the Japanese pattern tends to be reinforced by its benefits for structural competitiveness and for the development of favourable asymmetries in policy-level interactions with the USA and the industrializing East Asian states. Pressures to enhance structural competitiveness are felt at the corporate and policy levels in the USA, but with diverging perspectives which limit the possibilities for cooperation between managements and policy-makers.

Urgent imperatives for much more productive corporate–government relations are evident in Thailand, Indonesia, Malaysia and the Philippines. Gross macromanagement failures in these states have set demanding requirements for the development and regulation of sound financial systems, the implementation of effective fiscal and monetary policies, and the introduction of comprehensive structural policies. For the system-building tasks which are clearly necessary, the Japanese model of corporate–administrative partnership is especially appropriate. The US administration's advocacy of liberalization policies may discourage adoption of the Japanese model, despite its potent demonstration effect, but the status of the USA has been affected to a degree by the speculative activities of US financial institutions in the Thai, Indonesian and Malaysian currency crises. The most serious difficulties hindering reform in line with Japanese achievements, however, are the long-standing problems of governance in the army-dominated Indonesian regime, the weak representative government in Thailand, the politically more advanced system in Malaysia, and the somewhat less-advanced system in the Philippines.[80]

The Japanese pattern of corporate–government relations is highly productive because cooperation within the intercorporate system functions in responsive interaction with administrative consultation and advice. The pervasive relational basis for this alliance capitalism ensures implicit contracting with low risks and superior efficiencies. The wide-ranging corporate cooperation in this system can arouse concerns about economic imperialism in industrializing East Asian states, but sensitivity to this danger has motivated Japanese corporate emphasis on partnerships with host country enterprises and careful regard for local feelings. The feature of the Japanese system which appears to have made the strongest impression on ruling elites in the larger ASEAN countries is its process of administrative guidance, which encourages hopes of achieving rapid state-led outward-orientated industrialization. The potential efficiencies of promoting intercorporate solidarity like that in Japan clearly receive less attention at the policy level in the Indonesian regime and in the Malaysian administration, which relate to mainly Chinese business communities dependent on clientelist favours. In Thailand, intercorporate solidarity can develop more spontaneously, but the severity of the economic stresses since mid-1997 have dramatized the need for strong government in a context overshadowed by assertions of military interest in the formation of an effective administration.

In Indonesia, the need for strong macromanagement and reduced vulnerability to the manipulation of international financial markets has undoubtedly tended to make the ruling military elite more reluctant to allow gradual democratization, despite pressures from the politicized urban populations. Intra-elite rivalries relating to the issue of succession to General Suharto may well have been intensified by general perceptions of the requirement for effective government. In such rivalries, however, factional politics must be expected to relativize questions about entrusting more authority to technocrats, especially in view of the probability that a winning coalition will have to receive broad support from the upper echelons of the military establishment. In the business community, awareness of these probabilities is likely to motivate more a active cultivation of clientelist ties with figures in the military elite; while for those figures the utility of having that community in a subordinate role is likely to be even more apparent. The question of entrusting more authority to technocrats is probably seen to be linked with the advantages derived from military influence over the business community. Those advantages may indeed be responsible for reluctance to accept the functional logic of enhancing technocratic roles.

Thailand's political evolution, in which numerous weak, factionalized political parties have experienced insecurity under army-dominated regimes, has in effect allowed military leaders to cultivate a belief in their entitlement to dominate the executive. Motivations to provide efficient macromanagement, however, have been lacking, and the business interests of the military elite have clearly encouraged subjective preferences in dealing with a fragmented business community as well as a fragmented pattern of political organizations. Yet military leaders have to recognize that major international lending agencies and the US administration wish to deal with a representative government on issues of debt management and economic recovery. For such an administration, cooperation from the business community will be essential, but it must be stressed that losses of confidence have probably had divisive effects in that community, while virtually forcing a more active corporate exploitation of clientelist ties with military and political figures. The multiplicity of clientelist activities will of course make the formation of a corporate–government consensus for an innovative structural policy very difficult. Economic advice from international lending agencies, moreover, as a condition of assistance, must be expected to continue the emphasis on liberalization for the freeing of market forces.

Malaysia, at a considerably higher level of institutional development than Thailand and Indonesia, has administrative capabilities to promote corporate–government partnerships for a more functional structural policy. This would necessitate restraint on communal bias in infrastructure development and more equitable treatment of Chinese business interests. The longer-term effectiveness of the structural policy would depend on the scope and vigour of its technology component, into which private sector inputs would be essential. Orderly development of a more functional structural policy, influenced by Japanese achievements, could be aided by the quality of corporate–government interactions. These involve more mutual responsiveness than is possible in the authoritarian Indonesian context, despite the clientelism encouraged by the communal bias of the dominant Malay political party. Because of the small size of the Malaysian economy, however, the somewhat restricted scope for self-reliance in structural policy makes the treatment of foreign direct investment a major factor in corporate–government relations, and in this context opportunities for collaboration with Japanese firms assume much significance.

A relaxation of the communal bias in Malaysian policies would facilitate industrial and commercial partnerships with Singapore, which could compensate in part for Thailand's reduced significance as an adjacent trading partner. The prospect of Chinese interests in Singapore augmenting the role of the Chinese business community in Malaysian politics, however, has considerable influence on the attitudes of Malay political leaders. The scope for structural policy cooperation, moreover, could appear to be rather limited because of the strong foreign direct investment policy in Singapore, which has allowed the emergence of an almost overwhelming foreign economic presence. Yet Singapore's commercial links with the major industrialized states have become all the more important for Malaysian firms because of the regional effects of Thailand's economic decline.

In the Philippines, corporate–government interactions allow few opportunities for the consideration of structural policy initiatives. The liberal political tradition, with its clientelist blend, is well established. The large American business presence influences corporate–government relations on the basis of interests to ensure freedom for market forces and to limit the penetration of Japanese political and economic influence. As the Philippines continues to lag behind the Indonesian, Thai and Malaysian economies, the Japanese system of alliance capitalism can be considered to have great significance for policy-level discussions of ways to overcome the lag. Yet policy learning in the dynamics of the national system of corporate relations with the administration is made difficult by the proliferation of weakly aggregated interests in the Philippine form of agency democracy.

For South Korean corporate and government leaders the vulnerabilities of South-East Asian countries during the 1997 financial crises have probably validated the logic of structural policy partnership, despite strains that have affected that partnership under democratic government. Increases in economic liberalization, as advocated by the

US administration in the interests of reciprocity, are undoubtedly felt to entail serious vulnerabilities which would be difficult to overcome if the corporate–government partnership were weakened. Consensus on this is evidently being subjected to some stress because of pressures to meet US requests for increased economic openness, and because of rivalries between major South Korean firms for administrative favours in support of struggles for increased foreign market shares. Corporate–government exchanges in South Korea are influenced by a general strengthening of structural linkages with Japan which could sustain cooperation with the Japanese system of partnering between the enterprise and the administrative levels. Increasing intercorporate alliances are probably contributing to the growth of shared understanding of the advantages of wide-ranging collaboration between the two economies to cope with the growth problems of South-East Asian trading partners. The strong economic nationalism in Japanese alliance capitalism, however, is a major hindrance to the growth of political ties with South Korean peak economic associations and policy communities.

For the Japanese system of corporate–government partnering, the stresses in the South-East Asian economies have posed very difficult issues. These economies have great significance for the balanced and diversified expansion of the Japanese production system, in rivalry with the USA and, increasingly, with China. Japanese interests have been more seriously affected than those of the USA by the disruptions of the South-East Asian economies, and these have challenged the consensual Japanese corporate and administrative decision processes to work for more vigorous and more constructive engagement in that area. A concerted strategy for productive interactions with corporate and government elites in South-East Asia may be very difficult to develop, especially because of political uncertainties in Thailand and Indonesia, but there may well be an effectively coordinated focus on Malaysia. This country's level of economic development, its close links with Singapore, and the size and stability of its trade and investment links with Japan clearly invite much planning attention from Japanese managements and policy-makers. Malaysian policy has shown a favourable orientation, which was reflected in criticisms of US financial institutions involved in speculative attacks on South-East Asian currencies during 1997.

Corporate–government consultations in Japan have undoubtedly been intensified by the South-East Asian problems, and meanwhile they have certainly been obliged to take account of larger although less proximate issues in the regional processes of deepening integration. A reduction of the USA's role in the international monetary system, which is likely to follow the establishment of a European Monetary Union, will tend to reduce the status and bargaining strength of the United States in the Pacific. Opportunities may then be seen for more innovative Japanese entrepreneurship in that region, especially if the succession issue in Indonesia is resolved with prospects of continuing stability. Stronger Japanese corporate and political ties with Malaysia, Singapore and Indonesia would provide favourable conditions for involvement in the rebuilding of the Thai economy.

In the American pattern of corporate–government relations, perspectives on the Pacific have had to recognize diminished incentives for direct investment in South-East Asia and declining prospects for regional trade and investment liberalization. Short-term profits through manufacturing and resource extraction in continental South-East Asia have become less attainable, and a new awareness of the vulnerabilities of economic liberalization has influenced South-East Asian policy orientations. It has been clear, moreover, that the Japanese system of alliance capitalism has superior capacities for adaptation to the recessions and strains of the area. Perceptions of the weaker bargaining strengths of the Thai, Malaysian and Indonesian administrations on trade and investment issues, however, may well motivate US government endeavours to secure reductions of South-East Asian trade and investment barriers. American corporate demands for such reductions have undoubtedly been encouraged by assessments of South-East Asia's problems which have stressed the need to imposing market discipline on national economic policies.

Identities and compatibilities of interest between US firms and their national administration are changing with deepening integration, as international activities by those firms expand and induce reorientation by mainly domestic enterprises. The scale of this corporate internationalization, it must be stressed, is very great, and tends to increase fragmentation of the national intercorporate system. Increasing corporate internationalization, motivated basically by competition for world market shares, is responding to the need for acceptance by and interaction with multiple host governments and host intercorporate systems. This need is becoming stronger in European operations, and may become very much stronger if there are failures in Atlantic cooperation as a European Monetary Union is established, and if there is instability in US financial markets. In South-East Asia, problems of host country acceptance and treatment have tended to increase because of the altered status of US investors after the financial crises of the area. US firms whose identities have become more international can evidently expect to have more favourable conditions for their operations, especially in Malaysia and Thailand.

Greater fragmentation in the representation of corporate interests must be expected to increase the complexities and uncertainties of US policy-making on Pacific and Atlantic trade and investment issues. Trade and investment policy activism in the Pacific, on the basis of administrative efforts to aggregate diverse corporate interests, may provoke South-East Asian resistance while causing US firms to assume more international identities, and lose home country ties, for effective operations in the area. Problems of entrepreneurial coordination in the home economy, which will probably be made more difficult by the domestic effects of corporate internationalization for South-East Asian operations, are also likely to be made more difficult by the internationalization induced through operating conditions in Europe.

COMPARATIVE PERSPECTIVES

Systems of corporate–government interaction compete and cooperate across borders under pressures to raise levels of structural competitiveness and enhance national gains from deepening integration. In the Pacific there is far more cross-border competition than cooperation, and this contrasts with the mix in Atlantic relations, which includes relatively higher levels of cooperation based on cultural affinities, productive communication flows and institutional links. The Pacific pattern is distinguished by sharp contrasts between the Japanese and American systems which activate intense competition. In this competition the systemic logic of Japanese alliance capitalism remains strong and is reinforced by achievements in regional and world markets. In the American processes of corporate–government relations, political action by narrowly focused business groups has engrossing policy-level effects which divert attention from the gradual internationalization of US firms.

A thin network of Pacific business associations linked with the Asia Pacific Economic Cooperation forum facilitates some exchanges between US, Japanese and other Pacific organizations representing corporate interests. This has a potential for sponsoring constructive interpenetration of the regional forms of corporate–government interaction. Community-building efforts of the forum, however, have been set back by South-East Asian antipathies toward the USA, which were roused by that area's financial crises. Japanese corporate and government interests, moreover, have had to focus on problems of economic recovery in South-East Asia and on new opportunities to demonstrate solidarity with governments in that area seeking to promote growth on a more stable basis. The projection of the Japanese model of alliance capitalism has become more meaningful for South-East Asian elites, while western rationales for economic liberalization have tended to lose appeal.

In the regional context shaped by the South-East Asian financial crises, the bargaining strengths of governments on trade and investment issues have assumed increased importance. Elite recognition of the prospective common benefits of lowering trade and investment barriers has evidently tended to weaken because of a general lowering of trust and goodwill, and because the vulnerabilities associated with the liberalization of financial markets have been dramatized, as well as those caused by weak domestic regulation. Questions for governments and corporate groups about what increases in foreign market access can be secured through leverage against regional trading partners have become more prominent in policy communities. Japan's need for higher export earnings, to ensure a resumption of normal outward-orientated growth, has increased because of the problems in the South-East Asian economies; accordingly, greater access to the US market has become necessary. Hence imperatives for concerted entrepreneurship and for supportive government measures have become stronger, despite requirements to make trade and investment concessions for incremental reciprocity. The USA's need for higher export earnings has also increased, and the loss of opportunities in Southeast Asia must be compensated for mainly by expanded commerce with Japan, Europe and Latin America.

Corporate–government interactions in Japan, while imparting functional coherence to the national policy mix, can evolve more integrated approaches to expanded penetration of the US market from positions gained in the automobile, electronics and industrial equipment sectors. Bargaining strength to cope with US-administered and other forms of protection is being gradually increased, with growing asymmetries in investment interdependence and higher-volume Japanese manufacturing in the USA. The Japanese capacity for leverage, based on the partnership in alliance capitalism, can be used defensively with considerable advantage because of the strong pluralism which has divisive effects in the US system of arm's-length corporate–government relations. US attempts at trade and investment policy leverage tend to be hindered by opposition from special interest groups at home, in rivalry with other interest groups supporting such leverage.

The absence of close corporate–government cooperation in the USA and the higher degree of American corporate internationalization form an increasingly significant asymmetry in the dynamics of USA–Japan relations. There is a similar asymmetry in the management of the USA's economic relations with the European Union, and in this context, it must be stressed, the relatively easier processes of Atlantic interaction are about to encounter formidable challenges as a monetary union is formed in Europe. These challenges will set new imperatives for monetary cooperation between the USA and Japan while current issues of unequal structural interdependence in that relationship will undoubtedly remain outstanding. Highly constructive economic advice for firms and governments in the Pacific setting is becoming necessary, for systemic progress in the US political economy and functional interaction between Japanese alliance capitalism and more broadly coordinated corporate–government dealings in the USA. Collaborative engagement with issues of market failure and government failure that are assuming cross-border dimensions could then become more inclusive through the participation of industrializing East Asian states.

NOTES

1. See John H. Dunning, 'The global economy, domestic governance, strategies and transnational corporations: interactions and policy implications', *Transnational Corporations*, **1**(3), 1992, 7–45.
2. Ibid.
3. In the Japanese case, however, home government links remain very important. See Richard F. Doner, 'Japan in East Asia: institutions and regional leadership', in Peter J. Katsenstein and Takashi Shiraishi (eds), *Network Power: Japan and Asia*, Ithaca, NY: Cornell University Press, 1997 pp. 197–233.
4. See John Hagedoorn, 'Atlantic strategic technology alliances', in Gavin Boyd (ed.), *The Struggle for World Markets*, Cheltenham: Edward Elgar, 1998, pp. 177–91.
5. This consideration has been a factor in the failure of OECD talks on a Multilateral Investment Agreement in April 1998.
6. See Dani Rodrik, *Has Globalization Gone Too Far?*, Washington, DC: Institute for International Economics, 1997.
7. See comments on expansion of the Japanese intercorporate system in Doner, 'Japan in East Asia'.
8. Ibid.
9. Ibid.
10. See James O. Wilson, 'The corporation as a political actor', in Carl Kaysen (ed.), *The American Corporation Today*, Oxford: Oxford University Press, 1996, pp. 413–35.
11. Financial factors responsible for short termism are discussed in Charles W. Calomiris and Carlos D. Ramirez, 'Financing the American corporation: the changing menu of financial relationships', in ibid., pp. 128–86.
12. See Andrew MacIntyre (ed.), *Business and Government in Industrializing Asia*, Ithaca, NY: Cornell University Press, 1994, chs 7 and 9.
13. See references to South Korea in *Developing Economies*, Special Issue: 'Development mechanisms in Korea and Taiwan', xxxv(4), December 1997. See also Linsu Kim, *Imitation to Innovation: The Dynamics of Korea's Technological Learning*, Boston, Mass.: Harvard Business School Press, 1997.

14. See Gary Saxonhouse, 'Regional initiatives and US trade policy in Asia', *Asian-Pacific Economic Literature*, **11**(2), 1997, 1–14.
15. The US balance of payments deficit is expected to reach $230 billion in 1998; see International Monetary Fund, *World Economic Outlook, Interim Assessment, December 1997*, New York: IMF, 1997.
16. See International Monetary Fund, *International Capital Markets: Developments, Prospects, and Key Policy Issues*, New York: IMF, 1997, ch. 2.
17. See references to the mobility of capital in Rodrik, *Has Globalization Gone Too Far?*.
18. See Dennis J. Encarnation, *Rivals beyond Trade: America versus Japan in Global Competition*, Ithaca, NY: Cornell University Press, 1992, ch. 3.
19. See Kim, *Imitation to Innovation*.
20. See Jose Campa and Linda S. Goldberg, 'The evolving external orientation of manufacturing: a profile of four countries', *Federal Reserve Bank of New York Economic Policy Review*, **3**(2), 1997, 53–82.
21. See 'Foreign direct investment in the United States', *Survey of Current Business*, **77**(9), 1997, 75–118.
22. See Campa and Goldberg, 'The evolving external orientation of manufacturing'; and International Monetary Fund, *Direction of Trade Statistics Yearbook, 1997*, New York: IMF, 1997.
23. See Campa and Goldberg, 'The evolving external orientation of manufacturing'.
24. See Paolo Guerrieri and Carlo Milana, 'Changes and trends in the world trade in high technology products', *Cambridge Journal of Economics*, **19**(1), 1995, 225–42.
25. See Kim, *Imitation to Innovation*.
26. See cross-investment levels in 'Foreign direct investment in the United States'.
27. See Campa and Goldberg, 'The evolving external orientation of manufacturing'.
28. On the dynamic efficiencies, see Jens Laage-Hellman, *Business Networks in Japan*, London: Routledge, 1997.
29. See Frederic L. Pryor, *Economic Evolution and Structure: The Impact of Complexity on the US Economic System*, New York: Cambridge University Press, 1996.
30. On this trade policy activism, see Anne O. Krueger, *American Trade Policy*, Washington, DC: American Enterprise Institute, 1995.
31. Rises in stock prices have contributed to this trend. See *The Economist*, 18–24 April 1998, 67–9.
32. On these sectors see Campa and Goldberg, 'The evolving external orientation of manufacturing'.
33. On the organizational weaknesses of these associations, see William D. Coleman, 'State traditions and comprehensive business associations: a comparative structural analysis', *Political Studies*, xxxviii (2), 1990, 231–52.
34. See Rodrik, *Has Globalization Gone Too Far?*.
35. See Laage-Hellman, *Business Networks in Japan*.
36. On motivations for information sharing, see Ken-ichi Imai, 'Japan's corporate networks', in Shumpei Kumon and Henry Rosovsky (eds), *The Political Economy of Japan*, vol 3, Stanford, Cal.: Stanford University Press, 1992, pp. 198–230.
37. The worst problems appear to have been in Indonesia. See Hal Hill, *The Indonesian Economy since 1966*, Cambridge: Cambridge University Press, 1996.
38. See references to the Chinese in MacIntyre, *Business and Government in Industrializing Asia*.
39. See Imai, 'Japan's corporate networks'.
40. See Laage-Hellman, *Business Networks in Japan*.
41. See comments on the Japanese system, in W. Carl Kester, 'American and Japanese corporate governance: convergence to best practice?', in Suzanne Berger and Ronald Dore (eds), *National Diversity and Global Capitalism*, Ithaca, NY Cornell University Press, 1996, pp. 107–37.
42. Ibid.; and see OECD, *Economic Survey, Japan 1996*, Paris: OECD, 1996, ch. 5.
43. OECD, *Economic Survey, Japan 1996*

44. See OECD, *Economic Survey, Japan 1997*, Paris: OECD, 1997, ch. 4.
45. See Steven K. Vogel, 'International games with national rules: how regulation shapes competition in "global" markets', *Journal of Public Policy*, **17**(2), 1997, 169–93.
46. The cultural basis for collaboration remains strong. See Kumon and Rosovsky (eds), *The Political Economy of Japan*.
47. This appears to be true mainly in the outward-orientated manufacturing sectors: the construction, transport and agricultural sectors have experienced more divisive politicization. See Haruhiro Fukui and Shigeko N. Fukai, 'Japan in 1997', *Asian Survey*, XXXVIII (1), 1998, 24–33.
48. See Michael Hobday, *Innovation in East Asia: The Challenge to Japan*, Aldershot, UK: Edward Elgar, 1995, chs 4 and 5.
49. See *Developing Economies*, XXXV (4), 1997, special issue: 'Development mechanisms in Korea and Taiwan'.
50. On the political dynamics of the South Korean system, see Tong Whan Park, 'South Korea in 1997', *Asian Survey*, XXXVIII (1), 1998, 1–10.
51. See Hobday, *Innovation in East Asia*.
52. Ibid., ch. 5.
53. See Christopher Howe, 'The Taiwan economy: the transition to maturity and the political economy of its changing international status', *China Quarterly*, 148, December 1996, 1171–95.
54. See MacIntyre, *Business and Government in Industrializing Asia*, ch. 6; and Edmund Terence Gomez and K.S. Jomo, *Malaysia's Political Economy*, Cambridge: Cambridge University Press, 1997.
55. See symposium on Malaysia, *Developing Economies*, XXXV (3), September 1997.
56. See Iyanatul Islam and Anis Chowdhury, *Asia-Pacific Economies*, London: Routledge, 1997, ch. 12.
57. See Hill, *The Indonesian Economy since 1966*.
58. Ibid.; see also references to Indonesia in Denis Fred Simon (ed.), *The Emerging Technological Trajectory of the Pacific Rim*, Armonk, NY: M.E. Sharpe, 1995.
59. See Hill, *The Indonesian Economy since 1966*.
60. See Geoffrey Bascand and Assaf Razin, 'Indonesia's fiscal position: sustainability issues', in John Hicklin, David Robinson and Anoop Singh (eds), *Macroeconomic Issues Facing ASEAN Countries*, New York: IMF, 1997, 58–90.
61. See Simon (ed.), *The Emerging Technological Trajectory of the Pacific Rim*, ch. 7.
62. See Bascand and Razin, 'Indonesia's fiscal position', 61.
63. Ibid.
64. A new economic elite is emerging: see Margaret M. Pearson, *China's New Business Elite*, Berkeley, Cal.: University of California Press, 1997.
65. See Kaysen (ed.), *The American Corporation Today*, ch. 4.
66. See comments on the US business culture, in Mark Casson, Ray Loveridge and Satwinder Singh, 'Corporate culture in Europe, Asia and North America', in Gavin Boyd and Alan M. Rugman (eds), *Euro-Pacific Investment and Trade*, Cheltenham, UK: Edward Elgar, 1997, 96–129.
67. On the fragmentation of business associations, see Coleman, 'State traditions and comprehensive business associations'.
68. See 'Foreign direct investment in the United States'.
69. See Kester, 'American and Japanese corporate governance'.
70. See Rodrik, *Has Globalization Gone Too Far?*.
71. See Boyd, *The Struggle for World Markets*, ch. 4.
72. See Coleman, 'State traditions and comprehensive business associations'.
73. See Roger G. Noll, 'Structural policies in the United States', in Samuel Kernell (ed.), *Parallel Politics: Economic Policymaking in Japan and the United States*, Washington, DC: Brookings Institution, 1991, pp. 230–80.
74. On the dangers of speculation, see *The Economist*, 18–24 April 1998, 67–9; and Frederic S. Mishkin, 'Preventing financial crises: an international perspective', *Man-*

chester School Papers in Money, Macroeconomics and Finance, LXII, 1993, Supplement, 1–40.

75. See C. Randall Henning, 'Europe's monetary union and the United States', *Foreign Policy*, 102, Spring 1996, 83–104.
76. The difficulties which would have to be overcome are indicated in Coleman, 'State traditions and comprehensive business associations'.
77. Ibid.
78. See OECD, *Economic Survey, Canada, 1995, 1996 and 1997*, Paris: OECD.
79. See OECD, *Economic Survey, Mexico, 1995, 1996 and 1997*, Paris: OECD; and Frederic S. Mishkin, 'Understanding financial crises: a developing country perspective', *Annual World Bank Conference on Development Economics, 1996*, New York: World Bank, 1997, pp. 29–62.
80. The problems of governance have been reflected in the dimensions of macroeconomic problems: see Hicklin, Robinson and Singh (eds), *Macroeconomic Issues Facing ASEAN Countries*.

7. Corporate interaction, direct investment and regional cooperation in industrializing Asia

Michael G. Plummer

Economic growth in Asia over the past decade has been the envy of the world. During the 1980s and early 1990s, economic ties between East Asian countries intensified, and closer regional trade links have made an important contribution to the region's economic growth. Significantly, deeper regional integration in East Asia has coincided with greater overall openness of their economies and an ongoing liberalization of their trade and investment regimes. Through policy reform, the structure of East Asian countries' production is becoming increasingly based on comparative advantage, and their ability to absorb more sophisticated foreign technology was enhanced by rapidly growing direct foreign investment (DFI) flows. *Prima facie* evidence suggests that a virtuous cycle is at work in East Asia, with DFI contributing to export growth, which in turn creates pressures for further trade and investment liberalization and even greater volumes of DFI flows.

The increase in regional interdependence is unique in that it has not been due to one hegemon at the 'core' that leads integration, though surely Japan has played an important role. In fact, over the 1986–92 period, the sources of East Asian DFI were primarily intraregional: half of all DFI flows in the region originated in other East Asian countries (predominantly Hong Kong, Singapore, Korea and Taiwan); less than one-fifth originated in Japan and only one-tenth came from the United States and Western Europe.[1] The sectoral composition of DFI has also been changing. In earlier periods, investment from advanced industrial countries were channelled primarily into natural resource-based industries and related sectors, while in more recent years the newly industrialized economies (NIEs) have been investing primarily in manufacturing, especially in electrical machinery, electronics, non-ferrous metals and chemicals.

This chapter considers the emergence of Asian developing countries as a source of DFI in the region and their role in spurring regional

193

interdependence. While triad countries continue to be critical investors in the region, developed-country DFI in Asia has been extensively analysed elsewhere in the literature, as well as in other contributions to this volume. The role of developing Asian countries is often underestimated and, hence, the bulk of our analysis is focused on non-triad investment. We begin in the next section with a theoretical approach to corporate strategies and policy formation, with a special application to developing Asia. While this model can be generalized, it is particularly relevant in explaining the role that foreign investors have played in the Asian liberalization process. Next, as a large part of Asian economic integration is due to the interaction of (overseas and Mainland) Chinese firms, we consider the web of Chinese corporate connections in regional trade and investment. While the literature on the interactions of overseas Chinese in Asia is fairly extensive, it mainly pertains to social and cultural considerations rather than explicit empirical evidence. Hence, much of this analysis is anecdotal, except at the national level where data are more easily retrievable (but in which case analysis of overseas Chinese interactions are indirect). In the subsequent section we discuss the case of DFI in mainland China, where overseas Chinese are clearly the most important foreign investors.

However, it is not only the Chinese who have emerged as major investors in the region; DFI from Korea has increased rapidly since the mid-1980s when regulations on outward DFI began to be lifted and the structural change in the Korean economy provided a push to such investment. We therefore analyse some econometric evidence of the determinants of Korean investment abroad as an example of 'non-triad' DFI.

Policy-led regional economic integration has not been a force in Asian economic integration to date, but the creation of the ASEAN free trade area in 1992 is a sign of things to come. Arguably, formal economic integration accords will play an important part in facilitating corporate integration in the region. In the final section we consider new developments in regional integration, as well as the mechanisms through which these accords will affect corporate strategies, and we offer some concluding remarks.

A MODEL OF DFI AND POLICY FORMATION

Although there is no general consensus as to what the 'Asian model' of economic development is (or, in fact, if one exists), an important feature which is generally accepted as an integral component is the focus on outward orientation, as opposed to an import-substitution approach to industrialization. In fact, most Asian 'tigers' are essentially transitional economies, in which they are changing from import substitution to outward orientation and export promotion. They have succeeded to varying degrees; the Asian currency crisis of 1997 will no doubt affect the speed of economic reform, but it is not clear in which direction.

While the international trade aspects of an import-substitution paradigm have been analysed extensively in the literature, the role of DFI as an important force for liberalization has been almost totally ignored. Yet liberalization of trade policies in Asia has taken place simultaneously with rapid increases in DFI inflows.

In an import-substitution orientated regime, there exists an investment policy dimension that is predicated on the same notion that countries should be self-sufficient and, to the greatest extent possible, independent of 'core-country' dominance, which has not only detrimental economic but also political implications.[2] In principle, the rule-of-thumb is to restrict or even ban DFI from sectors in which indigenous investors are able to function, and to put very· stringent investment restrictions (for example, in the form of severe performance requirements) on others, especially in more advanced areas such as automobiles, electronics and capital equipment production in which there is little or no hope of successful domestic undertakings without foreign participation. In order to bring DFI into these latter areas, countries have to compensate for the high transactions costs of functioning in the inward-looking economy. This is redressed through the provision of tax and other fiscal incentives, but especially through high external protection, which is consistent with the overall development strategy anyway. Hence, DFI is directed to areas in which the country has comparative *disadvantage*.

The effects of DFI 'tariff hopping' has been explored fairly extensively in the literature.[3] Neoclassical theory argues that DFI in such sectors tends to stifle economic growth and development because it distorts relative prices, draws resources into inefficient sectors, creates incentives for rent-seeking, imposes demand constraints, and limits productivity-enhancing interaction with the international market place.

What do inward-looking policies imply for domestic policy formation? Import substitution is designed to reduce exposure to international markets; restrictive DFI policies also try to do this. In fact, DFI is permitted into the country *only as a means to support import substitution*; that is, DFI is allowed to flow to sectors in which the country has comparative disadvantage and, hence, can substitute for imports.

Investment and trade are 'path dependent', that is, increases in investment into the country will be followed by increases in trade, similarly,
increases in trade will be associated with increases in investment (Lee
and Roland-Holst, forthcoming; Petri and Plummer 1996). Hence, if
investment and trade policies become more restrictive, it follows that
the path will lead toward zero trade (extreme import substitution). This
appears to be the logical conclusion to an 'effective' import-substitution
regime.

However, this analysis is static in nature and arguably misses a critical
policy dynamic that might distort the ostensible linearity of such 'path
dependency', at least in the downward direction. In fact, it is possible
that the DFI–trade interdependency sows the seeds of policy reform
even in a standard import-substitution model.[4]

The argument could be advanced as follows. Suppose, as is typical,
that foreign investors are attracted to a country in order to gain a
special tax holiday and to enjoy protection in the manufacturing sector.
With captive internal markets, affiliates of foreign multinationals will
be able to reap extra-normal profits and, at least in the short run, may
have little incentive to alter the current policy regime. Nevertheless, the
presence of a foreign investor (who, since DFI in capital-intensive
sectors is not footloose, will be present in the country for at least the
medium term) adds an international dimension to the domestic
economy that would not exist if DFI were prohibited. Foreign affiliates
by their very nature are more dependent on imported inputs (often
from their parents); relative to domestic firms, they will suffer more from
a highly restrictive commercial policy regime and would tend to exert
more pressure for liberalization. And as changes in tariff structures
have the characteristics of being 'public goods', in that lobbying by one
firm in a given sector will affect all firms in the sector, the influence of
foreign affiliates may be disproportional. Additionally, since we have
assumed that DFI is permitted in capital-intensive and high-tech sectors
that often serve as inputs to the production of final goods, the effective
rate of protection for these goods will increase, *ceteris paribus*. This
allows the government to reduce nominal protection in the final-goods
sector without changing the amount of protection accorded domestic
value added.

Moreover, the evolving modern economy is characterized by an
increasing global division of labour in which international affiliates
become part of a larger production chain. Foreign affiliates in inward-
looking economies will be cut off from these networks, and the pace of
globalization of production makes such a situation increasingly costly.[5]
One might also consider the international ramifications of such incen-

tives for liberalization, as a country may need to be more responsive to the demands of foreign affiliates if they must compete for DFI with other countries.[6]

Linking the effects of trade policy innovations to changes in investment is certainly not new to the literature. However, existing work tends to focus on how altering tariffs induces changes in relative factor demands and, hence, factor returns (in the case of a fixed capital stock). If endogenous capital accumulation is permitted, protection could have a permanent effect on the growth rate, no doubt one incentive for an import-substitution regime. As noted by Baldwin and Seghezza (1996), there is a problem with this approach, not the least of which is that it ignores the stylized facts. They develop a dynamic model to test for 'trade-induced, investment-led growth' taking into account the cost of protection on imported intermediate goods, which has an 'anti-investment' aspect to weigh against the 'pro-investment effect'. While they do not consider DFI in the same way as we do here, the intuition is the same, in that they focus on the secondary distortions caused by the protective environment. On the other hand, Froot and Yoffie (1993) construct a model in which 'traditional' sectors not characterized by economies of scale will have a weakened incentive to protect (and, in fact, will push for liberalization) as production becomes increasingly mobile internationally. Ultimately over time, this will be true even for sectors exhibiting increasing returns:

> And to the extent that foreign direct investment occurs, and as long as it is an imperfect substitute for trade, it should diminish the force of increasing returns-based arguments for domestic protection. Foreign firms with local production (and local employment) will advocate liberalization.   (Froot and Yoffie 1993: 146)[7]

Figures 7.1 and 7.2 present our argument more formally from the perspective of foreign affiliates of multinationals ('foreign firms') operating in a developing country. Figure 7.1 shows the costs and benefits associated with a protected environment using the framework outlined above. Benefits from 'special preferences' take the form of special protection through tariffs and non-tariff barriers, fiscal incentives, and so on. We assume that these benefits can be quantified in money terms for the firm and reflected in a 45-degree line through the origin. The 'demand costs' (DC) associated with the protected environment are increasing in special preferences, as the efficiency costs associated with greater protection grow at an increasing rate.[8] Hence, the DC curve exhibits positive first- and second-order conditions; its slope will be a

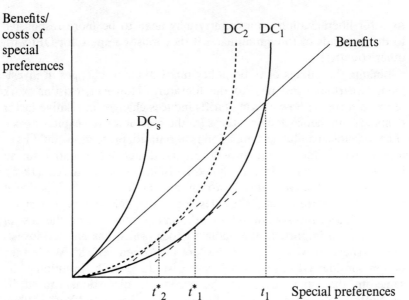

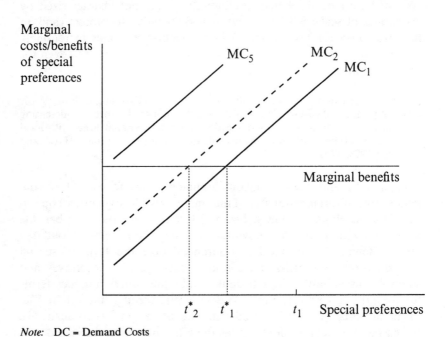

Note: DC = Demand Costs

Figure 7.1 Costs and benefits of a protective environment to foreign firms

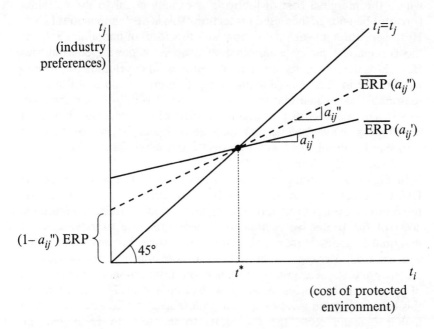

Notes:
1. ERP = $(t_i - a_{ij}t_i)/(1 \text{ X } a_{ij})$, $t_j = (1 \text{ X } a_{ij})$ ERP $+ a_{ij}t_i$
2. At t^*, $t_i = t_j =$ ERP.

*Figure 7.2 Costs of protection under alternative input–output coefficient
assumptions*

function of a number of national characteristics of the host country, for
example, its dependence on international trade. A country like Singapore, for example, will have an extremely steep DC curve (see DC), as
its international trade comes to over three times national value added.
However, the slope of the curve will also depend on the production
function of the industry, with more imported-input-dependent sectors
having steeper DC curves.

In addition, we could include the cost of lobbying in this model. After
all, this is the essence of the endogenous tariff literature: the higher the
level of protection that politicians grant, the greater the cost to
the economy[9] and, hence, the larger the cost to them in terms of votes.
Politicians force lobbyists to pay more in order to obtain marginal
increases in protection. The tariff level that optimizes the private-
welfare functions of economic agents and politicians will be the one

where the marginal cost of lobbying is exactly equal to the marginal (private) benefits of increased protection. This is the 'endogenous tariff'. However, while it is debatable how well this form of bargaining reflects the commercial policy determination process in developed countries (for which the model was created), the process in developing countries – particularly in Asia – is fundamentally different. While it still may be reasonable to assume that the costs associated with lobbying are positive, it is not necessarily true that these costs will be increasing in special preferences. Nevertheless, assuming zero, linear or increasing costs associated with lobbying will not affect our analysis here; rather, it will merely affect the slope of the DC line.

In Figure 7.1, foreign firms will break even at the point where the DC_1 curve cuts the benefits curve (t_1). However, from its perspective, the optimal level of protection will be at t^*_1, that is, where the marginal costs of the protective regime to foreign firms are exactly equal to marginal benefits. Now, suppose that, over time, the costs associated with protection change in the light of a more sophisticated division of labour (and, hence, greater reliance on international sources) and of dynamic inefficiencies spawned by the import-substitution regime. In this case, any given level of special preferences will be associated with higher demand costs; the DC shifts to the left (to DC_2) and the endogenous tariff decreases to t^*_2. In other words, foreign firms either reduce their lobbying activities or, perhaps, lobby proactively in favour of liberalization. Once again, the magnitude of the DC curve shift and, hence, the change in the endogenous tariff will be a function of both host-country-specific and industry-specific characteristics.

Another way to look at this problem from the foreign firms' perspective is to consider the effective rate of protection (ERP) facing the industry, which captures the degree to which actual value added in an industry is being protected.[10] Figure 7.2 focuses on the effects of a changing international division of labour on the structure of net benefits accruing to the foreign firm (that is, as proxied through ERP). We adopt the same notation from the ERP literature for simplicity. Advantages of a protective environment are grouped into t_{ji}, whereas the costs of the protected environment are denoted by t_i. Along the ERP ($...$) lines, the ERP is constant; as protection increases, the ERP lines show by how much industry preferences have to increase in order to prevent the ERP from changing, given a_{ij}. Hence, at $t_i = 0$, $t_j = (1-a_{ij})$ ERP and, of course, $t_i = t_j =$ ERP where ERP ($...$) crosses the 45-degree line (for example, at t^* in Figure 7.2).

The curves ERP (a_{ji}') and ERP (a_{ij}'') correspond to the same ERP under different assumptions of the input–output coefficient a_{ij}. The larger a_{ij} the greater the change required in t_j for a given change in t_i if the ERP is to remain constant. Therefore, with a changing international division of labour such that foreign affiliates engage in a greater degree of specialization and rely more on imported inputs, a_{ij} increases and, at the margin, the cost of the protected environment to foreign firms increases. This implies a stronger incentive to push for liberalization.[11]

It should be noted that many of the arguments developed above can be applied to domestic firms as well, especially in terms of the direction of the marginal incentives for libralization. In fact, it would be a great stretch indeed to attribute the rapid liberalization programmes of East Asian economies to foreign firms alone; clearly, many domestic firms, as well as growth-minded policy-makers with their minds on the economy rather than votes, played essential roles. In fact, while DFI can sometimes constitute a significant amount of capital formation in certain sectors, only in a few East Asian countries (for example, in city-states of Singapore and Hong Kong and in Malaysia) has DFI constituted much more than 10 per cent of domestic capital formation. However, as argued here, it is likely that affiliates of foreign firms will be affected more at the margin by these trends and, hence, will be more inclined to push for reform (though, clearly, they will not be the only ones).

In sum, in the modern international economy, there exist strong incentives for countries to keep open trade and investment regimes, and DFI can serve as an important catalyst, regardless of whether it comes from developed or developing countries.

OVERSEAS CHINESE AND CORPORATE RELATIONSHIPS

The private-sector economy in South East Asia is controlled largely by ethnic Chinese, a fact that has led to delicate social considerations and balancing over the years. For example, prior to the New Economic Policy in Malaysia in 1969, which led to a highly aggressive affirmative action programme in favour of indigenous Malays (*bumiputra*), up to 90 per cent of the private sector was controlled by ethnic Chinese; 25 years later, that ratio would fall to around two-thirds, but still a high proportion considering that ethnic Chinese in Malaysia comprise approximately one-third of the population. It is, perhaps, easiest to ascertain the magnitude of Chinese capital in South-East Asia in the cases of Malaysia and Indonesia, where they stand out culturally, but it is much more difficult to do so in the case of Thailand, where Chinese

over the years have been closely integrated into the indigenous popu-
lation. Clearly, the vast majority of the populations of Singapore, Hong
Kong and Taiwan is Chinese, and these economies form the core of
Chinese corporate interaction.

This is not to suggest that the *economies* of South-East Asia are
necessarily dominated by ethnic Chinese. After independence, South-
East Asian economies became largely state-directed, with abundant
natural resources allowing for the perpetuation of myriad state-owned
and/or state-directed enterprises. Hence, the private sector was
restricted to various degrees in each economy, thereby limiting the
potential for a strong 'dominance' on the part of the ethnic Chinese.
Yoshihara (1988) in his oft-cited study refers to the 'rise of ersatz
capitalism in Southeast Asia,' with ersatz capitalism denoting state-
control, rather than ethnic-Chinese or foreign dominance.

According to Yoshihara (1988: 51), in the resource-rich ASEAN
countries Chinese capital is dominant in the banking and light industries
sectors and has a substantial presence in property development, mining,
plantation agriculture, trade and machinery. Private indigenous capital,
on the other hand, is dominant in no sector and has a substantial
presence only in banking, property development and plantation agriculture. In all manufacturing sectors, indigenous capital plays a minor
role.

The large presence of ethnic Chinese in the private sector of South-
East Asia has been ascribed to many factors, including the influence of
colonialists in bringing Chinese into their colonies as merchants, as well
as cultural dispositions on the part of both the Chinese and the
indigenous population (Yoshihara 1988).[12] Thus, the success of Chinese
corporate strategies relied not only on a unique system of relationships
but also on state patronage at a crucial period.

Overseas Chinese corporate interactions tend to be based on informal
relationships that place a strong emphasis on trust. As these relationships often evolve in an underdeveloped legal environment –
compounded by problems associated with more than one country in
the case of an overseas joint venture – informal contracts and commitments must be enforced somehow, and this is done by reputation. If a
party reneges on a contact or does not pull through, this 'loss of face'
could be devastating and might severely impede the ability to undertake
future business.

Thus, it is understandable that business partnerships are arranged
between parties who are not only familiar to each other on a personal
level but also have established a strong bond of trust. These ventures
usually begin within families or extended families and often stay family-

centred (Yoshihara 1988). Moreover, in overseas Chinese communities, common regional roots and language tend to be important (according to the many Chinese dialects) and a strong emphasis is placed on interactions at the communal level.

These types of arrangements tend to be flexible, long-lasting, and lucrative, as evidenced by the great success of overseas Chinese. However, there have been social problems in host countries, as the Chinese are often seen to be exclusionary *vis-à-vis* non-Chinese. This in turn has lead to a less-favourable social and business environment for the Chinese, at times leading to bloodshed.

DIRECT INVESTMENT IN MAINLAND CHINA

Given the strong linguistic and cultural affinities between overseas Chinese and mainland China, it is not difficult to predict that ethnic Chinese capital would be among the first to take advantage of the opening up of the Chinese market which began with Deng's Four Modernizations in 1979. With rising wages in key markets such as Singapore, Hong Kong, Thailand and Malaysia, coupled with increasingly fluid international capital markets as the 1980s progressed, the locational advantages of cheap and abundant labour in mainland China and an increasingly hospitable local investment environment proved extremely attractive. Moreover, the traditional nature of doing business between ethnic Chinese made the lack of a strong legal framework less problematic in arranging business ventures, though they clearly influenced the type of arrangement.

A number of studies (for example, Thoburn *et al.* 1990) survey issues pertinent not only to the importance of overseas Chinese investment in China but also to the rationale for mainland China's courting of this capital. Four major motivations on the part of the Chinese government are frequently cited:

1. to diversify and modernize the economic structure of China;
2. to bring in foreign know-how, business practices, expertise and especially new technologies;
3. to tap into ready-made foreign markets and international production chains; and
4. to create additional sources of capital and foreign exchange.

These motivations are not unlike those of other developing countries; however, the size and transitional nature of the Chinese economy, coupled with the strong desire to catch up after years of autarky under Mao, in many ways made these needs more acute.

Pan and Tse (1996) test a series of hypotheses regarding investor motivations in China and corporate strategies. In particular, they focus on the strategies of foreign firms in forming cooperative relationships with *other* foreign firms. *Inter alia*, they find that a foreign firm would be more likely to bring another foreign firm into a cooperation venture as: (a) the risk level in China increases; (b) foreign firms choose a high-control mode of operation, such as equity joint ventures instead of contractual joint ventures; and (c) bilateral trade with China increases. Moreover, they note that Japanese firms in China are more likely to form a joint venture with another foreign firm than is the case for other triad countries.

Aggregate data on DFI give a strong indication of the importance of ethnic Chinese investment in mainland China at the macro level. Table 7.1 shows actual DFI flows in China by investing country/region. Total DFI flows into China have grown rapidly, from under $2 billion in 1985 to $3.5 billion in 1990.[13] More recent data show that DFI inflows in the 1990s were many times as large, growing to $34 billion in 1994 and $38 billion in 1995.[14] The data are more impressive when it is considered that before the 1980s DFI in China was essentially zero.

Table 7.1 Direct investment in China: actual investment flows ($ million)

	1985	1988	1990
Total	1956	3199	3487
of which			
Japan	315	515	503
United States	357	236	456
Hong Kong/Macau	956	2095	1913
Germany	24	15	64
France	33	23	21
United Kingdom	71	34	13
Australia	14	4	25
Singapore	10	28	50

Source: China Free Trade and Price Statistics/China Statistical Yearbook, various years.

Hong Kong/Macau continue to be the largest investors in China, particularly in Guangdong Province, with a total of $1.9 billion in 1990, which has increased from less than $1 billion in 1985. The second largest investors are Japan and the United States, with investments of $503 million and $456 million, respectively. However, Singapore exhibits the fastest increase in China over the 1985–90 period, rising from $10 million to $50 million. Official and unofficial investment from Taiwan, which is not reported in the statistics, and from Korea, whose presence is undoubtedly large in north-east China, are also large and are growing in importance (Kim 1995).

Clearly, the rapid increase in ethnic Chinese DFI is noteworthy. In fact, a great deal of DFI in China flows through Hong Kong in partnership with developed-country multinationals, which form joint ventures with Hong Kong firms due to its 'competitive advantage' in investing in China. While the return of Hong Kong to China in 1997 holds some political risks, it could reduce significantly the transactions costs of doing business in China through Hong Kong and, hence, the latter might serve as an even more attractive conduit of international investment into the mainland. This was probably a motivation behind the business community's pro-Chinese stance in the years leading up to the changeover.

Economic growth in China is concentrated in the coastal regions (see, for example, Lardy 1994). By far, Guangdong Province is the largest recipient of direct investment, with $1.2 billion in 1989 alone, followed by Shanghai ($422 million), Fujian ($329 million) and Beijing ($318 million).[15] This investment flows from Hong Kong or from Hong Kong–foreign joint ventures (often with Taiwan). Liaoning and Shandong Provinces, which have benefited from Korean DFI, also have DFI projects amounting to over $100 million. In part, these figures are a reflection of the increase in outward DFI from South Korea. This DFI flow has been induced by a combination of Korean restructuring, fundamental economic and political policy changes and rapidly rising wage rates. Thus, reforms in the NIEs as well as in China have generated the DFI flows to China (see Lee and Plummer 1992).

Direct Taiwanese investment flows appear to have concentrated mainly in Fujian Province. Total approved Taiwan investment flows in China came to $5.1 billion over the 1991–95/6 period, electronics and electrical machinery ($775 million), food and beverages ($591 million) and plastic products ($563 million) being the three largest sectors (Tu 1997). As noted above, these figures generally exclude DFI flows through Hong Kong and other vehicles. Interestingly, the size of Taiwanese investment in China has been kept relatively low by Taiwanese – rather than mainland Chinese – government restrictions, as officials are nervous about the political ramifications of an unduly large presence of Taiwanese investment in the mainland.

Thoburn *et al.* (1990) survey the distribution of foreign investment under various kinds of contracts in China. This is done for the 1985–8 period for both China and Guangdong Province, where the role of overseas Chinese capital is arguably strongest. They find that equity joint ventures in 1988 constituted 51 per cent of contracts in China compared to 39 per cent in Guangdong, whereas contractual joint ventures are more popular in Guangdong (39 per cent compared to 26 per cent). However, in both cases, the share of equity joint ventures had increased substantially since 1985. Moreover, the share of contracts associated with 'processing and assembly, compensation trade and international leasing' experienced a rapid growth rate for China and Guangdong, comprising 14 per cent and 18 per cent respectively, of all contracts in 1988.

DETERMINANTS OF OUTWARD DFI FROM INDUSTRIALIZING ASIA: THE CASE OF KOREA

There is no reason to believe that outward DFI from developing countries should be determined by different motivations than developed countries on the whole, though the divergent stages of economic development suggest that DFI would flow to different industries and countries than might be the case of developed-country DFI. It could be expected that the major contribution to the theory of the determinants of DFI (see, for example, Rugman 1980, and Dunning 1988) should, therefore, be generally independent of the stage of economic development of the capital-exporting country. In this section, we try to gauge the determinants of Korean DFI using a simple cross-sectional model. We limit the analysis to Korea, given the difficulties of obtaining reliable, disaggregated DFI data for the other NIEs.

As noted above, the Korean government severely restricted outward DFI outflows before 1985. Since then, they have been gradually liberalized, and Korea has emerged as an important investor not only in northeastern China but also in the ASEAN countries. Moreover, it has been involved in 'reverse DFI' in developed countries; that is, outward investment to the United States and Europe in order to set up distribution networks and acquire new technologies.

DFI theory suggests a wide variety of potential determinants to be examined in empirical analysis. While estimation of ownership and internalization motivations are beyond the scope of our study, we focus on locational considerations, which have been at the heart of empirical analysis of DFI determinants in the economics literature.

We use DFI data from the Bank of Korea, *Overseas Direct Investment Statistics*, 1992 and 1995, in order to gain intuition into the determinants of Korean investment abroad, including the trade–investment nexus.[16]

The model estimated includes standard variables suggested by theory, such as distance, general measures of market supply potential (GDP), and potential market demand (population), as well as exports. Because of this selection of variables, the model resembles the familiar gravity models of the empirical trade literature. Although sometimes criticized for their weak theoretical foundations in the trade context, gravity models also provide a natural framework for the analysis of DFI flows.

Our model specification is of the following form:

$$DFI = f \{GDP, POP, DIST, Asdum, EXP \ (t, t-1, t+1)\}$$

where:

GDP = host-country gross domestic product, a proxy for market poten-
    tial (supply side);
Pop = host-country population, a proxy for potential market demand;
DIST = distance between the investor and host countries, a proxy for
    transactions costs;
Asdum = a regional dummy variable for the ASEAN countries;
EXP = contemporaneous, lagged, and 'forward-loaded' Korean exports,
    a proxy for transactions costs and for market receptivity for the
    source country's products.

The leads and lags in exports were estimated as a means of avoiding the inherent simultaneity problems. However, as trade and investment decisions are undertaken simultaneously, it is unlikely that the simultaneity problem can be avoided entirely. Predictably, lag structure made very little difference in the results of the regressions.

The Korean DFI data are sufficient for regressions at the aggregate manufactures level and for labour-intensive manufactures. While it would have been useful to have further disaggregation, paucity of data precluded such analysis. The results are presented in Table 7.2 for both single-year (1992) and pooled data (1992 and 1995).

Several general results obtain. First, the R^2s are fairly low; in all cases, the model explained less than 20 per cent of the variance in the dependent variable. This is probably to be expected, given the relatively few degrees of freedom in the regressions and the complicated nature of outward Korean investment, in which the government continues to play an important regulatory role. Estimated coefficients on the size variables (GDP and population) tend to be of the expected sign (where statistically significant), suggesting that size does, indeed, matter. The positive estimate coefficients for the distance variable give credence to

Table 7.2 Determinants of Korean DFI

Independent variable	All manufactures		Labour-intensive manufactures	
	DFI 1992	Pooled[a]	DFI 1992	Pooled[a]
Constant	11681[b]	−1033[b]	−1707	−1768
GDP	−0.14	−1.2	0.46	−0.1
Pop	49.92[d]	7.9[c]	5.2[d]	6.6[d]
Distance	0.36	1.7[d]	0.43	0.35
ASEAN	2084[d]	985	1850[b]	3476[d]
Exp.^{2}	0.001[d]	0.001	0.01[b]	0.02[d]
Adj. R^2	0.19	0.06	0.19	0.13
N	67	155	37	83

Notes:
[a] In the pooled observations, a time binary variable was added in order to capture any difference between years. It was statistically insignificant except in the case of labour-intensive manufactures, where the estimated coefficient came to 1503 and was statistically significant at the 95 per cent level.
[b] Significance at the 85 per cent level.
[c] Significance at the 90 per cent level.
[d] Significance at the 95 per cent level.
Lag structure of exports makes little or no difference in the results of the regressions.

the argument that firms will choose to invest abroad – rather than export directly – over longer distances. Further, the regression results support the importance of the trade–investment link; exports are positively correlated with DFI. The ASEAN binary variable is statistically significant in three out of the four reported regressions and is always estimated to be positive (and tends to be larger) in the case of labour-intensive manufactures.

REGIONAL AND CORPORATE INTEGRATION IN EAST ASIA

Increasingly, developing countries have been placing a stronger emphasis on technology transfer in their multilateral and bilateral relationships. The evidence of this is ubiquitous, from the preponderance of requests for technical assistance in development aid and cooperation programmes to the 'virtuous cycle' of policy liberalization stemming from the desire to promote DFI capital inflows as a means of private-sector-led technology transfer. Regional economic integration accords can promote DFI inflows through reductions in transactions costs (whether they are border or non-border in origin); in doing so, they are able to establish an attractive business environment within which multinationals can easily profit from a vertical division of labour, as well as facilitating the emergence of multinationals within the developing region itself.[17] Of course, the same is true for developed countries. Also, as is noted in the theoretical model above (pp. 207), DFI inflows can set in motion a virtuous cycle of policy reform that will support the liberalization process.

Hence, regional economic integration accords can help to enhance the locational attractiveness of a region. In fact, particularly in the highly integrated world economy of the 1990s, the 'externalities' associated with good or bad policies in one country often spill over to its neighbours. Lower transactions costs in the region, by freeing up trade and investment, will through, say, a free-trade area and ancillary agreements not only make for a more attractive regional business environment but also highlight the importance of one country's investment policies for the rest of the region. Regional economic integration can help to internalize this externality by providing regional rules as well as constant dialogue and peer pressure.

Developing countries tend to place a stronger emphasis on technology transfer than, say, developed countries because of the greater technological gap which may be evident in not only production technologies, but also management techniques, other business practices, corporate culture and various training programmes. The ASEAN free-trade area (AFTA), for instance, was created mainly as an instrument to attract more DFI to the region at a time when competition for such flows was deemed to be increasing (especially from China, but also from South Asia and Latin America). Some have even described AFTA as more of an investment pact than a trade pact.[18]

Although the link between DFI and technology transfer has been firmly established, the relationship between trade and technology transfer is less well known. Through trade liberalization, countries are also able to stimulate technological development. For example, trade leads to the adaptation of new technologies from abroad by increasing the potential for success in using these technologies to crack foreign markets; also, increased competition forces domestic firms to place a higher priority on creating their own or importing new technologies (Pissarides 1995). This implies a strong incentive for developing countries which emphasize technology transfer (for example, all East Asian countries) to liberalize even unilaterally.

Moreover, in order to take best advantage of these new technologies, countries find that they must establish strong intellectual property protection laws and means of enforcement. Without an attractive, protective environment in which multinationals can operate and in which domestic firms can invest in new innovations, the process of technology transfer is significantly inhibited. Formal regional economic integration agreements can help in creating a strong underlying framework for the protection of intellectual property, and peer pressure in the implementation of associated laws.[19]

While there exists a substantial literature on the advantages and disadvantages of formal regional economic integration accords, the debate ultimately centres on the effect of such accords on domestic policy formation. For example, the North American Free Trade Agreement (NAFTA) was sold in the United States more as a means of encouraging further economic reform in Mexico than for its trade creation/diversion merits or de-merits. Most scholars, policy-makers, and business people would support formal regional integration if it leads to a more favourable policy environment. In Asia, where *de facto* formal accords did not exist until 1992 – when AFTA was formed – regional economic integration programmes were being developed as part of a *process* of economic reform, rather than as a separate policy strategy. There is a strong emphasis on 'open regionalism' in AFTA; the Philippines has tabled a proposal (backed by Singapore and Indonesia) to multilateralize intraregional tariff cuts. Moreover, the only region-wide arrangement in the Asia-Pacific, the Asia-Pacific Economic Cooperation (APEC) organization, appears to be committed to forming a region of 'open trade and investment' in a non-discriminatory way. This will lead to a more open environment in which to do business, particularly since most of the interaction in APEC and increasingly in AFTA regards nuts-and-bolts policies related to trade and investment facilitation measures, which often constitute the most important 'taxes' on regional trade and investment (Cecchini 1988).

Overseas Chinese have played a critical role in bringing the region together through trade and investment. It is likely that, as China continues to liberalize and Korea and Taiwan lift restrictions on outward and inward DFI, this will continue to be the case. In this chapter, we have reviewed the nature of Chinese corporate interactions and, more generally, the role of DFI originating from the NIEs, using the case of Korea as a (non-Chinese) example of a non-triad, new source of DFI in the region. However, the analysis was mainly at the macro level; to get the best picture of corporate interaction, alliances and strategies in developing Asia, one must rely on micro data and case studies. We have cited a number of studies which have shed some light on the many issues involved, but clearly more work remains to be done.

NOTES

1. United Nations (1995).
2. The political implications of a large foreign investment presence are especially important in the case of developing countries which are at early stages of building their nation-states (for example, in Asia) or those which have had a history of political and economic excesses in their relationship with a developed country (for Latin America, the United States; for Africa, Europe). The import-substitution paradigm becomes popular in such an environment even independently of any theoretical claims to economic effectiveness.
3. This body of analysis, most elegantly articulated by the 'immizerating-growth' literature, finds a key theoretical contribution in Bhagwati (1971).
4. A related point applied to the context of regional economic integration is found in Petri and Plummer (1996).
5. Of course, this will also be true of domestic firms. But foreign affiliates will tend to be more conscious of the problem and, in any event, more dependent on this global network of which they are a necessary part.
6. We would like to thank Professor Shigeyuki Abe for pointing out this possibility.
7. Hence, Froot and Yoffie (1993) approach the liberalization incentive from the *national* perspective; in this chapter we argue that foreign firms will play an important (though by no means unique) role in moulding this incentive.
8. While the existing endogenous protection literature also makes this assumption as a means of proxying costs from the *economy-wide* perspective (discussed below), we focus here on the firm: a more distorted environment makes doing business more costly on the supply side, and chokes off sales on the demand side.
9. This is because efficiency losses of protection are assumed to be increasing in special preferences.
10. We assume non-negative ERPs here because: (a) it is not clear in this model why a foreign firm would opt to enter into a country giving it a negative ERP; and (b) firms would certainly find it in their interests to lobby for liberalization in the case of negative ERPs, as the protective environment works to their detriment.
11. In theory, the change in the international division of labour could just lead the foreign firms to lobby for more protection, possibly creating an additional round of protection increases (particularly if product j is used as an intermediate input). But if we assume non-zero costs to lobbying and the general equilibrium effects of such a reaction, the probability of this response is lower.
12. Yoshihara (1988) is the most exhaustive book in the literature and surveys not only the origins of ethnic Chinese in the region but also histories of the more important families.
13. Plummer and Montes (1995).
14. These data are from ADB (1997) but should be treated with caution. As is noted elsewhere in this volume, DFI data are notorious for being inaccurate in both developed and developing countries. None the less, they serve as important indicators.
15. Plummer and Montes (1995).
16. For a closer examination of the trade–investment nexus and the Korean regressions in a cross-country context, see Kreinin *et al.* (1997), on which this section draws.
17. ASEAN multinationals, for example, have been increasing in number and importance since the creation of AFTA. In fact, some of the largest investors in Vietnam are ASEAN-based, with ASEAN DFI accounting for fully 20 per cent of the country's total.
18. Ariff (1996).
19. Having recognized this, the ASEAN countries have developed a regional framework for intellectual property protection.

REFERENCES

Ariff, Mohamed (1996), 'Outlooks for ASEAN and NAFTA externalities', in Shoji Nishijima and Peter H. Smith (eds), *Cooperation or Rivalry? Regional Integration in the Americas and the Pacific Rim*, Boulder, Col.: Westview Press, pp. 209–24.

Asian Development Bank (ADB) (1997), *Asian Development Outlook 1997 and 1998*, Manila: Asian Development Bank.

Baldwin, Richard E. and Elena Seghezza (1996), 'Testing for trade-induced, investment-led growth', NBER Working Paper 5416, Washington, DC: NBER.

Bhagwati, Jagdish N. (1971), 'The generalized theory of distortions and welfare', in J. Bhagwati *et al.*, (eds), *Trade, the Balance of Payments, and Growth*, Amsterdam: North-Holland.

Cecchini, Paolo (1988), *The Costs of Non-Europe*, Brussels: Commission of the European Communities.

Chen, Edward K.Y. and Teresa Y.C. Wong (1997), 'Hong Kong: foreign direct investment and trade linkages in manufacturing', in Wendy Dobson and Chia Siow Yue (eds), *Multinationals and East Asian Integration*, Ottawa: International Development Research Centre, ch. 4.

Dunning, John H. (1980), 'The eclectic paradigm of international production: a restatement and some possible extensions', *Journal of International Business Studies*, **19**(1), 1–31.

Froot, Kenneth A. and David B. Yoffie (1993), 'Trading blocs and the incentives to protect: implications for Japan and East Asia', in Jeffrey A. Frankel and Miles Kahler (eds), *Regionalism and Rivalry: Japan and the United States in Pacific Asia*, Chicago: University of Chicago Press, pp. 125–53.

Kim, Si Joong (1995), 'Structural change in the Korean economy and Korean investment in China and ASEAN', in Sumner J. LaCroix, Michael G. Plummer and Keun Lee (eds), *Emerging Patterns of East Asian Investment in China: From Korea, Taiwan, and Hong Kong*, New York: M.E. Sharpe.

Kreinin, Mordechai E., Michael G. Plummer and Shigeyuki Abe (1997a), 'Export and direct foreign investment links: a three-way comparison', paper presented at *International Links and Policy Formation*, Kobe, Japan, June.

——, —— and —— (1997b), 'Motives for Japanese DFI', mimeo.

Lardy, Nicholas R. (1994), *China in the World Economy*, Washington, DC: Institute for International Economics.

Lee, Hiro and David Roland-Holst (eds) (forthcoming), *Economic Development and Cooperation in the Pacific Basin: Trade, Investment, and Environmental Issues*, (New York: Cambridge University Press.

Lee, Keun and Michael G. Plummer (1992), 'Competitive advantages, two-way foreign investment, and domestic capital formation in Korea', *Asian Economic Journal*, **4**(2), 93–11.

Pan, Yigang and David K. Tse (1996), 'Cooperative strategies between foreign firms in an overseas country', *Journal of International Business Studies*, **27**(5), Special Issue.

Petri, Peter A. and Michael G. Plummer (1996), 'The determinants of direct foreign investment', Brandeis University Working Paper.

Pissarides, Christopher A. (1995), 'Trade and the returns to human capital in developing countries', mimeo, October.

Plummer, Michael G. and Manuel F. Montes (1995), 'Direct investment in China: an introduction', in Sumner J. LaCroix, Michael Plummer and Keun Lee (eds), *Emerging Patterns of East Asian Investment in China: From Korea, Taiwan, and Hong Kong*, New York: M.E. Sharpe.

Rodrik, Dani (1986), 'Tariff, subsidies, and welfare with endogenous policy', *Journal of International Economics*, **21**, 285–300.

—— (1996), 'Understanding economic policy reform', *Journal of Economic Literature*, xxxiv, March, 9–41.

Rugman, Alan M. (1980), 'Internalization as a general theory of foreign direct investment: a re-appraisal of the literature', *Weltwirtschaftliches Archiv*, **116**(2), 365–79.

—— (1981), *Inside the Multinationals: The Economics of Internal Markets*, New York: Columbia University Press.

—— and Richard Hodgetts (1995), *International Business: A Strategic Management Approach*, San Francisco: McGraw-Hill.

Thoburn, John T., H.M. Leung, Esther Chau and S.H. Tang (1990), *Foreign Investment in China under the Open Policy: The Experience of Hong Kong Companies*, Aldershot, UK: Avebury.

Tu, Jenn-hwa (1997), 'Taiwan: a solid manufacturing base and emerging regional source of investment', in Wendy Dobson and Chia Siow Yue (eds), *Multinationals and East Asian Integration*, Ottawa: International Development Research Centre.

United Nations (1995), *World Investment Report 1995*, New York: United Nations.

Yamazawa, Ippei and Akihito Asano (1996), 'Trade–investment and productivity nexus in Asia-Pacific: review of existing studies', Working Paper APEC/SC/HIT/DP, no. 7, March.

Yoshihara, Khnio (1988), *The Rise of Ersatz Capitalism in South-East Asia*, Singapore: Oxford University Press.

Zhang, Hai Yan and Daniel van den Bulcke (1996), 'International management strategies of Chinese multinational firms', in John Child and Yuan Lu (eds), *Management Issues in China. Vol. II: International Enterprises*, London: Routledge.

Zhang, Zhaoyang and Chen Kang (1997), 'China: a rapidly emerging light-manufacturing base in Guangdong Province', in Wendy Dobson and Chia Siow Yue (eds), *Multinationals and East Asian Integration*, Ottawa: International Development Research Centre.

8. Bank loan capitalism and financial crises: Japanese and Korean experiences

Terutomo Ozawa

Economic development – in essence, an expansion of the *real* sector's productive capacity – requires funding. Investments in productive capacity need to be financed by one means or another. Whether a country can do this job successfully depends on how effectively its financial industry (the *money* sector) can mobilize and utilize savings, domestic as well as foreign, and other financial resources to this end. In other words, economic development necessitates simultaneous and synchronized co-evolution in the country's real and money sectors. Money is not a 'veil' of the real sector; indeed, finance matters – and matters a lot for the process of economic development, which is nothing but a process of real capital formation.

There are three basic ways of funding capital formation: (a) to sell equity interests (stocks); (b) to borrow by issuing debt instruments (bonds and other securities); and (c) to use the banking system to create credit, namely bank loans. Capitalism that is dominated by the first two types of finance may be called 'securities-market capitalism' and is best exemplified by present-day Anglo-Saxon style capitalism. Conversely, capitalism that relies on bank loans to a much greater extent than securities may be identified as 'bank-loan capitalism', as is characterized by Japanese-style (and, in varying degrees, Korean-style and other Asian-style) financing of economic development. Because of the strongly speculative and high-risk nature of investment involved in the securities market, some call it 'casino capitalism' (Strange 1997). Both types of capitalism operate banking, but there are some institutional differences between Anglo-Saxon-style and Japanese-style banking.

Other than the institutional differences, the West itself has previously gone through the early stages of development in which their style of capitalism was once more proportionately dependent on bank loans than securities. In general, when a country is still in its early stages of

214

economic development – hence in a low state of financial development – it is expected that bank loans will be the primary source of finance, along with private finance (informal financial markets, such as borrowings from relatives and friends). The securities markets develop gradually as a long-term function of economic growth as discretionary personal savings (as opposed to bare minimum basic savings) rise in increasing amounts and savers begin to prefer risks (hence, higher yields) to safety.

In the context of the Asian experience, Japan, Korea and Taiwan in particular, actively made use of bank loans as a powerful policy instrument to achieve economic objectives. Partly because of their colonial ties with Japan, both Korea and Taiwan adopted Japan's financial system as a model in organizing their financial systems and in using them as a strategic instrument for industrialization. But they introduced their own innovative features which were different from the Japanese structure. Indeed, Japanese-style bank-loan capitalism has been quite different in many ways from the others, even from its Korean counterpart, its near clone in a number of ways.

Most interestingly, in the context of the recent financial turmoil in Asia, Japan and Korea both experienced an acute banking crisis, causing a credit crunch and aggravating their recessions. Moreover, Korea helplessly witnessed its won fall precipitously in value and had to seek an IMF rescue package of $58.5 billion in exchange for its promises of reforms. Japan, though not dependent on outside assistance, had to squeeze out $250 billion for the bailout of its banking sector. In fact, the two are (so far) the only 'northern' East Asian economies to be embroiled in banking débâcles, sharing a somewhat similar fate with their 'southern' brethren, notably Indonesia and Thailand. This chapter explores what has transpired in, and gone wrong with, Japan and Korea during the course of their pursuit of bank-loan capitalism.

TOWARD A THEORY OF GOVERNMENT-AUGMENTED BANK-LOAN CAPITALISM

CA-deficit-based versus central-bank-based finances

Any rapidly growing economy in the early phases of economic development must cope with the situation in which internal savings, however large they may be, tend to be exceeded by domestic investment. Hence, how to cover this inevitable deficiency of internal savings is a critical issue in formulating a successful strategy of rapid industrialization.

Basically, two possible solutions are available. One is a familiar text-book approach in which the market mechanism is relied on to solve the problem; the second is a relatively less-familiar approach in which a special institutional arrangement is crafted. The first approach is to let *macroeconomic* market forces work themselves out to bring about a natural solution or equilibrium. Any open economy which invests more than it saves (that is with the outcome of a familiar Keynesian disequilibrium situation: savings $<$ investment or aggregate supply $<$ aggregate demand), its current account (CA) is necessarily in the red (since CA = savings minus investment). That is, the country runs a current account deficit to be financed by capital inflows or external borrowings. Let us identify this solution as *CA-deficit-based finance*.

In fact, this type of finance is predicated as an ineluctable feature of any rapidly developing economy that adopts an outer-dependent strategy of industrialization in the stages theory of the balance of payments (Kindleberger 1963). As the country achieves economic development, however, this current account deficit situation will eventually be reversed and even turned into a substantial surplus. Over time, the country thus usually goes through the sequential balance-of-payments stages of immature debtor-borrower → mature debtor-borrower → debtor-lender and debtor-repayer → immature creditor-lender → mature creditor-lender → creditor-drawer and borrower (Halevi 1971). This scenario is also in line with what is called the 'theory of intertemporal production and trade' (Krugman and Obstfeld 1997). This intertemporal theory predicts that a rapidly developing country imports present output for domestic capital formation in exchange for future consumption; that is, borrowing from overseas to finance the current account deficit.

The second approach is to expand bank credit with the help of a country's central bank. This strategy is rather unorthodox and more institutionally embedded, in the sense that the central bank plays a coordinating function. This solution has been pursued with considerable success in Japan. Instead of borrowing from overseas, Japan employed a self-reliant method of financing economic development through domestic bank loans. Japan purposely avoided CA-deficit-based finance. We shall call it *central-bank-based finance*.

To the extent that both approaches are designed to cover the deficiency of domestic savings (that is, the lack of loanable funds), they are not mutually exclusive. Indeed, these two approaches may be combined. That is to say, a country may pursue *both* central-bank- and CA-deficit-based finance simultaneously, if it is willing to rely on foreign capital (foreign savings). Depending on what forms foreign borrowings may take (foreign direct investment, portfolio investment, and bank loans), however, there is a risk of exposing the debtor country to the whims of short-term capital flows and the foreign exchange market. Indeed, as will be detailed below, this has been the case with Korea's recent financial imbroglio.

Given the relatively low level of income – hence, the equally low level of national savings at the beginning of a developing country's growth – the only way to create loanable funds without borrowings from foreign countries is to make the most of the banking industry's credit-creating capacity with the help of its central bank. It goes without saying that the banking industry can create demand deposits (bank money) by a multiple out of any initial injection of deposits into the banking sector, a phenomenon known as bank money creation under a fractional reserve requirement. In addition, a bank can use the discount window of its central bank to secure additional reserves, against which the bank can then extend more commercial loans, thereby initiating a round of deposit creation within the banking industry. In the advanced countries, however, this new credit injection through the discount window is normally limited only for the short-run purpose of replenishing the depleted legal reserves.

Yet such a liquidity-creating facility can also be extended for the purpose of creating long-term credit for capital formation – but not for consumption purposes – in the economy under proper guidance and judicious supervision of the government. Theoretically speaking, then, the central bank is capable of creating an infinite amount of such assets (receivables from commercial banks) and thereby credit commercial banks' reserve accounts (which are entered on the liability side of the central bank's ledger). In other words, the central bank can create new purchasing power out of thin air, as it were. And this is the route any country can resort to if it chooses to do so. There is, however, an obvious need to channel credit (new purchasing power) to those economic agents who are capable of investing in, and creating, *new* productive facilities which will ultimately increase the real (not nominal) supply of goods and services; otherwise, such a monetary regime will culminate in hyperinflation, as has often been the case with many developing countries whose governments are often irresponsible in their budgetary management. Central-bank-based finance needs to be real-supply-focused so that economic development ensues. Interestingly enough, furthermore, this supply-side approach is the core mechanism of financing innovations that leads to the phenomenon of 'creative destruction' in Joseph Schumpeter's (1934), theory of economic development, although he did not mention the role of the central bank in credit expansion for development purposes – or for that matter, bank money multiplication under a fractional reserve requirement.

Schumpeter's theory of Bank Credit Expansion for Development

It is true that bank credit expansion always entails the risk of inflation. But Schumpeter argued that 'credit inflation' for capital formation at the hands of 'entrepreneurs' should be distinguished from credit inflation for consumption:

> But it is distinguished from credit inflation for consumptive purposes by a very essential element. In these cases also new purchasing power takes its place beside the old, prices rise, a withdrawal of goods results in favour of the credit receiver or of those to whom the latter pays out the borrowed sums. There the process breaks off: the goods withdrawn are consumed, the means of payment created remain in circulation, the credit must be continually renewed, and prices have risen permanently.
>
> In our case, however, the process goes *vi impressa* further. The entrepreneur must not only legally repay money to his *bankers*, but he must also economically repay commodities to the reservoir of goods – the equivalent of borrowed productive means; or, as we have expressed it, he must ultimately fulfil the condition upon which goods may normally be taken out of the social stream. The result of the borrowing enables him to fulfil this condition. After completing his business – in our conception, therefore, after a period at the end of which his products are on the market and his productive goods used up – he has, if everything has gone according to expectations, enriched the social stream with goods whose total price of the goods directly and indirectly used up by him. Hence *the equivalence between the money and commodity streams* is more than restored, the credit inflation more than eliminated, the effect upon prices more than compensated for, so that it may be said that there is no credit inflation at all in this case – rather deflation – but *only a non-synchronous appearance of purchasing power and of the commodities corresponding to it, which temporarily produces the semblance of inflation.*   (Schumpeter 1934: 110; italics added)

In short, what Schumpeter envisioned was that an additional aggregate demand initially created by entrepreneurs with bank credits would be fully – or even more than – matched by an additional supply of goods to be brought about through innovations, hence complete disappearance of inflationary pressure in the end.

Moreover, Schumpeter unequivocally stated that capitalism is driven by the money market in which 'What takes place is simply the exchange of present against future purchasing power' between 'entrepreneurs' on the demand side and 'producers of and dealers in purchasing power, viz. bankers' on the supply side (ibid.: 125). In other words, banks are the intermediaries for intertemporal trade in purchasing power. In fact,

Schumpeter argued: 'The money market is always, as it were, *the head-quarters of the capitalist system* from which orders go out to its individual divisions, and that which is debated and decided there is always in essence the settlement of plans for further development' (ibid.: 126).

It should be noted that Shumpeter recognized the role of securities (equity shares and bonds) in finance but that he considered them basically by-products or derivatives of the very process of development that would be brought about by bank loans in the first place. The shares and bonds are issued by already existing (not new) enterprises:

> If it is true that long-term enterprises are financed by *short-term* credit, every entrepreneur and every bank will try for obvious reason to exchange this basis as soon as possible for a *more permanent* one, indeed will regard it as an achievement if the *first stage* can be completely jumped in an individual case. In practice this approximately coincides with replacing purchasing power created *ad hoc* by that existing already. And this generally happens in the case of development in full swing which has *already accumulated reserves of purchasing power* – thus for reasons which our theory itself explains and which do not argue against it – and indeed *in two steps*. In the first place, *shares or bonds* are created and their amounts are credited to the enterprise, which means that *banking resources still finance the enterprise*. Then these shares and bonds are disposed of and gradually are paid for – not always at once, on the contrary the accounts of the subscribing customers are often only debited – by the subscribers out of *existing supplies of purchasing power or reserves of savings*. Thus, as it may be expressed, they are resorbed by the community's savings.   (Ibid.; III; italics added)

> And so the process of production can always be repeated anew with the help of renewal of credit, although this is *no longer* 'new enterprise' within our meaning. The credit instruments thus not only have *no* further influence upon prices, but they even lose that which they originally exercised. Indeed, this is *the most important of the ways in which bank credit forces its way into the circular flow, until it has so established itself there that analytical effort is necessary in order to recognize that its source is not there*.   (Ibid.: 112; italics added)

Schumpeter's perspective on shares and bonds is completely in agreement with the view that the securities markets or securities-market capitalism gain in importance as a country successfully industrializes (that is, at the time of 'development in full swing'). In the 'first stage' or the early stages of development, bank credit (bank-loan capitalism) serves as the driving force of innovations. This is especially so when a country is engaged in catch-up structural upgrading as a latecomer.

It is also worth stressing that the concept of innovation should not be narrowly defined as a mere technological breakthrough but that, as Schumpeter stressed, it covers a wide range of 'new things' in which an economy is involved: (a) 'the introduction of a new good'; (b) 'the introduction of a new method of production'; (c) 'the opening of a new market'; (d) 'the conquest of a new source of supply of raw materials or half-manufactured goods'; and (e) 'the carrying out of the new organisation of any industry' (ibid.: 66). For catching-up countries, emulation of what the firms in advanced countries are already doing constitutes entirely 'new' activities that add to the former's productive capacities, upgrading the level of 'circular flows'.

JAPAN'S 'HEADQUARTERS OF CATCH-UP GROWTH'

State-augmented Credit Creation and High Growth

In the case of Japan's 'first stage' of catch-up economic development, the banking system's traditional capacity to create credit was further augmented by the Bank of Japan, which was closely controlled by the Ministry of Finance. That is to say, central-bank-based finance was adopted. This centralized approach was a clear indication that the financial system was purposely used by the government as a policy instrument of economic development. The central bank pumped liquidity into the banking industry by way of augmenting commercial banks' reserves so as to make new purchasing power available for capital formation in the real sector. Hence, this government-augmented credit creation was something more than what Schumpeter had in mind when he stressed the role of the banking industry as 'the headquarters of the capitalist system'. The Japanese government further reinforced and enhanced the role of banking as the headquarters of a catch-up growth regime, to paraphrase Schumpeter's description.

In addition, the role of Schumpeterian entrepreneurs in prewar Japan was played not so much by individual entrepreneurs as by the *zaibatsu* groups, normally in close collaboration with the government, especially by the Ministry of Commerce and Industry (the predecessor of the Ministry of International Trade and Industry, or MITI). And these industrial groups, along with their satellite enterprises, were engaged in adaptive – if not original – innovations by absorbing on a massive scale modern technology from abroad, which quickly brought about a series of creative destruction in Japan's industrial structure. Luckily, Japan as a latecomer had a huge stock of borrowable industrial knowledge abroad (that is, a huge gap of technology). Indeed, catch-up growth is essentially a function of the absorption of knowledge from overseas.

Hence, in this latecomer version of the government-augmented Schumpeterian approach to economic development, *zaibatsu*-related large banks and holding companies were, early on, favourably treated, since they were the financiers of Japan's effort to promote heavy and chemical industrialization (originally designed to build up military strength). Japan avoided dependency on foreign loans. Hence, a regime of self-reliant central-bank-based finance was firmly established. Indeed, the banking industry was among the very first industries to be protected and promoted as a *strategic* national industry by the Meiji government, since it was designed to contribute to 'the wide spread development of many industries [in a manner] essential to industrial development' (Nakamura 1983: 60). And this distinct financial strategy continued up to the Second World War. For example, during the 1932–44 period, more than two-thirds of the funds of Japanese industry (excluding banks) were raised from the sources outside the businesses, and more than half of the total of such capital came from banks.[1]

Again, the postwar reconstruction and modernization of Japan's heavy and chemical industries naturally required a huge sum of capital – and foreign exchange with which to purchase advanced technology and capital goods. Japan was therefore desperately in need of capital and foreign exchange, but it again adopted a policy of financial independence (if not isolationism intended to minimize borrowings from foreigners). Japan's large banks, once again regrouped under the new system of *keiretsu* as soon as the Allies' occupation ended, played a pivotal role in capital financing. The stock markets were restored as a symbol of the capitalist system Japan readopted in the postwar period. They began to operate as an important source of capital but remained relatively shallow because the public preferred financial intermediation for what little they were initially able to save. Many new businesses starting from scratch in the early postwar period found indirect finance more suitable – and, in fact, the only way of securing funds, since the issue of equity shares was not an easy task for unknown enterprises. Moreover, bank-loan capitalism was deliberately instituted by the Japanese policy-makers, which did not leave much room for the securities markets to develop – hence for businesses either, large and small, to raise capital in the securities markets. As Hugh Patrick (1994: 371) concisely described:

> The post-war Japanese financial system owed much to its early post-war, war-time, and pre-war institutional heritage. The Ministry of Finance opted for a system of bank loan-based finance for industrial corporations. It used regulatory restrictions and economic incentives to severely inhibit corporate bond issue and the development of a secondary market. Essentially, only public utilities and long-term credit banks could issue bonds in any quantity,

and this was done mainly through non-arm's length placements. Equity issue was expensive for management-controlled firms, both because dividends were paid out of after-tax profits while interest payments were a deductible expense, and because the pre-war custom of new stock issue at par rather than market prevailed well into the 1970s. The issuance of commercial paper for short-term finance was not allowed until 1987. *Business, growing rapidly and always in need of new loans for working capital and fixed investment, had no choice but to borrow from banks.*

The basic rationale for Japanese policy-makers' discrimination in favour of bank finance over corporate bond or equity issue lay in their perception that savers in the early post-war period wanted safe, liquid, short-term financial assets. The inflationary experience was too traumatic and recent; financial and real wealth was low and relatively equally distributed; the stock market had difficulty absorbing the shares released through the zaibatsu dissolution programme. (Italics added)

The upshot was the low-level equity-to-debt ratio in corporate finance and the ever-declining ratio throughout Japan's high-growth era of 1950–74. For all industries it declined from 26.9 per cent in 1950 to 16.1 per cent in 1970, and for manufacturing it decreased from 31.4 per cent to 19.9 per cent over the same period (Caves and Uekusa 1976: 479). As a result, the equity-asset ratios of business enterprises in Japan remained exceptionally low in comparison with those in other industrialized countries. For example, 20.8 per cent in Japan (1968) as against 56.2 per cent in the United States (1968), 53.1 per cent in Britain (1967) and 45.0 per cent in Germany (1967) (Miyazaki 1980: 306).

And this rising leverage also meant a decline in what little dependence Japan initially had on foreign capital. For example, Japan's foreign debts accounted for merely 4.5 per cent of its total funds (and this ratio has declined ever since) during the post-Korean War economic expansion of 1954–7 when Japan was most dependent on borrowings from outside (Hamada and Horiuchi 1987: 233). As will be explained below, an end to the increasing leverage came as a slow growth era arrived in the early 1970s and as businesses improved their self-financing capability *pari passu* with the improvement in their export competitiveness, hence in Japan's balance of trade. That is to say, corporate Japan experienced 'development in full swing', thereby accumulating 'reserves of purchasing power', in Schumpeter's sense, and becoming less dependent on bank credit.

As illustrated in Figure 8.1, during the high growth period the Bank of Japan pumped funds into Japan's major city banks, which in turn extended industrial loans to their own groups of closely affiliated corporations, the groups known as the bank-led *kinyu* (or financial) *keiretsu*. There were six such major *kinyu keiretsu* which competed

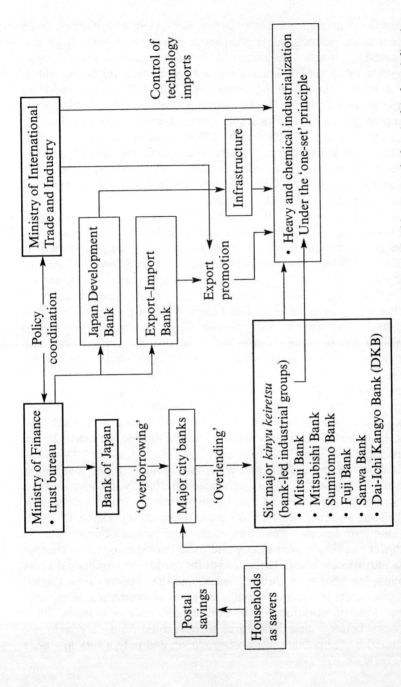

Figure 8.1 Japan's bank-loan capitalism during the high-growth period of heavy and chemical industrialization, 1950–74

223

vigorously in arranging a set of heavy and chemical industries (such as steel mills, petrochemical complexes, heavy machinery shops and shipyards): a practice popularly described as a 'one-set principle' (Miyazaki 1980: 53–75). The six *kinyu keiretsu* were led by the Mitsubishi Bank for the Mitsubishi group, the Mitsui Bank for the Mitsui group, the Fuji Bank for the Fuyo group, the Sumitomo Bank for the Sumitomo group, the Sanwa Bank for the Sanwa group, and the Dai-Ichi Kangyo Bank (DKB) for the DKB group. Observing the close intercorporate linkages in cross share-holding and directorship, not only between the lead *keiretsu* banks and their affiliated corporations but also among the non-bank firms, Gerlach (1992) nicknamed the Japanese brand of capitalism 'alliance capitalism'.

The end result was the two peculiar monetary phenomena in Japan: over borrowing ('overloan' as it was called in Japan) on the part of the corporate sector and overlending on the part of banks supported by the Bank of Japan. Overborrowing describes a situation in which corporations rely on borrowing from banks to an unusually high degree, and overlending means a condition in the private banking sector in which banks extend more in loans than the funds they receive from deposits or own capital, with the gap filled primarily by borrowings from the Bank of Japan (Suzuki 1987: 23–4). Both overborrowing and overlending are the distinct features of bank loan capitalism. It is worth stressing again that this form of credit expansion is well above and beyond the normal capacity of banks to create bank money under a fractional reserve requirement. It may not be amiss to say that the Bank of Japan was not a passive lender of last resort, as central banks are depicted in textbooks; on the contrary it was, indeed, an active lender of first resort.

Under heavy regulations and controls, Japan's banking institutions were also compartmentalized into specialized activities and markets (for example, separation of the lending business from underwriting and trading in securities and the trust business; separation of short- and long-term finance; separation of markets by size of customers via a two-tier banking system of city and local banks) in order to channel funds into specific areas. Three long-term banks – the Industrial Bank of Japan, the Long-term Bank of Japan, and the Nippon Credit Bank – were also created for the specific purpose of promoting heavy and chemical industrialization which could exploit scale economies. These long-term banks issued debentures to raise funds, but they were not purchased by the public since postwar Japan had only a very low asset level. Instead:

the debentures were *allocated* to city banks at *below-market interest rates.* BOJ [Bank of Japan] credit was then used to subsidize the city banks. Throughout the high growth period, the official BOJ discount was kept lower than the interbank deposit rate (the call loan rate). BOJ loans were *rationed* to banks, city banks being the *exclusive* recipients, and this was a major tool of base money control.   (Teranishi, 1994: 33)

Thus, both allocation and rationing measures in finance were used by the government for long-term investment in capital-intensive modern industries as well as in infrastructural facilities.

A special type of bank, called 'sogo banks', were also established to make available the funds for low-productivity small and medium businesses, since the Japanese economy was supported by a large number of these firms, which accounted for as much as 85 per cent of the total value of shipment in 1955 (the share was still 51.3 per cent in 1994).

Another unique feature of Japan's financial sector is that nearly one-third of total private savings has been captured by the Japanese government in the form of postal savings accounts. In fact, Japan's Postal Savings System may be aptly called 'the world's largest bank'. There are more than 20 000 post offices in Japan, many of which are in rural agricultural regions. This means that 'there are more postal savings windows than in all the branches of Japan's city banks combined' (ibid.: 128). The Postal Savings System as a depository of savings is managed by the Ministry of Posts and Telecommunications; but so far as the uses of funds are concerned, the Trust Bureau of the Ministry of Finance is mainly in charge of investments and loans of these funds. Funds are allocated for public purposes through the Japan Development Bank and the Export–Import Bank of Japan as the main conduits of finance.

In addition, the financial sector was isolated from the outside world in order to maintain an independent monetary policy and control. Up until 1970, indeed, international banking (via correspondent overseas banking without any branch banking across borders) alone was considered largely sufficient for the interest of economic development at home. Hence, only a limited form of cross-border banking was allowed (in the early years, only the Bank of Tokyo was given the unique role of a foreign exchange bank to facilitate Japan's international trade (as was the case with its predecessor, the Yokohama Specie Bank, during the Meiji period of industrialization) (Ozawa and Hine 1993).

This money-sector strategy was fully consistent – and so designed – with Japan's real-sector strategy for trade-based industrialization. Japan's overseas investment in the non-banking sector was initially controlled and subject to case-by-case screening and approval by the

Ministry of Finance, which made decisions in close consultation with other government agencies, notably the Ministry of International Trade and Industry (MITI). In other words, both Japan's money and real sectors were firmly in the grip of the Japanese government. Although no requirements for approval were officially announced, it was generally understood that foreign direct investment (FDI) must either promote exports from Japan or lead to the overseas development of natural resources vital to Japanese industry and that overseas production must not jeopardize the competitive position of other Japanese firms at home. These implicit requirements clearly meant that Japan's development strategy in the early postwar period was intended to develop export-competitive home-based manufacturing by importing whatever raw materials and fuels were necessary (that is, a 'workshop of the world' strategy), and that overseas investment was permitted only when it was capable of either promoting exports from Japan or developing the importable overseas resources vital to Japanese industry. In other words, like the money sector, the real sector too was totally devoted to Japan's trade primacy effort and FDI was assigned merely a supportive role. In short, Japan initially protected both the money (banking) and real (industrial) sectors simultaneously from outside competitors in order to build up trade-competitive industries at home.

Socially justifiable versus generative 'moral hazards'

Bank-loan capitalism during Japan's high growth era was closely con-trolled and fully supported by the government. Banks were able to extend industrial loans by simply borrowing from the Bank of Japan. No wonder, then, that their equity–asset ratio was kept at unusually low levels. Besides, there was no possibility of bank failure, as far as the major *keiretsu* banks were concerned: they were strategically too significant to be allowed to fail. The government would always come to the rescue if something ever went wrong to threaten the banks' financial health. Japan's high-growth strategy rested so much on the banks' capacity to provide whatever amount of capital was necessary to build up productive capacities. In fact, small and even weaker or inefficient banks were protected under the scheme popularly referred to as a 'convoy system', in which strong banks are obliged to guard weak ones. The result was that banks' operations became extremely asset-expansive as they eagerly extended loans.

Excessive asset expansion was an inevitable outcome of moral hazard. Banks – and, for that matter, the *keiretsu* groups – were made all the more risk-taking because they could count on the government for help.

Yet moral hazard was actually needed – and, in fact, taken advantage of – to promote large-scale investments in capital-intensive, scale-based industries, since these capital-intensive, scale-driven industries imposed high risks on the private sector. Without government support and *keiretsu* formation, individual enterprises alone might have been very reluctant to plunge into new large-scale industries. In this regard, this type of moral hazard, it could be argued, was socially justifiable, since it induced socially desirable investment in the modern sectors, thereby accelerating catch-up structural upgrading. It may be called 'socially justifiable moral hazard' (in contrast to what may be identified as 'degenerative moral hazard', as discussed below).

Moreover, Japan's banks held the shares of their closely affiliated corporations in the framework of *kinyu keiretsu* within the legal maximum of 5 per cent (earlier, 10 per cent) of the shares of each stock, usually as a symbol of long-term trust relationships with their intragroup clients, a system popularly known as the 'main bank' system (Aoki 1994: 56–7):

> There is . . . one city bank for each company among its major stockholders, called the main bank, which has the closest tie in terms of cash management, as well as short-term (and long-term) credits. The main bank plays the role of manager of a loan consortium when a group of banks extends major long-term credit to the company, and it is responsible for closely monitoring the business affairs of the company. If the company suffers a business crisis, the main bank assumes major responsibility for various rescue operations, which include the rescheduling of loan payments, emergency loans, advice for the liquidation of some assets, the facilitation of business opportunities, the supply of management resources, and, finally, reorganization to secure the claims of the consortium. In the normal course of events, however, the main bank exercises explicit control neither in the selection of management nor in corporate policymaking. Well-run companies that incur little or no debt from banks appear to be virtually free from banks' intervention, and their managements enjoy the highest degree of autonomy.

And in this system the banks' shares were in turn owned by their major corporate customers. This interlinked cross-holding of stock served to reduce the transaction costs associated with asymmetric information and opportunism, further deepening the intersectoral affiliation between banking and non-bank (industrial) firms. They came to establish affiliated relational banking instead of arm's-length, short-term banking relations, as is typical with Anglo-Saxon banking.

Summing up this unique nature of Japanese banking, Wallich and Wallich (1996: 279) noted:

The arm's-length, competitive principles of Anglo-Saxon-style banking did not mesh with the habits of Japan's clannish, cooperative business society. Before World War II the style of the major *zaibatsu* called for banks that were closely associated with them and were capable of supporting the complicated maneuvers of holding-company operations. After the war the largest banks replaced the *zaibatsu* holding companies in their function as leaders of 'groups', a role that also called for *a variety of capabilities not ordinarily associated with the concept of commercial banking.* (Italics added)

As explained in Chapter 3 of this book, Japan has climbed the ladder of structural upgrading starting from tier IV labour-driven 'Heckscher–Ohlin' light industries to tier III 'undifferentiated Smithian' heavy and chemical industries, tier II 'differentiated Smithian' industries and tier I 'Schumpeterian' innovation-driven industries. The high-growth period coincided with the phase of scale-dependent heavy and chemical industrialization. Japanese corporations were highly orientated to seeking market share rather than profit maximization in the short-run; so were their accommodating bankers, thereby becoming asset-expansive and asset-dominant in their operations. (Given a financial environment that was strongly protected by the government, it is no wonder that the banking industry came to develop a false sense of security which misdirected them in the recent past and led to the banking crisis at home.)

Japan's bank-loan capitalism worked nicely without generating any serious inflationary pressure. This is because, in the first place, high growth meant an ultimate expansion of real productive capacities and an increased supply of goods which swamped 'credit inflation' in the best Schumpeterian sense of credit-financed adaptive innovations. Moreover, whenever the Japanese economy was overheated in the wake of rapid capital investment, it inevitably encountered a balance-of-payments problem, as the resultant rise in Japan's imports tended to exceed that in its exports. This balance-of-payments bottleneck was experienced particularly during the tier III phase of heavy and chemical industrialization, when Japan was so dependent on imported raw materials, fuel and technologies (ores, bauxite, coking coal, crude oil, license fees, and so on). Instead of borrowing from overseas to finance a deterioration in the current account, the Bank of Japan quickly turned off its credit tap to induce an economic slowdown so that external balance would be restored. This balance-of-payments-guided monetary policy, which was geared to self-reliant finance, thus functioned just like a currency-board regime or a gold standard over the long haul. *Japan never allowed its economy to push its balance-of-payments deficit to the extent that it would become vulnerable to foreign lenders.* Japan thus managed very well the critical balance-of-payments deficit phase associated with the early phases of structural upgrading involving tier III heavy and chemical industrialization. By the end of the early 1970s Japan thus had success-fully emerged as a developed economy with a strong external balance.

The Victim of Success: Self-emaciation of the Banking Sector

Ironically, the very success of bank-loan capitalism came to undermine the privileged position of banks. As corporations became successful and profitable, with their own internal funds rapidly accumulating, they began to depart from the banks. Especially when Japanese industry successfully moved to the tier II phase of assembly-based industria-lization, in which higher value-added and more consumer-orientated industries such as autos and consumer electronics began to dominate the Japanese economy as the major growth industries, the manufac-turing sector became financially more and more autonomous and independent. For example, Toyota Motor Co. came to be known as Toyota Bank because of its huge accumulation of internal funds in the 1980s. In the meantime, banks began to wean themselves away from the Bank of Japan as their major source of funds, as the phase of capital-intensive heavy and chemical industrialization came to an end and as Japanese households began to save more and more out of their rapidly rising incomes. In 1965, for instance, Japan's household savings as a percentage of disposable income was already as high as 17.5 per cent compared to 15.9 per cent in Germany, 11.1 per cent in France, 6.0 per cent in the United States, and 6.1 per cent in UK. Japan's ratio further rose to 21.0 per cent in 1972 compared to 15.1 per cent, 12.1 per cent, 7.2 per cent, and 5.0 per cent in those countries respectively (Wallich and Wallich 1996: 257).

Moreover, the Japanese economy was forced to shift gear from high growth to low growth under pressures from both external and internal developments. Externally, the sharp appreciation of the yen in 1971 (the Nixon-initiated shift to floating rates) and the first oil crisis of 1973–4 jolted Japan as a workshop of the world. In 1974, for the first time in the postwar period, the Japanese economy registered a negative real growth rate of 0.7 for its GNP. Previously it had grown at an average annual rate of 9.7 per cent over the 1955–93 period. Internally, Japan as a resource-poor and geographically confined small island nation, hit the limit of tier III heavy and chemical industrialization, which caused serious environmental problems at home (since the heavy and chemical industries are pollution-prone) and trade frictions in secu-ring overseas resources (since they are highly resource-intensive). Japan had to move up the ladder of industrialization to the next phase of more environmentally compatible, higher value-added tier II 'differentiated Smithian industries' such as automobiles and electronics.

This period following the oil crisis brought about dramatic structural changes in the early 1970s which, practically overnight, rendered the heavily regulated financial system of the high-growth era outmoded and unfit for the subsequent period of low growth and the next phase of structural upgrading: 'Corporations reacted to low growth with austerity, that is, with caution about investment, employment, and borrowing, while households reacted to the decline in the growth of income by paying hitherto unknown levels of attention to the formation and management of savings' (Suzuki 1987: 4).

Another significant concurrent development was the emergence of the government sector as a deficit unit because of its expansionary financial policy pursued in the post-oil-crisis period (after 1974), thereby creating a supply of government securities in the money market. Thus, Japan's financial market experienced dramatic structural changes as the corporate sector declined in importance as the major deficit sector and the households continued to save while growing more sensitive to yields on their assets. And for the first time in the postwar period, Japan's underdeveloped (because of government restrictions) securities market began to develop due to the necessity to finance government deficits: an ironical turn of events that made Japan's financial industry yield-sensitive, that is, somewhat more market-conscious than regulation-constrained.

Moreover, the government's reliance on the bond market contributed to restructuring the mechanism of financial flows away from indirect finance and more towards direct finance channels, and this change put the banks in a bind. Since interest rates at banks were strictly controlled, they were not able to respond to the increased preference for high-yielding assets on the part of corporations and individuals (Suzuki 1987: 31). Households were later also attracted by the 1980 new provisions of the state-run postal savings programme that allowed the issuance of ten-year, high-yielding, fixed-interest deposits that could be withdrawn without penalties after only six months. Consequently, banks themselves had to introduce financial assets in order to survive the competition that stemmed from both the securities companies and the postal savings system.

The Bubble and its Consequences: Degenerative Moral Hazard

It was against the background of rapidly altered market conditions that a bubble economy (1987–90), stemming from and fed by speculative investments in real estate and stocks, occurred. It was actually created in the wake of the government's decision to adopt a low interest rate policy. The Plaza Accord of 1985 began to drive up the value of the yen phenomenally. Fearing a possible recession (dubbed the 'high-yen recession' in Japan), the Japanese government gradually lowered the discount rate from 5 per cent at the time of the Accord to 2.5 per cent in February 1987. The rate was thus cut by half over only a one-and-half year period. This low-interest policy was welcomed by the USA, which needed Japan's trade surplus to finance the then rapidly rising US federal deficits. Such finance was even called 'Japanese subsidization of American hegemony' (Gilpin 1987). Despite low interest rates in Japan, the yen continued to appreciate, reaching the level of ¥120 against the US dollar. The 'Black Monday' of 19 October 1987 further justified Japan in retaining an easy monetary policy because of the fear of any adverse effects on stock prices.

Because they had lost many large manufacturers as the prime borrowers – dependence on bank loans declined from 59 per cent in 1985 to 35 per cent in 1990 – the banks had to find new customers. Small and medium firms, real-estate firms and construction companies proved to be the banks' next major clients. The share of this group of borrowers grew to as much as one-third of total bank loans. Bank loans to real-estate firms alone accounted for one-quarter of the total. In addition, the banks channelled loans through non-banks (for example, housing-loan companies and consumer credit firms), since the latter were less stringently regulated than the banks themselves. These non-bank loans accounted for as much as 37.8 per cent of the total loans secured by the real estate firms (Noguchi 1992).

Low interest rates and the abundance of liquidity fuelled the rising prices of stocks and real estate. The Nikkei 225 Stock Price Index climbed from ¥13 000 in January 1986 to ¥39 000 at the end of 1989, a three-fold jump. Similarly, land prices (the average price of commercial real estate in Japan's six major cities) tripled. Behind this speculative boom was so-called *zai-tekku* or 'financial engineering' in which practically all the Japanese firms engaged in one way or another in the midst of *endaka fukyo* or 'high-yen recession'. Japan's government-manipulated banking system clearly brought about the problem of moral hazard, encouraging speculative investment in unproductive financial assets and land. This resultant ill effect may be identified as *degenerative* moral hazard in contrast to its socially justifiable counter-part discussed earlier.

With ever-soaring property values at home, many Japanese firms also turned their eyes to overseas real estate, especially in the US and Australia, where property values looked unrealistically cheap by comparison. Suddenly, Japan's real-estate investment abroad sky-rocketed in the late 1980s. The news of Japanese purchases of such trophy properties as the Rockefeller Center and the Four Seasons Hotel in New York City, the Pebble Beach golf course in California and the Watergate Hotel in Washington, DC, were headlines in the newspapers.

Concerned about the adverse social effect of the bubble on the public's wealth distribution, the Bank of Japan decided to burst the bubble by raising the discount rate to 3.25 per cent in May 1989 and to 4.25 per cent in December 1989. The Nikkei, which reached a record high of ¥38 915 on the last business day of 1989, tumbled to below ¥15 000 by the summer of 1992, marking a phenomenal 63.1 per cent decline. Land prices in Tokyo became less than half their high point in 1990. Capital losses stood at 86.9 per cent of GDP in 1992.

In the wake of the bursting of the bubble, real-estate firms and construction companies went bankrupt one after another. In 1990 alone, no fewer than 364 real-estate firms went out of business, leaving behind ¥660 billion ($4.9 billion at ¥135 per dollar) in outstanding debt. In 1991, many more firms collapsed, leading to a historic record high of nearly ¥3 trillion ($22.2 billion) of unpaid loans in the real estate industry alone (Noguchi 1992: 168). This brought disaster to Japanese banks. They became saddled with the ever-rising amounts of defaulted loans. The débâcle was then compounded by a continuous rise in non-performing commercial loans caused by the prolonged recession and weak recovery. In 1996 bad loans were estimated to be around $350 billion (but recalculated at around $600 at the start of 1998). Moreover, the falling stock prices threatened to undermine their ability to comply with the capital adequacy requirement (minimum 8 per cent capital-asset ratio) imposed by the Bank for International Settlements (BIS), since Japanese banks had a large amount of stocks of their affiliated corporations and were allowed to use paper profits on stock holdings as part of capital (that is, to value stock holdings at market prices).

In an ensuing prolonged recession, a series of bankruptcies occurred in the financial markets. Hanwa Bank, a large regional bank, closed in October 1996. Nissan Mutual Life Insurance collapsed in April 1997. And Hokkaido Takushoku Bank (Japan's tenth largest) and Nippon Credit Bank (Japan's Seventeenth largest bank) both filed for court protection from creditors in November 1997. Yamaichi Securities (the fourth largest securities firm) and Sanyo Securities (a medium-sized firm) also went bankrupt in November 1997. The depressed stock values and dwindling capital reserves forced banks to restrain lending, resulting in a credit crunch, especially after the Asian financial crisis erupted, starting in Thailand on 2 July 1997. The government was finally compelled to introduce a $270 billion rescue programme, along with a so-called 'Big Bang' reform plan, to overhaul the financial sector in early 1998.

Summing Up

In short, Japan's banking malaise has persisted over seven years, developing into a near crisis when large institutions began to collapse and a credit crunch developed in late 1997. The banking débâcle was totally home-made and self-inflicted. It had nothing to do with the volatility of foreign capital inflows, as was the case with other Asian crises. Japan continued to accumulate huge current account surpluses. The problem is that its banking industry has long outlived its one-time usefulness as a strategic industry but has still not yet been fully exposed to the 'survival of the fittest' rigours of market forces. The bank rescue programme itself has been implemented on the 'business-as-usual' basis of a convoy system, in which stronger banks applied for assistance, regardless of their need, along with weaker and near-insolvent banks lest the latter stand out, further undermining their positions and causing bankruptcies. What is really required is a slimming down of the over-blown banking sector through restructuring, including failures of inefficient institutions. If Japan had needed help from the IMF, it would surely have attached such a condition to it.

BANK-LOAN CAPITALISM AND A FINANCIAL CRISIS IN KOREA

Determined National Effort to Industrialize

The Korean government also adopted bank-loan capitalism as a policy instrument for industrial development, but it has been using it in a more centralized, top-down and micro-managed fashion. Korea's finance strategy has been closely geared to its export-led development strategy, which has been the country's hallmark ever since the inauguration of the first five-year development plan in 1962. The Korean banks were nationalized in 1961, following the military coup – it was only in the early 1980s that they were again privatized – and a number of new financial institutions were also created to perform specialized services to such areas as small and medium business financing, mortgages and foreign exchange operations. The Bank of Korea was established in 1950 under the law written by American advisers to ensure autonomy as a monetary policy institution. But its independent status was altered after the 1961 coup, and it was formally subordinated to the Ministry of Finance. Korea's financial industry, from top to bottom, all became handmaidens of the military government, which was fully determined to overcome the country's underdevelopment through implementing government-piloted industrialization programmes. Industrialization was a sheer necessity for national security reasons. The government quickly displaced the market-orientated banking system its predecessors had put in place. The central bank came under the bailiwick of the Ministry of Finance, which in turn was under the control of a powerful Economic Planning Board (EPB).[2]

To earn foreign exchange via exporting has been Korea's top priority. Particularly during the 1960s and 1970s, export promotion was 'so intense that economic planners set the goal of making all industries export-oriented, as manifested by the slogan "export-orientation of all industries"' (Park 1994: 168). 'Export Day' was nationally proclaimed for 30 November on the occasion of Korea's exports passing $100 million in 1964; and when Korea exceeded the $20 billion export mark on Export Day in 1981, more than 600 prizes were awarded by the government to numerous enterprises (Rhee *et al.* 1984: 24–33). All sorts of other export incentives were instituted. In this connection, bank credit was made abundantly available to promote and finance export activities. Korea's exports were thus institutionally driven and augmented.

Unlike Japan, whose credit expansion and investment decisions were mostly made by consultation between the government and industry (especially the *keiretsu* groups), the Korean financial system became a highly centralized, top-down conduit of directives: directives which the government practically handed down to industry. In lieu of Japan's 'main bank system' which was formed autonomously within each *keiretsu* on a basis of conventional customer relationships between banks and their affiliated corporations, Korea's 'principal transaction bank system' is officially designed by the regulations of the Monetary Board, and major banks were assigned to, and imposed on, *chaebols* mainly for supervisory purposes.

As Korea's tier IV labour-driven industrialization (1964–72) began to be constrained by rising wages, as happened in Japan, Korea went all out to enter the tier III phase of scale-driven industrialization (1973–83) by promulgating the Heavy and Chemical Industries Promotion Plan in June 1973. 'Six industries – steel, nonferrous metal, machinery (including automobiles), shipbuilding, electronics, and chemicals – were to be promoted at a total investment of $9.6 billion between 1973 and 1981' (Lee 1996: 30). Thus, Korea's new drive to structural upgrading encompassed *both* tier III heavy and chemical industries and tier II component-intensive, assembly-based industries, in a much more time-compressed fashion than in Japan.

This new plan called for promotional measures and much tighter control over finance to mobilize resources for heavy and chemical industries. As with Japan, the private sector on its own was reluctant to take on the risk of these capital-intensive and scale-driven industries unless it was supported and subsidized by the government. These investments and operations also required large-scale business organizations, so *chaebols* were promoted. Preferential loans were allocated to *chaebols* at below-market rates. In fact, the 'moral hazard' effect was needed – and socially desirable – to induce the Korean business conglomerates to enter the new fields. Thus, a regime of central-bank credit expansion was firmly established. Ro (1994: 156) observes:

> The Bank of Korea supplies credit to banks through two channels: *policy loans*, extended to encourage banks to support specific sectors in industry (examples are rediscounts of commercial paper and loans for export financing, agriculture and fisheries, and particular sectors, such as heavy and chemical industries), and *general loans* available to banks that have participated in preferential financing (Type A loans) or used mostly to control bank reserves (Type B).
>
> The Bank of Korea can affect the availability and cost of funds for banks by changing the *loan allotments* or *discount rates*; customarily, the rediscount rate is set lower than commercial bank rates, which are also fixed below market rates. In addition, *much of the bank's lending was to support policy loans* made by the commercial banks, and when there were rediscount applications, most of them were *automatically* approved. *This situation has limited the effectiveness of discount policy as an instrument for monetary control.* (Italics added)

In addition to preferential lending, the government found it necessary to protect what small domestic markets Korea had for heavy and chemical industry products by restricting imports so that local enterprises would be able to secure minimum-scale economies. Yet, at the same time, the protected Korean firms were all the more induced – or even required – to export their products, thereby adding to the basis for scale economies. They had to meet the test of the rigours of global market forces. Thus Korea's strategy was no longer a mere export-led development of light industries whose competitiveness derived from labour abundance. A new trade regime of import substitution and export promotion was adopted. This was a regime of 'import protection as export promotion' (Krugman 1984).

The upshot was the creation of 'Asia's next giant', which can be explained in terms of a new growth theory of late industrialization, a theory that defies many conventional ideas based on the free market (Amsden 1989). There emerged large-scale local enterprises and industrial complexes, such as Pohang Iron and Steel Company (1973), Changwon Machinery Industrial Complex (1974), Hyundai Shipbuilding Company (1973), Hyundai Automobile Company (1972–6), Ulsan Petrochemical Industrial Complex (1972) and Kumi Electronic Industrial estates (1971) (Lee 1996: 19). They were born as a result of a dynamic import substitution policy that forced the infant firms to benchmark on world-class standards, because the government was 'willing and able to exact performance standards from big business in exchange for trade protection and subsidies' (Amsden 1989: 321).

Korea's drive to heavy and chemical industrialization coincided with the first and second oil crises of 1974 and 1979 and the subsequent worldwide slumps, causing huge current account deficits (from –$309 million in 1973 to –$2023 million in 1974; from –$1085 million in 1978 to –$4151 million in 1979 and –$5320 million in 1980). Furthermore, Korea had to rely on foreign borrowings to finance the deficits.

It is worth noting that, although short-term debt increased at the end of the 1970s, it was part of the long-term trend in which Korea's external debt gradually shifted from long-term to short-term; long-term debt once accounted for as much as 98.54 per cent of total external debt in 1965 but then steadily declined to 70.58 per cent in 1983 (according to data in Amsden 1989: 95), a level still substantially high by today's standard. There was then no possibility of the sudden withdrawals of money that might cause a run on the country (this was in sharp contrast with the November 1997 financial crisis, examined below).

As the size and complexity of the Korean economy grew with rapid heavy and chemical industrialization, the government's micromanagement became increasingly inadequate. It was confronted with huge idle capacity in some of the targeted industries, accelerating inflation (a 29 per cent rise in consumer prices in 1980 and a 40 per cent jump in wholesale prices), and a growing current account deficit (–$5.3 billion) (Park 1994: 129). In fact, the deficit soared to as high as 8.7 per cent of GNP in 1980. In other words, central-bank-based as well as CA-deficit-based finance reached perilous levels for macroeconomic stability.

Unsatisfied with stage-managed economic performance, economic liberalism began to rise in the early 1980s, marking a turning point in Korea's economic policies. Financial liberalization programmes were introduced for the first time, including the deregulation of interest rates, although they were subsequently not implemented to the extent expected. An important change in the credit control system occurred, however, shifting its control objective from 'improving the capital structure and efficiency of use of capital by *chaebol* to restricting real estate acquisitions and investment in other companies'. As a result, business groups were forced to repay bank loans by divesting non-operating real-estate and affiliated companies.[3] In other words, this new programme was clearly designed to redress the adverse effect on society of degenerative moral hazard and to stem the concentration of economic power in large business groups.

The era of central-bank-based finance, initially intended to foster *chaebols* in connection with Korea's drive to heavy and chemical industrialization, was over by the start of the 1980s. In fact, the development of the securities markets, particularly for equities, has been promoted since the late 1960s, but most earnestly throughout the 1980s, especially during the latter half, in order to prepare for the opening of capital markets in the early 1990s (Park 1994: 137). More specifically:

> Government policies for broadening and deepening the equity market have focused on encouraging and at times forcing large business groups (the *chaebol*) to go public. To this end, the major *chaebol* have been denied additional bank credits above a certain level and have been required to repay bank loans with the funds raised by issuing stocks and bonds. (Park 1994: 138)

In other words, the government was intentionally encouraging a shift from bank credits to stocks and bonds, that is, a shift from bank-loan capitalism to securities capitalism in Korea's large-business sector finance:

> As a result of this tight credit control [on the *chaebol*], the share of the 30 largest groups' bank loans subject to credit control fell from 25.3 per cent of total bank loans in 1986 to 13.5 per cent in 1990 on a year-end basis ... [while] the share of small and medium companies in the total loans of deposit money banks rose from 31.5 per cent in 1986 to 56.8 per cent in 1991. (Nam and Kim 1994: 470–1)

The government's measures to promote securities, and including tax and other incentives for holding equities, contributed significantly to the bubble economy of 1986–8 in which stock prices skyrocketed and the total market value of listed stocks rose from less than 10 per cent of GNP in 1985 to 68 per cent in 1989. This short boom was created because in the latter half of the 1980s the Korean economy enjoyed large current account surpluses for the first time since 1977 when the current account recorded a temporary small surplus of $12 million. The current account turned from a deficit of $887 million in 1985 to a surplus of $4617 million in 1986, $9854 million in 1987, and $14161 million in 1989, though it dipped to $5055 million in 1990. This sudden surge in Korea's surplus was due in large measure to the sharp appreciation of the Japanese yen against the dollar after the Plaza Accord of 1985, which made Korea's then growing heavy and chemical industries ever more price competitive in the world market.

During that export-led boom, Korean firms' profits rose, and so did retained earnings (internal funds), thereby alleviating corporate dependence on outside funds. But the economy then experienced a downturn of the business cycle towards the end of 1989 which continued into 1993. The current account deficit as a percentage of GNP jumped, hitting a record high of 9.9 per cent in 1991.

Banking and Currency Turmoils

Until the financial crisis in the autumn of 1997, the Korean economy had been growing rapidly after the trough of the previous business cycle in early 1993. Business investment was the most dynamic component of domestic demand in the upturn of 1993–5, which registered a real GDP growth rate of 8.9 per cent in 1995. By the beginning of 1995, the share of business sector non-residential investment reached a record high of 25 per cent, a level rarely reached even during Japan's high-growth decade of the 1960s. Korean enterprises – and their exports in particular – became more price-competitive, 'with relative unit labour costs falling $5\frac{1}{2}$ per cent in 1992 and a further $3\frac{1}{2}$ per cent in 1993 – mainly as the result of the *appreciation of the yen*. This increased the profitability of exports, so encouraging companies to invest more' (OECD 1996: 19–21; italics added). Along with Korean industry's restructuring efforts following the marked increase in labour costs and the rise in the won's value which occurred in the late 1980s, the yen's appreciation helped the Korean economy to build up heavy and chemical industries, which were less labour-intensive; hence there was a rise in overall labour productivity growth in manufacturing.

Before the recent financial crisis, the Korean economy had been performing relatively well – at least, on the surface. As shown in Table 8.1, its macroeconomic indicators did not show any sign of vulnerability.

The central government budget had been more or less balanced, and the rate of inflation (measured in terms of consumer prices) rose to almost 5 per cent at the end of 1996 but started to slow down in 1997. Korea could not be faulted for its macroeconomic stabilization performance. In fact, the IMF gave the following assessment:

Table 8.1 Korea's economic indicators

	1995	1996	1997[a]
Real GDP growth (% change)	8.9	7.1	6.0
Consumer prices (end of period, %)	4.7	4.9	4.2
Central government balance (% of GDP)	0.3	0.3	−0.5
Current account balance ($ bn)	−8.9	−23.7	−13.8
External debt ($ bn)	78.4	104.7	101.5

Note: [a] The first three quarters.

Source: *IMF Survey*, 26(23), 1997.

> Until the present financial crisis, Korea's macroeconomic performance in 1997 was *broadly favorable*. Notwithstanding a sharp slowing of domestic demand, real GDP grew by 6% during the first three quarters and inflation declined slightly to 4%. Subdued import demand and rapid growth of exports caused the external current account deficit to narrow in the 2nd quarter, and a current account deficit of 3% of GDP is expected in 1997. (International Monetary Fund, World Economic Outlook, December 1997)

The current account deficit did increase to $23.7 billion in 1996 from $8.9 billion in 1995, but it was steadily improving throughout 1997. Nevertheless, the deficit was still large in absolute terms, if not as a ratio of GDP. Consequently, external debt hit a record high of $104.7 billion; the problem resided in the nature of private external debt, which consisted mostly of short-term bank loans from overseas. Moreover, it was not so much due to the strength of the Asian financial virus that was spreading from the South-East Asian economies as to the weakened immunity, as it were, of the Korean economy that Korea succumbed to the virus. As the IMF succinctly summarized:

> [Despite the favourable macroeconomic performance,] since the beginning of the year, an unprecedented number of highly leveraged conglomerates (*chaebols*) have moved into bankruptcy. This reflected a number of factors, including *excessive investment* in certain sectors, such as steel and autos, and a weakening in the profitability associated with the *cyclical downturn*. The bankruptcies severely weakened the financial system and nonperforming loans rose sharply to the equivalent of 7½% of GDP. At the same time, the *steep decline in stock prices* has cut the value of banks' equity and further

> reduced their net worth. These developments exacerbated the existing weak-
> nesses in the banking system . . . The weak state of the banking sector has
> led to *successive downgrades by international credit rating agencies* and a
> sharp tightening in the availability of external finance.   (Ibid. Emphasis
> added)

Overcapacity and bankruptcies occurred in part because of a slowdown in export expansion, which was caused by the sharp depreciation
of the currencies of Korea's close competitors, China and Japan.[4] China
devalued the yuan as much as 33 per cent on 1 January 1994, which put
competitive pressure on Korea's still surviving labour-intensive industries (such as textiles and clothing). The Japanese yen began to
depreciate steadily after its record high value in 1995. It depreciated as
much as 36 per cent from ¥80 to the dollar in April 1995 to ¥125 to the
dollar in November 1997, which helped Japan's export industries but
simultaneously damaged Korea's price competitiveness in heavy and
chemical industries such as steel, petrochemicals, shipbuilding, autos
and auto parts and semiconductors.

What worsened Korea's trade balance was also the sharp slowdown
of the once-booming South-East Asian economies on which Korea's
exports have come so much to depend. The share of East Asia (minus
Japan) in Korea's total exports was 25.5 per cent in 1985, but ten years
later it rose to as much as 46.8 per cent in 1995.[5] On the other hand,
the shares of North America and Japan declined from 39.7 per cent
and 15.0 per cent, respectively, in 1985, to 20.9 per cent and 13.9 per
cent in 1995 (OECD 1996: 25). On the other hand, both 1994 and 1995
saw imports zoom at an annual rate of close to 23 per cent:

> First, investment in machinery and equipment – the fastest growing compo-
> nent of domestic demand – relies heavily on imports of capital good imports.
> Moreover, the production of export goods requires large inputs of raw
> materials and semi-finished manufactures. Second, the strong demand for
> textiles, clothing and footwear has boosted imports from nearby Asian coun-
> tries (such as China, Philippines and Vietnam) where labour costs are
> markedly lower.   (Ibid.: 31–2)

In the meantime, Korea's current account deficit came to be increasingly financed by short-term foreign private capital. Private capital flows
basically take the forms of (a) direct investment; (b) portfolio investment; and (c) loans from foreign banks. Direct investment is the best
way to finance a deficit, since it is not only long-term in commitment
but also instrumental in bringing modern technology, managerial skills
and access to overseas markets. Portfolio investment is made by institutional investors such as mutual funds, pension funds and hedge funds.

It is highly volatile 'hot' money. Loans from foreign banks are less footloose but are still short-term in commitment. In fact, both portfolio investment and loans constitute an important 'trigger' cause of financial crises once investors and lenders lose confidence in the borrower countries, since portfolio investors pull money out quickly and banks refuse to roll over loans.

Which type of private capital inflows did Korea become dependent on? Recently, Korea emerged as a net FDI investor overseas as its outward FDI expanded. Consequently, it became dependent on bank loans and portfolio investment from overseas. In June 1997, for example, its ratio of foreign bank debt to GDP stood at 23 per cent, which was much lower than Thailand's 45 per cent, Indonesia's 35 per cent and Malaysia's 30 per cent. But the problem was that Korea had the highest ratio of short-term debt to official reserves in the region, which was more than 300 per cent, and 'by December, before the IMF stepped in, it had risen to 14 times' (*The Economist*, 7 March 1998). What mattered most was not so much the relative size of private borrowings as a proportion of GDP but what forms it took and how large it was relative to official reserves. As mentioned earlier, in the 1960s and 1970s Korea's current account deficit was covered mostly by long-term official borrowings, in part because the private sector was not yet capable of raising funds overseas at a favourable interest rate, and in part because of restrictions on external capital transactions. Now that Korean industry has become world-class with many globally known corporations, the private sector has attracted many willing foreign investors and lenders, as financial transactions have been increasingly liberalized. Structurally, therefore, Korea became vulnerable to footloose money as it borrowed short to invest long in its industries which were already at overcapacity. The ratio of corporate debt to equity was no less than 330 per cent during the 1986–8 period, although it declined to 290 per cent by the middle of 1995 (OECD 1996: 23).

Summing Up

In short, once foreign lenders and banks lost confidence in the Korean economy because of signs of a slump and corporate bankruptcies, it was quickly trapped in a vicious cycle. As illustrated in Figure 8.2, the cycle generated a downward spiral: excessive investment → cyclical downturn, worsened by the depreciations of the Chinese yuan and the Japanese yen → bankruptcies → non-performing local bank loans → steep decline in stock prices → loss of confidence by foreign lenders

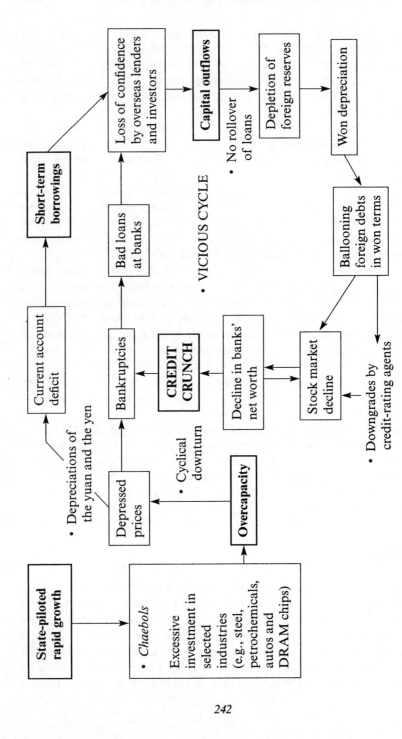

Figure 8.2 Korea's financial crisis

and banks (less portfolio investment inflows and Korean banks' difficulty rolling over loans from overseas) → decline in the value of banks' equity and net worth → credit crunch → downgrades by credit rating agencies → further loss of confidence by foreign lenders and banks → an ever-deepening trap or vicious cycle.

CONCLUSIONS

No doubt, bank-loan capitalism is a powerful institution through which to foster industrialization in the early phases of economic development. Yet this system requires capable bureaucrats and dedicated politicians who are devoted to the enhancement of national economic welfare and prestige. Central-bank-based finance of capital formation is most appropriate during the stage of building heavy and chemical industries which are capital-intensive, scale-based and risky from the private investors' point of view. The social benefits of external economies, both cross-sectional and longitudinal, and increasing returns far exceed the private benefits. Moral hazard, then, should indeed purposely be capitalized on in order to channel funds into strategic industries (thereby turning moral hazard into the socially justifiable type). Even in the West, when these industries came into existence, they were in the early stages heavily subsidized or even directly built up by central governments for the national goals of imperialism (up to the Second World War) or for the execution of war itself.

Without resort to a centralized way of fostering heavy and chemical industries in terms of finance, they would not have developed as swiftly and as successfully as they have done in Japan and Korea. Central-bank-based finance no doubt proved to be a success so far as that specific phase of industrialization is concerned. The trouble with Japan is that the institutions and mentality of bank-loan capitalism still continue without much alteration. When the Japanese economy graduated from the phase of tier III heavy and chemical industrialization in the early 1970s, such a system became obsolete because, by then, industry had become substantially autonomous in financial capacities as internal funds accumulated. In the meantime, the household sector was generating high savings, and direct finance was increasingly desired by both lenders and borrowers. The upshot was the so-called 'departure from banks' phenomenon, which made banks rather superfluous in corporate finance. Yet the government was slow to deregulate and reform the financial industry.

Protected from failures ('too strategic to fail') as a legacy of government-augmented bank-loan strategy, banks were therefore induced to engage in speculative investment under the influence of degenerative moral hazard. Low-interest policy caused the banking sector to become bloated with excess liquidity which was then poured into the stock and real-estate markets, culminating in a short-lived bubble and leaving hundreds of billions of non-performing loans in the hands of banks. It was a self-choreographed tragedy. It had nothing to do with volatile foreign capital inflows and sudden outflows (or the refusal of loan roll-overs), as was the case with Korea – and other Asian economies.

When Korea caught the financial flu from the South-East Asian economies, it was about to graduate from bank-loan capitalism, so far as the large business sector is concerned. In fact, the Korean government was more consciously and more purposely promoting the development of the securities markets for stocks, bonds and other securities than its Japanese counterpart. Bank-loan capitalism did serve the Korean dream of rapid catch-up industrialization. The only mistake it made was that the government allowed CA-deficit-based finance to expand excessively, especially in short-term foreign debts. In both Japanese and Korean experiences, a big irony is that credit flooding (credit overcreation) eventually culminated in a credit drought (credit crunch) because of the banking crisis.

In concluding this chapter, a few words are warranted about the financial crises experienced by other Asian nations. Prior to the turmoils, Thailand, Malaysia and Indonesia all had relatively stable macro-economic conditions; on the whole, their government deficits were manageably small and prices were stable. Yet they all had growing current account deficits. In other words, analogous to Korea, they were unwittingly trapped into CA-deficit-based finance under untrammelled market forces. Their foreign borrowings similarly took the form of short-term capital inflows.

The crux of the problem was that all the three governments began to liberalize their financial sectors and made themselves vulnerable to the risk of volatile foreign money *before* they developed modern financial institutions and capabilities. Because of the problems of asymmetric information and moral hazard, deregulation and liberalization of the financial industry without first forging a strong bank supervisory system is a prescription for disaster (Mishkin 1997: 57). As Hugh Patrick (1994: 342) put it: 'Financial liberalization does have costs. Market interest rates are more volatile than controlled ones, and this generates swings in asset prices. *Hedging is feasible for individual players, but not for the system as a whole*' (italics added). In 1987, Thailand initiated a series of deregulations of interest rates and banking operations and opened the Bangkok International Banking Facilities, or BIBF, which led to substantial capital inflows when rising local interest rates created rising differentials *vis-à-vis* the rest of the world. Borrowed money from overseas was then poured by inadequately supervised banks into the speculative land and stock markets. Indonesia, too, had a similar experience, as its financial liberalization measures introduced in 1983 and 1988 resulted in large interest differentials (5–10 per cent), causing rapid capital inflows. In 1994, Malaysia, which also moved to liberalization, even directly regulated unwanted capital inflows because of the fear of inflation by, among other things, limiting foreign exchange liabilities of banks and banning the sale of short-term securities to foreigners. Thus, all these countries were subject to danger from the volatility of 'hot money' because of the uncontrollable rises in interest differentials, in exactly the same manner in which Mexico was ultimately victimized by the sudden withdrawal of foreign money in December 1994 (Hayakawa 1997).

Interestingly enough, it was reportedly not so much currency speculators (of the likes of George Soros, who sold borrowed local currency forward in hopes of precipitating a devaluation) but local borrowers who caused the day of reckoning in the foreign exchange market.[6] The local borrowers of loans in dollars actively hedged against the exchange risk by selling local currency forward, the risk-averting activities which, in their simultaneous outcome, inevitably ended up by driving down the value of local currency to such a level that confidence was lost and herdlike action ensued. Hedging was thus quite rational and feasible for individual players but proved risk-inflicting and deadly for the country as a whole. There is definitely a high cost to financial liberalization which needs to be heeded and avoided in the critical early stages of development; local banks were particularly ill-equipped and inexperienced to lend wisely – and, above all, were poorly supervised. Marketization does not eliminate the involvement of government. On the contrary, it calls for a strong and judicious regulatory role, possibly including temporary controls on volatile capital inflows.

NOTES

1. The data are from Goldsmith (1986: 127).
2. 'The Economic Planning Board has played a central role in preparing and implementing Korea's various economic plans and policies ever since the EPB was established in 1961. As soon as Park Chung Hee took power he created the Economic Planning Board by combining the Bureau of the Budget of the Ministry of Finance, the Bureau of Statistics of the Ministry of Home Affairs, and the planning functions

of the Ministry of Reconstruction. The Minister of the EPB was given the concurrent title of Deputy Prime Minister and authorized to control, co-ordinate, and adjudicate among other ministries on economic matters. DPM presides over the fortnightly Economic Ministers' Meeting attended by eleven economic ministries and the Minister of Foreign Affairs' (Song 1990: 141).

3. 'As a result, 309.9 billion won of borrowing from banking institutions, equal to 2.7 per cent of the broadly defined money supply, was repaid by selling real estate and 166 member companies were disposed of by the end of 1984. Of the real estate sold, 56 per cent (in terms of value) was purchased by individuals and companies not subject to credit control, and the rest was sold to the Land Development Corporation, a government-invested corporation'.

4. In its 1996 survey report, the OECD presciently expressed concern about the adverse effect of the yen's depreciation on the Korean economy: 'One downside risk ... concerns the exchange rate, notably *vis-à-vis* the Japanese currency. A further appreciation of the won against the yen could affect the Korean export performance, with possible adverse implications for Korean business investment. This would particularly hurt the small labour-intensive manufacturing sector which already has significant financial problems' (OECD 1996: 38).

5. East Asia (minus Japan), for Korea, includes nine economies: Hong Kong, China, Taipei, Singapore, Malaysia, Thailand, Indonesia, the Philippines and Vietnam.

6. For example, Indonesian companies borrowed hundreds of millions of dollars to avoid punishingly high Indonesian interest rates. At the first whiff of trouble, they hedged their dollar debts: 'For a fee, [they] bought the right to sell rupiah for dollars in the future at a set price. It was a maneuver that, when repeated by scores of other Indonesian borrowers [along with many foreign investors], pushed down the rupiah's value' ('Money trail: speculators didn't sink Indonesian currency; local borrowing did', *Wall Street Journal*, 30 December 1997, A1.

REFERENCES

Amsden, Alice H. (1989), *Asia's Next Giant: South Korea and Late Industrialization*, New York and Oxford: Oxford University Press.

Aoki, Masahiko (1994), 'Toward an economic model of the Japanese firm', in Kenichi Imai and Ryutaro Komiya (eds), *Business Enterprise in Japan: Views of Leading Japanese Economists*, Cambridge, Mass.: MIT Press, pp. 39–71.

Caves, Richard E. and Uekusa, Masu (1976), 'Industrial organization', in Hugh Patrick and Henry Rosovskly (eds), *Asia's New Giant: How the Japanese Economy Works*, Washington, DC: Brookings Institution, pp. 459–523.

The Economist (1998), 'East Asian Economies', 7 March, a special survey, 1–18.

Gerlach, Michael L. (1992), *Alliance Capitalism: The Social Organization of Japanese Business*, Berkeley, Cal.: University of California Press.

Gilpin, Robert (1987), *The Political Economy of International Relations*, Princeton, NJ: Princeton University Press.

Goldsmith, Raymond (1986), *The Financial Development of Japan, 1868–1977*, New Haven, Conn.: Yale University Press.

Halevi, Nadav (1971), 'An empirical test of the "balance of payments stages" hypothesis', *Journal of International Economics*, 1, 103–17.

Hamada, Koichi and Horiuchi, Akiyoshi (1987), 'The political economy of the financial market', in K. Yamamura and Y. Yasuba (eds), *The Political Economy of Japan*. Vol. 1: *The Domestic Transformation*, Stanford, Cal.: Stanford University Press, pp. 223–60.

Hayakawa, Masahisa (1997), 'ASEAN Shokoku ni okeru Naigai Kinri Kakusa to Tanki Shihon Ryunyu' [Internal and external interest differentials and short-term capital inflows in ASEAN Countries], *Kaigai Toshi Kenkyu Shoho*, **23**(4), 34–73.

Johnson, Chalmers (1982), *MITI and the Japanese Miracle*, Stanford, Cal.: Stanford University Press.

Kindleberger, Charles P. (1963), *International Economics*, 3rd edn, New York: Irwin.

Krugman, Paul (1984), 'Import protection as export promotion: international competition in the presence of oligopoly and economics of scale', in H. Kierzkowski (ed.), *Monopolistic Competition and International Trade*, Oxford: Oxford University Press, pp. 180–93.

Krugman, Paul (1994), 'The myth of Asia's miracle', *Foreign Affairs*, **73**(6), 62–78.

Krugman, Paul and Maurice Obstfeld (1997), *International Economics: Theory and Policy*, Reading, Mass.: Addison-Wesley.

Lee, Chung H. (1995), *The Economic Transformation of South Korea: Lessons for the Transition Economies*, Paris: OECD.

Lee, Hyung-Koo (1996), *The Korean Economy: Perspectives for the Twenty-first Century*, Albany, NY: State University of New York Press.

Mishkin, Frederic S. (1997), 'Understanding financial crisis: a developing country perspective', in Michael Bruno and Boris Pleskovic (eds), *Annual World Bank Conference on Development Economics, 1996*, Washington, D.C.: World Bank, pp. 29–62.

Miyazaki, Yoshikazu (1980), 'Excessive competition and the formation of keiretsu', in Kazuo Sato (ed.), *Industry and Business in Japan*, White Plains, NY: M.E. Sharpe, pp. 53–73.

Nakamura, Takafusa (1983), *Economic Growth in Prewar Japan*, New Haven, Conn.: Yale University Press.

Noguchi, Yukio (1992), *Baburu no Keizaigaku: Nihon Keizai ni Nani ga Okkottanoka* [Economics of Bubble: What Happened to the Japanese Economy], Tokyo: Nihon Keizai Shimbunsha.

OECD (1996), *OECD Economic Surveys: Korea, 1996*, Paris: OECD.

Ozawa, Terutomo and Sue Hine (1993), 'A strategic shift from international to multinational banking: a "macro-developmental" paradigm of Japanese banks qua multinationals', *Banca Nazionale del Lavoro Quarterly Review*, no. 186, 251–74.

Park, Yung Chul (1994), 'Korea: development and structural change of the financial system', in Hugh Patrick and Yung Chul Park (eds), *The Financial Development of Japan, Korea, and Taiwan: Growth, Repression, and Liberalization*, New York and Oxford: Oxford University Press, pp. 129–87.

Patrick, Hugh T. (1994), 'Comparisons, contrasts, and implications', in Hugh Patrick and Yung Chul Park (eds), *The Financial Development of Japan, Korea, and Taiwan*, New York and Oxford: Oxford University Press, pp. 325–72.

Rhee Yung Whee, Bruce Ross-Larson and Garry Pursell (1984), *Korea's Competitive Edge: Managing the Entry into World Markets*, Baltimore, Md.: Johns Hopkins University Press.

Ro, Sung-Tae (1994), 'Korean monetary policy', in Stephan Haggard, Richard Cooper, Susan Collins, Choongsoo Kim and Sung-Tae Ro, *Macroeconomic*

Policy and Adjustment in Korea, 1970–1990, Cambridge, Mass.: Harvard University Press, pp. 145–84.

Schumpeter, Joseph A. (1934), *The Theory of Economic Development* (first published as vol. XLVI in the Harvard Economic Studies Series), New York and Oxford: Oxford University Press, 1961.

Song, Byung-Nak (1990), *The Rise of the Korean Economy*, Hong Kong: Oxford University Press.

Strange, Susan (1997), *Casino Capitalism*, Manchester: Manchester University Press.

Suzuki, Yoshio (ed.) (1987), *The Japanese Financial System*, Oxford: Clarendon Press.

Teranishi, Juro (1994), 'Japan: development and structural change of the financial system', in Hugh Patrick and Yung Chul Park (eds), *The Financial Development of Japan, Korea, and Taiwan*, New York and Oxford: Oxford University Press, pp. 27–80.

Wallich, Henry C. and Wallich, Mabel I. (1996), 'Banking and finance', in Hugh Patrick and Henry Rosovsky (eds), *Asia's New Giant: How the Japanese Economy Works*, Washington, DC: Brookings Institution, pp. 249–315.

9. Pacific collective management

Gavin Boyd

In the vast area of the Asia Pacific Economic Cooperation (APEC) forum the dimensions of the structural and policy interdependencies between its members raise questions about its potential for evolving a system for the comprehensive management of those interdependencies in the common interest, and about the significance of such a system in the global political economy. The structural interdependencies of the area are large and have been rising rapidly, mainly because of the dynamism of high-growth East Asian countries. Vital policy interdependencies have developed, primarily because of the magnitude of the structural linkages and especially because of imbalances in those linkages which are seen to need collaborative measures to ensure a fairer spread of the gains from trade and transnational production. APEC has made a modest start in promoting such collaboration, and it could lead to transregional cooperation with the expanding European Union, and have extensive consequences for order and growth in the rest of the world.

Where political and business elites begin to develop a sense of regional identity, through participation in consultative groups with an area focus, the potential for promoting regional economic integration and building a structure for collective management depends on the pattern of affinities that can facilitate the growth of productive exchanges between national policy communities. Such exchanges, aiding the development of rapport on ways of harmonizing and integrating trade, structural, fiscal, monetary and financial policies, can open up opportunities for higher and more balanced interdependent growth, if there is substantial cooperation by firms. Such firms, if engaged in transnational production, are likely to operate on an increasingly global basis, but with corporate cultures and identities that remain significantly national, and can thus be responsive to the policy concerns of their home governments.

In the APEC context, affinities conducive to the development of cross-border understandings between policy communities and corporate associations are few, and there are numerous sharp cultural and political contrasts. The multiplication of commercial exchanges gradually moderates the divisive effects of those contrasts, but competitive pressures motivate ventures in corporate collaboration that are mainly national, especially in East Asia. Business associations give little impetus to the growth of political exchanges which might activate trade- and investment-facilitating measures for progressive regional market integration.

The policy orientations of APEC members express interest in regional trade and investment liberalization, as this can promise higher growth, depending on the terms of whatever arrangements might be negotiated and even more on the capabilities and strategies of the firms which would be contending for regional market shares. The liberalizing arrangements, it is commonly understood, would be the outcome of complex bargaining processes, dominated by the USA and Japan as economic powers whose varied domestic groups would be able to demand side payments. Exploitation of the expanded opportunities for regional commerce would be expected increasingly to become a series of contests between leading American and Japanese firms. The American enterprises would be advantaged by their domestic and European market strengths, while the Japanese corporations would benefit from relational cooperation in their industry groups and between those groups and their national government.

Ongoing regional structural change, resulting mainly from the operations of Japanese and American international firms, is forcing new assessments of the likely gains from alternative outcomes of APEC negotiations. This is happening in a context that has been profoundly affected by the disruptions of East Asian financial markets in 1997–8. These have had far-reaching consequences in a larger context of globalization that has challenging implications for all APEC members, especially the USA. For the United States, more than for other industrialized states, globalization entails a mix of gains and costs that necessitates adjustments which are difficult. There are problems of governance; and the scale of foreign production by US firms is very large in relation to exports, which of course include high-volume intrafirm trade.

Within APEC, the US administration is the main advocate of regional trade and investment liberalization, which it seeks for anticipated gains as a result of reduced protection in East Asian trading partners, and with confidence that it can secure favourable terms for such liberalization through its position of strength in the North America Free Trade Area (NAFTA). Short-term concerns focus on prospects for securing increased access to the Japanese market, while in the longer term more attention can be given to opportunities for commerce with the large

Chinese economy.[1] Japanese policy, while endorsing the objective of liberalization, reflects an understanding that solidarity between Japanese business groups ensures superior effectiveness in coping with the trade and investment barriers of industrializing East Asian countries.[2] There may also be awareness that American trade policy activism can have alienating effects in those countries, which could indirectly benefit Japanese interests.

US policy-makers have not proposed the formation of a system of regional economic cooperation: APEC would evidently remain a consultative association after the projected trade and investment liberalization, and in this association the USA would have much freedom for the independent management of its foreign economic relations. Substantially increased consultative activity does not appear to be favoured, as this could entail the acceptance of informal accountability to other members. Japanese attitudes also indicate reluctance to become involved in intensified regional consultative activity. There are understandable preferences for bilateral dealings with industrializing East Asian states, in which differences in bargaining power can be used to maximum effect. Similar preferences are more evident in American policy, although US diplomatic capabilities are better suited to conferencing.

The prospect of unevenly bargained Pacific trade and investment liberalization is a challenge for observers sensitive to the interests and rights of the diverse communities in the area who are being affected by the structural transformations that result from its complex contests for market shares. In these structural transformations the linkages expanding through transnational production and trade are causing market efficiencies and failures to assume cross-border dimensions. Associated with these are government efficiencies and failures which are at variance with the imperatives for cooperation that can be seen in the dynamics of the regional political economy.

PACIFIC REGIONALISM AND GLOBALIZATION

The linking of economic structures and markets across borders through transnational production and trade tends to be initially regional because of the effects of geography, cultural affinities and the interests of governments in managing the interdependencies that develop with neighbouring economies. These interests tend to become more significant in policy processes where commercial exchanges and social ties facilitate transnational representations of concerns about trade and investment. Forms of regional cooperation between governments develop through bargaining processes in which decision-makers interact on the basis of a variety of considerations about the actual and prospective sharing of benefits, and terms are fixed through many types of leverage. Large states commonly extract concessions from smaller states which seek better access to their markets; but where bargaining strengths are roughly balanced, arrangements can be more evenly negotiated.

Transregional commerce assumes more importance as corporate contests for market shares intensify. Firms which strengthen their positions in more or less integrated regional markets acquire capabilities for transregional operations. These tend to develop on a global scale, causing trends toward concentration, as the more competitive enterprises displace their weaker competitors. Through these trends, the successful corporations commonly lose home country attachments and loyalties, interact with numerous host governments, contract alliances with other multinationals, and become less dependent on trade, investment and the technological and other advantages provided in the regional context. Rivalries between governments striving to raise levels of structural competitiveness thus become more complex, extending outside the regional patterns in which those governments are located, but meanwhile posing issues of collective management within those patterns. Potentials for collaboration to raise *regional* structural competitiveness, through common policies, can thus become significant, as has been evident in the European Union.[3]

The globalization of corporate activities, with the multiplication of transregional structural interdependencies, is not significantly complemented by transregional and global cooperation between governments, and evokes only modest responses from systems of regional economic cooperation. Policy processes remain national, limiting the potential to develop regional systems, and motivating individual efforts to assert interests transregionally. Corporate associations for political action retain their national character, as do political parties, and generally do not bond effectively with their counterparts in other members of a regional pattern of economic cooperation. International corporate alliances, formed for technological, production and marketing advantages, tend to be narrowly focused on commercial interests, and have shifting instrumental concerns; they do not usually result in the establishment of associations for transnational political action.

Major industrialized states, especially the USA, have facilitated and in many ways have given impetus to the global expansion of corporate operations. High levels of capital mobility have resulted from the liberalization of financial markets, which was primarily a consequence of endeavours by American administrations to increase the openness of national economies with high savings levels and to facilitate US trade and foreign direct investment. Patterns of interest representation to influence financial policies in the USA and other industrialized states have been elitist and highly specialized, and the structural consequences of high capital mobility have generally had low impacts on American and European policy communities focused on trade, growth and employment issues. The liberalization of trade in goods, because of the more visible and more immediate effects on domestic economic sectors, has been much slower than the opening up of financial markets, and has also been mainly an outcome of American advocacy. This has stressed the common benefits attainable through general increases in market openness, but has evidenced very active concerns with export promotion in order to reduce large trade deficits. The size of the domestic market has ensured strong leverage in market-opening diplomacy, but persistent fiscal deficits have ensured high levels of internal demand, drawing in high-volume imports.

The American economy has become globalized on a scale much greater than that of Japan, and this has much significance for the APEC area. The proportion of national manufacturing that is outward-orientated is moderate, compared with other industrialized states, but foreign production and sales by foreign affiliates of US firms are at much higher levels and are spread very widely in the world economy.[4] The US corporate presence in Europe is a potentially dominant complex of regional market strengths, and there is a relatively stronger presence in Latin America. Only in East Asia is there potent rivalry with moderate but increasing global dimensions: this is a major area of Japanese foreign production and commerce.

The United States, on the basis of its interests and capabilities, can promote trade and investment liberalization in the Atlantic, Latin American and Pacific contexts, while the European Union's options are limited to the Atlantic and Latin America. Japan's capabilities for competitive foreign economic diplomacy are limited to the Pacific and, although substantial as noted, are subject to constraints, especially because of its dependence on access to the US market.[5] Japanese globalization, in rivalry with the USA, is aided by superior structural competitiveness, but has to cope with the disadvantages of inferior market strengths in Europe and Latin America.

Of the industrializing East Asian states, only the members of the Association of Southeast Asian Nations (ASEAN) have become linked in a consultative grouping; their association, however, is a loose organization, at a low level of regional integration and with little promise of development. Intrazonal levels of understanding and cooperation appear to have been badly affected by the disruptions of the Thai, Indonesian, Malaysian and Philippine economies which began in 1997. These forced intense policy level concentrations on issues in their inter-actions with the International Monetary Fund (IMF), in which individual accommodations were sought; there was no concerted effort as little solidarity had developed in ASEAN and its members remained heavily dependent on external markets, especially that of the USA.[6]

Since 1997, attitudinal cleavages across the Pacific have become more significant obstacles to trade and investment liberalization and to initiat-ives for more active regional cooperation. Commitments to such liberalization which had been made in principle by APEC members were subject to reservations because of marked cultural differences between North American and East Asian participants, and because of perceptions of basic conflicts of interest. American political and business elites tended to see the dynamic East Asian economies as states achieving high export-led growth through the exploitation of opportuni-ties in the US market while restricting their imports.[7] For East Asian elites, gains in penetrating the American economy were necessary to ensure the development of their own firms, which would be disadvan-taged in open competition against enterprises with secure bases in the large US market.

The 1997–8 disruptions in the East Asian economies, which drama-tized the macromanagement deficiencies of governments and the scale of the speculative activities which they had tolerated, caused resentment against US financial enterprises whose manipulation of financial markets had contributed to sharp currency depreciations in South-East Asia and South Korea. There was also resentment at perceived US influence on the conditions attached to adjustment assistance provided by the IMF. Governments receiving assistance were required to open their financial markets to foreign investors, and this provided opportuni-ties for American and other multinational enterprises to acquire national firms. Meanwhile the acceptance of dependency status entailed weaker bargaining strength in interactions with the USA on issues regarding the implemention of APEC commitments to regional trade liberalization.

In the regional pattern of bargaining capabilities and policy orien-tations, Japan has been adversely affected by the disruptions of economies in industrializing East Asia.[8] These have been major desti-nations of Japanese foreign direct investment, which has been shaping an integrated production system, virtually an extension of the industrial establishment in the home economy. The adjustment and developmental needs of the affected industrializing states have made Japanese economic cooperation all the more necessary for them, and accordingly Japan has exceptional opportunities to continue building links with them. There is scope to develop a comprehensive pattern of East Asian economic collaboration, while strengthening a regional corporate presence that would limit penetration of the area by American firms.

China, moving from the periphery into a more active role in the regional political economy, is an increasingly significant rival for Japan and for the American presence in East Asia, because of growing economic links with industrializing neighbours.[9] These links have been growing through the development of informal ties with Chinese business communities in South-East Asia. The Chinese regime is not a fully acceptable partner in APEC discussions of regional trade and investment liberalization because of its high degree of formal and informal authoritarian methods of macromanagement. Its vast internal market, however, is a potent attraction for Japanese and American firms, and this would undoubtedly have a strong influence on Japanese and US negotiating strategies in any regional interactions on trade and investment liberalization.

PACIFIC DEVELOPMENTAL ISSUES

Trade and investment linkages between the APEC states make up a complex pattern of structural interdependencies, with many asymmetries that are associated with imbalances in the spread of gains and with the efficiencies and deficiencies of market functions extending across numerous borders. Governments in the area compete to raise levels of structural competitiveness so as to secure more gains for their economies, but contrasts in their capacities have become sharp since the disruptions of financial markets in 1997–8. Imperatives for collective adjustment have been evident, but the severe stresses, it must be reiterated, have forced national administrations to concentrate on their own macromanagement problems. There has been little trust in the goodwill and capabilities of governments in East Asian neighbours. General awareness of the requirements for the development of sound financial systems has increased, but rationales for opening these systems to foreign penetration have not been persuasive.

The structural interdependencies are developmental, as order, growth and employment in each country are affected by the expansion of transnational production and trade, thus challenging the structural policy capabilities and orientations of governments, while making policy choices more dependent on measures taken by other national adminis- trations and on the investment and production options chosen by international firms. For several South-East Asian governments a very prominent problem is the geographic dispersal of manufacturing oper- ations by transnational enterprises whose direct investment has been attracted in the hope of securing technology transfers.

In a region where trade and investment liberalization are uneven, community formation is at a low level and there is an imbalance in the spread of bargaining power between its members, the feasibility of advances into differing forms of economic cooperation varies greatly. Competition policy issues assume immediate importance, and prospects for some cooperation on these are likely to be more significant than the scope for structural policy cooperation, which would require con- siderable trust and goodwill. The potential for collaboration in all the areas of economic policy would depend on the learning and attitudinal effects of initial and subsequent ventures in any of those policy areas.

Competition policy issues emerge because progress towards market integration accelerates concentration trends through increased mergers and acquisitions and the more rapid displacement of less-competitive firms. A variety of government measures typically contribute to these trends, reflecting rivalries to enhance structural competitiveness and resorts to leverage by larger states against smaller ones. The increasing scope for more competitive behaviour by firms has important impli- cations for the spread of gains between the countries whose economies are being linked. There are incentives to use competition measures protectively, to assist disadvantaged national firms, but also to coordi- nate those liberalizing decisions which can promise increases in efficiencies and fairness, however difficult this may be to assess.

Competition policy measures commonly overlap with regulatory prac- tices relating to product standards, labour issues and environmental concerns: these can affect opportunities for competition, despite being outside the competence of competition authorities. Diverse regulatory practices in Japan have been the targets of US trade policy activism seeking to increase the scope for competition in the Japanese market. Reductions in formal trade barriers between industrialized states over the past decade, however, have been accompanied by general increases in regulatory practices that have affected the degrees of economic openness and opportunities for competition.[10] The involvement of a number of regulatory authorities, in the USA as well as in Japan, has greatly complicated questions of competition policy cooperation.

Competition policy issues have increasing structural significance as markets become more closely linked. Structural policy concerns have become more active in the USA because of persistent trade deficits. Such concerns can cause a US administration to favour liberal shifts in anti-trust enforcement, so as to facilitate the mergers and acquisitions that enable very large American enterprises to become internationally more competitive. The limited scope for structural policy in the American political system makes relaxations of anti-trust enforcement on efficiency grounds justifiable through references to the increasing regionalization and globalization of national markets.[11] A liberal trend in the European Union's competition policy, encouraging the emergence of larger and more efficient firms, has been a challenge for US anti-trust policy authorities.[12]

Financial policy options, meanwhile, demand more attention from governments. Imperatives for structural competitiveness necessitate efforts to increase efficiencies in domestic financial systems for the funding of national industries, while limiting capital flight into international financial markets which reward high short-term profitability and are subject to much volatility. Such imperatives have become stronger in industrializing East Asian states because of serious weaknesses in their systems of financial guidance and regulation.[13] In the USA, high-volume speculation is a cause of volatility that can be destabilizing. In Japan, speculation has been limited by stable shareholding and by regulatory functions with generally high degrees of effectiveness. Continuity in the domestic funding of industry has in general been maintained.[14]

Both in the Pacific and globally, efforts by the USA to promote the liberalization of financial markets have stressed the potential common benefits of channelling savings into their most productive uses, but this has been understood to refer to processes of selection according to short-term profits, influenced by the requirements of firms with strong positions in world markets, and by speculative manipulations, notably in the United States.[15] For Japan and the industrializing East Asian countries, the importance of stable high-level domestic funding of outward-orientated industries has been far more significant than the potential benefits of financial liberalization for the world economy. Policy choices, however, have been complicated because of the increasing significance of opportunities for direct investment in the USA, and because varying degrees of openness to incoming foreign direct investment have become necessary for reciprocity and for access to advanced technology.

Financial policy options in the Pacific have to be considered in the context of monetary relations. A prominent feature of the regional pattern is the substantial degree to which the management of US government debt is dependent on the confidence of Japanese investors. Overshadowing this is the prospect of strains in Atlantic monetary relations as the formation of the European Monetary Union reduces the international role of the US currency, while making Atlantic monetary cooperation more uncertain.[16] This prospect indicates requirements for US monetary cooperation with Japan; but levels of confidence and goodwill in the relationship appear to have been reduced since the 1997–8 East Asian financial crises. On the Japanese side, difficulties in the relationship since the 1970s have caused awareness of macromanagement problems in the USA and of the significance of Japanese investor confidence as a restraint on American trade policy activism. The attitudes of US policy communities, meanwhile, have been strongly influenced by an awareness of Japanese informal barriers to imports and to incoming foreign direct investment.[17]

American encouragement of fiscal expansion in Japan has been a factor in the recent history of bilateral interactions. Increased Japanese demand for imports has been hoped for, although with the expectation that currency depreciation would make Japanese exports more competitive. Neither government has shown interest in bringing fiscal interdependence into APEC discussions, although other members of that forum are very much affected by trends in USA–Japan macroeconomic relations. The well-established preference in US policy is to manage the relationship bilaterally, but with additional leverage, where feasible, through enlisting European cooperation. The Japanese preference, understandably, is to maintain a high degree of independence in fiscal policy, especially in view of the uncertainties regarding the macroeconomic interdependence between the European Union and the USA.

Questions about surveillance of the financial, monetary and fiscal policies of industrializing East Asian states have been raised by many observers since 1997; there have been proposals that the principal responsibility should be assumed by the International Monetary Fund and that it should cover all Third World countries. An APEC structure for this type of function has not been suggested and clearly would be difficult to advocate, as it would have to be established through intensive interactions between the USA and Japan and then made acceptable to the prospective East Asian governments whose performance would be under constant review. A role for the International Monetary Fund would have to be made possible primarily through collaboration between the USA and its European members, and this would almost certainly be difficult. Questions about the equity of the weighted voting in the Fund would acquire new prominence, especially because Germany's economic strength is under-represented.

REGIONAL LIBERALIZATION AND INTEGRATION

Spontaneously concerted reductions of trade and investment barriers within APEC have been advocated, including proposals for 'open regionalism', with suggestions that East Asian preferences and concerns with status would be met through the encouragement of unilateral liberalizing decisions and that discrimination against outside states should be avoided. The USA's very active promotional diplomacy, however, has evidenced basic concerns with negotiating regional increases in economic openness, through bargaining methods seeking reciprocity in response to offered concessions.[18] The proposed terms of liberalization would relate primarily to issues of bilateral market access with individual East Asian members, while the liberalization of trade and investment between those members would·be a secondary consideration.

If the practical effects of a negotiated Pacific liberalization assume a hub-and-spoke configuration, the USA would be advantaged, giving it increasing leverage to enhance the degree of market access secured in each of the cooperating regional partners and scope to manage its regional economic diplomacy quite independently. A virtual hub-and-spoke arrangement could develop without much guidance or design through a sequence of US bilateral efforts to promote liberalization that would appear to be necessary because of the lack of solidarity between the East Asian partners. Their individual interests in the American market would in several cases be stronger than their interests in each other's markets. While the Association of Southeast Asian Nations (ASEAN) would have to be involved, as a subregional organization, its decisional weaknesses would oblige the USA to conclude separate agreements with each member, which could then be combined into a regional package of concessions, exceptions and side payments.

Japan's less active role in APEC liberalization endeavours reflects a well-developed form of hub-and-spoke structural statecraft, implemented through informal methods in cooperation with firms which are closely associated with each other in the national intercorporate system.[19] The development of the resultant pattern of structural interdependencies does not depend on advances in regional economic liberalization, but it could be hindered by competing American diplomacy. In the present regional context, Japan tends to develop broader and more stable structural bonds with industrializing East Asian states through more comprehensive partnership arrangements, in which official aid is liked with high-volume, coherently patterned direct investment. An integrated regional production system is centred on Japan, serving mainly the US and the home markets, but contributing to the growth of commerce between the East Asian host countries. The Japanese corporate presence is larger and has been growing faster than that of the USA. Its acceptability is affected by limited openness to exports of manufactures from the East Asian host countries, but can be aided by negative responses from those states to US market-opening leverage. In rivalry with US firms seeking acquisitions in the disrupted East Asian markets, Japanese enterprises tend to be advantaged by their willingness to take minority positions in host country firms, while providing much managerial expertise.[20]

Trade liberalization in ASEAN is a commitment made by its members in 1992, on the basis of apparently modest expectations of increasing trade in manufactures within their association, although high proportions of these exports are produced for outside markets, especially the USA, mainly by Japanese and American firms. Much of this manufacturing in mature and higher-technology sectors is dispersed across borders in assembly-type operations which allow little scope for technology transfers or for the implementation of structural policies by host governments.[21] In the direct investment flows shaping this pattern the very strong Japanese corporate presence tends to produce a hub-and-spoke configuration which could be expected to become more dominant if ASEAN trade liberalization proceeds, and even more dominant if it does not. Policy orientations in the member states, it must be stressed, have been diverted from subregional trade issues by intense pressures to cope with the disruptions of the area's economies, and solutions have been sought mainly through individual dealings with international lending agencies, Japan and the USA, with rivalries to secure large-scale adjustment assistance. Capacities to bargain with industrialized states on trade issues have been weakened by the new forms of financial dependence, but the solidarity to cope with this problem has been lacking

The larger ASEAN members, like other industrializing states, have been committed to general trade liberalization under the Uruguay Round agreements which established the World Trade Organization. Tariff reductions and the phasing out of quotas are intended to ensure freer trade with outside countries and within the association. The benefits of liberalization for exports of low-technology manufactures to major advanced-country markets, however, have been limited by American and European evasion resulting from the influence of protectionist groups.[22] This evasion has been possible because of the absence of a strong coalition of Third World interests. US pressure on the larger ASEAN states to implement their Uruguay Round commitments, in order to avoid loss of access to the American market, is a major challenge which must cause anxieties about the honouring of any obligations which might be accepted in an APEC trade liberalization agreement. The formal content of such an agreement, with its exceptions and side payments, would almost certainly be an outcome of numerous unequal bargaining processes.

The difficulties of implementing growth strategies based on exports of low-technology manufactures are especially significant for the larger ASEAN members, as their levels of industrialization lag behind those of South Korea and Taiwan. Reliance on the attraction of foreign direct investment into manufacturing at medium and higher technological levels thus tends to increase, and is being in effect encouraged by the economic reverses of 1997–8. Investment bidding competition is thus likely to add to the divisive factors that have been tending to weaken ASEAN's significance as a subregional organization. Japanese and American firms, as the main beneficiaries of the investment bidding rivalry, must be expected to have increasing scope to strengthen structural interdependencies between each of the larger ASEAN members and the Japanese and US economies. Two interpenetrating hub-and-spoke patterns may thus become increasingly evident, in a context in which secondary trade and investment links between ASEAN members will continue to develop mainly through collaboration between South-East Asian Chinese business communities.

A regional liberalization package, comprising mainly exchanges of trade concessions between the USA and individual East Asian states and arrived at principally because of American quests for equivalent increases in economic openness, but made possible through Japanese participation, would influence trade patterns in ways that would be increasingly affected by direct investment flows. These could strengthen either or both emerging hub-and-spoke configurations, depending on the concessions secured by the USA and Japan and on the strategies implemented by their firms. In the present pattern of regional economic relations, trade between the large industrialized and the numerous small and medium-sized industrializing states is evolving under diverse discriminatory arrangements, including voluntary export restraints and anti-dumping measures, as well as quotas, and tariffs that discourage the processing of primary products. Although industrialized states have accepted Uruguay Round commitments to phase out these forms of trade discrimination, many of them are continuing in ways that avoid technical violation of the commitments or that discourage Third World complaints to the World Trade Organization.[23] In APEC trade liberalization negotiations, the East Asian industrializing states would have to reckon with the influence of protectionist groups, especially in the United States, that would seek to perpetuate the established methods of trade discrimination.

COMPETITION POLICY PROBLEMS

In the current uneven pattern of deepening Pacific integration competition policy issues demand attention in discussions of trade and investment liberalization. These issues are posed not only because of the use of transnational market power by international firms but also because diverse policies implemented by governments assist the acquisition of such power, resulting in conflicts of interest which involve domestic firms also. Differing institutional arrangements and regulatory perspectives further complicate competition policy issues in the area. The establishment of a common competition authority would not be feasible for the APEC forum, especially in a period of East Asian adjustment to severe financial crises. Discretionary cooperation between the governments with the more highly interdependent economies could be expected to evolve, depending on basic policy orientations and institutional compatibilities.

Competition policy problems are intractable in the USA–Japan relationship, in which structural competition is basically rivalry between relationally linked Japanese enterprises and large American firms engaged in tacit but less active cooperation under the constraints of anti-trust policy. The greater openness of the American economy and the high degree of individualism in its culture provide wide opportunities for Japanese firms producing and distributing in the USA. The Japanese economy, because of its regulatory and structural policy measures and strong relational ties in its intercorporate system, is much less open to US and other foreign enterprises.[24]

Cooperation between the USA and the European Union provides little guidance for US initiatives which seek similar collaboration with Japan. Because of the structural and policy asymmetries in the relationship, the USA has incentives to work for collaboration so that the scope for corporate operations will become more balanced. Japanese policy preferences are to retain the advantages of the present pattern of disparities. A persuasive rationale is that these advantages, while substantial, are cumulative. A further consideration is that it is in Japan's interest to avoid being drawn into bargaining processes in which decisional problems in the USA's strongly pluralistic political system might be overcome through an intensification of economic nationalism: very strong US leverage could then be experienced.[25] Corporate solidarity in Japan could thus have to give way to demands for managed trade, and that solidarity could be weakened by increasing links between Japanese and American firms.

Competition policy issues in the USA have become highly complex because the openness of its economy has facilitated a great multiplication of links with foreign markets, resulting in a proliferation of opportunities for international mergers, acquisitions, alliances and restrictive practices. Questions of efficiency and fairness which anti-trust authorities have had to consider primarily in the national context have assumed external dimensions. Meanwhile, much litigation in the USA, encouraged by laws authorizing anti-trust enforcement, has led to a vast and somewhat incoherent accumulation of regulatory and judicial decisions, reflecting awkward jurisdictional separations. Uncertainties about institutional responsibilities and decisional criteria, together with trends in the evolving regulatory and judicial pattern, have to be reckoned with by other governments dealing with the USA on questions of competition policy cooperation.[26] As the most active exchanges have been with the European Union, there has been some pressure to rationalize the institutional arrangements and the criteria, but the long-standing fragmentation of authority in the US system has prevented change.

Because of the institutional factors and the diversity and ambiguity of criteria, the formation of an effective policy community for comprehensively constructive dialogue with foreign governments would be very difficult. Collaboration to form an international competition authority, in the Atlantic context or under the World Trade Organization, would also be difficult, especially because of the prospect of subordinating present US institutions to such an authority. The external reach of anti-trust policy that can be considered necessary because of the regionalization and globalization of the American economy thus has to be made effective through bargaining, as cases arise, and through unilateral assertions of external jurisdiction. Under guidelines for anti-trust enforcement in the USA, actions may be taken against foreign anti-competitive behaviour which is claimed to affect US exporters as well as consumers.[27]

Relative bargaining strengths tend to assume greater significance as issues multiply in the expanding external area of US competition policy. Tendencies to extend jurisdiction in that area, resulting from and encouraging the use of opportunities for litigation, have serious implications for developing countries.[28] Of the APEC members, the industrializing East Asian states whose economies have been disrupted by financial crises are those whose interests could be most affected. Their disadvantages could be reduced if an East Asian Economic Caucus were formed, but the divisive consequences of their financial crises have made the formation of such a caucus less likely.

For US interests in the APEC area, the business practices that have most significance as international competition policy issues are those of Japanese firms. These, while hindering access to the Japanese market, present extensive collaborative barriers to penetration of the industrializing East Asian economies and result in growing concentrations of market power within the USA. Anti-trust enforcement in the United States, however, remains markedly domestically orientated because of case loads and the home country political concerns of the administration, and in part because of the problems of coordination between the principal authorities for enforcement: the Anti-trust Division of the Department of Justice and the Federal Trade Commission, which has the status of an independent agency.[29] Japanese involvement in concentrations of market power within the USA are significant for the domestic anti-trust concerns, but on a minor scale; those concerns have focused on the activities of US enterprises with strong positions in the home economy. On questions of Japanese limitation of US corporate opportunities in industrializing East Asia, the two principal US authorities would have to collaborate with the US Department of Commerce, at the risk of jurisdictional conflicts. With such collaboration, moreover, cooperation would have to be sought from governments in industrializing East Asia.

US policy concerns have been felt in industrializing East Asia through pressures for trade and investment liberalization, while endeavours to extend the external reach of competition policy have been directed mainly at Europe. The pressures for liberalization have had competition policy effects, and the East Asian governments coping with external financial dependence have been obliged to accept US acquisitions of national firms which would otherwise have remained under home ownership. The adoption of new competition policy measures by these governments has been discouraged by the risks of provoking stronger demands for liberalization, which could be exerted through the International Monetary Fund as well as directly by the US administration.

Japanese competition policy is informal, discretionary and based more on the self-regulating capacities and the collective interests of the national intercorporate system. Concepts of structural competitiveness shared by technocrats and the managerial elite strongly influence the orientation of competition policy, primarily on the basis of concerns with enhancing the capacities of national firms to penetrate foreign markets. Competition in the Japanese political economy is fundamentally cooperative, and the ethos of this highly functional combination is appropriately identified by the term alliance capitalism. The need for regulatory activity is seen to be limited because of spontaneous order in the intercorporate system and because of perceived imperatives to restrain competition while encouraging concerted entrepreneurship.[30] The nation's superior achievements in outward-orientated growth, despite resource deficiencies, have inspired general confidence in the established pattern of alliance capitalism.

Considerations of efficiency and fairness, which tend to be difficult to reconcile in other industrialized states, are felt to be compatible in a broad consensus which sustains Japanese competition policy as a form of administrative–corporate partnership. The blend of competition and cooperation has well-recognized efficiency effects, and the cultural basis for this blend has a high degree of vitality because the political economy has experienced little foreign penetration while achieving its successes in world markets. Some strains have developed in the system of alliance capitalism, however, because of the disruptions associated with the collapse of a speculative property boom in the early 1990s, large increases in foreign production by Japanese firms coping with appreciation of the yen, and stresses in the financial system associated with losses experienced by Japanese firms in industrializing East Asian states during 1997–8.[31] Corporate competition appears to have become somewhat less restrained by cooperative motivation, although the efficiencies of collaboration have become more significant for the economy's overall adjustment and growth.

For the USA, Japanese competition policy is a factor in the rivalry for higher levels of structural competitiveness and in the difficult interactions to achieve parity in degrees of economic openness. Japanese firms operating in the USA collaborate with each other very actively but informally, and, in the absence of explicit agreements to cooperate in ways that could be considered anti-competitive, are not vulnerable to anti-trust litigation. Risks of exposure to such litigation are encountered only in dealings with American enterprises. Such risks can increase if there is greater reliance on US subcontractors or if there are alliances with American corporations for the development of new technology, production sharing or market sharing. Manufacturing investment in response to investment bidding by American state governments can reduce the risk of vulnerability to anti-trust litigation.

Industrializing East Asian states experience the cumulative effects of expanding cooperation between Japanese firms attracted into manufacturing and resource-based ventures. The cooperation tends to result in the formation of an integrated presence in each host country; these become linked with similar neighbouring presences to constitute a co-ordinated pattern. Host country treatment of each presence and of proposals for new ventures is influenced by awareness of the solidarity between Japanese firms and of the interests of their home government in their operations. Bargaining capabilities and inclinations to use these for more beneficial relationships with the Japanese business communities can decrease, while opportunities for host country firms are in effect restricted, unless there is a significantly competitive European or American corporate presence.[32]

Competition policies in most industrializing East Asian states have been strongly influenced by imperatives to attract foreign direct investment since the financial crises of 1997–8. These imperatives have overshadowed fundamental requirements for strong structural policies to promote basically self-reliant growth by national firms funded by domestic savings and linked by relational bonds that facilitate concerted entrepreneurship. Such policies could promise more equal and more productive interactions with incoming foreign firms, encouraging faster resolution of the adjustment problems associated with the financial crises of the area. In the larger ASEAN countries, increased reliance on the attraction of foreign direct investment has reflected the constraints of weak technocratic capabilities and deficiencies in political will at leadership levels, as well as low confidence in the potentials of domestic business communities. Stronger technocratic capabilities and more effective leadership in Taiwan and South Korea have made possible continued structural endeavours that emphasize self-reliance, but these have been more difficult in South Korea than in Taiwan, where the economy has been less vulnerable to destabilization by incoming short-term investment flows.[33]

FINANCIAL POLICIES

The disruption of financial markets in East Asia has dramatized several issues for industrializing and industrialized states concerned with the management of their own economies and with the development of structural interdependencies through regional trade and investment liberalization. For the industrializing states, stable high-level domestic funding of national firms has become a more vital imperative. Hence, outflows of investment into the operations of American, Japanese and European multinationals with strong positions in global markets have to be restricted. Differences in stages and levels of industrial development and in capacities for bargaining over trade and investment issues make the domestic funding imperative increasingly important for governments in industrializing East Asia. These differences also make it all the more necessary for them to implement structural policies designed for functional partnerships with appropriately motivated transnational enterprises based in industrialized states. For the USA and Japan, the East Asian financial crises have increased the gravity of the problems in world financial markets, which have been growing more serious for more than two decades because of failures in international economic cooperation. Volatile high-volume non-productive operations in global financial markets, especially by US firms, attracts much investment into this rent-seeking, which is linked with large-scale speculative operations within the USA that threaten to have destabilizing effects.[34]

Financial markets in most industrializing East Asian states have not been sufficiently developed and regulated for the funding of national industries. Degrees of liberalization in these markets, responding to US leadership and pressures for global financial liberalization, opened up opportunities for external financing of industrial growth. Short-term inflows, encouraged by high growth levels, contributed to much speculative activity in these states, at a cost to the funding of industry. When this speculative activity became unsustainable, outflows of the foreign funds, together with flights of domestic capital, caused sharp declines in currency and stock markets, with failures in financial institutions and a general loss of confidence.[35] The administrative deficiencies of governments became more evident, particularly because of greatly increased dependence on external financing.

American and IMF pressures for increased financial liberalization have been experienced by industrializing East Asian states, while their underdeveloped financial systems have been disrupted. Increased involvement by external financial enterprises has been expected to be a source of market discipline for sound development, as if the option for institutional and regulatory improvement without further liberalization were not viable. External discipline, it has been implied, has been necessary because of the weaknesses of regulatory structures in the East Asian states, but Taiwan's record of institutional and policy development has indicated that the establishment of a financial system for the support of outward-orientated industrialization can proceed with formal and informal controls over involvement in world financial markets. Administrative improvement for the development of basically similar financial systems is clearly a fundamental imperative in the larger ASEAN countries. The necessary efforts could be coordinated within the association if there were sufficient political will, and the common benefits could be very substantial.

Financial development under diverse regulatory arrangements in industrializing East Asian states has generated pressures for domestic liberalization, and then for the use of opportunities for free involvement in international financial markets. Well-developed regulatory systems have ensured adequate control over both processes in Taiwan in the interests of structural competitiveness, but the regulatory mechanisms in South Korea have been less effective. Those in the larger ASEAN countries have been weak, allowing unsustainable borrowing that became severely destabilizing. External pressures to allow the entry of American and other foreign financial institutions have been difficult to counter where financial crises have forced dependence on the IMF and other international lending agencies. Such pressures have been experienced by South Korea, but Taiwan's more stable and more functional system has been less vulnerable to external leverage.

Of the larger ASEAN countries, Thailand and Indonesia, because of the severity of their economic crises, have become especially vulnerable to the external pressure for financial liberalization. Responses by Thailand's weak representative administration are likely to be accommodating, but the Indonesian administration can be expected to be more assertive in its efforts to achieve self-reliant recovery and growth. Japanese support, extended because of Indonesia's central importance as the largest resource-rich ASEAN member, could be of vital significance.

For the United States, the encouragement of financial liberalization in the industrializing East Asian states would expand opportunities for trade in financial services that can benefit the balance of payments and assist the marketing of US government debt. These opportunities are very significant because savings levels in industrializing East Asia have been high and confidence in local institutions has diminished. In financial services trade, US enterprises have superior competitiveness and this will have added significance for the United States as the European Monetary Union becomes a major entity in global finance. Economic recoveries in industrializing East Asia, which could be assisted by US financial institutions supporting host country manufacturing and resource-based industries, will increase the area's interest in investment opportunities within the USA, while tending to draw more imports from the United States. Altogether, deepening US financial involvement, depending mainly on the extent to which it contributes to adjustment and growth, may result in more active rivalry with the strong Japanese presence in industrializing East Asia.

The US administration has to reckon with a reduced role for its currency in global finance after the establishment of the European Monetary Union, and with possible strains in Atlantic cooperation affecting the interdependence of US and European financial markets, especially if European regulatory endeavours are directed at the estab- lishment of a more-integrated and more-stable regional system of financial administration. Possible problems in Atlantic relations have to be considered in conjunction with the risks of a financial crisis in the United States, due to unsustainable speculation in stock markets. The risks of such a crisis have to be assessed with an awareness of regulatory problems in the securities industry and in the fragile banking sector.[36] The possible effects of a crisis in high-volume speculation on inter- national currency markets also has to be taken into account. Incentives to work for increased financial and monetary cooperation with Japan can be seen in the assortment of factors of major significance for US policy at the global level and in Atlantic relations, although in the Pacific context opportunities for increased competition against the Japanese presence evidently tend to have a stronger influence on US policy.

For the USA's regional concerns, the APEC forum has apparently become a less useful association: scope for independent diplomacy in bilateral dealings seems to have become operationally more significant, and on financial policy issues the USA's interests in liberalization can be pressed in association with IMF rationales for liberalization as a condition for adjustment assistance. Although attitudinal changes in East Asia since the financial crises have been unfavourable, the prospec- tive utility of US independent advocacy of financial liberalization may be seen to have increased. The USA remains the most important trading partner of the majority of the industrializing East Asian states, and its imports from them have increased with the depreciation of their cur- rencies. Japan has been more seriously affected than the USA by the disruption of their economies, and thus has also become more depen- dent on access to the US market.

Japanese policy confronts difficult problems in industrializing East Asia because opportunities to assist the development of strong financial systems in the area are limited, open opposition to the further liberaliz- ation of these systems has to be avoided so that the USA will not be antagonized, and grants or loans to assist economic recoveries could be imprudent if prospects for administrative improvement in the affected countries remained unfavourable. Advantage can be taken of financial liberalization by those countries, but competition against the anticipated expanding American role would be quite unequal. The regional development of Japanese financial institutions has been set back by the stresses affecting Japanese regional production and commerce, and the international competitiveness of US financial institutions is likely to remain superior.

Liberalization in Japan that would allow increases in the modest American financial presence continues to be an unacceptable option,[37] and the available leverage for resistance is substantial because of the importance of Japanese investor confidence for the management of US government debt. This confidence will be of increasing significance for the USA as the formation of the European Monetary Union changes the international role of the American currency. Japan, however, has incentives to cooperate more with the USA on Pacific issues because of the increased importance of the US market for Japanese exports, and the modest reciprocation to US economic openness will clearly have to increase in the area of services trade. Japan also has incentives to cooperate with the USA on issues of global finance that may become difficult to manage in Atlantic relations. If strains in those relations are considered probable, the USA's interest in Japanese cooperation could increase.

On the Japanese side, as for the USA, independent management of regional financial policy issues has evidently become much more important than discussion of them in the APEC forum. Separate bilateral dealings with other members provide much scope for initiative and for the use of bargaining capabilities, in a context in which the potential for collaboration between industrializing East Asian states has been reduced. In the relationship with the USA, however, management of the evolving pattern of financial interdependence has become exceptionally complex in ways that have global significance because of the involvement of European interests.

Low interest rates in Japan, intended to assist growth and moderate upward pressure on the currency caused by trade surpluses, have been enabling American and other financial institutions to borrow yen, convert to US dollars, and purchase US government bonds at significantly higher interest rates, while taking advantage of tax havens, including the Cayman Islands. Similar opportunities for large-scale rent-seeking have been exploited through borrowing in European countries. Returns from investment in US government debt have been reinvested in higher-yielding international markets which US global investors have been able to exploit because of superior expertise in speculative operations. Uncertainties about business conditions in Japan contributed to shifts by international investors from yen to dollar securities, adding to appreciation of the US currency, which further aided the expansion of Japan's exports.[38]

Opportunities to place funds in high-growth East Asian countries have been especially significant for the US global investors, and their portfolio operations in those countries have benefited from the vigorous exporting which sustained the high growth in those countries, despite the resultant deficits in US trade. Resumptions of that high growth, following the depreciation of East Asian currencies, will accord with the interests of the global investors and with their preferences for increased financial liberalization in the area. The high-growth East Asian countries, however, will have to recognize imperatives to restrict speculative inflows and to emphasize self-reliant financing of their industrial development, to maintain minimal vulnerability to external manipulation.

A fundamental problem for Japan is the drain of funds into the financing of US government debt and the subsequent reinvestment by US financial institutions into industrializing East Asian countries associated with the integrated Japanese production and marketing system in the area. The speculative inflows of US funds have increasing destabilizing potential that can threaten long-term Japanese interests in the stability and growth of industrializing East Asia. These interests necessitate the encouragement of policy mixes to promote orderly productive corporate operations rather than rent-seeking in association with foreign speculators. At home, meanwhile, Japanese policy has to find ways of directing low-cost funds into the support of foreign production by the nation's firms while reducing flows into the speculative activities of US financial enterprises and contributing to the funding of US government debt through purchases by Japanese rather than through lending to American financial institutions. That change is advisable in order to secure profits currently acquired as rents by US financial institutions and to strengthen leverage in the financial interdependence between the two countries.

MONETARY AND FISCAL ISSUES

Financial liberalization causes the management of monetary policy to become more vulnerable to external influences, including especially inflows and outflows of short-term funds and direct investment and disturbances in international markets for goods. Vulnerability to shifts

in the activities of domestic enterprises also increases, and can be dramatized by failures of financial institutions and by flights of capital. Fiscal
policies, meanwhile, notably through reliance on external financing,
can make monetary policy management more difficult. Financial crises,
attributable mainly to the speculative exploitation of varying complexes
of vulnerabilities, tend to follow sequences in which market participants
react slowly and then over-react, with very disruptive effects. Slow
reactions by regulators and policy-makers are also common in these
sequences, because of concerns to avoid losses of status and to avoid
difficult decisions.

In industrializing East Asia, slow and inadequate administrative
responses to emerging financial crises have been the consequence of
methods of personal rule through soft authoritarianism, as in Indonesia,
and of executive disunity, as in Thailand's weak parliamentary system.
Currency depreciations resulting from the crises have posed severe
problems in the management of monetary policies, with drastic effects
on business confidence; this has been evident especially in the flights of
capital which have aggravated the difficulties of monetary management.

Across the APEC area the increasing interdependence in the management of monetary policies that has resulted from varying degrees of
financial liberalization has assumed a configuration which is dominated
by the USA and Japan. Their policy interdependence has been the
principal feature of a global pattern in which diverse asymmetries have
been sources of constraints and opportunities, to which policy communities have responded with frequently diverging preferences, under the
influence of anticipated forms of market discipline. National administrations in this pattern have differed in their capacities for and
orientations towards the management of monetary policies, and the
contrasts have reflected competing as well as complementary roles in
the global monetary system.

Japanese policy is implemented with a degree of monetary sovereignty considerably higher than that of the USA. The Japanese political
economy is significantly more integrated, and its monetary policy is
made effective by technocrats functioning with dedicated expertise,
substantially insulated against political pressures but in intensive consultations with corporate elites in the national system of alliance
capitalism.[39] The role assumed in the international monetary system,
while larger than Germany's, will have a somewhat lower ranking as
the European Monetary Union is established. Options in relations with
that Union will complicate those in the Pacific with the USA, and in
the changed pattern of bargaining strengths Japan will have incentives

to build a stronger system of monetary links with industrializing East Asian states.

The principal objective of Japanese monetary policy is to restrain the appreciation of the yen which tends to result from large balance of payments surpluses, caused principally by high-volume exports. Monetary expansion has been serving this objective, and it has been aided by extensive use of the US dollar in the commerce of Japanese firms, especially in East Asia. Domestically, inflationary tendencies have been countered by fiscal discipline and by slow increases in wage levels, made possible by the distinctive system of industrial relations which in effect restricts the scope for collective bargaining while ensuring continual increases in productivity.

As low interest rates have encouraged outflows of investment in search of higher yields, especially to the USA, these outflows have moderated an appreciation of the yen which had been a significant trend during the first half of the 1990s, while discouraging foreign inflows. The relative decline of the currency contributed to export increases in the later 1990s and to slack growth in imports. Domestically based growth was low because of severe problems in the financial system, as many institutions, following the collapse of a property boom, were burdened with bad loans totalling about 10 per cent of GDP. Bank lending to the private sector was at low levels during 1996–7. Business confidence was adversely affected by the prospect of a slow and difficult recovery, due to the fragility of numerous financial enterprises and to the high costs of government measures to restore stability to the system. Regulatory responses to the weaknesses and failures of financial institutions after the collapse of the property boom was slow, and evidently discouraged optimism regarding the administration's capacity to cope with further problems in the sector.[40]

Fiscal policy, which had become expansionary in order to promote recovery from a recession after the collapse of the property boom, has been restrictive during the later 1990s, to reduce deficits caused by the endeavours to revive growth and to cope with losses in the financial sector. Public sector investment, which has been high relative to other industrialized democracies, notably for the development of transport systems, housing and urban development, is being reduced to meet a fiscal deficit target of 3 per cent of GDP by 2003. There is pressure from the USA to increase public spending, so that higher consumer demand will draw in more imports, but, as in the past, this is being resisted. Allocations to assist economic recoveries in South-East Asia and South Korea have become necessary for the protection of Japan's regional interests but have been difficult to make without increasing the fiscal deficits and slowing growth in the home economy.

The USA's capacity to pressure the Japanese administration into fiscal expansion, it must be stressed, is limited because of the importance of Japanese investor confidence to the American economy. The available leverage, moreover, is likely to be further weakened by the establishment of monetary union in Europe, which will substantially reduce the role of the US currency in world finance and may well cause it to depreciate, while making Japanese monetary cooperation more desirable for the USA. The likely effects of monetary union in Europe overshadow Japanese monetary and fiscal options as they affect the nation's interests in the APEC area. These interests clearly necessitate substantial strengthening of the trade and investment links with industrializing East Asian states, with assistance for their recoveries. Japanese funds available at currently low interest rates could provide valuable support for those recoveries, with long-term benefits for the home economy, subject to improvement in the local systems of financial administration. These long-term benefits indicate the advisability of finding ways to redirect flows of low-interest funds away from the financing of speculative operations by US securities firms and banks.

It is in Japan's interest to work for more favourable and less risky asymmetries in the monetary and financial interdependence with the USA, while strengthening economic ties with industrializing East Asian states, with of course emphasis on long-run stability and increasing symmetries conducive to such stability. This objective could be served through leadership and support for the development of much more active trade and investment links among industrializing East Asian states, as well as among those states and the home economy. Vulnerabilities associated with asymmetric interdependence with the USA could thus be moderated, while more control could be exercised over the evolution of that interdependence.

All this would require more comprehensively constructive interaction with elites in industrializing East Asia and, therefore, a substantially improved capacity for regional economic statecraft. However Japanese technocrats, corporate elites and politicians may focus more narrowly on perceived immediate interests in East Asia, because of the gravity of the area's financial difficulties and uncertainties about the potential for administrative development in the affected countries. Relationships with policy communities in industrializing East Asia have been distant because of the inward-looking orientations of most of those communities and the relative insulation of Japanese policy processes against foreign penetration. Failures to work toward broad rapport with elites in industrializing East Asia may in effect leave the evolution of economic bonds with that area to be determined almost entirely by the operations of the nation's major firms.[41] A configuration with hub-and-spoke features could thus become more evident, with overall growth lower than what would be possible in an emerging East Asian economic community and with less effective competition against the American corporate presence.

Monetary and fiscal issues for the USA in the APEC context have larger global dimensions than those for Japanese policy-makers, but have to be managed with greater decisional problems because of the strong pluralism in the US political economy and its lower degree of integration. Fiscal policy in this system has been persistently more expansionary because of the difficulties of aggregating and reconciling allocative demands. The inflationary effects and those on the trade balance have been the main problems for monetary policy, which has responded with alternating concerns for the interests of US manufacturers and financial institutions, and with occasional criticism from the administration and Congress.[42]

Coherent expressions of policy preferences from the private sector are lacking, and varying assertions of these preferences influence the Treasury and the independent Federal Reserve in the management of monetary policy. The principal domestic consideration is restraint on inflation, necessitated by fiscal deficits and by the expansionary effects of speculation in the nation's stock markets. This is primarily a Federal Reserve responsibility, exercised through efforts to restrain increases in the supply of credit. These efforts can entail conflict with the Treasury, which is more sensitive to their effects on the administration's domestic political interests, especially during election years. Over time, attempts at credit tightening by the Federal Reserve have tended to encourage inflows of foreign funds, which increase inflationary pressures.

Stock market speculation which tends to move to unsustainable levels can precipitate a financial crisis. Prevention of such a crisis through monetary tightening that slows growth has been a major concern for the Federal Reserve since the 1987 stock market crash. The disruptions of East Asian economies during 1997–8, and related movements of capital to the USA, have raised questions about the sustainability of high upward movements in US stock markets. Large funds were injected into the financial system to restore stability after the 1987 crash, but in the event of a further crash such measures might be less effective because of the increased internationalization of US financial markets.

Monetary restraint for price stability and the moderation of stock market speculation exert upward pressure on the dollar in international currency markets, conflicting with the downward pressures caused by balance of payments deficits. In the APEC area some depreciation of the yen and large depreciations of currencies in industrializing East Asia have caused rising US trade deficits, thus activating demands by exporters for monetary loosening. Meanwhile, the large inflows into the USA attracted by interest rates higher than those in Japan, and supplemented by capital flight from industrializing East Asia, contribute to the upward pressure on the dollar, thus further encouraging demands for monetary loosening that would lower the exchange rate and enable more competitive exporting.

The complexity of the issues in US monetary policy and the potential for change in the interacting factors causing these issues appear to reinforce a long-standing emphasis on maintaining a high degree of independence in the management of this policy, while seeking accommodative shifts in Japanese and European macroeconomic policies. The emphasis on independence reflects the magnitude of the domestic interests that can be affected by monetary tightening and loosening and the apparent significance of shared concerns in the Federal Reserve and the Treasury, to cope with conflicts between their preferences without any encumbering foreign commitments.

For external cooperation, the US monetary authorities have to look primarily to Japan, in view of the changes in relative bargaining strengths and perspectives in Atlantic relations that must be expected to follow the establishment of the European Monetary Union. US bargaining strength in the relationship with Japan will remain potent, despite unfavourable shifts in the financial interdependence with that country. Attitudinal factors affecting the possibilities for rapport on the dynamics of that interdependence and for the coordination of approaches to its management are probably tending to increase US reliance on bargaining leverage to secure accommodating shifts in Japanese policy. Pressure for Japanese fiscal expansion, however, is likely to remain unsuccessful.

In industrializing East Asia, a major implication of issues in the USA–Japan monetary relationship appears to be that probable failures to resolve those issues will intensify USA–Japan rivalry in the area, with American financial enterprises aggressively expanding their operations, notably to assist acquisitions by US manufacturing firms. Meanwhile substantial increases in US trade deficits with the area, attributable to depreciations of its currencies, will trigger US anti-dumping measures which the targeted countries will be reluctant to counter through the World Trade Organization and which will discourage their exporters.

The possible problems in relations with the USA will tend to force policy-level concentration on each industrializing state's own endeavours to secure accommodation of its interests in the unequal interactions. The logic of working for monetary, financial and structural cooperation with each other is thus likely to receive little attention unless highly constructive initiatives are taken by Japan for the sponsorship of East Asian regional collaboration. Within the Association of Southeast Asian Nations, it must be stressed, potentials for constructive leadership must be expected to remain weak because of heightened uncertainties about each national administration's capacity to promote economic recovery and to manage any collaborative arrangements with other members.

APEC's CONFIGURATION

The APEC area is experiencing deepening integration with multiple asymmetries, increased imbalances in the spread of bargaining power, severe adjustment and recovery problems in its industrializing members, little development of transnational policy communities, and considerably conflicted relations between its two leading states. The projected formation of a large region of liberalized trade and investment can be envisaged as an outcome of intensive and prolonged US bargaining with individual East Asian states. Such a drive could well be motivated in part by hopes of coping with reduced American status in the world economy, due to the enlargement of the European Union and the establishment of its monetary union. The implementation of a large design for regional liberalization, however, could be difficult because of opposition from labour unions and protectionist groups in the USA, as well as conflicts between the administration and Congress. In industrializing East Asia, moreover, intensive Japanese economic diplomacy could rather effectively discourage cooperation with the US endeavour, thus ensuring delays longer than the time frames within which a US administration would have to operate.

Asymmetries in the regional pattern are becoming more pronounced because of the disruptions of East Asian economies. In the larger ASEAN members, the necessary adjustments and the slackening of growth are in effect prolonging dependence on exports of low-technology manufactures and primary products by national firms, and on outward-orientated assembly-type manufacturing by mainly Japanese and US enterprises. Low levels of technological competence and weak technocratic capabilities contribute to the persistence of these types of dependence. The structural interdependencies which are evolving with

the USA and Japan are becoming more imbalanced in their technological and financial dimensions. The extensive collaboration between
Japanese firms is responsible for a coherent spread of asymmetries
and for considerable control over their evolution.[43] The less patterned
operations of US firms, however, are related to the large role of the
USA as the principal market for East Asian exports. The attractions of
this market encourage quests for improved access, and these provide
occasions for the use of superior bargaining power.

Policy communities in the region have almost exclusively national
orientations and these change little, as levels of cross-border interaction
are low. Consultations within APEC are on a modest scale, reflecting
the reluctance of most member governments to promote and support
frequent substantive dialogues between their officials, legislators and
corporate groups. Exchanges in the USA–Japan relationship, managed
almost entirely bilaterally in line with apparent preferences on each
side, are intermittent high-level adversarial processes in which neither
side seeks the broader dialogue between policy communities that would
be conducive to understanding and consensus.

ASEAN, having been weakened by the failures of its member governments to build solidarity for collaborative engagement with their
economic crises, has done little to sponsor exchanges between the policy
communities of its governments. The strong emphasis on top-level
control of the legislature, the bureaucracy and the business community
in Indonesia and the more moderate form of executive direction in
Malaysia have limited the scope for initiatives aimed at forming consultative links at working levels that would give impetus to regional
economic cooperation.[44] Efforts to bring the Burmese military regime
and the communist administration in Vietnam into the association as
effective members, moreover, have caused a focus on political and
security issues while restricting opportunities for intensive interaction
over issues of regional economic collaboration.

The lack of unity and institutional development in ASEAN causes
US and Japanese policy to concentrate on bilateral dealings with its
members. The rivalry in these interactions, as it involves advantages for
the USA because of the size of its economy and the great importance
of its market, reveals many opportunities for US initiatives but poses
many uncertainties for each ASEAN state. Utilizing the US-Japanese
rivalry to secure better terms of interaction on trade and investment
issues has become more difficult, moreover, because of the weakened
bargaining capacities of the ASEAN states whose economies have been
disrupted.

China has assumed somewhat increased significance in the regional economic relations of the USA and Japan because of the crises in the larger ASEAN countries. Dealing bilaterally with China, while informally limiting exchanges with that regime as well as with ASEAN members in the larger APEC context, is clearly a US and also a Japanese preference and reflects concerns to limit opportunities for the development of Chinese economic and political ties with ASEAN members. The US interest in separate interactions with each member for trade and investment liberalization could be hampered by increasing Chinese influence in the area. The comparable Japanese interest could also be adversely affected by such a trend, but Japanese concern could be expected to be less evident because of the greater significance of the Chinese market for the Japanese economy.[45] US public criticisms of the Chinese regime, especially because of its human rights record, probably have some indirect influence on ASEAN policy-makers. ASEAN's efforts to bring Burma and Vietnam into its grouping appear to have been motivated by hopes of limiting the development of Chinese influence in those two states.

The USA's regional policy, emphasizing bilateral approaches to the formation of a preferential trade area, has evoked East Asian resistance, which has undoubtedly become stronger since the 1997–8 crises. In part, this resistance appears to have been encouraged by expectations of using the World Trade Organization as a means of restricting unilateral tendencies in US policy, possibly with the support of the European Union. Before the 1997–8 crises East Asian governments had shown support for regional liberalization through spontaneous market-opening decisions which would encourage reciprocity without initiating formal negotiations. Risks to national status would thus be avoided, and the conventions that would be established would hopefully prevent resort to aggressive unilateralism by any participating government.[46] Preferences for this approach have probably become stronger because of the changes in regional bargaining strengths since the East Asian crises, while the World Trade Organization has evidently been seen as a global institution in which relative capacities for leverage are more favourable than in the APEC context. The European Union's interests in the region have been growing rapidly, and European exports to East Asia began to exceed those to North America in 1996. In that year a consultative European Union–East Asian forum, the Asia–Europe Meeting (ASEM) held its first meeting.

Spontaneous market-opening decisions by APEC members, while observing liberalization commitments under the World Trade Organization, could contribute to the formation of a regional community through substantive reciprocation that would build trust and goodwill.

The acceptance of principles, norms and rules would build an elite regional political culture conducive to a balanced spread of gains from commerce, with stability that would facilitate long-term planning and with collaborative adjustment to any stresses. With these considerations, the East Asian preferences could be advocated persuasively, indicating possibilities for conflict-free regional economic integration that would ensure general increases in growth.

It would have to be anticipated, however, that implementation of the spontaneous market-opening decisions by East Asian governments would be discretionary, to a considerable extent, and that resultant uncertainties would discourage export and direct investment ventures by outside firms. Reciprocal liberalization, moreover, on whatever terms, would of necessity have to be formalized by the USA, to provide a clear legal basis in line with measures governing US commerce as a whole. East Asian firms could thus be advantaged in regional commerce while US enterprises would have to reckon with variable and unpredictable East Asian entry barriers. On the East Asian side, such barriers would tend to be considered justifiable because of the USA's greatly superior bargaining strength and the capacities of its large firms to penetrate foreign markets.

At the global level, for purposes of involvement in the World Trade Organization, the East Asian states have to accept formalized arrangements for liberalization, despite biases in these that result from the dominant negotiating roles of the European Union and the USA. On this basis, the USA can press the logic of liberalization through specific negotiated arrangements in the APEC area, to reduce uncertainties about the treatment of imports and incoming foreign direct investment. For this purpose, intensive discussions with numerous members of East Asian policy communities would clearly be very helpful, well in advance of attempts to launch formal negotiations.

The US administration is well placed to sponsor such intensive discussions in cooperation with the Pacific Basin Economic Council, an association of business leaders in APEC countries which has a secretariat in Honolulu.[47] Collaboration could be sought from APEC administrations, whose contributions could include teams of officials, legislators and academics. US initiatives to launch the discussions could overcome suspicion and resentment in East Asia regarding American interests in regional trade liberalization and the USA's identification with pressures from the International Monetary Fund for such liberalization.[48]

The intensive regional discussions, while hopefully assisting the development of APEC understandings about imperatives for liberalization in the common interest and the growth of trust regarding general good-will in the implementation of arrangements for freer commerce, could take up basic structural issues. Those most vital for the region would concern the cross-border effects of the changing pattern of transnational production and the related evolution of market efficiencies and failures. There could be increasing recognition of problems of coordination and adjustment as the interactive effects of expanding direct investment flows become more relevant for structural and trade policies. Regional direct investment conferences could be proposed to facilitate collabor-ative corporate planning of complementary manufacturing, resource extraction and infrastructure ventures. Technocratic contributions to these conferences could be advocated, as these could assist interactive entrepreneurial learning for purposes of cooperative planning.

Forms of alliance capitalism, evolving on the basis of complementary technological and production-sharing interests, principally between Japanese and US firms, could expand and become regionally more inclusive as the direct investment conferences increased productive interactions among managements and between managements and tech-nocrats. Wider exploration of the opportunities for alliance capitalism would be made possible by the conferences, and managements would become more sensitive to the interests of other firms and of govern-ments represented in the conferences.

All the encouragement of corporate cooperation could be open to objections that the main results of the conferences would be increased collusion, with greater oligopolistic exploitation of markets and more extensive discrimination against small and medium-sized firms. Enter-prises and governments in industrializing East Asia could have good grounds for apprehension. Monitoring of the entrepreneurial collabor-ation by technocrats responsive to the region as a whole would clearly be necessary, and this need would have to be met through a regional institution. Responsibilities for structural and competition issues would have to be assumed by that institution, especially to balance tendencies by firms and governments to further their perceived particular interests. Recognition of the need for such an institution would be a necessary advance in the evolution of the USA's regional policy.

Altogether, conferencing to reconcile US preferences for formal lib-eralization with East Asian preferences for informal discretionary liberalization could lead to broadly collaborative exploration of the scope for concerting entrepreneurial and structural endeavours. Per-spectives derived from economic nationalism and narrowly perceived corporate interests would hopefully become open to concerns about regional growth and welfare. Views on the efficiency effects of competition could become more realistic through an understanding of the market and structural changes caused by trends towards increasing concentrations of corporate strengths and through an appreciation of the potentials for enhancing entrepreneurial activities cooperatively as well as through rivalry.

The conferencing would facilitate recognition of imperatives to manage, in the general interest, structural interdependencies which are arising in the present pattern of regional commerce, with growing asymmetries, and which will increase, with greater imbalances, in the unevenly negotiated phases of liberalization that can be anticipated if there are no major initiatives to transform APEC into a community. Because of the diversity of the region, the achievements that could be hoped for through conferencing would require highly constructive endeavours to build rapport on a doctrine of collective management which would affirm not just the importance of market integration for increases in gains from trade but also the responsibilities of governments for the development and coordination of their structural policies, in consultative partnerships with their own and foreign firms.

. The involvement of the transitional Chinese political economy would be a source of difficulties in the conferencing, unless this were restricted to the area's market economy states. The Chinese regime's representatives could have some very useful learning experiences, notably regarding the capacities of industrialized democracies to go beyond trade liberalization into collective management endeavours. These representatives, however, would be under pressure to conform to their regime's views and preferences, based on concepts of national socialism that require emphasis on independent development and resistance to foreign ideological penetration. A high degree of coercive domestic control enables the regime to manage competitive devaluations that can adversely affect the trade balances of South-East Asian countries with similar roles in regional commerce. A large devaluation at the beginning of 1994 contributed to a deterioration of trade balances in Thailand, Malaysia and Indonesia, where the reluctance of the authorities to engineer devaluations opened the way for speculative attacks on the currencies of those states.[49]

The great size of the Chinese economy and its efforts to achieve a higher level of industrialization, financed through export revenues and aided by the attraction of foreign direct investment, challenge the market-economy APEC states to plan for regional community building in highly innovative ways. Working simply for regional trade and investment liberalization, with unqualified faith in market forces, will probably do little to encourage constructive change in the Chinese regime.

Imperatives for collective management, it must be stressed, have to be recognized in the APEC pattern of structural interdependencies. The principal responses that have to be made to these imperatives, in line with the common interests of most APEC members, could well encourage Chinese involvement in the evolution of a system of regional alliance capitalism, operating in partnership with the coordinated structural policies of the market economy states.

APEC AND THE WORLD ECONOMY

For the USA, the most active promoter of economic liberalization in the APEC area, the opening of markets across the Pacific, while potentially valuable because of high growth records in East Asia, is an endeavour which assists attempts to increase commercial liberalization at the global level. At the same time achievements at that level, and in other regional contexts including Latin America, can support promotional activity directed at East Asia. Bargaining strength, meanwhile, used regionally and globally, is enhanced by the consolidation of the USA's central position within the North America Free Trade Area (NAFTA). Japan's economic diplomacy, less clearly and less actively committed to economic liberalization, is on a restricted scale, due to more regionally focused interdependencies and political links and to smaller resources for bargaining, as well as, more specifically, to constraints related to dependence on the large US market. The Chinese regime's economic diplomacy, which is much more restricted in scope, concentrates narrowly on the external interests of its form of national socialism and is not significantly active at the global level, where the USA's major role is matched only by the European Union.

The deepening and enlargement of the European Union has had no demonstration effects in the APEC area. The development of the advanced European system of regional integration has not led to Pacific recognition of the logic of structuring arrangements for the collective management of the interdependencies which arise with regional market integration. The commonly recognized reason for this is the diversity of the APEC area, but very prominent factors in that diversity have been the preferences of the US and Japanese administrations for retaining high degrees of autonomy in their external economic relations. The evolution of the European Union has been significant for the USA and Japan mainly because of the importance of access to its market and because of the potent bargaining strength which it has acquired in the world trading system.

Because APEC has been weakened by the financial crises in industrializing East Asia and the related growth of East Asian antipathies towards the USA, it is not likely to evolve into a system of regional cooperation capable of relating effectively to the European Union for partnership in collective management. The principal transregional relationship of significance at the global level will remain that between the European Union and the USA. This may well be subjected to serious strains as European Monetary Union reduces the international role of the US currency and opens the way for a stronger assertion of European interests in promoting stability in international financial markets.

Japan, despite heavier dependence on the US market and increased vulnerability to US pressures, will have strong incentives to broaden trade and investment links with the European Union, especially if strains between the USA and the Europeans are managed ineffectively by the US administration and if the US economy is affected by financial crises. Constructive European initiatives would encourage positive Japanese responses, and these in turn could activate stronger European engagement with issues in the global economy. Such issues, it should be emphasized, would have assumed greater prominence if anticipated stresses had developed in European monetary relations with the USA.

All the strains in APEC, together with the danger of stresses in the policy interdependence between the USA and the European Union, necessitate close study of the principles of international economic cooperation that have been asserted in the endeavours to liberalize trade and investment regionally and globally. Rationales for these endeavours have affirmed the potential benefits of integrating markets, so as to allow firms to operate with greater economies of scale and scope and with increasing technological advances. Only in Europe, however, has it been recognized that, in the common interest, regional market integration requires a system of regional market governance in which the rising structural and policy interdependencies will be managed for the common good. The moral imperative which has been given practical expression in Europe, despite difficult problems of advanced political development in each of the cooperating states, has a clear application in the Pacific. This has been obscured by conventional wisdom about the area's cultural differences, and more recently about the causes of its financial crises, but the expanding dimensions of the interdependencies that have evolved do require new and highly constructive partnership endeavours, to build a regional community firmly committed to collaborative macroeconomic and microeconomic management. The challenge that can be seen is very demanding and will have to be met with strong moral commitments, not crude assertions of narrowly perceived interests.

NOTES

1. See comments on US trade policy in Robert Z. Lawrence, 'Trade liberalization issues in industrial countries', in Chorng-Huey Wong and Naheed Kirmani (eds), *Trade Policy Issues*, Washington, DC: International Monetary Fund, 1997, pp. 69–86; and Gary Saxonhouse, 'Regional initiatives and US trade policy in Asia', *Asian-Pacific Economic Literature*, **11**(2), 1997, 1–14.
2. See Jens Laage-Hellman, *Business Networks in Japan*, London: Routledge, 1997, ch. 7.
3. See references to problems of European competitiveness in Gavin Boyd (ed.), *The Struggle for World Markets: Competition and Cooperation between NAFTA and the European Union*, Cheltenham: Edward Elgar, 1998.
4. See Sylvia E. Bargas, 'Direct investment positions for 1996', *Survey of Current Business*, **77**(7), 1997, 34–41
5. See comments on pressures affecting Japanese trade policy in Yumiko Mikanagi, *Japan's Trade Policy*, London: Routledge, 1996.
6. See Prem-Chandra Athukorala and Jayant Menon, 'AFTA and the investment–trade nexus in ASEAN', *World Economy*, **20**(2), 1997, 159–74.
7. See perceptions reflected in Laura D'Andrea Tyson, *Who's Bashing Whom? Trade Conflict in High Technology Industries*, Washington, DC: Institute for International Economics, 1992.
8. See International Monetary Fund, *World Economic Outlook, Interim Assessment*, Washington, DC: IMF, December 1997, ch. 6.
9. See OECD, *China in the 21st Century: Long Term Global Implications*, Paris: OECD, 1996; and Robert Taylor, *Greater China and Japan: Prospects for an Economic Partnership in East Asia*, London: Routledge, 1996.
10. See Giandomenico Majone, 'From the positive to the regulatory state: causes and consequences of changes in the mode of governance', *Journal of Public Policy*, **17**(2), 1997, 139–67. On regulatory factors affecting international trade, see OECD, *Regulatory Reform*, vol. II, Paris: OECD, 1997, ch. 5. See also Sanoussi Bilal, 'Political economy considerations on the supply of trade protection in regional integration agreements', *Journal of Common Market Studies*, **36**(1), 1998, 1–32.
11. Anti-trust enforcement has evidenced increasing emphasis on economic efficiency, rather than on the adverse effects of concentrations of market power. See John E. Kwoka Jr and Lawrence J. White (eds), *The Antitrust Revolution*, 2nd edn, New York: HarperCollins, 1994. US anti-trust policy, however, lacks coherence: see Lawrence J. White, 'Competition policy in the United States: an overview', *Oxford Review of Economic Policy*, **9**(2), 1993, 133–511; and Marc Allen Eisner, 'Bureaucratic professionalization and the limits of the political control thesis: the case of the Federal Trade Commission', *Governance*, **6**(2), 1993, 127–53.
12. See Andre Sapir, Pierre Buigues and Alexis Jacquemin, 'European competition policy in manufacturing and services: a two speed approach?', *Oxford Review of Economic Policy*, **9**(2), 1993, 113–32. See also Lee McGowan and Stephen Wilks, 'The first supranational policy in the European Union: competition policy', *European Journal of Political Research*, **28**(2), 1995, 141–69.
13. See IMF, *World Economic Outlook, Interim Assessment, December 1997*, ch. 6.
14. See W. Carl Kester, 'American and Japanese corporate governance: convergence to best practice?', in Suzanne Berger and Ronald Dore (eds), *National Diversity and Global Capitalism*, Ithaca, NY: Cornell University Press, 1996, ch. 4. Strains in the

Japanese financial system are discussed in IMF, *World Economic Outlook, Interim Assessment*.

15. See references to the funding of industry, in Colin Mayer, 'New issues in corporate finance', *European Economic Review*, 32, June 1988, 1167–89.
16. See C. Randall Henning, 'Europe's monetary union and the United States', *Foreign Policy*, 102, Spring 1996, 83–104.
17. See Tyson, *Who's Bashing Whom?*.
18. See Saxonhouse, 'Regional initiatives and US trade policy in Asia'.
19. See Richard F. Doner, 'Japan in East Asia: institutions and regional leadership', in Peter J. Katzenstein and Takashi Shiraishi (eds), *Network Power: Japan and Asia*, Ithaca, NY: Cornell University Press, 1997, pp. 197–233.
20. See references to partnering endeavours in ibid.
21. See Athukorala and Menon, 'AFTA and the investment–trade nexus in ASEAN'.
22. See Laura Baughman, Rolf Mirus, Morris E. Morkre and Dean Spinanger, 'Of tyre cords, ties and tents: window dressing in the ATC?', *World Economy*, **20**(4), 1997, 407–34.
23. The WTO agreement places no significant restraints on trade policy leverage by large states. See Alan V. Deardorff, 'An economist's overview of the world Trade Organization', in *The Emerging WTO System and Perspectives from East Asia*, Joint *US–Korea Academic Studies*, 7, 1997, 11–36.
24. See contrasts in Jose Campa and Linda S. Goldberg, 'The evolving external orientation of manufacturing: a profile of four countries', *Federal Reserve Bank of New York Economic Policy Review*, **3**(2), 1997, 53–82.
25. On the strong pluralism in US policy processes, see comments about protectionism in Bilal, 'Political economy consideration . . .'; and discussion of problems in presidential leadership, in M. Stephen Weatherford, 'The puzzle of presidential leadership: persuasion, bargaining, and policy consistency', *Governance*, **7**(2), 1994, 135–64.
26. See White, 'Competition policy in the United States'.
27. See Alexis Jacquemin, 'Towards an internationalisation of competition policy', *World Economy*, **18**(6), 1995, 781–90.
28. Ibid.
29. See White, 'Competition policy in the United States'.
30. On the cooperative spirit in the Japanese system, see Doner, 'Japan in East Asia'.
31. See IMF, *World Economic Outlook, Interim Assessment*.
32. These consequences can be attributed to the interfirm collaboration discussed in Doner, 'Japan in East Asia'.
33. See indicators of Taiwan's performance in OECD, *Economic Outlook*, 62, 1997, 141–5.
34. See discussion of indicators of a financial crisis in Frederic S. Mishkin, 'Preventing financial crises: an international perspective', *Manchester School Papers in Money, Macroeconomics and Finance*, Supplement, LXII, 1993, 1–40.
35. See IMF, *World Economic Outlook, Interim Assessment*.
36. See William D. Coleman, *Financial Services, Globalization and Domestic Policy Change*, London: Macmillan, 1996, ch. 7.
37. US direct investment in banking in Japan at the end of 1996 was $379 million, that is smaller than the US banking presence in Singapore, Taiwan and Thailand (*Survey of Current Business*, **77**(7), 1997, 36).
38. See International Monetary Fund, *International Capital Markets: Developments, Prospects, and Key Policy Issues*, Washington, DC: IMF, 1997, pp. 2–20.
39. See C. Randall Henning, *Currencies and Politics in the United States, Germany, and Japan*, Washington, DC: Institute for International Economics, 1994, ch. 4.
40. See IMF, *World Economic Outlook, Interim Assessment*.
41. The pattern of cooperation reviewed in Doner, 'Japan in East Asia', may alter because of policy-level indecision, causing Japanese firms to make more independent decisions in industrializing East Asia.

42. See Henning, *Currencies and Politics . . .* ch. 6.
43. See Doner, 'Japan in East Asia'.
44. See Andrew MacIntyre (ed.), *Business and Government in Industrialising Asia*, Ithaca, NY: Cornell University Press, 1994, chs 6 and 9.
45. See Taylor, *Greater China and Japan*.
46. See Andrew Elek, 'APEC beyond Bogor: an open economic association for the Asian-Pacific Region', *Asian-Pacific Economic Literature*, **9**(1), 1995, 1–16.
47. The Pacific Basin Economic Council publishes occasional policy papers. See May 1996 paper 'Implementing free trade and investment in the Pacific region'.
48. On the USA's association with IMF pressures, see Martin Feldstein, 'Refocusing the IMF', *Foreign Affairs*, **77**(2), 1998, 20–33.
49. See Chan Huh and Kenneth Kasa, *A Dynamic Model of Export Competition, Policy Coordination and Simultaneous Currency Collapse*, Federal Reserve Bank of San Francisco, Center for Pacific Basin Monetary and Economic Studies, Working Paper PB 97–08.

Index

Acer 144
alliance capitalism 6, 134, 151, 154, 162, 281
Asia Pacific Economic Cooperation forum 1, 2, 44–7, 110, 124, 187, 249
  community formation 9, 110, 187
  competition policy 262
  financial policies 266
  globalization 10, 283
  Japanese involvement 259
  market penetration 154
  monetary cooperation issues 271
  regional trade 95, 96, 110, 154, 259
  trade cooperation 93
  US involvement 6, 259, 280
Association of Southeast Asian Nations (ASEAN) 1, 2
  Chinese firms 42, 80, 114, 141, 201, 210
  community formation 278
  developmental problems 261, 277
  economic growth 76
  financial markets 267
  market efficiencies 161
  political development 7, 76
  relations with
    Japan 77
    USA 259, 280
  structural policies 5, 157
  trade 260
AT&T (Japan) 127
Australia 130

bank loan capitalism 215
bargaining strengths 8, 253, 259

China 9, 113, 172
  direct investment 203
  economy 9, 79, 172, 205
  multinationals 130, 142
  political system 9, 172, 279

  relations with
    Japan 278
    Southeast Asia 113, 203
    USA 278
Chinese firms 42, 80, 114, 141, 201, 210
competition policies 256, 262
corporate–government interdependencies 151, 154
corporate strategies 96, 153, 154

Daewoo 127, 141
Dai-Tchi Kango Bank 137
Dong Peng Group 144

East Asian financial crises 21, 19, 267
East Asian economic growth 55, 214
economic integration 41, 92, 105, 109, 249
European Monetary Union 258
European Union 258
Exxon 127

financial institutions
  Indonesia 170
  Japan 85, 164, 220
  Malaysia 34, 254
  Philippines 34, 254
  South Korea 85, 233
  Thailand 34, 85, 171
  United States 178, 268, 275
financial policies 215, 253
flagship model 132
flying geese paradigm 62
Ford 127
foreign direct investment 194, 256
Fujitsu 137
Fuyo 137

General Electric 127
General Motors 127

higher technology markets 10, 58
Hitachi 127

IBM 127
import substitution 195
Indonesia 169
  Chinese community 169
  economy 12, 169
  financial sector 170
  government–business relations 169
  political system 169, 182
  technocratic competence 169
industry groups 215
information revolution 83
international Monetary Fund 23, 258,
    267
intra-industry trade 74
investment issues 145
Itochu 127

Japan 214
  bubble economy 231
  · competitiveness 85
  competition policy 264
  corporate culture 133
  corporate finance 85, 163, 220, 229
  corporate strategies 96, 153, 154
  demonstration effects 150, 182
  exchange rate 229
  financial institutions 3, 84, 164, 220
  fiscal policy 258, 273
  foreign direct investment 2–4, 66,
    96, 99, 103, 266
  foreign trade 96, 99, 156, 259
  intercorporate system 133, 152,
    162, 182
  Liberal Democratic Party 164
  macromanagement 164, 214
  manufacturing, outward
    orientation 156
  market efficiencies 158
  market failure 160
  Ministry of International Trade and
    Industry 220
  monetary policy 66, 272
  multinational firms 43, 129, 133
  regulatory measures 85
  relations with
    China 102
    East Asian industrializing

      countries 55, 102, 188, 269,
        274
    USA 3, 11, 13, 270
  technology 66

Krugman, on East Asian crises 29

LG Group 141
Latin American 99, 111
Liberal Democratic Party 164

macromanagement 107, 116, 164
Malaysia 34, 168
  Chinese firms 168
  economy 168
  foreign trade 168
  government–business relations 183
  growth strategy 168
  multinationals 130
  political system 183
  technocratic capabilities 168, 183
market efficiencies and failures 15, 16,
    154, 157, 159
Marubeni 127
Matsushita 127
Mitsubishi 127, 136
Mitsui 127, 136
Mobil 127
monetary policy
  Japan 66, 272
  USA 11, 269, 275
multinational firms 116, 118, 126

NEC 138
Nippon Life Insurance 127
Nippon Tel & Tel 127
Nissho Iwai 127
North America Free Trade Area 95,
    99, 104, 111
North American Business Networks
    131

oligopoly power 159

Pacific collective management 249
  competition policy issues 262
  financial policies 266
  monetary and fiscal issues 271
  trade liberalization 250
Philippines 172, 174

financial sector 172
government–business relations
    172, 184
technocratic capabilities 172, 184
political development 16, 92, 149

Samsung 140
Sanjiu Group 143
Sanwa 137
South Korea 153, 233
    chaebols 139, 165
    economy 155, 233
    financial sector 85, 233
    foreign direct investment 71, 206
    multinationals 128, 129, 139
    political system 165, 184
    relations with Japan 71
    structural policy 71, 184, 234
    technocratic capabilities 166
structural competitiveness 8, 255
structural interdependencies 13, 255
Sumitomo 127, 136

Taiwan 167
    foreign direct investment 73, 205
    multinationals 130, 144, 167
    political system 167
    relations with
        China 205
        Japan 71
        USA 167
    structural policy 71, 167
    technocratic capabilities 167
technology 117, 209

Thailand 171
    economy 12, 171
    financial sector 85, 171
    political system 171, 183
    relations with Japan 12
    technocratic capabilities 171
Toyota 127

United States 174
    APEC involvement 250
    competition policy 263
    corporate governance 176
    Federal Reserve 26
    financial sector 178, 268, 275
    firms 174
    foreign direct investment 2, 96
    foreign trade 11, 86–7, 96, 250, 253
    globalization 253
    intercorporate relations 175, 178
    manufacturing, outward
        orientation 156
    market efficiencies 158
    monetary policy 11, 269, 275
    multinational firms 5, 128, 152, 174
    political systems 177
    relations with
        ASEAN members 4, 186
        European Union 10, 11, 189
        Japan 3, 13, 186, 258
    trade policy 177

Wal-Mart 127
World Trade Organization 11, 260,
    262, 263